Russia, the Soviet Union, and Imperial Continuity in International Law

Russia, the Soviet Union, and Imperial Continuity in International Law

LAURI MÄLKSOO

Professor of International Law, University of Tartu, Estonia

OXFORD
UNIVERSITY PRESS

OXFORD
UNIVERSITY PRESS

Great Clarendon Street, Oxford, OX2 6DP,
United Kingdom

Oxford University Press is a department of the University of Oxford.
It furthers the University's objective of excellence in research, scholarship,
and education by publishing worldwide. Oxford is a registered trade mark of
Oxford University Press in the UK and in certain other countries.

Published in the United States of America by Oxford University Press
198 Madison Avenue, New York, NY 10016, United States of America.

British Library Cataloguing in Publication Data
Data available

Library of Congress Control Number: 2025942453

ISBN 9780198955931

DOI: 10.1093/9780198955962.001.0001

The manufacturer's authorised representative in the EU for product safety is
Oxford University Press España S.A. of Parque Empresarial San Fernando de Henares,
Avenida de Castilla, 2 – 28830 Madrid (www.oup.es/en or product.safety@oup.com).
OUP España S.A. also acts as importer into Spain of products made by the manufacturer.

Acknowledgements

Research for and writing this book was supported by grant PRG969 of the Estonian Research Council. The key period for working on the book was my fellowship at the Institut d'études avancées (IEA) in Paris during the academic year 2023–4; during two months within this period, I also received support from Fondation Maison des Sciences de l'Homme in Paris. I would like to thank Saadi Lahlou, Paulius Yamin, Lisette Winkler, Miruna Achim, Michael Livermore, Patricia Mindus, Henrik Palmer Olsen, Sophie von Stumm, and the other colleagues and fellows of IEA Paris for the time we all spent together at the charming Hôtel de Lauzun on the Ile Saint-Louis in Paris. Moreover, I am deeply grateful to Paris Nanterre University's Faculty of Law, in particular Professors Mathias Forteau and Pierre Bodeau-Livinec, for accommodating me at Nanterre during my IEA fellowship and giving me the opportunity to teach international law masters students there. I am also very grateful to Professors Diego P Fernández Arroyo, Jean d'Aspremont, Samantha Besson, and Léna Gannagé, of other leading Paris research institutions for taking an interest in my research and showing me Paris from their unique perspectives. In Paris, I was also lucky to be able to interact with US researchers on imperial history: Professors Jane Burbank, Frederick Cooper, and Jennifer Pitts.

Some of the seeds for this book were planted during my fellowship at the Woodrow Wilson Center for International Scholars in Washington, DC during the academic year 2017–18, and I would like to thank Matthew Rojansky and William E Pomeranz at the Kennan Institute for the excellent working conditions during this fellowship. One of the privileges of being at the Woodrow Wilson Center for International Scholars was convenient access to the National Library of Congress. For example, I discovered for myself the key work of the Soviet international lawyer Evgeny Pashukanis during this fellowship.

Ideas for this book were tested at conferences at the University of Kiel (thank you, Andreas von Arnauld and Kenneth Chan!), at the Collège de France (thank you, Samantha Besson!), at the London School of Economics (thank you, Lora Izvorova and Gerry Simpson!), at the University of Washington (thank you, Guntis Šmidchens!), at the University of Göttingen (thank you, Frank Schorkopf and Andreas Paulus!), at the Leibniz Institute for East and

Southeast European Studies (IOS Regensburg; thank you, Cindy Wittke!) and at other universities.

Among the articles and chapters which I have published over recent years on Russia, the Soviet Union, and the history of international law, and which have been helpful for preparing the empirical basis for this book, are the following:

'Two Empires: China, Russia, and the Soviet Union in the History of International Law', in: Ignacio de la Rasilla, Wang Jiangyu, Congyan Cai (eds) *All Under Heaven. Histories of International Law in China*, OUP, 2026 (forthcoming)

'Soviet Approaches to International Law', in: Robert Kolb, Momchil Milanov (eds), *The Cambridge History of International Law*, Vol IV, CUP, 2025, 686–716

'The Historiography of International Law in Russia and Its Successor States', in: Randall Lesaffer, Anne Peters (eds) *The Cambridge History of International Law*, Vol I, CUP, 2024, 273–92

'The Contested Politics of History in International Law: A Reply to Anne Orford', 36 *Temple International and Comparative Law* 2022, 117–27

'The Legacy of F F Martens and the Shadow of Colonialism', 21 *Chinese Journal of International Law* 2022, 55–77

'Russia's 2020 Constitutional Amendments and International Law', 115 *American Journal of International Law* 2021 No 1, 78–93

'The Treaties of Brest–Litovsk, Versailles and Moscow: Contesting Sovereignty and Hegemony in Eastern Europe in 1919–1939', 62 *German Yearbook of International Law* 2019, 189–209

'The Controversy over Human Rights, UN Covenants and the Dissolution of the Soviet Union', 61 *Japanese Yearbook of International Law* 2018, 260–83

'The Soviet Approach to the Right of Peoples to Self-Determination: Russia's Farewell to Jus Publicum Europaeum'19 *Journal of the History of International Law* 2017, 200–18

However, the only article from which I have used some passages directly in this book is the 2022 *Chinese Journal of International Law* article on Martens and colonialism.

Historical research needs time and is often the result of encounters whose significance is often revealed only years later. For example, I am thinking of a car excursion in 2009 from Tbilisi to Mtskheta with the late Georgian international lawyer Levan Aleksidze (1926–2019); conversation with him opened my eyes to some aspects of comparative 'imperiology' concerning the Russian Empire and the Soviet Union. I am glad that some references in my book also draw attention to Aleksidze's important work.

Moreover, historical study often requires a sort of detective work as well, so when doing this research I sometimes chased one or another book or journal series in various university libraries. From a German seller of antiquarian books, I was able to buy for the University of Tartu library the full collection of *Soviet Yearbooks of International Law* which formerly belonged to a GDR international lawyer, Edith Oeser (1930–2005), some of the volumes with a dedication by Grigory Tunkin. Furthermore, I have been fortunate to use several other excellent libraries for my research: besides my own University of Tartu, also the libraries of the University of Glasgow (thank you, Christian Tams and Akbar Rasulov!), the University of Cambridge, the Max Planck Institute for Comparative Public Law and International Law at Heidelberg (thank you, Philipp Glahé!), the Peace Palace library in The Hague, and the Central European University in Budapest. At my home institution, the University of Tartu, I owe particular thanks to Sille Avalo, Terje Hannus, Merilin Kiviorg, Anu Laumets, Katre Luhamaa, Marju Luts-Sootak, Priit Pikamäe, Mari Ann Simovart, Gaabriel Tavits, Ave Tiisler, René Värk, and my former and current PhD students Sevanna Poghosyan, Artur Simonyan, Pierre Thévenin, and Liina Lumiste, for supporting the research for this book in various ways, especially when I was away doing research in Paris.

I also owe much thanks to my editor at OUP, Robert Cavooris, for supporting and helping to shape this book project from the beginning. Initial conversations with Robert helped me to formulate what I wanted to aim at with this book. Mirza Rizwaan Ahmad of OUP was also very helpful during the final stages of the editorial process.

I am also very thankful to Christopher Goddard, who carefully proofread my text as language editor.

Last but surely not least, my amazing family—Elizabeth, Elias, and Andreas—thank you for always being there for me, even when I was often absent because of this project.

Finally, with respect to all the individuals mentioned, I also want to emphasize that any responsibility for the views and arguments, as well as any errors, in this book is solely mine.

Contents

1
Introduction

The Relevance of the History of International Law for Situating Russia's War Against Ukraine

This book is a critical history of international law in the Russian Empire, the Soviet Union, and to some extent also the post-Soviet Russian Federation, with a focus on the continuity of Russia's imperial practices and discourses in international law. The context for writing it is, inevitably, the Russian Federation's full-scale invasion of Ukraine on 24 February 2022. The Russian government has attempted to justify its aggression against Ukraine with a mix of narratives and claims based on international law but also very much on interpretations regarding the history of the Russian Empire and the Soviet Union, including their constitutional history. Arguments on what the right of peoples to self-determination implies in international law are an aspect of these claims, in the context of ethnic Russians and native Russian speakers living beyond the borders of the Russian Federation. When one listens to President Putin or other leading Russian politicians or clerics such as the head of the Russian Orthodox Church, Patriarch Kirill, it seems that Russia's 'special military operation' against Ukraine is all about the legacy of 'historical Russia' (code for the Russian Empire) and certain historical and legal continuities which determine claims in the contemporary world as well.[1]

Russia's war against Ukraine has given work to international lawyers in governments and international organizations who in their memorandums and meetings discuss the legal qualification of Russia's war against Ukraine, mechanisms of individual accountability and state responsibility, sanctions, and so on. As the results of votes at the UNGA demonstrate, the global consensus is

[1] See V Putin, 'On the Historical Unity of Russians and Ukrainians', 12.07.2021, http://www.en.kremlin.ru/events/president/news/66181; 'Exclusive: Tucker Carlson Interviews Vladimir Putin', 6.02.2024, https://www.youtube.com/watch?v=fOCWBhuDdDo; Dmitry Medvedev, 'Rossia i Polsha: zametki k 4 noiabria', *Rossiiskaia Gazeta*, 01.11.2023, https://rg.ru/2023/11/02/rossiia-i-polsha-zametki-k-4-noiabria.html; Russian Orthodox Church, 'Sviateishii patriarkh Kirill: Te, kto budut sokhraniat' vernost' dukhovnomu edinstvu nashei Tserkvi, v kontse kontsov pobediat', 28.08.2024, http://www.patriarchia.ru/db/text/6154796.html.

Russia, the Soviet Union, and Imperial Continuity in International Law. Lauri Mälksoo, Oxford University Press.
 DOI: 10.1093/9780198955962.003.0001

that Russia's war against Ukraine violates the prohibition of the use of force in the UN Charter (Article 2 paragraph 4) and constitutes aggression.[2] Since Russia started its full-scale war against Ukraine in 2022, international law scholars have been offering their initial analyses of the situation in journal symposia such as the *American Journal of International Law*.[3] Russia's use of force and policies in Ukraine is widely seen as violating international law, even its *jus cogens* norms.[4] At the same time, when finalizing this book project in 2025, it was already visible how facts on the ground created by Russia will have some significance in Ukraine, which will be a major challenge to contemporary international law.

Among Western governments and some scholars, one popular insight is that Russia's war against Ukraine is in its essence an imperialist war.[5] One may think, for example, of Putin's ontological claim that Ukrainians do not 'exist' as a nation separate from Russians.[6] That Russian foreign policy had taken a 'neo-imperialist' turn was recognized in international relations literature even before Russia's full-scale invasion of Ukraine.[7] There is an understanding that, under Putin, an 'imperial presidency' has developed in Russia, and in particular Russia's constitutional amendments of 2020 expressed a neo-imperial version of Russia's identity.[8]

At the same time, there are quite different understandings of the essence of Russian imperialism, or indeed imperialism generally. For example, Anastasiya Kotova and Ntina Tzouvala see in Russia's decision to attack Ukraine a reflection of 'inner-imperialist rivalries',[9] suggesting that imperialism is a more systemic feature of the current world, and that among the great powers Russia has not been alone in acting imperialistically, even in the context of Ukraine. 'Inner-imperialist contradictions' was of course already a trope in Soviet

[2] UNGA Resolution ES 11/1, March 2, 2022.

[3] See, eg, the 2022 AJIL Agora Essays "The War in Ukraine and the Future of the International Legal Order" and the AJIL Unbound 2022 symposium "Ukraine and the International Order".

[4] See, eg, Júlia Miklasová, *Secession in International Law with a Special Reference to the Post-Soviet Space*, Brill, 2024, 708.

[5] For a discourse on governments, see Patryk Labuda, 'Memory Wars at the United Nations After Russia's 2022 Invasion of Ukraine', 07.01.2025, Lawfare blog, https://www.lawfaremedia.org/article/memory-wars-at-the-united-nations-after-russia-s-2022-invasion-of-ukraine. For scholarly views, see, eg, Alexander Etkind, 'Russia Against Modernity', Polity Press, 2023, 13 et seq.

[6] See V Putin, 'On the Historical Unity of Russians and Ukrainians', 12.07.2021, http://www.en.kremlin.ru/events/president/news/66181.

[7] See, eg, Domitilla Sagramoso, *Russian Imperialism Revisited. From Disengagement to Hegemony*, Routledge, 2020, 343.

[8] William Partlett, *Why the Russian Constitution Matters. The Constitutional Dark Arts*, Hart, 2024, 7, 138–43, 157.

[9] Anastasiya Kotova, Ntina Tzouvala, 'In Defense of Comparisons: Russia and the Transmutations of Imperialism in International Law', *AJIL* No 116, 2022, 713.

approaches to international law.[10] In Western critical anti-capitalist literature, the war in Ukraine is somehow also a result of Western imperialism, aiming to turn Ukraine into a 'de facto colony of Europe'.[11] The rhetoric of US President Trump about Canada, Gaza, Panama, and Greenland indeed demonstrates that imperialism is not confined to Russia.

This book aims to put the Russo–Ukrainian war in its historical context but also goes much beyond that war, using it as an opportunity to examine the history of international law in Russia and the Soviet Union. What concerns us here is the genealogy or 'archaeology' of imperialist ideas and practices in Russia's and Soviet historical interactions with international law. Taking the imperialist features of Russia's aggression against Ukraine as a starting point, we are interested in unearthing and clarifying the history of such ideas and patterns in Russia's interactions with international law. What role has the idea of Russia *qua* Empire played in its historical interactions with international law and how has this idea transformed over time, including during the crucial Soviet period? These are the central questions which this book aims to answer.

To illustrate the relevance of the history of international law in terms of understanding Russia's aggression against Ukraine since 2014—and especially since 2022—five aspects can be highlighted.

First, the history and transformations of Russia's constitutional identity and self-understanding. On 1 July 2020, following the initiative of President Putin, Russia amended its constitution. These amendments included references to state continuity and succession with the Soviet Union, as well as the statement that Russia 'respects the memory of the defenders of the Fatherland and protects the historical truth' (Article 67.1 paragraph 3). In an interview justifying the need for constitutional amendments, President Putin called Vladimir Lenin's decision in and after 1917 to reconstruct the Russian Empire along federalist lines (including the union republics' constitutional right to secession) a 'ticking time bomb', and also claimed that in 1991 'some republics left the center with more than what they came with', namely with territorial gifts from Russia.[12] This makes the history of the creation of the Soviet Union on the ruins of the tsarist Russian Empire relevant for understanding contemporary

[10] See, eg, Yu Shishkov, 'Novyi etap mezhimperialisticheskikh protivorechii', *MZh* No 3, 1967, 88–99.

[11] See, eg, Eric Draitser, 'Ukraine and the March of Empire', in: Immanuel Ness, Zak Cope (eds) *The Palgrave Encyclopedia of Imperialism and Anti-Imperialism*, Vol I, Palgrave Macmillan, 2016, 430–45 at 437.

[12] Artem Girsh, 'Putin rasskazal o "mine zamedlennogo deistvia" v Konstitutsiii SSSR', *Vedomosti*, 05.07.2020, https://www.vedomosti.ru/politics/news/2020/07/05/833979-putin-rasskazal-o-konstitutsii.

conflicts between the states which once formed part of the Russian Empire and the Soviet Union.

Second, justification of the war by some international lawyers in Russia. On 7 March 2022 the presidium of the Russian Association of International Law, an organization of scholars and other international law experts in Russia, published a statement justifying and excusing Russia's actions against Ukraine.[13] While this document mostly repeats the Kremlin's narrative about the 'special military operation', things fall into place when we consider the rich history of how Russian and Soviet international lawyers have been engaged with international legal justifications of their country's wars, military interventions, and conquests. As we will demonstrate in this book, this—with justifications of a war that Russia initiated—is how the discourse about European international law started in the Russian Empire in the early eighteenth century. This is also relevant for understanding the fact that the Constitutional Court of the Russian Federation approved Russia's annexation of four regions of Ukraine in 2022,[14] although 143 states out of the UN's 193 member states considered it illegal under international law in the relevant UNGA resolution.[15]

Third, treaties and attitudes towards treaties, their violation, and their termination. When attacking Ukraine, Russia violated (besides the UN Charter itself) the 1994 Budapest memorandum and the Russian–Ukrainian border treaty of 28 January 2003 in which Russia recognized Ukraine's 1991 borders. However, there is a fundamental question: what are treaties, philosophically speaking, and how have they been understood in Russian and Soviet traditions of international law? We should also note that, in Moscow's own narrative, it was not Russia but *Ukraine* that violated international treaties: the Minsk agreements of 2014–15. The Minsk agreements are in themselves a fascinating example of what is tolerable and what is not according to fundamental principles of international treaty law. Although supportive references were made to the Minsk agreements both by the UN Security Council (UNSC)[16] and the International Court of Justice (ICJ)[17] ('Package of Measures for the Implementation of the Minsk Agreements'), it should be acknowledged at least in retrospect that Ukraine was forced to sign the Minsk agreements under

[13] Statement of the Presidium of the Russian Association of International Law, 7.03.2022, http://www.ilarb.ru/html/news/2022/7032022.pdf, 4.

[14] Russian Constitutional Court ruling, 02.10.2022, No 39-П/2022.

[15] UNGA Res ES 11/4, 07.04.2022.

[16] UNSC Res 2202 (2015).

[17] ICJ, Application of the International Convention for the Suppression of the Financing of Terrorism and of the International Convention on the Elimination of All Forms of Racial Discrimination (*Ukraine v Russian Federation*), Request for the Indication of Provisional Measures, Order of April 19, 2017, para 104.

military coercion from Russia. That the Ukrainian government did not itself officially say so at the time was the result and expression of the very same coercion and power dynamics. This raises fundamental questions about the validity of treaties in international law, nowadays under the Vienna Convention on the Law of Treaties. The question of the validity and termination of treaties has a rich history in the Russian Empire and the Soviet Union; this book maps the discussions and arguments in Russian and Soviet international legal theory and practice, spanning several hundred years.

Fourth, how far should Russia's rights or veto power extend with respect to its neighbours? In December 2021, before starting its full-scale war against Ukraine, Moscow presented a demand that NATO's military infrastructure in Central and Eastern Europe be rolled back to the *status quo* effective in 1997, before NATO's Eastern enlargement beyond East Germany. Doing so would affect not only Ukraine (which according to this logic would of course never be allowed to join NATO) but also Poland, Hungary, Czechia, Slovakia, Romania, Bulgaria, the three Baltic States, several Balkan states, and of course also Finland and Sweden, which joined NATO after Russia's aggression against Ukraine. However, the question of legitimate security concerns and spheres of influence also has a fascinating history because in the early nineteenth century the Russian Empire intervened militarily in Central Europe in defence of the principle of monarchical legitimacy. Moreover, in the twentieth century, the Soviet Union did the same in Hungary and Czechoslovakia in the name of socialist international law and proletarian internationalism. Russia and the Soviet Union have a long history of trying to set conditions for statehood of smaller states in Central and Eastern Europe, including military intervention, occupation, and demands for the neutral status of small states.

Fifth, the discourse which the Russian government used when going to war against Ukraine can properly be understood considering the earlier history of international legal arguments and discourses, especially from the period of the Cold War. For example, just before the Russo–Ukrainian war, Russia's foreign minister Sergey Lavrov referred at the OSCE to the principle of indivisibility of security,[18] which Moscow said had not been respected vis-à-vis the Russian Federation. Contemporary international lawyers from countries other than Russia may not necessarily be aware of such a principle as part of international law. Apparently, it implies that security-related decisions should not be made against objections and in this sense to the disadvantage of the

[18] See Łukasz Kulesa, 'Contested Interpretations of the Indivisibility of Security', PISM, 03.02.2022, https://pism.pl/publications/contested-interpretations-of-the-indivisibility-of-security.

other state concerned (a sort of veto power). However, in terms of the history of such claims in Moscow, it is of importance that during the last decades of the Soviet Union, Soviet international lawyers argued that indivisibility of security had become an international legal principle, at least in Soviet security relations with the US and NATO.[19] This claim is a somewhat forgotten aspect in the history of Western–Soviet interactions in international law.

Altogether, the history of international law matters for a deeper understanding of the Russo–Ukrainian war; indeed, one of the best ways to understand this war (which is not the same as justifying) is historically. At the same time, it is not my argument that the history of international law points at the inevitability of the present condition or unavoidability of Putin's decision to launch his 'special military operation'. The Russian government's decision to attack Ukraine was still exactly that—a decision. In 2014 and in 2022, a different future for Russia and Ukraine, as well as for Russian–Western relations, would have been possible.

The Book's Argument and Its Context in the Literature

Even though decisions and specific personalities play a big role in history, each major country's tradition of international law also involves something of path dependency. Certain historical discourses, patterns, and practices keep returning, even allowing for noteworthy transformations, changes, and new interpretations over time. It would be a mistake not to take such patterns seriously as by neglecting them in analysis one ends up being shocked and surprised every time they happen again. This book deals with the question of how much of the international legal tradition in Russia and the Soviet Union has revolved around the imperial idea, the Russian Empire's vast territory, and its leading status in the world. My main argument in this book is that there has been a strong imperial continuity in Russia and the Soviet Union concerning its own state identity as well as in its discourses and uses of international law in geopolitically important contexts. Yet paradoxically, a quite notable part of the historical literature of international law and imperialism has looked the other

[19] V K Sobakin, 'Printsip ravenstva i odinakovoi bezopasnosti', *SGP* No 10, 1982, 85–92; E I Skakunov, '"Vseobiemliushaya bezopasnost": model perestroiki mezhdunarodnykh otnoshenii', *SGP* No 5, 1987, 102–11; L A Ivanashchenko, 'Printsip ravnoi bezopasnosti storon i ego znachenie dlia sovremennogo mezhdunarodnoga prava', *Soviet YBIL*, 1976, 57–68; G I Tunkin, 'Sovetskaya programma mira i nekotorye problemy mezhdunarodnoga prava', *Soviet YBIL* 1971, 13–28 at 21; S A Malinin, 'Aktual'nye problemy mezhdunarodnoi bezopasnosti v svete reshenii XXVI s'ezda KPSS', *Soviet YBIL* 1981, 26–41 at 30.

way and has not much discussed Russia as an example of imperialism in international law, or seriously problematized the continuity in imperial Russian, Soviet, and post-Soviet traditions of international law.

Some examples from scholarly literature are the following. Concerning pre-Bolshevik history in Russia, some interpretations diminish the imperialist weight of the Russian Empire in international law before 1917. For example, Arnulf Becker Lorca sees the Russian Empire—in the context of *jus publicum Europaeum* of the pre-World War I era—only as a 'semi-peripheral' state.[20] But the issue is more fundamental with evaluations of the Soviet legacy in international law. In 2007, Professor John Quigley of Ohio State University School of Law published a book in which he highlighted the positive and progressive features of Soviet contributions in the realm of law, to an extent also touching upon international legal initiatives.[21] In a much more recent book, the editors maintain that the Soviet revolution of 1917 in Russia inspired anti-imperialist movements throughout the world.[22] Several chapters in their book deal with Soviet alternative approaches to international law, from legal theory to use of force and investment law. However, when inspiring anti-imperialist movements in the world, what was the Soviet attitude towards the earlier imperialism of the Russian Empire: was the previous imperialism of tsarist Russia discontinued or not? The question is not tackled much in the co-edited volume, but it also concerns the legacy of the Russian Bolshevik revolution of 1917. Moreover, Western literature contains interpretations which are quite appreciative of aspects of the Soviet approach to the right of peoples to self-determination and somewhat sympathetic towards Soviet attitudes to international law during the Cold War.[23] Some views in contemporary scholarship celebrate Lenin's stance on self-determination as 'progressive' while in contrast US President Woodrow Wilson is seen as someone who partly just appropriated Lenin's ideas and turned them into something else, and something weaker, in the political process.[24] Moreover, in a recently published edited volume,

[20] Arnulf Becker Lorca, *Mestizo International Law. A Global Intellectual History 1842–1933*, CUP, 2014, 119–25.

[21] John Quigley, *Soviet Legal Innovation and the Law of the Western World*, CUP, 2007.

[22] Kathryn Greenman, Anne Orford, Anna Saunders, Ntina Tzouvala, 'International Law and Revolution: 1917 and Beyond', in: Kathryn Greenman et al (eds) *Revolutions in International Law: The Legacies of 1917*, CUP, 2021, 2.

[23] Bill Bowring, 'The Soviets and the Right to Self-Determination of the Colonized. Contradictions of Soviet Diplomacy and Foreign Policy in the Era of Decolonization', in: Jochen von Bernstorff, Philipp Dann (eds) *The Battle for International Law. South-North Perspectives on the Decolonization Era*, OUP, 2019, 404–25; Boris N Mamlyuk, 'The Cold War in Soviet International Legal Discourse', in: Matthew Craven, Sundhja Pahuja, Gerry Simpson (eds) *International Law and the Cold War*, CUP, 2020, 339–75.

[24] See Adom Getachew, *Worldmaking after Empire. The Rise and Fall of Self-determination*, Princeton UP, 2019, 42.

Raluca Grosescu and Ned Richardson-Little see socialism (including Soviet socialism) as a 'driver of progressive projects' and combatting 'Western imperialism'.[25] Umut Özsu observes correctly that during the decolonization period, the Soviet Union sided with non-aligned states at the UN and wanted the right of peoples to self-determination in Africa and Asia to be interpreted broadly.[26] Other authors writing on the history of international law and the Soviet Union add more critical notes as well. For example, in his history of the negotiation of the Geneva Red Cross conventions of 1949, Boyd van Dijk maintains that Moscow had no desire to accept any legal restraint on its ongoing efforts to subjugate Eastern Europe and that, 'like other imperial powers', it expected to be able to control application of the Geneva conventions in the context of insurgencies which might happen in territories under its own control.[27]

In contrast to some of these works—which tend to downplay the imperialist energy and continuity of the Soviet Union and/or the Russian Empire—my book shows the continued imperial and imperialist legacy and trajectory of international law in Russia and invites readers to take this imperialist legacy seriously when examining the global history of imperialism and international law.

In 2015 I wrote a book entitled *Russian Approaches to International Law*,[28] to which the current book can be seen as a sequel, also because it is with the same publisher. My 2015 book engaged with the work accomplished by the notion of 'civilization' in Russian thinking about international law and examined to what extent Russia's post-Soviet concept of international law has differed from Western understandings. My 2015 book's main observation—that at various times, Russia has emphasized its civilizational distinctness from the West, which in turn has had repercussions for its conceptualization and use of international law—has since then been further confirmed and consolidated in state practice and *opinio juris* in Russia.[29] At the same time, my 2015 book

[25] Raluca Grosescu, Ned Richardson-Little, 'Socialism and International Law: Legacies of Innovation, Contradiction, and Failure', in: Raluca Grosescu, Ned Richardson-Little (eds) *Socialism and International Law. The Cold War and Its Legacies*, OUP, 2025, 1, 12.

[26] Umut Özsu, *Completing Humanity. The International Law of Decolonization, 1960–82*, CUP, 2024, 29.

[27] Boyd van Dijk, *Preparing for War. The Making of the Geneva Conventions*, OUP, 2022, 143.

[28] Lauri Mälksoo, *Russian Approaches to International Law*, OUP, 2015.

[29] See, eg, The Concept of the Foreign Policy of the Russian Federation, 31.03.2023, 4 (referring to Russia's 'special position as a unique country–civilization') with various implications for international legal policies further in the document, https://mid.ru/en/foreign_policy/fundamental_documents/1860586/. In Russian scholarship, see, eg, Yuri I Skuratov, 'Evraziiskaya kontseptsia "mnogonarodnoi natsii" i ee zhanchenie dlia razvitia Rossiiskoi gosudarstvennosti', *Moscow JIL* No 4, 2019, 18–30; Yuri I Skuratov, 'Evraziiskie osnovy mezhdunarodno-pravovoi politiki Rossiiskoi Federatsii', *Moscow JIL* No 1, 2021, 28–45.

mostly bypassed Soviet theory and practice of international law. In contrast, the present book also reconstructs the Soviet period in Russia's history and in international law discursively, linking it to debates about imperialism as well as Russia's pre- and post-Soviet history. Compared to my earlier research, I also present here a more critical view of the leading tsarist international lawyer Fedor Martens, as I discuss his entanglements in tsarist Russian imperialist and colonialist projects.

A connection exists between ideas about Russian civilization and the Russian Empire. Emphasizing Russia's civilizational distinctness has been one of the ways to protect and advance the interests of the Russian Empire—while during the twentieth century, the idea of Soviet communism was another.[30] Of the two ideas and concepts, the Empire has been the continuous and constant one. When the communist idea was dominant, ideas of Russia's civilizational distinctiveness, for example among the Russian Eurasianists who were in exile after 1917, were criticized as 'fascist'[31] in Soviet literature. However, nowadays Russia's President Vladimir Putin, who is influenced by Eurasianist ideas and has favourably referred to the emigrant thinker on Russian statehood Ivan Ilyin (1883–1954), whose thought at least the North American historian and public intellectual Timothy Snyder has characterized as fascist,[32] criticizes Lenin as a political leader who put a 'time bomb' under the building of 'historical Russia'.[33] But in several ways, both of these ideological perspectives—Eurasianism and Soviet communism—wanted the best for the Empire, even though the domestic nature and ideology of the Empire was different.

What is Imperialism and How Does it Relate to Russia?

An important point to note about debates and interpretations in international law is that the very notions of empire and imperialism are contested.[34] For the

[30] This is frankly admitted, eg, in Sergey N Baburin, *Mir imperii. Territoria gosudarstva i mirovoy poryadok*, Izdatel'stvo R. Aslanova 'Yuridiceshki tsentr Press', 2005, 520.

[31] M Korbut, 'Evraziistvo kak beloemigrantski fashizm i ego agentura v SSSR', *SGIRP*, No 9, 1931, 110–29 and No 10, 1931, 106–22 (inter alia criticizing the Eurasianist book of N N Alekseev 'Teoria gosudarstva', 1931).

[32] Timothy Snyder, *The Road to Unfreedom. Russia, Europe, America*, London: Blackwells, 2019. See also Timothy Snyder, 'Ivan Ilyin, Putin's Philosopher of Russian Fascism', 16.03.2018, *The New York Review*.

[33] Artem Girsh, 'Putin rasskazal o "mine zamedlennogo deistvia" v Konstitutsii SSSR', *Vedomosti*, 5.07.2020, https://www.vedomosti.ru/politics/news/2020/07/05/833979-putin-rasskazal-o-konstitutsii.

[34] See, eg, Ntina Tzouvala, *Capitalism as Civilization. A History of International Law*, CUP, 2020, 218 (contesting the understanding of imperialism in the scholarship of Anne Peters); B S Chimni, 'Anti-Imperialism. Then and Now', in: Luis Eslava, Michael Fakhri, Vasuki Nesiah (eds) *Bandung, Global*

following discussion, it is therefore crucial that I lay out how I understand and use those concepts in this book. Semantically, I see a slight difference between the adjectives 'imperial' and 'imperialist'. 'Imperial' pertains to the Empire and—as Russia was officially an empire until 1917—there is no controversy in characterizing its pre-1917 international legal practices and discourses as pertaining to the Empire and thus imperial.[35] Historically, powers which call themselves empires are often simultaneously also 'imperialist' (expansionist), a circumstance that usually finds a reflection in their international law practice and discourses. However, a further important question is: to what extent can we still also characterize as 'imperialist' international legal practices and discourses of major states which explicitly understand themselves as revolutionary and 'anti-imperialist'? The Soviet Union is a major case of interest in this regard. We need to look behind the labels and self-representations and will critically examine practices and discourses in the context of international law.

In 1721, with new conquests in Northeastern Europe, Tsar Peter the Great declared what was previously known as the Grand Duchy of Muscovy to be the Russian Empire. Ruled by the Romanov dynasty, the Russian Empire formally existed until 1917. Over the eighteenth and nineteenth centuries, the Russian Empire continuously expanded territorially by annexing formerly Polish and Lithuanian, Swedish, Ottoman, Persian, and Chinese territories or those belonging to smaller states (for example, the Kingdom of Kartli–Kakheti in today's Georgia). The history of the Russian Empire and of Russian imperialism as such has been extensively studied.[36] At the same time, the history of imperialism in Russia and its connection with international law has only recently been seriously taken up by researchers.[37] The history of European imperialism is nowadays one of the main themes in critical literature on international law, but curiously enough, Russia—and especially the Soviet Union—are notably absent, even invisible, in this literature, where the main energy has

History, and International Law. Critical Pasts and Pending Futures, CUP, 2017, 35, 47; see also Wolfgang J Mommsen, *Theories of Imperialism*, translated from the German by P S Falla, Random House, 1980.

[35] See, eg, Williard Sunderland, 'Russian Empire, 1552–1917', in: Philippa Levine, John Marriott (eds) *The Ashgate Research Companion to Modern Imperial Histories*, Ashgate, 2012, 223–42.

[36] See, eg, Ariel Cohen, *Russian Imperialism. Development and Crisis*, Praeger, 1996; Dominic Lieven, *Empire. The Russian Empire and Its Rivals*, Yale UP, 2001; Jane Burbank and Frederick Cooper, *Empires in World History: Power and the Politics of Difference*, Princeton UP, 2010; Kimitaka Matsuzato (ed) *Imperiology. From Empirical Knowledge to Discussing the Russian Empire*, Slavic Research Center, 2007; Victor N Zakharov, 'The Russian Empire: Main Features and Particularities', in: Mary N Harris, Csaba Lévai (eds) *Europe and Its Empires*, Edizioni Plus—Pisa UP, 2008, 47–58.

[37] See Andreas von Arnauld, Thomas Kleinlein, Nele Matz-Lück (eds) *German Yearbook of International Law*, Vol 66, 2023, with the focus section on Russia, imperialism, and international law.

been devoted to the study of the history of West European empires. However, as this book will demonstrate, the Russian Empire played a prominent role in the historical interplay between international law and imperialism. Moreover, the changing challenges to the Empire decisively shaped international legal doctrines and discourses in Russia. This book postulates that, in Russia, no other factor was as crucial for the evolution of the national tradition of international law as the needs of and challenges to the Empire.

The end of tsarist Russia in March 1917 accelerated centrifugal tendencies in the Russian Empire. In 1917, the Russian provisional government hastily undertook changes in the territorial administration of some European parts of the Empire, which to an extent acknowledged the Empire's multinational composition and emerging claims for self-determination. Elements of ethnic-based autonomy were introduced in some western territories of the Empire such as the Baltic provinces. However, still no territory was supposed to secede from the Russian Empire under the post-tsarist provisional government of Russia in 1917. Then, in November 1917, the Bolsheviks came to power and the Russian Empire became Soviet Russia, which represented a further significant transformation. At least rhetorically, the Bolsheviks declared their vocal support for the right of peoples to self-determination, even up to the point of separation from Russia. Starting from December 1917, several territories seceded or attempted to secede from the Russian Empire, particularly in its European part. However, in all these non-ethnic-Russian secessionist territories 'bourgeois' factions clashed with Soviet-supported forces or war broke out with Soviet Russia, also about the borders of the new states, for example in Poland. The Soviet Russian government militarily and politically supported the communist factions in separatist territories while claiming that national Soviet formations *were* the manifestation of the proclaimed self-determination of peoples. Between late 1918 and 1922, several separate Soviet republics, such as Russia, Ukraine, Byelorussia, and the Caucasus republics, co-existed alongside each other; the constitutional or international legal nature of their relationship at the time remained ambivalent and was disputed both then and later. After the Bolshevik victory in the Russian Civil War, on 30 December 1922 these Soviet republics concluded a treaty establishing the Soviet Union, a state that existed until December 1991, when the Russian Federation replaced the Soviet Union in international organizations such as the UN as the Soviet Union was dissolved.

The Soviet government had proclaimed the right to separate from Russia and eventually—but only after military conflicts or civil wars in which the Bolsheviks could not prevail—concluded peace treaties with 'bourgeois' governments of states which had seceded from Russia. The peace treaties of 1920 with some of the newly emergent nations (Estonia, Latvia, Lithuania, and Georgia) highlighted the right of peoples to self-determination as a ground of secession from Russia. However, one needs to look deeper into this, as Soviet practice—for example, in Georgia—very soon, and even during Lenin's lifetime, started to differ starkly from the rhetoric of those treaties. It can be debated whether, for Lenin, self-determination of peoples and separation from Russia was a strategic and moral necessity or merely a tactical concession, as there are also citations in his work which highlight that he thought of self-determination of peoples in Russia as something historically temporary.[38] Lenin's views on self-determination were later subject to openly imperialist Soviet reinterpretations. Moreover, Lenin did not decide Soviet policy on self-determination alone: for example, Stalin wrote in 1920 that demands to separate from Russia had to be rejected because they 'contradict the interests of the popular masses both at the center and the periphery'.[39]

One of the main intrigues explored in this book is to what extent—notwithstanding revolutionary domestic changes and the loss of certain territories at the western border—Soviet Russia and the Soviet Union continued Russia's imperialist and great power identity in contexts relevant for international law. To be sure, noteworthy and in some sense radical changes took place in Soviet Russian international legal policies and discourses in and after 1917; after all, even the official name of the country itself was changed. However, transformations and breaks of continuity were true in some respects while in other aspects pertaining to the Empire continuity with tsarist Russia was claimed directly, especially in the context of territorial rights and prerogatives. Moreover, Soviet Russia and the Soviet Union soon compensated themselves for the old Russian Empire's territories lost in the west as they expanded further into Central Asia in the 1920s, at the expense of the former tsarist Russian vassal states of Bukhara and Khiva, now the Soviet republics of Bukhara and Khorezm, which were soon officially integrated into the Soviet Union. Indeed, the whole political landscape of Central Asia was further reformed, up to the very names of territorial entities. The biggest transformation in Soviet Russia and the Soviet Union, compared to the tsarist Empire, was constitutional: that the territory of the Russian Empire (minus those non-Soviet states which had genuinely separated from Russia) was reorganized

[38] We will come back to these references and their relevance later in the book.

[39] Jossif Stalin, 'Oktiabrski perevorot i natsional'nyi vopros. Sbornik stat'ei po natsional'nomu voprosu', Mosow: Giz, 1920, cited in: N Cheliapov, 'Partia i natsional'nyi vopros', *SGIRP*, No 5–6, 1930, 101–21 at 107.

based on the federalist-ethnic principle. However, the unity of most of the Empire's territory was preserved.

In 1939–45, the Soviet Union not only reversed most Russian territorial losses of 1918–20 but also made new acquisitions, including in territories which had never belonged to the Russian Empire, such as Galicia (the Lviv region in today's Ukraine and formerly part of Poland and the Austro–Hungarian Empire) and Tuva (formerly a part of Mongolia, which itself had been a part of the Chinese Empire). During the Cold War, rivals of the Soviet Union, especially Mao Zedong's People's Republic of China, regularly referred to Soviet practices of international law such as the so-called Brezhnev doctrine—particularly in the context of the Soviet-led military intervention against Czechoslovakia in 1968—as imperialist and hegemonic.[40] The communist Chinese concept for such Soviet practices was 'social-imperialism'. However, during the 1960s, when the PRC started to challenge the Soviet Union's borders in Central Asia and the Far East, asserting that the borders were the result of unequal treaties of the colonial era, Soviet scholars responded that China itself had been a conquering and expanding empire in the past, in regions such as Xinjang and Tibet.[41] In several aspects, as the Ukrainian–American historian Taras Hunczak (1932–2024) argued, the Russian Revolution of 1917 profoundly transformed Russian imperialism, and—indirectly—imperialism and empires elsewhere.[42]

After the collapse of the Soviet Union in 1991, the same question arose regarding the Russian Federation as was asked after 1917 about Soviet Russia and, starting from the end of 1922, the Soviet Union: as a subject of international law, is it the same state as before, a new one, or a partly old/partly new one? While questions of state identity are asked from the perspective of history and politics more generally, they also have more specific meanings in the context of international law. From the perspective of international legal theory (or doctrine), the mainstream view is that either the old state continues to exist as a subject of international law, or it does not, in which case state succession occurs. This concerns inheritance of rights and duties by the new state(s). Today, the question of the Russian Federation's international legal identity (vis-à-vis

[40] See, eg, Wei Chi, *The Soviet Union under the New Tsars*, Foreign Languages Press, 1978, 1; Jerome Alan Cohen, Hungdah Chiu, *People's China and International Law. A Documentary Study*, Vol I, Princeton UP, 1974, 140–56; Vol II, 1447–96; Theodor Schweisfurth, *Sozialistiches Völkerrecht? Darstellung—Analyse—Wertung der sowjetmarxistischen Theorie vom Völkerrecht 'neuen Typs'*, Springer, 1979, 139, 157.

[41] V M Khvostov, 'Kitaiski "schet po reestru" i pravda istorii', *MZh* 1964, No 10, 21–7 at 25–6.

[42] Taras Hunczak (ed) *Russian Imperialism from Ivan the Great to the Revolution*, Rutgers UP, 1974, 13.

the Soviet Union) is not one of only abstract academic interest, as Ukraine has questioned the Russian Federation's seat as a permanent member of the UN Security Council, inherited from the Soviet Union.

What is Colonialism and How Does It Relate to Russia?

If an empire can experience complex ideological transformations and, in that sense, a self-proclaimed 'anti-imperialist' power like the Soviet Union can also pursue imperialist policies, then what about another related concept: colonialism? Emerging literature in international relations scholarship has drawn our attention to Russia's 'colonialist' history and related patterns in Russian foreign policy discourse, particularly vis-à-vis Ukraine.[43] Two comparative constitutional law scholars—William Partlett from Melbourne and Herbert Küpper from Regensburg—have offered a thought-provoking conceptual framework, interpreting the Russian Empire, the Soviet Union, and the territories which they formerly owned and dominated through the lens of colonialism.[44] In a similar vein, the historian and international relations scholar Alexander Etkind has used the concept of colonialism quite broadly in the context of the history of the Russian Empire, for example characterizing in that way not only the Russian occupation of East Prussia in 1757–62 but also Russia's annexation of Poland and the Baltic provinces in the eighteenth century.[45] However, contemporaries of these events and annexations did not think of Russia's military occupations or conquests in Central and Eastern Europe in terms of 'colonialism'. The idea of colonialism was linked in people's minds with the idea of civilization. When Muscovy took the Baltic provinces from Sweden in the Great Nordic War (1700–1721), its main writer and legitimizer, the diplomat Petr Shafirov, made the argument—endorsed by Tsar Peter the Great—that Russia itself could be considered as sufficiently 'civilized' and was entitled to take part in European affairs.[46] Arguments about colonization in Central and Eastern Europe were rather made by Germans, who also assumed the existence of a *west–östliches Kulturgefälle* in Europe. For example, the

[43] Maria Mälksoo, 'The Postcolonial Moment in Russia's War against Ukraine', 25 *Journal of Genocide Research* 2022, 471–81; Kseniya Oksamytna, 'Russia's Status as a Colonial Power', 01.11.2024, E-International Relations, https://www.e-ir.info/pdf/106552.

[44] William Partlett, Herbet Küpper, *The Post-Soviet as Post-Colonial. A New Paradigm for Understanding Constitutional Dynamics in the Former Soviet Empire*, Edward Elgar Publishing, 2022.

[45] Alexander Etkind, *Internal Colonization. Russia's Imperial Experience*, Polity Press, 2011, 177.

[46] P P Shafirov, *A Discourse Concerning the Just Causes of the War Between Sweden and Russia: 1700–1721*, with an introduction by W E Butler, Oceana Publications, 1973.

nineteenth-century Baltic German international lawyer August Bulmerincq (1822–90) talked about the Baltic provinces of the Russian Empire as at least historically *German* (rather than Russian) 'colonies', referring to the thirteenth-century German crusaders' conquests and states in that part of Europe as well as Christianization efforts, but also the perceived cultural superiority of the Germans vis-à-vis the numerically smaller local peoples.[47] In that sense, from an international legal perspective at least, it seems historically anachronistic to associate Russia's eighteenth-century occupation of East Prussia or its annexation of Poland and the Baltic provinces with 'colonialism'.

International law in the eighteenth century and particularly in the nineteenth century assigned a special regime for Europe. This was based on the distinction between 'civilized' and 'uncivilized' peoples and the term 'colonies' was used when the land of the 'uncivilized' was seized by conquest (and settled) by Europeans. Usually, a large sea or ocean lay between conqueror and conquered. A specific feature of the Russian Empire, imperialism, and colonialism is that, being a Eurasian continental power, the Russian Empire conquered adjacent territories, declaring the new territories part of Russia but without calling them 'colonies'. Nevertheless, when the tsarist Russian Empire expanded to Siberia, the Caucasus, and Central Asia, colonialist practices and attitudes were predominant.[48] In conquered Asian and Caucasian territories, the Russian Empire's practices were as severe as behaviour for which West European maritime empires became notorious in their own conquered territories.[49] Additionally, at its Caucasian and Central Asian borders, tsarist Russia also used a specific legal institute of colonial international law, namely protectorates. This happened as far back as the late eighteenth century in Kartli–Kakheti (today's Georgia) and in the late nineteenth century in Central Asia, with Bukhara and Khiva. Until 1917, the Russian Empire's laws treated indigenous peoples in conquered Asian territories as inferior people (*inorodtsy*).[50] The reasons why the Russian Empire preferred not to call its conquests outside Europe 'colonies' have been discussed among historians, and the matter was also to an extent debated among the elites of the Russian Empire.[51] At the same time, the US historian Michael Khodarkovsky concludes that in substance

[47] August Bulmerincq, 'Rußland. Die deutschen Ostseeprovinzen', in J C Bluntschli, K Brater (eds) *Deutsches Staatswörterbuch*, Vol 9, Stuttgart: Expedition des Staatswörterbuchs, 1865, 1–63.

[48] Alexander Etkind, *Internal Colonization*, 69–78.

[49] See, eg, on the conquest of Tartarstan and Chechnya in Johannes Socher, *Russia and the Right to Self-Determination in the Post-Soviet Space*, OUP, 2021, 70 et seq.

[50] See, eg, L A Challandes, *Russkoe gosudarstvennoe pravo*, Tipografia Shnakenburga, 1908, 55–6.

[51] Michael Khodarkovsky, 'Between Europe and Asia. Russia's State Colonialism in Comparative Perspective, 1550s–1990s', 52 *Canadian-American Slavic Studies* 2018, 1–29.

(although not in form), the Russian Empire was no different in its conquests in Asia from colonialist Western European empires.[52] Researchers of colonial empires (with 'overseas' colonies) admit that in important ways, these empires had much in common with continental empires such as the Russian Empire.[53]

That imperial Russia before 1917 did not call its conquests in Asia or Caucasus 'colonies' had, at the time, more domestic than international significance. As pointed out by the Russian Empire's leading international lawyer, Fedor Fedorovich Martens (1845–1909)—as well as, later, the German diplomat and historian of international law Wilhelm Grewe (1911–2000)— by the nineteenth century, 'colony' had become a term of constitutional rather than international law.[54] From the perspective of international law, a colony was still part of an empire's territory, even though important constitutional differences may have existed between the motherland and the colony in empires that included colonies. Later, in international law in the 1960s, the 'salt-water doctrine' became central for an understanding of colonies and colonialism in the context of the right of peoples to self-determination.[55] In a way, the 'salt-water doctrine' of self-determination acknowledged the non-colonial status of the Soviet Union, although substantively, the criterion of an ocean in between the territories remained quite arbitrary. The UN understanding favoured the continental empires, by leaving their colonial practices out of the spotlight during decolonization. However, this distinction is emphasized in Russian international law scholarship: Russia was a 'unique' empire because it was not a 'colonial' empire.[56]

One fascinating aspect of the Russian history of imperialism and colonialism in the context of international law is how the Soviets dealt with the tsarist legacy when they came to power. They proclaimed equality between the peoples of the former Russian Empire—Lenin famously called the tsarist Empire 'the prison house of peoples'—and took at least a rhetorical distance from tsarist policies and discourses, referring to both as 'imperialist' and 'colonialist'. After 1917, Soviet Russia highlighted this new perspective in its treaty practice with 'eastern' countries. For example, the Treaty of Friendship signed by Persia and Soviet Russia on 26 February 1921 called the previous Russian governments 'colonizing' (Article 1) and the Russian Empire's previous policies towards

[52] Ibid.

[53] Pierre Singaravélou (ed) *Les empires coloniaux (XIX–XXe siècle)*, Paris: Éditions Points 2013, 15.

[54] F de Martens, *Traité de droit international*, Tome I, Paris: Librairie Marescq Ainé, 1883, 314; Wilhelm G Grewe, *Epochen der Völkerrechtsgeschichte*, Baden-Baden: Nomos, 1984, 552.

[55] James Summers, *Peoples and International Law*, 2nd revised edn, Brill, 2014, 117.

[56] Maxim A Isaev, 'K voprosu o mezhdunarodno-pravovom statuse Velikoga kniazhestva Finliandskogo', *Moscow JIL* No 2018, 33–43 at 35.

Persia 'colonial and capitalist' (Article 9, 10).[57] In Soviet historiography, it was also common to speak critically of Russian 'imperialism', referring to the tsarist period.[58] Soviet legal authors had no problems with labelling tsarist Russian practices 'colonialist'—especially in Central Asia and the Caucasus.[59] By way of further example, Soviet scholars acknowledged that tsarist Russia, having separated (Outer) Mongolia from China during the First World War, effectively turned the region into its own 'colony'.[60] In Southeastern Europe, Soviet scholars characterized some tsarist Russian border territories—for example Bessarabia—as an 'economically backward colony'.[61] The Russian Empire seized Bessarabia from the Ottoman Empire, which Russian legal scholars in the nineteenth century, particularly Martens, considered less 'civilized' than Europe (including Russia).

However, especially after the victory in the Second World War, a transformation soon emerged in attitudes between those Soviet international lawyers who conceptually prioritized the socio-economic and ideological changes in Russia since 1917 and those who, in the bigger picture of things, preferred continuity with the former Russian Empire. This second group of scholars proudly argued that the Soviet Union had been the same state as the Russian Empire all along. After the Second World War, negative appraisals regarding the tsarist Empire started to fade away in Soviet international law scholarship, with the Russian Empire's legacy in international law being referred to more and more positively, most strikingly in the work of the Soviet international lawyer—and after 1953 also ICJ judge—Fedor Kozhevnikov (1903–98).[62] In practice, the Soviet government also made sure that, notwithstanding constitutional norms and ideas about the self-determination of peoples and the proclaimed sovereignty of the Soviet republics, secession from the Soviet Union could only be

[57] Persia and the Russian Socialist Federal Soviet Republic, Treaty of Friendship, signed at Moscow on 26 February 1921, LNTS 1922, 400–13.

[58] See, eg, M P Viatkin (ed) *Iz istorii imperializma v Rossii*, Moscow: Izdatel'stvo Akademii Nauk SSSR, 1959; A M Davidovich, 'Sushchnost i evoliutsia samoderzhavia v epokhu imperializma', *SGP* No 6, 1970, 71–9 at 72.

[59] I Levin, 'Sredniaya Azia: primer konsolidatsii natsii v usloviakh diktatury proletariata', *SGP* No 6, 1934, 74–82 at 78; S Radzhapov, 'Etapy razvitia sovetskogo gosudarstvennogo stroya v Srednei Azii', *SGP* No 11, 1948, 61–7 at 61; G T Taymanov, 'Kazakhskaya SSR v Sovetskom mnogonatsional'nom gosudarstve', *SGP* No 4, 1954, 27–38 at 29; Kh P Vakhidov, 'Politicheskie vzgliady prosvetitelei narodov Srednei Azii vtoroi poloviny XIX. v', *SGP* 1955, No 7, 100–8 at 101, 108; A Kh Dudaev, 'Sozdanie i razvitie checheno-ingushskoi natsional'noi sovetskoi gosudarstvennosti', *SGP* 1964, No 6, 117–22 at 117.

[60] I Trainin, 'Antiimperialisticheskie avanposty na Dal'nem Vostoke', *SGP* No 4, 1932, 135–56 at 151.

[61] A A Karlov, 'Obrazovanie i razvitie sovetskoi natsional'noi gosudarstvennosti moldavskoga naroda', *SGP* No 6, 1964, 111–17 at 111.

[62] F I Kozhevnikov, *Russkoe gosudarstvo i mezhdunarodnoe pravo (do XX veka)*, Moscow: Zertsalo, 2006 (original: Moscow: Iuridichekoe izdatel'stvo Ministerstva iustitsii SSSR, 1947).

mentioned at a merely theoretical level (although it formed part of the Soviet constitution). Here it is worthwhile examining the international and constitutional legal doctrines and methods of argumentation used by Soviet lawyers to explain and justify Soviet state practice, which often failed to correspond with the initial Soviet rhetoric on self-determination.

Why the History of Russian Imperialism Has Often Been Neglected in the Literature on International Law

As already indicated, one of the challenges at the beginning of this book is that, at least until recently, Russian and Soviet imperialist practices and discourses have been relatively marginal in the Western literature on the history of international law and imperialism. An interesting question is why this has been so. To start with, the literature on the history of international law involves a certain conflation of the concepts of 'imperialism' and 'colonialism'.[63] As Russia did not formally have colonies in the same way as did the West European empires, this conflation itself may, for some legal scholars, leave the Russian Empire at the margins—or even out of the picture altogether—of imperialism in the history of international law. In this type of literature, 'imperialism' and 'colonialism' are often treated as two sides of the same coin; for the one to be seen and critically acknowledged, the other ought to appear on the other side as well. In any case, the history of imperialism in international law has so far been written primarily by scholars who have been more familiar with or interested in the history of the West European empires, the British and French, but also the Spanish, Dutch, Portuguese, and Belgian Empires, and also from the perspective of US historical involvement with imperialism.[64] In the critical literature on postcolonial international law, Russia is mostly absent—a blank sheet.[65]

[63] See, eg, A Anghie, 'Imperialism and International Legal Theory', in: Anne Orford, Florian Hoffmann (eds) *The Oxford Handbook of the Theory of International Law*, OUP, 2016, 157 (wondering why imperialism has not been a central concern of the theory of international law and postulating that one reason was that 'colonial questions' were seen as pragmatic, political issues).

[64] Antony Anghie, *Imperialism, Sovereignty, and the Making of International Law*, CUP, 2005; Jennifer Pitts, *Boundaries of the International: Law and Empire*, Harvard UP, 2018; Lauren Benton, Lisa Ford, *Rage for Order. The British Empire and International Law, 1800–1850*, Harvard UP, 2018; Inge Van Hulle, *Britain and International Law in West Africa. The Practice of Empire*, OUP, 2020; Martti Koskenniemi, Walter Rech, Manuel Jiménez Fonseca (eds) *International Law and Empire. Historical Explorations*, OUP, 2017; Benjamin Allen Coates, *Legalist Empire. International Law and American Foreign Relations in the Early Twentieth Century*, OUP, 2016; David Armitage (ed) *Theories of Empire, 1450–1800*, Ashgate, 1998.

[65] See, eg, CL Lim, *The Aims and Methods of Postcolonial International Law*, The Hague Academy of International Law, Recueil des cours, Vol 437, 2024.

But further reasons explain why the Russian Empire, and especially the Soviet Union, have been relatively ignored in the critical literature on the history of empires in international law. The first Soviet leader, Vladimir Lenin (1870–1924), argued influentially that imperialism was the 'highest stage of capitalism'; it logically followed that the Bolsheviks finished with imperialism—and simultaneously finished with capitalism—in Russia the moment they came to power. Besides Lenin, the Soviet politician and writer Nikolay Bukharin (1888–1938) propagated a similar linkage between imperialism and capitalism.[66] Quite interestingly for international lawyers, in the interwar Soviet Union, Evgeny Bronislavovich Pashukanis (1891–1937), a legal scholar who became a leading voice in Marxist theory of law, and also specifically in international law, dedicated an entire study to the further development of Lenin's concept of imperialism, focusing on economic factors of capitalism.[67] In this Soviet Leninist approach, imperialism was the problem of Western capitalist states, but no longer a problem of Soviet Russia or the Soviet Union. In post-Soviet Russia, too, the view that the Soviet Union presented a challenge to capitalist imperialist powers has been upheld in the scholarship.[68]

In his book on neo-colonialism, Kwame Nkrumah—President of Ghana in the period 1960–1966 and one of Africa's leading politicians during the process of decolonization—proceeded semantically from Lenin's concept of imperialism.[69] Soviet discourse on self-determination of peoples, which was directed to the outside world, was influential and Moscow was quite convincing in criticizing the imperialist record of West European colonial empires. The US scholar Adom Getachew has demonstrated how, during the interwar period, the Pan-Africanist movement already drew on and was deeply influenced by Lenin's account of self-determination.[70] Several intellectual leaders of this movement were either employed or heavily influenced by the Communist International (Comintern; also 'Third International'). At the same time, this Moscow-based organization—conceived by the Soviets as a sort of alternative to the 'capitalist' (and thus 'imperialist') League of Nations—also created

[66] Robert Know, 'Marxist Approaches to International Law', in: Anne Orford and Florian Hoffmann with Martin Clark (eds) *The Oxford Handbook of the Theory of International Law*, OUP, 2016, 306–26 at 313.

[67] E B Pashukanis, *Imperializm i kolonial'naya politika. Chast' pervaia: ekonomika imperializma. Kurs lektsii, chitannykh v I MGU*, Moscow: Izdatel'stvo kommunistischeskoi akademii, 1928, 3.

[68] Boris Kagarlitsky, *From Empires to Imperialism. The State and the Rise of Bourgeois Civilisation*, Translated by Renfrey Clarke, London: Routledge, 2014, 296–7.

[69] Kwame Nkrumah, *Neo-Colonialism, the Last Stage of Imperialism*, New York: International Publishers, 1965.

[70] Adom Getachew, *Worldmaking after Empire. The Rise and Fall of Self-determination*, Princeton UP, 2019, 68.

bitter personal disappointments for them.[71] Nevertheless, a certain takeover of Soviet ideas of self-determination of peoples seems to have taken place among some leaders of colonized peoples, according to which imperialism was an intrinsic problem for the capitalist West but no longer for Soviet Russia. It helped that Soviet Russia and the Soviet Union were globally the first systemic critics of—Western—imperialism and colonialism.

The international lawyer Ntina Tzouvala has offered a critical reading of the notion of 'civilization' in the history of international law. Her understanding of imperialism is essentially also a Leninist one. She refers to imperialism as a specifically capitalist phenomenon and writes of the 'tendency of capitalism for unlimited expansion'.[72] However, the Soviet Union, which was not capitalist, was still also expansionist. Apart from the expansionist secret protocols of the Nazi–Soviet Non-Aggression Pact of 23 August 1939—which laid claim to the territory of six neighbouring sovereign states, all of which in 1939–40 suffered Soviet aggression—Soviet Russia's general declared aim, ever since the 1918 constitution, was that other countries, too, would establish the rule of the proletariat and then evolve into communism.[73] As this book will demonstrate in detail and in the context of international law, in practice communism in the Soviet Union became closely intertwined with the Russian imperialist tradition and agenda. Thus, conceptually limiting and linking 'imperialism' only to capitalism would make us myopic about the imperialism/expansionism of non-capitalist powers such as the Soviet Union. Therefore, in this study, I understand 'imperialism' as an obsession with territory and territorial expansion notwithstanding the predominance of capitalism, socialism, or other economic systems. Apart from this, as we shall soon see, Muscovy started its territorial expansion long before capitalism: during the feudal era.

We can also illustrate this historical conundrum regarding imperialism during the Soviet period with an anecdote from the diaries of Grigory Ivanovich Tunkin (1906–93), one of the leading international lawyers of the Soviet Union. In June 1964, Tunkin attended a session of the UN International Law Commission in Geneva, and recorded in his diary a breakfast conversation with Manfred Lachs (1914–93), the representative of Poland, who later became a judge at the ICJ. Lachs told Tunkin: 'I consider you to be an example. You represent a great power, one of the two presently existing great powers. But I do not feel in your interventions that you defend the interests of a great power

[71] Ibid, 67–70.

[72] Ntina Tzouvala, *Capitalism as Civilization. A History of International Law*, CUP, 2020, 2, 219.

[73] Art 4 of the 1918 Soviet Russian constitution expressed 'absolute resolve to liberate mankind from the grip of capital and imperialism', https://www.constituteproject.org/constitution/Russia_1918.

against small countries.' To which Tunkin, according to his own diary, responded: 'I said that I represent not simply a great power, but a socialist power which adheres to the principle of equality. "We have", I said, "no companies interested in the suppression and exploitation of other peoples".'[74] Indeed, this was the typical Soviet self-image; as Lilya Artemevna Modzhoryan (1911–96), later a professor at MGIMO University, wrote in 1953: 'A socialist state does not need foreign expansion. It does not need colonial conquests.'[75] However, Russian history reveals that apparently companies are not the only actors that favour expansion to other countries.

The Polish international lawyer Lachs himself favourably commented on creation of the Warsaw Pact in 1955.[76] What he may or may not have known was that after 1956 Tunkin *qua* international lawyer had justified the Soviet military intervention against Hungary.[77] Later, after 1968, Tunkin also justified the Soviet-led military intervention against Czechoslovakia.[78] With the rise of the *Solidarność* (Solidarity) movement and strikes as well as the proclamation of martial law in Poland by General Jaruzełski, other Soviet international lawyers implicitly threatened Poland that intervention based on the principle of socialist international law (and proletarian internationalism) remained an option on the table for the Soviet Union.[79]

Russian and Soviet 'contributions' to the history of imperialism and colonialism have remained less than visible in global history, including in the context of international law. Vasily Klyuchevskii (1841–1911) and other famous Russian historians who took a favourable view of the Russian colonization of Siberia and other territories in the East took the concept of 'colonialism' and in a way turned it around, arguing that Russia had also 'colonized itself'.[80] The historian Alexander Etkind also concludes that Russia was at different stages of history, in being both 'colonized and colonizing'.[81] However, to an extent the concept of Russia's 'self-colonization' confuses situations in which the Russian

[74] William E Butler and Vladimir G Tunkin (eds) *The Tunkin Diary and Lectures. The Diary and Collected Lectures of G I Tunkin at The Hague Academy of International Law*, Eleven international publishing, 2012, 26.

[75] L A Modzhoryan, 'Bor'ba demokraticheskogo lageria za natsional'nuyu nezavisimost' i natsional'nyi suverenitet', *SGP* No 1, 1953, 52–65 at 56.

[76] M Lachs, 'Varshavskii dogovor i problema kollektivnoi bezopasnosti v Evrope', *MZh* No 10, 1955, 55–62.

[77] G I Tunkin, 'Novyi tip mezhdunarodnykh otnoshenii i mezhdunarodnoe pravo', *SGP* No 1, 1959, 81–94 at 86.

[78] G I Tunkin, 'V. I. Lenin i printsipy otnoshenii mezhdu sotsialisticheskimi gosudarstvami', *Soviet YBIL* 1969, 16–32 at 25.

[79] E T Usenko, 'Mezhdunarodno-pravovye problemy rashirenia i uglublenia sotrudnichestva sotsialisticheskikh gosudarstv', *Soviet YBIL* 1982, 28–40 at 29, 32.

[80] Alexander Etkind, *Internal Colonization*, 70.

[81] Ibid, 57.

Empire was in a classic way conquering and colonizing neighbouring territories and peoples. Moreover, a remarkable history remains to be explored further in the context of international law, namely the history of Russia taking established concepts and changing their meaning for its own purposes.

Proceeding from Lenin's understanding of imperialism, the Soviet Union presented itself as a vehemently anti-imperialist power. Criticism of old-world imperialism became prominent as a discourse about Soviet Russia exiting the First World War. For this purpose, the Bolsheviks criticized the war as an imperialist war as well. In the context of international law, Moscow asserted that it was a 'great power' (*velikaya derzhava*), especially after the victory in 1945, though by its nature a good, humanist, and benevolent power, not an imperialist one. For example, during the 1950s–80s, few articles in the leading thematic Soviet periodicals *Soviet State and Law* (*Sovetskoe gosudarstvo i pravo*) and the *Soviet Yearbook of International Law* do not juxtapose the Soviet Union and its socialist bloc to the (negatively framed) 'imperialist states' of the West. A whole genre of specialized literature in the Soviet Union vehemently criticized American imperialism in the context of international law.[82] During the Cold War, the Soviet self-image sometimes acquired comical propagandistic dimensions in international legal narratives, for example when Soviet legal scholars critically asserted that 'imperialist' powers had the proclivity to systematically violate international treaties whereas the Soviet Union itself 'always fulfilled its treaty obligations and demanded the same from others'.[83] Naturally, views can be found in the post-Soviet Russian international law literature which emotionally reject the idea that the Soviet Union could have been an

[82] See, eg, O V Bogdanov, 'Amerikanskaya mezhdunarodno-pravovaya doktrina na sluzhbe imperialisticheskoi ekspansii', *SGP* No 5, 1952, 70–72; G Zadorozhnyi, 'Amerikanskii zhurnal mezhdunarodnoga prava'—propovednik mezhdunarodnoga razboya i bespravia, *SGP* No 12, 1952, 80–87; G Zadorozhnyi, 'Amerikanskaya pravovaya doktrina - zleishii vrag mezhdunarodnoga prava', *SGP* No 1, 1953, 66–74; E Petrov, 'Amerikanskie imperialisty—zlostnye narushiteli rezhima voennoga plena', *SGP* No 12, 1952, 48–61; K Ya Chizhov, 'Amerikanskii imperializm - razrushitel' mezhunarodnoga prava', *SGP* No 2, 1953, 52–9; S A Gonionsky, 'Organizatsia amerikanskikh gosudarstv—orudie monopolii SShA', *SGP* No 5, 1953, 144–51; M Lazarev, 'V narushenie suverennykh prav narodov. (O voennykh bazakh USA na inostyrannykh territoriakh)', *MZh* No 10, 1956, 77–88; L A Modzhoryan, 'Amerikanskie doktriny grabezha i razboya: ot Monroe do Johnsona', *SGP* No 9, 1965, 57–64; I I Lukashuk, 'Mezhdunarodno-pravovoi nigilizm vo vneshnei politike SShA', *SGP* No 7, 1982, 121–9; Yu Deporov, 'Agressia SShA protiv Grenady i mezhdunarodnoe pravo', *SGP* No 5, 1984, 80–5; M M Avakov, A I Grinberg, 'SShA: kurs na podryv mezhdunarodnoga pravoporiadka', *SGP* No 6, 1984, 84–92; I P Blishchenko, V F Shavrov, 'SShA: doktrina i praktika protiv mezhdunarodnoi zakonnosti', *SGP* No 10, 1984, 110–16; A Natalin, 'Protivopravnost "strategicheskoi oboronnoi initsiativy" SShA', *SGP* No 11, 1985, 113–19; N B Krylov, *Na vesakh Femidy: SShA i mezhdunarodnoe pravo*, Molodaya gvardia, 1986. (Series 'Imperializm: sobytia, fakty, dokumenty); I I Rogachev, 'Interventsia SShA v Paname i mezhdunarodnoe pravo', *SGP* No 8, 1990, 109–17.

[83] A N Talalaev, *Pravo mezhdunarodnykh dogovorov. Tom 2. Deistvie i primenenie dogovorov. Dogovory s uchastiem mezhdunarodnykh organizatsii*, Zertsalo, 2011 (Originally, Moscow: Mezhdunarodnye otnoshenia, 1985), 4, 11.

empire.[84] Even today, in the context of Russia's current war against Ukraine, some authors in the West are still hesitant to put anything more definitive than a question mark to the statement that Russia is an imperialist power.[85]

Focus on International Legal Discourse as a Method

The main sources of international law comprise treaties and customary law. However, the problem is that these two do not speak to us directly; we need international lawyers as intermediaries. According to Article 38 paragraph 1 p. d of the ICJ Statute, teachings by the most highly qualified publicists of the various nations are merely a 'subsidiary means' for determining rules of law. However, the present study is of the positions taken by Russian and Soviet international lawyers and puts consciously at the centre-stage their analysis and discourse about international law.

The focus on discourses and discursive strategies has become popular in studies of the history of international law.[86] It is easy to see why: it enables us to learn what the arguments were about in struggles concerning international law, how international legal disputes played out in dynamic historical settings, and in what directions international lawyers from various powers tried to deploy narratives. International law has not been carved in stone. To advance certain types of claims and outcomes, choices were made, and priority was given to some readings of international law as opposed to others. Usually, such arguments were made in contestation with rival powers. This understanding of discourses as something essential for an understanding of international law is influenced by the tradition of critical legal studies, which sees law as indeterminate.[87] According to the critical school, it is the very essence of international law that as a 'language' it enables opposing arguments. This perspective is further highlighted by the fact that judicial settlement of international legal disputes has been a relatively marginal phenomenon in Russian and Soviet history. For a moment in time, the Russian Empire promoted Fedor (Fréderic de)

[84] V A Drozhzhin, 'Byl li Sovetskii Soyuz imperiei?', *Moscow JIL*, 1996, 22–7.

[85] Sergei Fediunin, Hélène Richard, 'La Russie est-elle impérialist?', *Le monde diplomatique*, January 2024, https://www.monde-diplomatique.fr/2024/01/FEDIUNIN/66451.

[86] See, eg, Jochen von Bernstoff, Philipp Dann (eds) *The Battle for International Law. South–North Perspectives on the Decolonization Era*, OUP, 2019, 2, 138; Ntina Tzouvala, *Capitalism as Civilization. A History of International Law*, CUP, 2020, 8–14.

[87] Martti Koskenniemi, *From Apology to Utopia. The Structure of International Legal Argument*, CUP, 2006; see also *Jan Klabbers, International Law*, CUP, 2013, 13, 19–20.

Martens (1845–1909) as the 'chief arbiter of the Christian world'.[88] However, Russia's own disputes with other nations rarely ended up in arbitration or judicial settlement. The Soviet Union further distanced itself from the legally binding settlement of international disputes. It is also in this context that the views of international law writers and scholars become particularly relevant.

As a key method, this study takes seriously—and explores—the discourses of Russian and Soviet international lawyers. This enables us to see how things were seen and understood, what normative meaning was given to events, not just what happened. International law is a field in which some assumptions in the discourse analysis literature in international relations can be contested. For example, the Danish international relations scholar Lene Hansen highlights the political importance of 'official' discourses: essentially, what governments say. According to Hansen, academic discourses are (at least relatively speaking) marginal compared to 'official' discourses.[89] Although practices in different countries and traditions may vary, in international law its prominent representatives often represent and mix 'official' and 'academic' angles. Prominent international lawyers advise and represent governments; indeed, international lawyers with a history of working with the government sometimes gain distinct visibility and prominence. Since the international judge as such has been of relatively marginal importance in the history of the international law of Russia and the Soviet Union, at least in politically significant cases, international lawyer–academics could speak and write as if they were 'quasi-judges' but simultaneously also as advocates and propagandists for their countries. This is particularly so in centralized totalitarian states such as the Soviet Union, where the role of international lawyer–academics was widely seen as helping and defending their country with arguments echoing the government's foreign policy views and where dissident views about the interpretation of core state interests in the context of international law were not permitted. Beyond the Soviet Union, Russian international lawyers have often been in dialogue with national doctrines and essentially discussed problems of international law with the perspective of how best to protect Rusia's national interest.[90] In this book, I will critically study these semi-official academic

[88] V V Pustogarov, *Our Martens: F. F. Martens, International Lawyer and Architect of Peace*, edited and translated by W E Butler, The Hague: Kluwer Law International, 2000.

[89] Lene Hansen, *Security as Practice. Discourse Analysis and the Bosnian War*, London: Routledge, 2006, 57.

[90] See, eg, the dialogue with Russia's 2022 Maritime Doctrine and the best plausible claims which Russia can make in the Sea of Okhotsk in: V V Gavrilov, R M Nurimbetov, 'Istoricheskie prava gosudarstv na morskie akvatorii i pravovoi status Okhotskoga moria', *Moscow JIL* No 4, 2022, 44–55 at 46, 54.

discourses and arguments about international law and their interlinkages with state practice in Russia and the Soviet Union.

We can wonder—if international law is to a significant extent 'indeterminate', plausibly enabling lawyers and diplomats to present opposing arguments—to what extent the history of international law should also be considered 'indeterminate'. Sometimes fierce disagreements arise about how properly to approach the study of the history of international law. Contextualist and critical approaches to the history of international law have been juxtaposed.[91] Professor Anne Orford of Melbourne University has discussed the tension between approaches by contextualist historians interested in international law and critical international lawyers interested in the past of their field.[92] Some historians have critically asserted that international lawyers do not always 'properly' tackle the history of their field methodologically and jump too easily to political conclusions, or perhaps nurture a political agenda before approaching the history of international law in the first place. In her analysis, Orford demonstrates that there is no one-size-fits-all school to study the history of international law; indeed, history itself remains a methodologically diverse field. Orford also argues that any approach to the history of international law inevitably involves its own politics. Writing 'objective' history, perhaps in the sense of the nineteenth-century Prussian historian Leopold von Ranke (1795–1886), who aimed at writing history 'as it actually happened', is nowadays considered not realistic. Orford makes the study of the history of international law challenging when she argues that 'there is [. . .] no method that will establish that our account of facts or our version of truth is the correct one'.[93]

That may be true about methods but a study of the history of international law, or indeed any history, must still be based on the premise that historical truth, at least about events, can be established. History in terms of international law cannot be endlessly indeterminate. We must maintain the capacity to point out when states, diplomats, or international lawyers make things up, when they lie about history and facts. On 1 September 1939, Hitler claimed that Poland had attacked Nazi Germany, but we know for a fact that this was not so and that the opposite was the case. The Soviet history of international law is also rich in claims and arguments about history which are demonstrably untrue; for example, that Finland attacked the USSR in 1939[94] (or at least 'provoked' the

[91] Ignacio de la Rasila, *International Law and History. Modern Interfaces*, CUP, 2021.
[92] Anne Orford, *International Law and the Politics of History*, OUP, 2021.
[93] Ibid, 320.
[94] See, eg, E A Korovin, 'Vazhnyi istoricheskii dokument. (Po povodu spravki Sovinformbiuro 'Falsifikatory istorii'), *SGP* No 4, 1948, 1–7 at 5; Yuri G Barsegov, *Territoria v mezhdunarodnom prave*, Moscow: Gosudarstvennoe izdatel'stvo iuridicheskoi literatury, 1958, 152.

Winter War);[95] that the Katyn massacre of some 22,000 Polish officers during the Second World War was a Nazi—not Soviet—crime; or that the 'elections' which the Soviet Union organized in occupied Estonia, Latvia, and Lithuania in 1940 were genuine and democratic.[96] In such historical contexts, there must remain a method to establish that a certain account of facts is correct, even if the interested power or its advocates among international lawyers have maintained or even continue to vehemently maintain the opposite. Although Soviet foreign minister Vyacheslav Molotov maintained until the end of his life—apparently in the interests of *raison d'état*—that there were no secret protocols to the Nazi–Soviet Non-Aggression Pact of 23 August 1939,[97] these protocols undoubtedly existed; as a matter of fact, Molotov personally signed them in the name of the Soviet Union, while Nazi Germany and the Soviet Union both acted on the basis of the protocols, and the contemporary Russian government has exhibited the Soviet original copy of the protocols at an archive exhibition in Moscow.

The main approach or method adopted in this book is that I connect the main events in Russian and Soviet state practice of international law—especially related to the status and expansion of territory—with Russian and Soviet international legal discourses. When I refer to international law discourses, then a key empirical element in this book consists in materials published in leading periodicals of international and constitutional law such as the *Revue de droit international et de législation comparée* ('the *Revue*') in the late nineteenth century and the journals *Sovetskoe gosudarstvo i pravo* (in its early decades after 1917 *Sovetskoe gosudarstvo i revolyutsia prava* and since 1992 *Gosudarstvo i pravo*), the *Soviet Yearbook of International Law* in the twentieth century, and the *Moscow Journal of International Law* in the twenty-first. This amounts to a vast body of material and a significant amount of detail as the number of texts reviewed on international law is quite extensive. Nevertheless, this constitutes the central empirical axis and novelty of this book. These Soviet materials and discourses on international law have been insufficiently examined and considered, especially nowadays, decades after the end of the Cold War.[98]

[95] This was a widespread Soviet trope—see, eg, V N Durdenevsky, 'Sovetskaya territoria v aktakh mezhdunarodnoga prava za 30 let. (1917–1947 gg)', *SGP* No 12, 1947, 58–65 at 63; M A Avakov, *Pravopreemstvo Sovetskogo gosudarstva*, Moscow: Gosudarstvennoe izdatel'stvo yuridicheskoi literatury, 1961, 90.

[96] See, eg, R Yu Auling, 'Sozdanie i razvitie Sovetskogo gosudarstva v Estonii', *SGP* 1955, No 5, 24–30.

[97] Claudia Weber, *Der Pakt. Hitler, Stalin und die Geschichte einer mörderischen Allianz*, München: C H Beck, 2019, 163 (referencing the book by Felix Chuev, *Sto sorok besed s Molotovym*, Moscow, 1991).

[98] Important exceptions are Johannes Socher, *Russia and the Right to Self-Determination in the Post-Soviet Space*, OUP, 2021 and Michael Riepl, *Russian Contributions to International Humanitarian Law. A Contrastive Analysis of Russia's Historical Role and Its Current Practice*, Baden-Baden: Nomos, 2022; Kaj Hobér has also referred to international law-related articles published in the journal *Sovetskoe*

However, they reveal important aspects: for example, when leading Soviet international lawyers such as Korovin and Tunkin uninhibitedly discussed the consequences of socialist international law.

The journals and yearbooks considered in this book had different audiences. The *Revue*, which was published in Belgium, was primarily oriented to (French-speaking) European international law elites while the Soviet journals were primarily oriented domestically and to an extent also to other socialist countries. This is fascinating precisely because this is international law as explained by Soviet lawyers to Soviet and socialist audiences. The Soviet journals and yearbooks on international law represented official Soviet discourse and thinking, at least as presented to Soviet citizens. All these materials reveal significant aspects of both tsarist Russian—in addition to Soviet—claims in and arguments about international law, as well as often revealing the imperial logic behind such claims. It is particularly fascinating to follow exchanges in which an actual debate took place among Soviet international lawyers, for example, on questions regarding the history of Soviet federalism, the state identity of the Soviet Union (compared to the Russian Empire), and the conditions under which the principle of *pacta sunt servanda* could be overridden under treaty law and philosophy. Usually, the stances taken in such debates also reflect geopolitical challenges to the Empire.

The book follows chronological logic. The following elements pertaining to the fate of the Russian Empire are highlighted in the international legal discourses examined. First, Russia's identity and self-image and its implications for the state's international legal subjectivity and claims, especially claims regarding its territory. In the specific terminology of international law, this concerns state identity and continuity (or succession), but also how solutions in Russian and Soviet constitutions reflected their understandings. The main insight here is that both the Soviet Union and, after 1991, the Russian Federation adopted flexible understandings of state continuity/succession which ultimately ended up defending Russia's imperial state identity and continuity. Second, attention is paid to the nature of treaties and doctrines about their validity and termination in Russian and Soviet practice and writings on international law. Treaties have served as facilitating and fixing Russia's territorial conquests; but often before conquest could happen, an earlier treaty needed first to be pushed aside—that is, violated. Thus, we will examine how stable political treaties were in reality and how easy it was to terminate them unilaterally,

gosudarstvo i pravo in: Kaj Hobér, *The Perestroika Era and International Law*, Edward Elgar Publishing, 2024, 28, 44, 78.

violate them, or ignore them, according to tsarist Russian and Soviet doctrines and theories of international law. Third, attention is paid to specific Russian and Soviet imperial doctrines, justifications, and framings in international law during each period. These are the doctrines and theories that comprise the foundations (or bigger picture) of international law in a certain way that highlights the indispensable and legally recognized role of 'great powers' (*velikie derzhavy*) in the international community, Russia's role in maintaining the balance of power, and specific international legal doctrines supporting Russia's imperial interests such as the doctrine of monarchical legitimacy in the context of the nineteenth century or the theory of socialist international law, used by the Soviet Union during the Cold War.

For readers who are not familiar with the Russian language, I have added English translations of the titles to the texts referred to in the bibliography section of the book. However, for reasons of space, these translations do not appear in footnotes on each page.

2

The Russian Empire until the Crimean War (1853–6)

'Restoring' Muscovy's Patrimony

Russian historians of international law have shown a special interest in the treaties which Kievan Rus concluded with Byzantium during the ninth and tenth centuries.[1] Academic preoccupation with these treaties was particularly marked during the late tsarist period.[2] This apparent search for state continuity or pedigree of sorts reflects— besides the historical prestige of Byzantium and Orthodox Christian regionalism[3] in Eastern Europe at the time—the idea that Kievan Rus was a *Russian* state, a predecessor of the later Russian Empire. But was it? Such an exclusive identity may have made sense in the nineteenth century when the territory of the Russian Empire also included Ukraine.[4] Of course, for historians of international law, ancient Byzantine treaties with Kievan Rus are interesting in themselves, even without searching for symbolic state continuities.

[1] R L Khachaturov, *Mezhdunarodnye dogovory Rusi s Vizantiei, zaklyuchennye v X veke*, Moscow: A-prodzhekt, 2015; K S Rodionov, 'Pravda o dogovorakh X veka, zaklyuchennykh Vizantiei s kievskimi knyaziami Olegom (911 g) i Igorem (945 g), *Russian YBIL* 2019, 284–305; M Yu Braichevsky, 'O pervykh dogovorakh Rusi s grekamy', *Soviet YBIL* 1978, 264–84; M Yu Braichevsky, 'K voprosu o pravovom soderzhaniy pervogo dogovora Rusi s grekami (860–863 gg)', *Soviet YBIL* 1982, 276–97; F I Kozhevnikov, *Russkoe gosudarstvo i mezhdunarodnoe pravo (do XX veka)*, Moscow: Zertsalo, 2006, 22–3, 116, 153–4.

[2] See, eg, Nikolay Lavrovsky, *O vizantiiskom elemente v yazyke dogovorov russkikh s grekami*, St Petersburg: Tipografia Imperatorskoy Akademii Nauk, 1853; N Marks (ed) *K tysiacheletiu dogovora Olega 911-go goda. Dogovory russkikh s grekami i predshevstvovavshie zakliucheniu ikh pokhody russkikh na Vizantiu. Chast' pervaya. Vremya Olega; Chast' vtoraya. Vremya Igorya i Sviatoslava*, Moscow: Moskovski arkheologichesky institut, 1912; G M Barats, *Kritiko-sravnitel'nyi analiz dogovorov Rusi s Vizantiei: Vosstanovlenie teksta, perevod, kommentarii i sravnenie s drugimi pravovymi pamyatnikami, v chastnosti—s Russkoyu Pravdoyu*, Kiev: Tipografia 1-i Kievskoi Arteli Pechatnogo Dela Trekhsvyatitel'skaia No 5, 1910.

[3] See Michel de Taube, 'L'apport de Byzance au développement du droit international occidental', *RCADI* 1939, Vol 67, 233–339.

[4] On how the memory of Kievan Rus divides Russia and Ukraine, see Andreas Kappeler, *Ungleiche Brüder: Russen und Ukrainer vom Mittelalter bis zur Gegenwart*, 6. Auflage, München: C H Beck, 2022.

Russia, the Soviet Union, and Imperial Continuity in International Law. Lauri Mälksoo, Oxford University Press.
 DOI: 10.1093/9780198955962.003.0002

In Russian lands, Moscow started to rise under Mongol–Tartar rule (ca 1240–1480). According to Rais Abdulkhakovich Tuzmukhamedov (1926–96), a Soviet international lawyer, the Russian Empire and the Soviet Union borrowed extensively from the Mongol–Tartar state, the Golden Horde, its practices of empire-building, and its ways of conducting international relations.[5] The idea that Muscovy borrowed extensively from the Golden Horde was also popular with Russian Eurasianists during the interwar period, especially Nikolai Trubetskoy (1890–1938).[6] In Muscovy, the aspiration to be a successor of old (Kievan) Rus[7] and at the same time borrowings from the Mongol–Tartar Golden Horde also created a unique mixture of expansionist claims and practices.

At the end of the fifteenth century, Muscovy concluded its first written agreements with European states: in 1490 with Austria and in 1493 with Denmark.[8] What 'international law' meant in those times is debatable as the grand dukes of Muscovy did not yet use this concept regularly in their international communication and disputes with other states; nor indeed did the West European states. Muscovy enthusiastically gathered both the lands of ancient Rus as well as other former constituent parts of the Golden Horde. In the words of the US historian Henry R Huttenbach:

> Thus, if the rulers of Muscovy marched westward as the descendants of the Roman emperors and the spiritual heirs of the Byzantine emperors, they marched eastward as the successors of the khans of the great Eurasian empire of the Mongols of which they had once been part.[9]

For example, in the East, Muscovy conquered the khanates of Kazan (1552) and Astrakhan (1556), neither of which had ever belonged to Kievan Rus. Nevertheless, Muscovy justified its conquests with dynastic claims: that these lands on the Volga River were Muscovite patrimony, still ancient lands of Rus; a statement which was 'proved' with reference to dynastic claims reaching back to Kievan days. Andreas Kappeler, a Swiss historian and expert on the

[5] Rais A Tuzmukhamedov, 'Nekotorye mezhdunarodnye i mezhdunarodno-pravovye aspekty sozdania, sushchestvovania i padenia Zolotoi Ordy', *Moscow JIL*, No 1, 1995, 116–24 at 117–18.

[6] See Jane Burbank, Frederick Cooper, *Post-Imperial Possibilities. Eurasia, Eurafrica, Afroasia*, Princeton UP, 2023, 71.

[7] See F Kozhevnikov, *Russkoe gosudarstvo i mezhdunarodnoe pravo (do XX veka)*, Zertsalo, 2006, 26.

[8] G B Gal'perin, 'Voprosy mezhdunarodnopravovoga priznania edinogo rossiyskogo gosudarstva XV-XVI vv', *Soviet YBIL* 1969, 261–77 at 263.

[9] Henry R Huttenbach, 'The Origins of Russian Imperialism', in: Taras Hunczak (ed) *Russian Imperialism from Ivan the Great to the Revolution*, Rutgers UP, 1974, 18–44 at 34.

formation of the Russian Empire, remains sceptical about the historical truthfulness of these claims.[10] Another renowned historian of Eastern Europe, Serhii Plokhy, argues that on several occasions such claims were based on Muscovite domestic chronicles which were conveniently rewritten on the occasion of new conquests. For example, when Muscovy's Tsar Ivan III subjugated Novgorod—an independent Russian republic—in 1471, the Russian chronicles were rewritten to highlight Muscovy's continuity with Kievan Rus and its former territorial possessions.[11]

In 1547, the Muscovite ruler Ivan Grozny proclaimed himself tsar (or caesar). The most consequential international legal claim by Muscovy over the sixteenth and seventeenth centuries related to the title of tsar and Muscovy's demand that European states recognize its ruler with nothing less than that specific title. This was on the one hand a claim that Muscovy's position would not derive from the West, especially from the Holy Roman Empire or the Pope; the title of tsar came from God.[12] For example, the Tsars Ivan III and Ivan Grozny rejected the offers of the Emperors of the Holy Roman Empire to recognize their title as tsar because the way they were formulated—from Muscovy's perspective—would have meant symbolically subordinate status vis-à-vis the Holy Roman Empire.[13] Fedor Kozhevnikov, who in 1953 became the Soviet judge at the ICJ, summed up the situation in the following way:

> Muscovite diplomacy successfully uses legends and historical facts for the juridical foundation for the legality of recognizing the tsar's title as Muscovy's rulers.[14]

One of these legends invoked in the sixteenth-century chronicle *Tale of the Princes of Vladimir* was that a forefather of Rurik, from whom the Muscovite rulers claimed direct continuity, had been the Roman Emperor Augustus.[15]

What is particularly relevant in the context of international law is that the title of tsar was simultaneously also a claim to the lands which Rus had

[10] Andreas Kappeler, *The Russian Empire: A Multiethnic History*, Routledge, 2013 (2001 Taylor & Francis), 21–6.
[11] Serhii Plokhy, *Lost Kingdom. The Quest for Empire and the Making of the Russian Nation. From 1470 to the Present*, Basic Books, 2017, 9–10.
[12] V I Zuev, 'Prioritet russkoy pravovoy mysli v sozdanii i razvitii teorii suvereniteta', *SGP* No 3, 1951, 24–37 at 27.
[13] Gal'perin, 'Voprosy mezhdunarodnopravovoga priznania edinogo rossiyskogo gosudarstva XV-XVI vv', 1969, 270–1.
[14] Kozhevnikov, *Russkoe gosudarstvo i mezhdunarodnoe pravo (do XX veka)*, 2006, 85.
[15] Ibid.

arguably lost in the past, when Rus came under Mongol–Tartar rule and things fell apart.[16] Thus, a very practical element in the Muscovite rulers' titles of 'tsar' and 'ruler of all Rus' in practice meant that Muscovy had territorial claims to its Western neighbours—Poland, Lithuania, and Sweden. Muscovy's struggle for recognition of the title of tsar was simultaneously also a programme for recovery of lands arguably lost in the past and now 'occupied' by its neighbours.[17] Lithuanian expansion to the lands of Rus has also been narrated in Lithuanian historical scholarship.[18] Based on these ideas of its own historical patrimony, Muscovy did not recognize, for example, the river Ugra—currently located in the Smolensk and Kaluga oblasts of the Russian Federation—as a legitimate border between itself and the Kingdom of Lithuania, even though it served in that function for a while. Because of Muscovy's territorial pretensions linked to the title of tsar, for a considerable time Lithuania, Poland, and Sweden—Muscovy's immediate Western neighbours— refused to formally recognize the claim by the rulers of Muscovy to the title of tsar. For example, the title of tsar appeared in the Muscovite version of the treaty of 1549, but not in the Lithuanian version. In 1551 and 1552 the Lithuanian Rada (Senate) and the Muscovite Duma had to negotiate because negotiations between the sovereigns had become impossible due to Ivan Grozny's insistence on the title 'tsar'. The same situation recurred in later decades.[19] In the course of the sixteenth and seventeenth centuries, Muscovy protested on every occasion that its rulers' title of tsar was, in its own view, not adequately respected by European peers in diplomatic correspondence.[20]

The memory of these distant disputes and conflicts has not disappeared in contemporary foreign policy discourse. For example, on 15 September 2022, the (then) Twitter account of the Russian Ministry of Foreign Affairs, citing the Ministry's spokesperson, Maria Zakharova, announced: 'The Battle of Orsha of 1522 between Muscovy & the then Lithuania is glorified in Lithuania & Ukraine on an annual basis. Russophobes can manipulate history as much as

[16] E A Korovin, *Istoria mezhdunarodnogo prava. Vypusk I (ot drevnosti i do kontsa XVIII veka). Posobie k lektsyam*, Moscow: Voenno-yuridicheskaya akademia Krasnoy Armii i Vyshaya Diplomaticheskaya Shkola MID SSSR, 1946, 45–9, 83. Cf Kozhevnikov, *Russkoe gosudarstvo i mezhdunarodnoe pravo (do XX veka)*, 2006, 83.

[17] Gal'perin, 'Voprosy mezhdunarodnopravovoga priznania edinogo rossiyskogo gosudarstva XV-XVI vv', 1969, 269.

[18] Arturas Dubonis, 'Dve modeli litovskoy ekspansii na Rusi (XIII-nachalo XIV v). Ovladenia Polotksom i Novogrudkom', in: A E Titkov (ed) *Istorichesky vestnik, Tom 7, Litva, Rus i Polsha XIII-XIX vv*, Moscow, 2014, 54–85.

[19] Walter Leitsch, 'Russo-Polish Confrontation', in: Taras Hunczak (ed) *Russian Imperialism from Ivan the Great to the Revolution*, Rutgers UP, 1974, 131–66 at 139.

[20] Korovin, *Istoria mezhdunarodnogo prava. Vypusk I (ot drevnosti i do kontsa XVIII veka)*, 1946, 47 et seq

they want, in the end it all comes down to peace treaties, which fixed Moscow in achieving its goals.'[21]

At the same time, the tsars of Muscovy occasionally also made it clear to their main Western neighbours—Poland and Sweden—that they did not consider their rulers equal to themselves. This illustrates an ambition to be the more significant state; to establish a hierarchy between powers. For example, Tsar Ivan Grozny wrote to the Swedish King Erik XIV that he was as far above Erik as 'the sky is from the earth'.[22] The tsars refused to address Swedish and Polish kings—sovereigns on Muscovy's Western border—with the characteristic friendly denomination of the time, 'brother'. Evgeny Korovin (1892–1964), a leading Soviet Russian international lawyer, wrote that Muscovy's diplomatic efforts at the time were motivated by the 'struggle for equal rights, for the dignity of Russia as a great power, its status among other international actors'.[23] This was a popular Soviet trope: 'The whole history of the struggle of rulers of Moscow for the title of tsar and later emperor was a struggle for independence, equality and sovereignty of the state of Moscow.'[24] Even the authoritative course on international law of the perestroika era in the Soviet Union emphasized:

> [In the sixteenth century] Russia returned to its place among the great powers. [. . .] the Muscovite state never recognized the right of the Roman Emperor to award the tsar's (royal) power as was done by many West European countries. The smallest protocolary strangulations of Russia's independence were decisively brought to a stop.[25]

What is noteworthy in the history politics of this narrative is that Russia only 'returns', an understanding of history that justifies various seizures. They are not conquests but the 'return' of territories. This trope identifies Kievan Rus and Muscovy with Russia, talking of the 'restoration' of a certain great power status but also a territorial reach which Kievan Rus was assumed to have enjoyed among European states before the Mongol–Tartar invasion.

A comparative context of Muscovy's disputes regarding the title of tsar with European states was that, before the seventeenth century at least, it was common in Europe to think of states in terms of their rank and hierarchy within

[21] MFA Russia (@MFA_russia) Twitter account, 15.09.2022.
[22] Korovin, *Istoria mezhdunarodnogo prava. Vypusk I (ot drevnosti i do kontsa XVIII veka)*, 1946, 48
[23] Ibid, 49.
[24] Zuev, 'Prioritet russkoy pravovoy mysli v sozdanii i razvitii teorii suvereniteta', 1951, 26.
[25] R A Müllerson, G I Tunkin (eds) *Kurs mezhdunarodnogo prava. Tom 1. Ponyatie, predmet i sistema mezhdunarodnoga prava*, in: V N Kudriavtsev (general ed) *Kurs mezhdunarodnoga prava v semi tomakh*, Nauka, 1989, 51.

the European community. In Western Europe, in 1504, Pope Julius II published a regulation which established twenty-eight ranks for states. According to this scheme, the Holy Roman Emperor was followed by the Roman king; the kings of France, Castile, Aragon, and England; and so on.[26] As a result, a monarchy's place in the ranking order was a legitimate concern. The idea of equality of sovereign states, big or small, had not yet been firmly established in international law.

Muscovy's political publicists in the sixteenth and seventeenth centuries—among them, Ivan Peresvetov, Maksim Grek, and Yuri Krizhanich—discussed Messianic ideas about the reach of Muscovy's power far beyond its borders, and in particular the need to liberate Orthodox Christian populations from Ottoman rule.[27] The author of the idea that Moscow was the 'third Rome', Philotheus of Pskov (Filofei; 1465–1542), also spoke out against freedom of science and scientific research, even for the tsars,[28] thus expressing the opposite to emerging Renaissance ideas in Western Europe. In his history of international law scholarship in Russia, Vladimir Hrabar (also called Grabar) (1865–1956) discusses these authors when addressing Muscovy's proto-international legal claims and positions.[29] The main point seems to be that Muscovy had convinced itself that it was morally, dynastically, and—simply in terms of justice—entitled to expand its territories or, as it claimed, to restore its ancient patrimony. In this sense, territorial expansion was Muscovy's key international programme in the early modern era, although this was not framed as conquest but as liberation and restoration of rightful patrimony.

In terms of the birth of international legal arguments, Muscovy's expansion to the Urals and Siberia from the sixteenth century was not accompanied by any specific claims or debates which would, for example, resemble Spanish theological–moral quasi-legal debates about the conquest of the New World (America). When advancing in Siberia, the Russians were of course confronted with the indigenous population. However, there emerged no Muscovite legal–political reflections *à la* Francisco de Vitoria (1483–1546) or Bartolomé de las Casas (1484–1566) in Spain on whether Muscovy had the

[26] D V Aleksandrikov, 'Vlianie Velikoy oktyabrskoy revolyutsii na razvitie i utverzhdenie printsipa ravenstva gosudarstv v mezhdunarodnom prave', *Soviet YBIL* 1968, 106–120 at 107. Cf Martens 1883, 384.

[27] Korovin, *Istoria mezhdunarodnogo prava. Vypusk I (ot drevnosti i do kontsa XVIII veka)*, 1946, 65.

[28] N M Zolotukhina, 'Iz istorii russkoi politicheskoi mysli kontsa XV-nachala XVI v: teoria "Moskva—tretii Rim"', *SGP* No 1, 1977, 100–6 at 106.

[29] V E Grabar, *The History of International Law in Russia, 1647–1917. A Bio-Bibliographical Study*, translated and edited by W E Butler, Clarendon Press, 1990, 14 et seq.

right to conquer the militarily weak and non-Christian natives in Siberia. In contrast, Antony Anghie—international lawyer and a leading critical historian of European imperialism in international law—has emphasized the importance of Vitoria's work for the emergence of European international law and, in the end, for legitimizing European colonial conquests and imperialism.[30] Later, the Soviet and even the post-Soviet Russian narrative often highlighted that when Muscovy and later the Russian Empire expanded to regions such as Siberia, the Caucasus, or what is nowadays Kazakhstan, various ethnic groups and regions became part of Muscovy (Russia) 'voluntarily'. This highlights at least the discursive difference with West European empires, where violent conquest as such has at least recently been acknowledged. However, the reality of Russia's conquest in the East was often different from the purported voluntary nature of its expansion: indeed, the subjugation of populations was a violent and often lengthy process of conquest.[31] Debates about agreements concluded in the process of conquest were a part of this phenomenon because Muscovy considered acts of subjugation as final whereas the local rulers sometimes did not, seeing—instead of final subjugation to Muscovy—arrangements for protection which could be renegotiated and even reversed, if necessary by rebellion.

In 1654, Muscovy concluded an agreement with the Ukrainian hetmanate—the Pereyaslav Agreement—which later became a source of intense academic and political debate, particularly between Russian and Ukrainian authors, arguing over its exact nature and consequences.[32] The Pereyaslav Agreement became a subject of memory debates and even memory wars when the question of Ukraine's relationship with the Russian Empire or the Soviet Union came up. During the Soviet period, and particularly in 1954, the Pereyaslav Agreement was widely celebrated as the act of Ukraine's voluntary unification with Russia.[33] However, during the Russo-Ukrainian war in 2022 a scene was aired on Russian television in which the chairman of the Russian Constitutional Court, Valery Zorkin, brought a French map from the seventeenth century to the Kremlin; in examining it, both President Putin and Zorkin emphasized

[30] Antony Anghie, *Imperialism, Sovereignty and the Making of International Law*, CUP, 2005.

[31] See, eg, Alton S Donnelly, *The Russian Conquest of Bashkiria 1552–1740. A Case Study in Imperialism*, Yale UP, 1968, 173.

[32] See, eg, V A Myakotin, *'Pereyaslavskii dogovor' 1654-go goda*, Izdatel'skoe obshchestvo 'Edinstvo', 1930; Vyacheslav Prokopovych, 'The Problem of the Juridical Nature of the Ukraine's Union with Muscovy', *The Annals of the Ukrainian Academy of Arts and Sciences in the US* No 4, 1955, 917–80.

[33] See K A Sofronenko, 'Vossoedinenie Ukrainy s Rossiei (1654–1954 gg), *SGP* No 1, 1954, 55–70; B M Babii, V A Chekhovin, 'Vydaiusheesya sobytie v istorii nashey Rodiny (K 325-letiu vossoedinenia Ukrainy s Rossiey), *SGP* No 3, 1979, 26–31.

that no 'Ukraine' was depicted on it.[34] At the same time, a Soviet historian of international law noted with a certain pride that in 1649 the Ukrainian hetman Bogdan Khmelnitsky had concluded an agreement with the Ottoman Empire on free navigation of merchant ships in the Black Sea.[35] In order to do that, the hetmanate must have enjoyed international legal subjectivity, at least in the eyes of the Ottomans: so Judge Zorkin's French map can only be a fragment of the whole picture. In the late seventeenth century, Muscovy expanded, especially at the expense of the Kingdom of Poland. In particular, the Moscow treaty of 1686 turned out highly successful for Muscovy as it expanded by some 2000 square miles.[36] As already indicated, in Soviet Russian historiography these territorial changes were not understood as conquests but as Muscovy returning original Russian lands to itself.[37]

The Great Nordic War and Petr Shafirov: Russia's First Argument in European International Law

Muscovy started to talk more specifically in language referring to international law when it started the Great Nordic War (1700–21) against Sweden. The war started when the army of the Russian Tsar Peter I attacked Swedish forces at the battle of Narva in 1700; a battle which the Russians lost. However, at the latest with the battle of Poltava in 1709, the fortunes of war turned: in the end, Russia won the war and gained Ingria (where St Petersburg was founded in 1703) as well as Estonia and Livonia (which comprised most of today's Latvia). Sweden recognized the transfer of Ingria, Estonia, and Livonia to Russia in the 1721 Treaty of Uusikaupunki (Nystad).[38] As a result of this successful war, Peter the Great declared himself Russian emperor in 1721. From then on, the Russian emperors demanded respect for this title from their European peers, just as earlier Russian rulers had demanded recognition of their title of tsar. The leading tsarist-era Russian international lawyer, Fedor Martens, highlighted the importance of the Peace Treaty of Uusikaupunki (Nystad), as only after

[34] Erin Burnett (CNN), 'Putin's Latest Move Includes a Map of the 17th Century', 23.05.2023, https://edition.cnn.com/videos/world/2023/05/23/erin-burnett-monologue-map-putin-ukraine-17-century-ebof-vpx.cnn.

[35] V I Lisovsky, 'Dogovor getmana Bogdana Khmel'nitskogo s sultanom Turtsii o svobodnom plavanii torgovykh sudov po Chernemu moryu', *Soviet YBIL* 1959, 401–5.

[36] See further L R Lewitter, 'The Russo-Polish Treaty of 1686 and its Antecendents', IX *The Polish Review* No 3–4, 1964.

[37] Kozhevnikov, *Russkoe gosudarstvo i mezhdunarodnoe pravo (do XX veka)*, 2006, 33.

[38] For a contemporary Russian reception of this treaty, see N A Narochnitskaya, G A Sanin, I V Nogaev (eds) *Nishtadtsky mirnyi dogovor i rozhdenie Rossiyskoi imperii 1721–2021*, Veche, 2021.

that did Russia have 'permanent and regular relations with Western Europe' and become 'an indispensable member of the European community'.[39]

The Great Nordic War is an under-studied example of Muscovy's history politics and its early use of international law. Essentially, in the context of this war, Russia claimed that everything was the other way round: it was not that Muscovy had attacked Sweden; rather, it framed Sweden as the aggressive party at fault for the war. Later, especially the Soviet historiography of international law echoed the officially endorsed justifications of how Russia was merely defending its 'vital interests' in the Great Nordic War at the shores of the Baltic Sea.[40] The echo of this Russian and Soviet framing of the history of the Great Nordic War is also reflected in some Cold War-era international law works in the West. For example, William E Butler—American historian of international law and translator of Russian and Soviet works on international law—referred to the 'war between Sweden and Russia' (in that order) in his publication of Petr Shafirov's text on the just causes of the Great Nordic War, even though it is a historical fact that it was Russia that started the war.[41] On the other hand, emphasizing Sweden as the 'symbolically initial' party of the war even in the title of Shafirov's book actually well reflects what Russian propaganda at the time wanted Europeans to think. This way of framing wars was later repeated on other occasions in Soviet history: for example, in a radio speech Soviet foreign minister Molotov referred to the 'Polish–German war' when justifying the Soviet army's entry into Eastern Poland on 17 September 1939.[42]

Shafirov's text was written in the Russian language in 1716 but published only after Russia's victory in the Great Nordic War, in 1722. It was apparently also the first ever Russian text translated into and printed in English. Since the mid-twentieth century, Shafirov's treatise has repeatedly been called 'the first original work on international law in the Russian language' and also a 'work dedicated to the problem of just war and the form of its declaration'.[43] In other publications, it is simply referred to as 'the first Russian work on international law'.[44] William E Butler also took over the trope from Hrabar and other Soviet authors since the 1940s that Shafirov's text was 'the first original work *of an*

[39] Martens, *Traité de droit international*, 1883, 137.

[40] Korovin, *Istoria mezhdunarodnogo prava. Vypusk I (ot drevnosti i do kontsa XVIII veka)*, 1946, 80.

[41] P P Shafirov, *A Discourse Concerning the Just Causes of the War Between Sweden and Russia: 1700–1721*, with an introduction by W E Butler, Oceana Publications, 1973.

[42] Claudia Weber, *Der Pakt. Hitler, Stalin und die Geschichte einer mörderischen Allianz*, CH Beck, 2019, 82.

[43] V N Durdenevsky/S B Krylov (eds), *Mezhdunarodnoe pravo*, Yuridicheskoe izdatel'stvo ministerstva iustitsii SSSR, 1947, 63.

[44] Lev Berdnikov, *Jews in Service to the Tsar*, translated by Nora Seligman Favorov, Russian Information Services, 2009, 79.

unofficial nature on international law in the Russian language', and yet Butler also added that Shafirov's was 'an isolated and lonely monument, unemulated by another Russian work of comparable scope or originality for many decades'.[45] That Shafirov's text was of an 'unofficial nature' is perhaps true simply in the formal sense that it did not go out in the name of Russia as a state but under the abbreviation 'PS'. However, the person behind this abbreviation, namely Petr Shafirov, was the vice-chancellor of the Russian Empire. Shafirov had been the Russian negotiator of the 1711 Treaty of Pruth with the Ottoman Empire, which involved a very difficult negotiating situation for Russia and Peter the Great's army. But Shafirov's career had been far from linear: he was accused of corruption and at some point, Peter the Great even ordered Shafirov's mock execution; the Tsar's pardon and Shafirov's internal exile in a Russian province were announced at the very moment when he expected his execution to be carried out.

As propaganda and justification material, Shafirov's text was used domestically in Russia very widely: its 1722 print run produced 20,000 copies and sold at discount prices throughout the Russian Empire.[46] Thus, in practice it was an *ex post facto* justification of Russia's war aims in the Great Nordic War. In any case, we should examine Shafirov's text and its arguments more closely. It turns out that Shafirov's text was less of a 'work dedicated to the problem of just war and the form of its declaration'[47] but more of a justification for violating treaties which Muscovy had previously—before the Great Nordic War—concluded with Sweden. In contemporary terms, we could compare Shafirov's text with a passionate and politics-laden oral presentation which a state's diplomatic representative would present to the ICJ in contentious proceedings; at least, it is a distant predecessor of this genre.

The background for the emergence of Shafirov's text was that Peter the Great and Russian diplomacy were facing an image problem in Europe because in 1700 Muscovy had started the Great Nordic War in violation of previous peace treaties with Sweden, especially the Treaty of Stolbovo (1617)[48] but also the Peace Treaty of Cardis (Kärde; 1661). According to these treaties, the border between Russia and Sweden was considered settled and was recognized by both parties. True, there had been signs of turbulence, as there had

[45] W E Butler, 'P P Shafirov and the Law of Nations, in: P P Shafirov (P.S.), *A Discourse Concerning the Just Causes of the War Between Sweden and Russia: 1700-1721*, with an introduction by W.E. Butler (Oceana Publications 1973), 39.

[46] Butler, ibid.

[47] Durdnevesky/Krylov, *Mezhdunarodnoe pravo,*1947, 63.

[48] See NP Lyzhin, *Stolbovskiy dogovor i peregovory emu predshestvuyushie*, Tip. Imp. Akademii Nauk, 1857.

been quarrels over interpretation of the thirty articles of the Cardis treaty and Muscovy had complained of Sweden's infringements of some of these articles. However, in 1666 Muscovy agreed to make the Cardis treaty 'permanent' and to accept Swedish diplomats in the capital, Moscow, on a permanent basis.[49] In October 1683 the treaty of Cardis was confirmed, with great pomp and circumstance, by a Russian embassy in Stockholm, while a Swedish embassy travelled to Moscow to confirm the treaty on behalf of King Charles XI in June 1684.[50]

Swedish writers such as the King's official historian, Olaus (Olof) Hermelin (1658–1709), who had experienced Muscovy's geographical proximity at first hand as a professor in Sweden's province of Livonia, attacked Russia for having violated these treaties as well as the laws and customs of war.[51] Hermelin questioned whether Russia was a 'civilized' country, for example writing about Peter the Great:

> Er hat ja diesen Krieg nicht erhoben / sein oder seiner Bunds-Genossen Beschimpffung /davon nichts zu hören/ zu rächen / sondern nur sein barbarisches wesen in die manierlich eingerichtete Europäische Länder einzuführen.[52]

Hermelin concluded that the Russians were 'Verstörer des Rechtes aller Völker'.[53] For the context of these accusations, we should keep in mind that the question of *bonne foi* was a central one in eighteenth-century European discussion on the nature of treaties; it was damaging for the reputation of a ruler for him to be called 'perfidious'.[54]

Before becoming a part of Sweden in the sixteenth century, since the thirteenth century, Estonia and Livonia had been ruled by the Teutonic Order and bishoprics which were vassals of the Holy Roman Empire, while Denmark had also ruled Estonia in the thirteenth and early fourteenth centuries. The

[49] Ragnhilde Marie Hatton, 'Russia and the Baltic', in: Taras Hunczak (ed) *Russian Imperialism from Ivan the Great to the Revolution*, Rutgers UP, 1974, 106–30 at 117.

[50] Ibid, 118.

[51] Olaus Hermelin, *Gerechte Ablehnung derer lasterhafften Beschuldigungen, womit der Moscowitische Czar Seinen Krieg, damit Er Schweden, wieder Eyd, und noch neulich versicherte Treu und Glauben, angegriffen, zu beschönigen gesuchet hat*, nach dem Lateinischen Original übersetzt, Stockholm, 1701. On Hermelin and Swedish war propaganda during the Great Nordic War, see Sven Olsson, *Olof Hermelin. En karolinsk kulturspersonlighet och statsman*, Gleerupska Univ-Bokhandel, 1953, 177 et seq.

[52] Ibid, 55 ('He did not start the war in order to take revenge for insults to him or his countrymen – which did not happen – but in order to introduce its barbaric essence in civilized European countries').

[53] Ibid, 57 ('violators of the laws of all peoples').

[54] Marc Bélissa, 'Peace Treaties, Bonne Foi and European Civility in the Enlightment', in: Randall Lesaffer (ed) *Peace Treaties and International Law in European History. From the Late Middle Ages to World War One*, CUP, 2004, 241–53 at 243.

Teutonic crusader states in the Baltics were stable polities by the standards of their age and had seen both peaceful times and wars and military raids with Muscovy, as well as their Russian neighbours that had later been absorbed by Muscovy, namely the republics of Novgorod and Pskov. Sometimes the Teutonic Order was even the more successful party in these wars and raids, for example under its Master (*Landmeister*) Wolter von Plettenberg (1450–1535). Nevertheless, in 1489 the Austrian emperor Friedrich III sent a mission to Moscow which inter alia demanded that the citizens of Pskov should be prohibited from making military raids into Livonia.[55] So even if there had been a tribute situation in the eleventh century in parts of pre-German conquest Livonia—such as in Tartu, which the Kievan prince Yaroslav the Wise conquered in 1030 and maintained for three decades—there had first and foremost been centuries of Livonian independence from Rus, Muscovy, and other Russian polities. Nevertheless, in his text, Shafirov made the argument that up until their existence in the sixteenth century, the Teutonic Order had been *vassals* of Muscovy, though admitting that they had not fulfilled their duty most of the time. Moreover, the main reason why the Teutonic Order had been in the position of Muscovy's vassals was because their state had been established on 'ancient Russian land'.

This argument by Muscovy and Shafirov was not new; it had been made by Muscovy's Tsar Ivan Grozny when he started the Livonian War (1558–83), with the aim of seizing Estonia and Livonia from the Teutonic Order.[56] Even then, the Baltic (Livonian) negotiators rejected the notion of any historically established tribute but were eventually forced to accept payment of tribute to avoid Muscovy's impending military attack, a threat which could in this way only be postponed for some years.[57] Just as Muscovy initiating the Great Nordic War against Sweden in 1700 was justified in Soviet Russian historiography of international law, so was Ivan Grozny's starting the Livonian War against the Teutonic Order in 1558.[58] Moreover, at least as an echo, the historical interpretation that even in 1700 Muscovy was merely interested in 'ancient Russian lands' in the Baltics has not disappeared from Russian political discourse. For example, in June 2022, President Putin, when publicly meeting 'young scientists and entrepreneurs' in St Petersburg, compared

[55] Martens, *Traité de droit international*, 1883, 131.

[56] See Margus Laidre, *Domus belli. Põhjamaade saja-aastane sõda Liivimaal 1554–1881*, Argo, 2015, 132–5.

[57] Balthasar Russow, *Liivimaa provintsi kroonika*, translated by Jüri Kivimäe, Tänapäev, 2022, 126 et seq.

[58] Kozhevnikov, *Russkoe gosudarstvo i mezhdunarodnoe pravo (do XX veka)*, ., 2006, 29, 36.

himself to Tsar Peter the Great and said the following about the Great Nordic War:

> You might think he was fighting with Sweden, seizing their lands. But he seized nothing; he reclaimed it! It seems it has fallen to us, too, to reclaim and strengthen.[59]

Returning to Shafirov's text, we can further quote from the original English translation of his text:

> Accordingly the Bishops and Heer-meisters (Commanders of the Teutonick Order) who governed over the said cities, owned the Russian Monarchs for their supreme Lords, and paid a yearly Tribute to them as Vassals; Concerning which Affair many original Writings and Records are still extant to this Day in the Russian Chanceries at Moskow, Novgorod and Pleskow. [. . .] And though the said Provinces some times, in troublesome Conjectures, departed from the Russian Obedience, yet they were reunited to Russia either by treaties or by Force of Arms.[60]

Then how did Shafirov deal with the Swedish accusation that, by attacking Narva in 1700, Tsar Peter I had violated perpetual peace treaties between Muscovy and Sweden such as the Treaties of Stolbovo and Cardis (Kärde), which recognized Livonia as part of Sweden? One argument was *tu quoque* and a reminder of the more distant past, namely that during the earlier Livonian War in the sixteenth century, after Muscovy's initial successes in the war Sweden had concluded a treaty with Muscovy in 1564 which recognized Livonia as belonging to Muscovy ('as belonging to his Czarish Majesty by Inheritance and Property, and being under his Protection').[61] Later on, in 1572, the tsar's Ambassador to Sweden had repeated the same claims:

> the Russian Ambassador maintained their Master's ancient and just Pretentions to the said Provinces, asserting that the Heermeister had always been his Czarish Majesty's Subject and Vassal, and paid Tribute to him.[62]

[59] Sarah Rainsford, 'Putin and Peter the Great: Russian leader likens himself to 18th Century tsar', *BBC*, 11.06.2022, https://www.bbc.com/news/world-europe-61767191.

[60] P S, *A Discourse concerning the Just Reasons Which his Czarish Majesty, Peter I., Czar and Emperor of all the Russians, etc, had*, 1717, 242–3 (Edited by W E Butler).

[61] Ibid, 245.

[62] Ibid, 246.

If—so went Shafirov's question—previous treaties could be changed by the party who prevailed militarily in the past, then why not during the Great Nordic War? It did not matter so much that some treaties had been called 'perpetual'.

Shafirov's other argument was to distance Muscovy from Tsar Boris Godunov (1552–1605), under whose regency the Peace Treaty of Stolbovo with Sweden had been concluded in 1617:

> so the Usurper little concerned himself about the interests of the Empire, but only made it his Business how by yielding up one Province and Town after the other, he might live in Peace with the neighbouring Powers. [...] This conduct so much incented the whole Nation, but particularly the principal Men of the Empire.[63]

As a result, '[t]his extorted Treaty was concluded between the two Parties, by the Mediation of the Ambassador of England, on the 27th of February, 1616, in the Village of Stolbowa'.[64] Shafirov failed to mention that when the Treaty of Stolbovo had been concluded, it was also widely celebrated in Muscovy. For example, the Soviet international lawyer Fedor Kozhevnikov wrote about this event:

> The treaty of Stolbovo may not be considered as a mistake of Russian diplomacy. To the contrary, in these historical circumstances, peace with the Swedes was necessary. It then freed Moscow's hands in the struggle with Polish aggression.[65]

It has been debated to what extent Shafirov's treatise on Muscovy's war aims and justifications in the Great Nordic War was about 'international law'.[66] However, references not only to treaties but also to the concepts of 'law' and 'rights' were present in Shafirov's argument, for example when he argued that:

> Peter I has in Truth had rightful Causes, supported by all the Laws of the World, to recover those Provinces (which) had been torn off and extorted

[63] Ibid, 250.
[64] Ibid, 269.
[65] Kozhevnikov, *Russkoe gosudarstvo i mezhdunarodnoe pravo (do XX veka)*, 2006, 32.
[66] Pärtel Piirimäe, 'Russia, the Turks and Europe: Legitimations of War and the Formation of European Identity in the Early Modern Period', 11 *Journal of Early Modern History* 2007, 63–86 at 64.

> from his Empire. [. . .] There were ancient Causes for it, sufficiently justiciable by the Laws of Nature and Nations, beyond all Reproaches of Conscience.[67]

Shafirov also referred to the law of nations in his criticisms of Swedish conduct of military operations:

> We might allege many other Instances, how the Swedes proceeded contrary to the Usage and Customs of War, and the general Law of all civilized Nations.[68]

The part on the laws of war and accusations of war crimes was particularly topical in Shafirov's narrative because—for example in Estonia and Livonia in the early 1700s[69] (the Sheremetev campaign) and in Finland (the so-called Great Wrath in 1714–21)— Muscovy's military had been accused of widespread massacres against the civilian population in conquered Swedish territory. However, as is typical of the genre of war justifications, Shafirov turned the accusations around and made war crimes appear as if primarily a Swedish practice.

Shafirov's text ended with an expression of satisfaction that, after having gained military victory over Sweden, Russia was now the country of which the Swedes were most afraid:

> By the Assistance of Almighty God, Russia has become so formidable that we now see a Nation who were the Terror of almost all Europe, vanquished by the Russians. And I dare say, Thanks to God alone, they dread no power whatsoever so much as Russia.[70]

One of the conclusions based on the actions of Peter the Great in the Great Nordic War and the war pamphlet of Shafirov was that even after solemn treaties establishing the sovereignty of neighbours and a different state of affairs which had lasted for several decades or even centuries, Muscovy could come back with the argument that certain territories outside its borders were in fact 'ancient Russian patrimony', which served to justify conquest. Earlier 'perpetual' treaties could be cast aside in this process because, for Muscovy, they apparently only reflected the balance of power and interests at any given historical moment.

[67] P S, *A Discourse concerning the Just Reasons Which his Czarish Majesty, Peter I., Czar and Emperor of all the Russians, etc, had*, 1717, 270-1 (Edited by W E Butler).

[68] Ibid, 342.

[69] See Christian Kelch, *Liivimaa ajaloo järg* (Continuation of the History of Livonia), Tänapäev, 2024, 125 et seq, 333.

[70] P S, *A Discourse concerning the Just Reasons Which his Czarish Majesty, Peter I., Czar and Emperor of all the Russians, etc, had*, 1717, 349 (Edited by W E Butler).

Shafirov's treatise can be seen as a foundational 'speech act' in the Russian Empire's relationship with international law; as a starter of the Russian discourse on international law. With Shafirov speaking, Russia arrived in the European community of nations and its international law, *jus publicum Europaeum*. Politically, it is fascinating that Russia comes to be perceived as a 'European' state and a participant in *jus publicum Europeaum* only after it beats Sweden militarily and conquers European (and by predominant population, Western Christian) territories in the Great Nordic War (the Baltic provinces). In our time, Shafirov's justificatory text has been reprinted in Russia with no critical (but only approving) historical commentary, as an early and authoritative example of international legal scholarship and the international legal publicist tradition in Russia.[71] It is that, too, but especially concerning the unilateral termination (violation) of earlier treaties, the reading offered above gives a more critical explanation as to in what sense this is the case.

Eighteenth and Early Nineteenth Centuries: Further Annexations and the Principle of Monarchical Legitimacy in International Law

In terms of Russian publicist–academic discourses of international law, there is not much to discuss about the eighteenth and early nineteenth centuries. However, this does not mean that the Russian Empire's role in the practice of international law in Europe was insignificant during these times.

Since the Treaty of Utrecht (1713), balance of power has been formally recognized as one of the underlying principles of international law in Europe.[72] This principle justified military intervention when some monarch's might became too threatening for other European states but it could also serve as a blueprint for voluntary restraint, for example in matters of inheritance between monarchs. In their treaty of alliance, concluded in Amsterdam on August 4 (15), 1717, Russia, Prussia, and France pledged to stand for 'general silence' in Europe (Article 5). This reference has been understood in Russian historiography of international law in such a way that since Peter the Great, Russia had become

[71] V A Tomsinov, 'Predislovie', in: P P Shafirov, Rassuzhdenie, kakie zakonnye prichiny Petr I, tsar' i povelitel' vserossiiski k nachatiu voiny protiv Karla XII, korolya shvedskogo, v 1700 godu imel, Zertsalo, 2008, VII–XII.

[72] Grewe, *Epochen der Völkerrechtsgeschichte*, Nomos, 1984, 393–4. See also Frederik Dhondt, *Balance of Power and Norm Hierarchy: Franco-British Diplomacy after the Peace of Utrecht*, Brill, 2015; Stella Ghervas, *Conquering Peace. From the Enlightment to the European Union*, Harvard UP, 2021, 34 et seq.

an indispensable empire in the European balance of power system.[73] With the treaty of Amsterdam, Russia and the other treaty powers undertook to guarantee the balance of power already expressed in the earlier Treaty of Utrecht.[74]

There were specific diplomatic events in which the Russian Empire played a decisive role. Russia mediated peace between Austria and Prussia at the Congress of Teschen in 1779.[75] In 1778, war almost broke out between Prussia and Austria over the inheritance of Bavaria; both parties requested Russia's mediation. In this spirit, the Congress of Teschen was the Russian Empress Catherine II's initiative. Eventually, Austria abandoned its claim over Bavaria, enabling war between Prussia and Austria over Bavaria to be averted.[76] This event has subsequently been highlighted as a successful example of dispute resolution by mediation. Moreover, the Empress played a leading role in establishing the institution of armed neutrality in 1780. This was undertaken during the American War of Independence in the context of attacks by the British Navy against neutral ships.[77]

However, application of the principle of the balance of power also led to controversial results in Europe, particularly from the perspective of smaller states. In 1772, 1793, and 1795, Prussia, Russia, and Austria partitioned Poland, which in the end ceased to exist as an independent state. The liquidation of Poland as a sovereign state was justified by reasons of balance of power: along with others, that 'anarchy' in Poland, due to its constitutional situation, presented a threat to its neighbours.[78] However, the partitions of Poland also led to important legal and moral debates in Europe which reveal much about the transformations in international law in Europe during the nineteenth century. Several West European international lawyers and publicists criticized the liquidation of an entire state—which had played a very important role in Central and East European history—as an immoral and even illegal act. The nineteenth century witnessed a struggle of ideas between natural law and legal positivism in legal thinking and thus, especially after the French Revolution, the layers of existing law and just (or future) law, *lex lata* and *lex ferenda*, or law and morality generally, became conflated in legal–political debates and arguments, as indeed they almost always do. In terms of legal technique, the partitions of Poland were

[73] Kozhevnikov, *Russkoe gosudarstvo I mezhdunarodnoe pravo (do XX veka)*, 2006, 48.
[74] Ibid, 159.
[75] See F Martens, *Actes concernant le congrès de Teschen*, St Petersburg, 1888.
[76] See also Martens, *Traité de droit international*, 1883, 147–8.
[77] Carl Bergbohm, *Die bewaffnete Neutralität 1780–1783. Eine Entwicklungsphase des Völkerrechts im Seekriege*, Puttkammer & Mühlbrecht, 1884. See also Grewe, *Epochen der Völkerrechtsgeschichte*,1984, 450–7 and Skordos, *Südosteuropa und das moderne Völkerrecht.*, 2021, 86 et seq.
[78] Martens, *Traité de droit international*, 1883, 144; Grewe, *Epochen der Völkerrechtsgeschichte*, 1984, 396.

formalized through treaties between Russia, Prussia, and Austria: the treaties were concluded at St Petersburg.[79] Thus, at least Russia could argue—and in fact did argue when Martens and the Russian Ministry of Foreign Affairs published these treaties in 1875—that the partitions of Poland were accomplished by one of the main instruments of international law: treaties. It was another question whether these treaties were morally defensible.

Shafirov had observed in his time that Muscovy had gained various territories 'either by treaties or by Force of Arms'.[80] Over the eighteenth and nineteenth centuries, treaties continued to play an important role in the enlargement of the Russian Empire. A case in point is the Kingdom of Kartli–Kakheti (Eastern Georgia), whose ruler Erekle II concluded the Treaty of Georgievsk with the Russian Empire in 1783. Kartli–Kakheti had been a vassal state of Persia, a status that Russia had also recognized for Kartli–Kakheti in its treaty with Persia, the Treaty of Resht (1732).[81] However, with the Treaty of Georgievsk, things changed and Georgia became a vassal State of Russia.[82] The Georgian international lawyer Levan Aleksidze (1926–2019) characterized the Treaty of Georgievsk as a treaty of submission which deprived Kartli–Kakheti of its full sovereignty.[83] At the same time, Kartli–Kakheti remained a specific subject of international law, a vassal state or protectorate (different scholars had different interpretations about the exact classification of this treaty).[84] The kingdom's right to enjoy foreign relations became restricted. Writing in the Soviet Union in 1963, Aleksidze had to navigate the sensibilities of Moscow when characterizing the treaty and the nature of the Russian–Georgian relationship in the past. Aleksidze suggested that Kartli–Kakheti exchanged a 'coerced dependence on Persia' for a 'voluntary' one on Russia.[85] However, in 1800–1, the Russian Empire annexed the Kingdom of Kartli–Kakheti regardless; a step which Aleksidze, writing during the final years of Khrushchev's rule in the Soviet

[79] See, eg, F F Martens, *Sobranie traktatov i konventsii zakliuchennykh Rossieiu s inostrannymi derzhavami*, vol II, Tipografia Bencke, 1875. 25.07.1772 Convention conclue a St Petersburg concernant le partage de la Pologne at 21; 23.12.1794 Declaration relative au partage de la Pologne at 214; 13.10.1795 Convention conclue entre la Russie et la Prusse concernant le partage de la Pologne, avec la participation de l'Autriche at 261.

[80] P S, *A Discourse concerning the Just Reasons Which his Czarish Majesty, Peter I., Czar and Emperor of all the Russians, etc, had*, 1717, 243 (Edited by W E Butler).

[81] Reza Sardari, *Un chapitre de l'histoire diplomatique de l'Iran. Les Traités entre l'Iran et la Russie depuis le XVIe siècle jusqu'à 1917*, Maurice Lavergne, Imprimeur, 1941, 61.

[82] Levan Aleksidze, 'Mezhdunarodno-pravovaya priroda Georgievskogo traktata 1783 goda', in: *International Law and Georgia (From Antiquity to Present). Selected Papers Published in 1957–2012*, Ivane Javakhishvili Tbilisi State University, 2012, 189–219.

[83] Ibid, 193, 200, 215.

[84] See, eg, Otfried Nippold, *Le Géorgie du point de vue du droit international*, Paris: Édition du Bureau de presses géorgien, 1920.

[85] Aleksidze, 'Mezhdunarodno-pravovaya priroda Georgievskogo traktata 1783 goda', 2012, 205.

Union, boldly dared to characterize as the Russian Empire's violation of the terms of the Treaty of Georgievsk.[86] This statement was possible because, at the time, it was tolerable to say that the Russian Empire had been an 'imperialist' state, whereas one could not, of course, have publicly indicated the same thing about the Soviet Union. That the Russian annexation of Georgia violated the terms of the earlier Treaty of Georgievsk was also a view shared by the Iranian legal scholar Reza Sardari.[87] Nevertheless, reflecting the political limits of his time and situation, Aleksidze further concluded that the Treaty of Georgievsk was 'objectively a progressive phenomenon' as it integrated Kartli–Kakheti with Russia, which was 'more developed' than Persia or the Ottoman Empire, and 'put an end to the physical destruction of the Georgian people'.[88] Avoiding such legal semantics and intricacies of argument, in 1983 a Soviet postage stamp simply declared the 1783 Treaty of Georgievsk to be 'the first manifest of friendship and brotherhood between the Russian and the Georgian peoples'.

Another Russian territorial acquisition was Moldova. In 1812, the eastern part of the Principality of Moldova, known as Bessarabia, was united with the Russian Empire. The Principality of Moldova (in Russian: Moldavia) had been a significant state of the medieval and early modern era, particularly under Stefan the Great, who died in 1504. [89] However, for several centuries before annexation by Russia, the Principality of Moldova had been a vassal state of the Ottoman Empire. The Soviet historiography of international law highlighted that leading Moldovan intellectuals and statesmen such as Nicolae Milescu (1636–1708) and Dimitrie Cantemir (1673–1723) advocated for the principality's dependency on Russia as opposed to Ottoman suzerainty because—an apparent paradox—this would help Moldova 'to preserve its statehood'.[90] However, unification of the principality's territory with the Russian Empire in 1812 meant that Moldova's statehood was not preserved. Furthermore, with respect to the Ottoman Empire, the historian Will Smiley has argued that the Russian Empire developed certain regional and bilateral norms and practices together with it, particularly concerning the treatment of prisoners of war.[91]

[86] Ibid, 219.

[87] Sardari, *Un chapitre de l'histoire diplomatique de l'Iran* 1941, 64.

[88] Aleksidze, 'Mezhdunarodno-pravovaya priroda Georgievskogo traktata 1783 goda', 2012, 219.

[89] On the historical distinction between Moldova, Moldavia, and Bessarabia, see Rebecca Haynes, *Moldova. A History*, Bloomsbury, 2020, 3.

[90] Yu A Baskin, P V Sovetov, 'Voprosy mezhdunarodnoga prava v dogovornoy praktike i politicheskoy literature Moldavii XIV-XVIII vv.', *Soviet YBIL* 1962, 189–210 at 204.

[91] Will Smiley, *From Slaves to Prisoners of War. The Ottoman Empire, Russia, and International Law*, OUP, 2018. See also V V Poznakhirev, 'Osobennosti dogovorov o sdache krepostey (kapituliatsii), zaklyuchennykh v khode russko-turetskikh voin XVIII–XIX vv', GP No 12, 2015, 93–101.

The Russian–Jewish emigrant scholar Boris Mirkine-Guetzévitch (1892–1955), who wrote a study on the influence of the French Revolution on international law in Eastern Europe, observed that imperial Russia's foreign policy was continuously characterized by the desire for territorial expansion, which Mirkine-Guetzévitch, 'for the sake of brevity', called the 'territorial principle'.[92] In the nineteenth century, Russia's preference for territorial expansion became intertwined with battling against liberal ideas in European politics, especially the democratic ideas of the French Revolution. During the rule of Tsars Alexander I and Nicholas I, it was the foreign legal policy of the Russian Empire to keep Europe safe for multinational empires ruled by autocratic emperors. Therefore, St Petersburg promoted the principle of monarchical legitimacy in European international law and, if necessary, supported intervention in defence of that principle. When the power of a monarch in Europe was threatened by revolutions and popular uprisings, particularly those fuelled by ethno-national sentiment, the Russian Empire worked towards keeping the monarch in power and keeping control over the situation. This policy was particularly marked during the activity of the Holy Alliance in 1815–30, which was an initiative of the Russian Emperor Alexander I.[93] This means that the Russian imperial vision of the international legal order in Europe at that time was one of multinational empires where populations were ruled by a monarch whose legitimacy came from God, but certainly not from the people(s) as democratic legitimacy. In 1848, Russia suppressed the Hungarian Revolution, to defend the principle of monarchical legitimacy in the Austrian Empire. Historians of international law have argued that during the first half of the nineteenth century and compared to liberal West European powers, a separate stream of more conservative international law flowed in Eastern and Central Europe,[94] shaped particularly by the Russian Empire, together with Austria and Prussia.

The period after the Congress of Vienna was also a period in the history of international law in Europe which saw far-reaching deviations from the premise that (European) states are equal in their sovereignty. On several occasions, the great powers of the Holy Alliance made decisions about smaller powers without consulting them.[95] This period was one of those in European history in which the status and special powers of *puissances principales de*

[92] Boris Mirkine-Guetzévitch, 'L'influence de la révolution française sur le développement du droit international dans l'Europe orientale', *RCADI*, Vol 22, 1929, 295–457 at 337, 349, 351.

[93] Wilhelm G Grewe, *Epochen der Völkerrechtsgeschichte*, Baden-Baden: Nomos, 1984, 505.

[94] V N Durdenevsky, S B Krylov (eds), *Mezhdunarodnoe pravo*, 1947, 8.

[95] Karol Wolfke, *Great and Small Powers in International Law from 1814 to 1920. (From the Pre-History of the United Nations)*, Travaux de la Société des sciences et des lettres de Wroclaw, 1961. See also Grewe, *Epochen der Völkerrechtsgeschichte*, 1984, 505.

l'Europe (or *premieres puissances* or *puissances du premier ordre*) were institutionalized, a 'directorate of great powers' to which Russia belonged.[96]

Already in the late eighteenth century, the Empress Catherine II had proudly declared that she 'had possessions in three parts of the world',[97] meaning not only Europe and Asia but also America. The 1823 Monroe doctrine of the US, which opposed any European intervention in the Western hemisphere, was inter alia a response to the European doctrine supporting intervention in the name of monarchical legitimacy. There was a possibility, based on what Russia had proposed and what was decided at the Congress of Troppau in 1820, that the Holy Alliance would support military intervention in South America to preserve the 'legitimate' colonial possessions of the Spanish and Portuguese empires and monarchs.[98] Moreover, with the Ukase of 4/16 September 1821, Russia claimed Alaska and, beyond it, further parts of North America, although in 1825 it reached an agreement with both the US and Great Britain which reversed at least some of these extensive claims.[99] In 1867 the US purchased Alaska from the Russian Empire, which was in deep financial need after its defeat in the Crimean War in 1856.

When using *jus publicum Europaeum* after the eighteenth century, Russia could take advantage of the fact that international law at the time did not outlaw war, conquest, and annexations. In this spirit, a special role in extending the Russian Empire was played by treaties. However, in practice such treaties were usually only of a mainly temporary quality. That is, when the balance of power tilted further in Russia's favour, a previous treaty-based arrangement was unceremoniously abandoned. For example, in the Treaty of Küçük Kaynarca (1774), Russia and the Ottoman Empire agreed not to intervene in the political, civil, and domestic matters of the Crimean khanate.[100] However, in 1783 Russia seized and annexed Crimea regardless, 'practically bloodlessly'.[101] When a territory had become Russian, it was defended as Russian territory with all the force of military power as well as legal–political arguments; territorial retreat was exceptional. The history of international law in the Russian Empire over the eighteenth to nineteenth centuries is simultaneously a history of territorial expansion.[102]

[96] Grewe, *Epochen der Völkerrechtsgeschichte*, 1984, 503.
[97] Durdenevski/Krylov (eds), *Mezhdunarodnoe pravo*, 1947, 63.
[98] Durdenevsky/Krylov (eds), ibid, 70; Grewe, *Epochen der Völkerrechtsgeschichte*, 1984, 506.
[99] Martens, *Traité de droit international*, 1883, 466–7.
[100] See Igor I Lukashuk (ed) *Osnovnye printsipy mezhdunarodnoga prava*, in: V N Kudriavtsev (ed) *Kurs mezhdunarodnoga prava v semi tomakh*, Vol 2, Moscow, Nauka, 1989, 131.
[101] Viatcheslav Svetlichnyi, 'Kratkii ocherk istorii rossiiskogo diplomaticheskogo predstavitel'stva v Krymskom khanstve', *MZh* No 12, 2013, https://interaffairs.ru/jauthor/material/997.
[102] Cf Vladislav l Tolstykh, *Kurs mezhdunarodnoga prava*, Prospekt, 2018, 96 et seq.

3

The Late Russian Empire (1856–1917)

1870 and the Problem of *Clausula Rebus Sic Stantibus*

For European international relations and law in the nineteenth century, the Crimean War (1853–6) constituted a watershed.[1] One of the events that preceded the war—the Russian occupation of the Danube principalities, which were under the suzerainty of the Ottoman Empire—was seen as a violation of international law (treaties).[2] In the Crimean War, the alliance of England, France, Sardinia, and the Ottoman Empire achieved a military victory over the Russian Empire. The war ended with the Paris Peace Treaty, which inter alia foresaw the neutralization of the Black Sea; Russia was no longer supposed to keep its navy there and committed not to build new fortifications on the northern shore of the Black Sea as well as to demolish existing ones.[3] The point in this peace settlement was not only the navy and fortifications as such but whether Russia counted as a great power in the Black Sea region, without limits set by other European powers.

The Franco–Prussian war broke out in 1870. Russia announced on 30 October that year that it would move its navy back to the Black Sea, contrary to the stipulations of the Paris Peace Treaty. When doing so, St Petersburg referred to the fundamental change of circumstances as justification for its disregard of the Paris Treaty. In November 1870, Russia's foreign minister, Prince Gorchakov, announced that '*l'Europe aujourd'hui n'est plus celle qui a signé le traité de 1856*'.[4] Gorchakov argued that other powers, too, had violated the Black Sea neutrality stipulations of the Paris Peace Treaty and that

[1] See, eg, Fréderic de Martens, *Traité de droit international*, Tome I, Paris: Librairie Marescq Ainé, 1883, who starts to count a new sub-period in the evolution of international law from the end of the Crimean war in 1856. On the international legal claims and arguments in the Crimean war, see further Hendrik Simon, *A Century of Anarchy? War, Normativity, and the Birth of Modern International Order*, OUP, 2024, 154 et seq.

[2] Adamantios Theodor Skordos, *Südosteuropa und das moderne Völkerrecht. Eine transregionale und globale Geschichte im 19 und 20 Jahrhundert*, Wallstein Verlag, 2021, 77.

[3] Martens, Traité de droit international, 1883, 182.

[4] Erich Kaufmann, *Das Wesen des Völkerrechts und die clausula rebus sic stantibus*, J C B Mohr, 1911, 15.

Russia, the Soviet Union, and Imperial Continuity in International Law. Lauri Mälksoo, Oxford University Press.
 DOI: 10.1093/9780198955962.003.0003

new developments in naval technology put Russia at risk; Russia needed to respond. In the twentieth century, Soviet international legal scholars approvingly repeated the official line as stated by Gorchakov: it was not Russia but other powers such as England and France which had 'systematically violated' the terms of the 1856 Paris Peace Treaty on the neutrality of the Black Sea.[5]

As a sidenote, it is of interest that, in 2014, Russia's foreign minister, Sergey Lavrov, opened a monument to Alexander Gorchakov at the elite MGIMO University in Moscow, which is designed to work in close cooperation with the Russian foreign ministry. Gorchakov became known for his policy circular of 1856 which said: *La Russie ne boude pas; elle se recueille* ('Russia is not sulking, she is composing herself').[6] This phrase of Gorchakov's has often been approvingly referred to in Putin's Russia and the apparent parallel found here is that, in some periods, Russia has been kept down by historical events, especially by hostile Western powers—but it rises again, through its own strength and determination. In the context of interest to us here, we can take note of the fact that, in 1870, Russia's 'thinking things over' led to the sudden Russian 'self-liberation' from the constraints laid down by the Treaty of Paris (1856). However, if Gorchakov and his doctrine and policies were an inspiration for Moscow's MGIMO University in 2014, then it also cannot be ignored that even in 2008 the Russian Federation had started to challenge post-Soviet borders in South Ossetia and Abkhazia, contrary to Russia's earlier agreements and her recognition of those borders, and that 2014 was the year of Russia's annexation of Crimea and the beginning of the war in the Donbas.

The violation of a relatively recent treaty in 1870 triggered a diplomatic crisis, and the leading European powers gathered for a conference in London to discuss the situation, including the principled question whether a fundamental change of circumstances could ever constitute an excuse or justification for violating or bypassing earlier treaty stipulations. Of course, this whole theme did not come up just in 1870–1; it had been an older issue in the interpretation of state obligations as well as in international law literature.[7] For example, the English international lawyer Richard Zouche (1590–1661) cited a diplomatic incident between England and Holland in 1585 in which the position of Queen Elizabeth I was understood to mean that promises remained in

[5] Kozhevnikov, *Russkoe gosudarstvo i mezhdunarodnoe pravo (do XX veka)*, 2006,162–3.

[6] On Gorchakov's reception in Russia's foreign policy discourse, see, eg, Amir Bilialitdinov, 'Kniaz' Gorchakov kak zerkalo russkoi tsiklichnosti. K 220-letiu so dnia rozhdenia samogo populiarnogo v proshlom ministra inostrannykh del', *MZh* No 8, 2018, https://interaffairs.ru/jauthor/material/2067 .

[7] See György Haraszti, 'Treaties and Fundamental Change of Circumstances', *RCADI* Vol 146, 1977, 5–93 at 10 et seq.

force only if the underlying state of affairs remained the same, and that parties were not bound by a contract that might cause public injury.[8] However, over the following centuries, at least international legal doctrine moved towards strengthening the principle of *pacta sunt servanda*. This meant that, from the perspective of this fundamental principle, *rebus sic stantibus* was a problematic exception.

The London Conference was organized in particular at the initiative of England and Prussia.[9] Its sessions took place from 17 January to 14 March 1871. The conference adopted the following declaration:

> [I]t is an essential principle of the Law of Nations that no Power can liberate itself from the engagements of a Treaty, nor modify the stipulations thereof, unless with the consent of the Contracting Parties by means of an amicable arrangement.[10]

This is an important statement in the historical evolution of international treaty law because, essentially, the Vienna Convention on the Law of Treaties (1969) voices the same restrictive approach towards *rebus sic stantibus* in its Article 62(1). However, its historical context was also that other European powers were 'reminding' the Russian Empire of what treaties meant.

In London in 1871, the Ottoman Empire, as the state geographically most affected by the Russian revisionist move, argued that too little time had passed since 1856 in order for *clausula rebus sic stantibus* to even be seriously considered.[11] At the same time, it is important to note that Russia's policy to put its navy back in the Black Sea remained a *fait accompli*; the Russian move worked out in terms of *Realpolitik*. Just as with the Great Nordic War, the Russian lesson to the world was that things could be accomplished by bold strategic moves and by letting one's military power (or the threat of it) do the work. One just had to wait for the right time to arrive. What is also interesting is that although Russia signed the London Declaration of 1871, in the substance of the matter St Petersburg apparently did not change its mind to the same degree on the question of the political nature of international treaties and how they can be terminated. Russia continued pushing for an interpretation that highlighted

[8] Cited in Alexander Orakhelashvili, *International Law and International Politics. Foundations of Interdisciplinary Analysis*, Edward Elgar Publishing, 2020, 69.

[9] Kaufmann, *Das Wesen des Völkerrechts und die clausula . . .*, 1911, . . ., 14.

[10] See David J Bederman, 'The 1871 London Declaration, *rebus sic stantibus* and a Primitive View of the Law of Nations', *AJIL* No 82, 1988, 1–40 at 3.

[11] Kaufmann, *Das Wesen des Völkerrechts und die clausula . . .*, 1911, 17.

clausula rebus sic stantibus (fundamental change of circumstances) to allow unilateral revision of treaty stipulations. We can even say that during the late tsarist era this view developed into the Russian doctrine on the law of treaties. Moreover, as we will see later, it continued to be a popular position in the Soviet Union and beyond and was always linked with the size of the territory of the Empire. Erlend M Leonhardsen has observed that Russia seemed to be the most frequent invoker of the principle of *clausula rebus sic stantibus* during both the tsarist and the Soviet periods, usually in the context of shifts in the balance of power.[12]

During the First Hague Peace Conference in 1899, the Russian delegation emphasized that any convention adopted by the Conference could restrict the freedom of action of the parties only as long as circumstances remained unchanged. On the other hand, if the circumstances changed, the rights and obligations deriving from a convention would also have to be modified.[13] Later Soviet international law scholarship was also fully aware of the fact that in 1899 the Russian Empire proposed to the First Hague Peace Conference a resolution acknowledging a decisive role for the principle of *clausula rebus sic stantibus* and hence the volatile and dynamic nature of all political treaties.[14] However, this was not received with approval by other participating states at The Hague, not least because other European powers had already expressed their opposite views with the London Declaration in 1871. During the Soviet period, the understanding of the Russian history of international law was so intertwined with state propaganda that Kozhevnikov even argued that during the second half of the nineteenth century—precisely when the Russian Empire by its actions triggered the *clausula rebus sic stantibus* debate in European diplomacy and international law—'loyal implementation of international obligations' was characteristic of Russian foreign policy.[15] Writing during the late Soviet period, one of the foremost Soviet authors on international treaty law, Anatoly Nikolaevich Talalaev (1928–2001), asserted that during earlier centuries

[12] Erlend M Leonhardsen, 'Pride and Perseverance: Strategic Use of Rebus Sic Stantibus in Russian Foreign Policy 1870–1950', *German YBIL* No 63, 2020, 581–620 at 591–3.

[13] 'Ces traités lient la liberté d'action des parties tant que restent invariables les conditions pratiques dans lesquelles ils se sont produits. Ces conditions venant à changer, les droits et les obligations découlant de ces traités changent aussi nécessairement' *(Conférence internationale de la paix, La Haye, 18 mai–29 juillet 1899,* La Haye, ministère des Affaires étrangères. Annexes au rapport de la convention pour le règlement pacifique des conflits internationaux. Annexe A, Documents émanés de la délégation russe, 161–2). Cited also in György Haraszti, 'Treaties and Fundamental Change of Circumstances', *RCADI* Vol 146, 1977, 21.

[14] See V Chikvadze (ed) *Kurs mezhdunarodnoga prava v shesti tomakh*, Vol II (Osnavnye printsipy mezhdunarodnoga prava), Nauka, 1967, 277 (referring to the conference proceedings, 1899, 29.07.1899, 161).

[15] F Kozhevnikov, *Russkoe gosudarstvo i mezhdunarodnoe pravo (do XX veka), 2006*, 161.

Russian state practice strengthened the principle of *pacta sunt servanda* in international law, as popes in particular had weakened it by issuing indulgences in the context of treaty violations.[16] Talalaev also justified Russian actions in 1870 by maintaining that West European powers had started to violate the neutrality of the Black Sea right after conclusion of the Paris Peace Treaty in 1856, so that the treaty had thus become a 'fiction'.[17]

Martens on International Treaties

The international lawyer formulating Russian official views on this question at the First Hague Peace Conference was Fréderic de (aka Fedor Fedorovich) Martens (1845–1909), who was usually wearing two hats at the same time during his career. He was an influential legal counsellor at the Russian imperial Ministry of Foreign Affairs (MFA) and simultaneously Professor of International Law in the Russian Empire's capital city, at the University of St Petersburg. Whereas Shafirov in the early eighteenth century had been a high official and influential diplomat at the court of Tsar Peter the Great, Martens played the dual role of both international law expert (professor) and counsellor in the foreign ministry. Martens's popular textbook on international law and his polemical articles invoking international law made no mention of his continuous employment at the foreign ministry, but only of his status as Professor of International Law at St Petersburg University. Practical diplomacy dominated in his life to the extent that, at least once, Martens confided to his diary that he was 'bored' with his lectures at the University of St Petersburg after five months of high-profile diplomatic and academic conferences in Western Europe.[18] In his scholarly writings on international law, Martens defended the legal views and positions which Russia propagated in its international relations, such as in 1870 regarding the earlier Paris Peace Treaty, as well as at The Hague in 1899 regarding international treaties generally. For example, in his influential textbook on international law, first published in 1882, Martens wrote on the nature of international treaties as follows:

[16] A N Talalaev, *Pravo mezhdunarodnykh dogovorov. Tom 1. Obshchie voprosy*, Moscow: Zertsalo, 2011 (Originally, Moscow: Mezhdunarodnye otnoshenia, 1980), 18.
[17] Ibid, 23.
[18] E R Voronin (ed) *Prakticheskoe mezhdunarodnoe pravo i diplomatia F.F.Martensa. Iz dnevnikov, traktatov, konventsii*, Moscow: MGIMO-Universitet, 2023, 374.

> The binding force of international treaties not protected by means of enforcement is based on the voluntary limitation of their will by those States which enter into the agreement. [...] Interest and own advantage force States to conclude international treaties, and interest and advantage ensure recognition of their being binding. [...] As regards the moral force of obligations, its significance in international relations should not be exaggerated. [...] On this basis one may put the rule that the degree of being binding and implementation of international treaties is determined by the extent of their conformity to the real reasonable needs of States and their mutual relations. [...] The true reason for the frequent violation of treaties is not a 'conflict of interest', but the fact that treaties often are concluded without knowledge and sufficient respect for mutual reasonable relations and advantage of the contracting parties. The 1856 Treaty of Paris serves as evidence in those provisions which concerned Russia and ran counter to its basic rights as an independent power. Russia could and had to reject these provisions, and she acted as predicted in advance and was well-known to the Contracting Powers at the Paris Congress.[19]

Thus, writing in 1882, Martens made his central argument about treaties that Russia's 'self-liberation' from its treaty constraints in 1870 had been legitimate and was covered by realist philosophy on the role of treaties in international law. In the same textbook, discussing international treaties, Martens concluded that *clausula rebus sic stantibus* was one of the grounds for the termination of treaties.[20] He explained further:

> With regard to a change of circumstances under which the conclusion of a treaty proceeded, it should be noted that the last is always signed with the tacit assumption that it will have force so long as the conditions under which it was signed remain unchanged. This so-called *clausula rebus sic stantibus*, to be sure, often concealed an arbitrary violation of treaties and was understood in the sense that any change of circumstances entails a legitimate basis for termination of the operation of a treaty. But abuses do not, of course, prove that the rule itself had no significance. It follows from the essence of

[19] F F Martens, *Contemporary International Law of Civilized Peoples. General Part*, translated and edited by W E Butler, The Lawbook Exchange, 2021, 148, 308–9. (Equally: F F Martens, *Sovremennoe mezhdunarodnoe pravo tsivilizovannykh narodov*, Moscow, 1995, Vol I, 150, 266–7; Martens, *Traité de droit international*, 1883, 513–4.)

[20] Martens, *Contemporary International Law of Civilized Peoples*, 2021, 290; Martens, *Traité de droit international*, 1883, 558.

> international treaties that a State may reasonably oblige itself only in view of a State goal, and any obligation concluded by it exists as long as it is consistent with this purpose. Therefore, the operation of a treaty terminates under such a change of the mutual provision of the parties which makes the said purpose unachievable and the further recognition of the treaty places the State in danger.[21]

Of course, the problem remained how to distinguish between 'abusive' and legitimate references to *clausula rebus sic stantibus*. Nevertheless, Martens assumed that this was possible; in any case, he maintained that Russia's use of *clausula rebus sic stantibus* in 1870 had not been abusive. Just so that there was no misunderstanding about his views on this central topic of international law, Martens made the same point in his diaries as well: if circumstances underlying a treaty change, the treaty becomes void.[22]

In the late Soviet period, when the Soviet Union had territorially expanded and once its borders after World War II and the Helsinki Accords of 1975 seemed settled, the international lawyer Oleg Ivanovich Tyunov (1937–2017) observed that Martens's enthusiasm for *clausula rebus sic stantibus* in international treaty law was characteristic of 'bourgeois authors'.[23] However, we will see later that Soviet authors on international treaty law, such as Evgeny Pashukanis in the 1930s and Vladimir Shurshalov (1913–1990) in the 1950s, had also been fully approving of Martens's views on *clausula rebus sic stantibus*. So apparently the inclination in Russia to favour the argument of *clausula rebus sic stantibus* was not linked to the views of the bourgeoisie only.

Martens's argument on *clausula rebus sic stantibus* goes hand in hand with the Russian Empire's state needs after 1870, when Russia restored its status as a great power in Europe. In this sense, these views of Martens were not random scholarly views; they were simultaneously Russian state doctrine, and their support in Russian scholarship was more widespread.[24] A concrete example in Martens's diaries illustrating this approach to international treaties

[21] Martens, *Contemporary International Law of Civilized Peoples*, 2021, 337. Martens, *Sovremennoe mezhdunarodnoe pravo tsivilizovannykh narodov.*, 1995, 291; Martens, *Traité de droit international*, 1883, 560–1.

[22] E R Voronin (ed) *Prakticheskoe mezhdunarodnoe pravo i diplomatia F.F.Martensa*, 2023, 83 (Entry for 26.01.1887).

[23] O I Tiunov, 'Printsip dobrosovestnogo sobliudenia mezhdunarodnykh obiazatel'stv i doktrina *rebus sic stantibus*', *Soviet YBIL* 1978, 101–12 at 105.

[24] For other examples from Russian pre-1917 international law scholarship, see A N Talalaev, *Pravo mezhdunarodnykh dogovorov. Tom 2. Deistvie i primenenie dogovorov. Dogovory s uchastiem mezhdunarodnykh organizatsii*, Moscow: Zertsalo, 2011, 216–17 (Original: Mezhdunarodnye otnoshenia, 1985).

came during the Russo–Japanese war of 1904–1905, which Russia lost. During the Portsmouth Peace Conference in 1905, the head of the Russian delegation, Sergei Yul'evich Witte (1849–1915), was initially hesitant about the formulation that Southern Sakhalin would pass from Russia to Japan 'en pleine souveraineté et à perpétuité'. Martens wrote about this moment in his diaries:

> Gr.[af] demanded that this article and these words be changed. I explained to S. Yu. that these are ordinary words for territorial concessions that mean nothing. If Russia can take back half of Sakhalin, then it will take it, and words will not mean anything. Witte agreed with me.[25]

Martens's views on the role of treaties in international law were grounded in extensive empirical–historical research. His international law scholarship paid particular attention to the study of the Russian Empire's treaties with European powers because, using the MFA archives, he edited a fifteen-volume collection of Russia's treaties with the Austrian, German, British, and French Empires. Regarding this series, the editorial choices and Martens's extensive comments to the treaties were sometimes criticized in other European states for telling the history of these European bilateral or plurilateral treaties primarily from the perspective of Russian imperial interests and in that sense failing to achieve a balance on the history of these treaties, alliances, motives of the parties, and other aspects. One critic of Martens's method on international treaties was the Baltic German historian Carl Schirren (1826–1910),[26] whom Martens called in his diary 'the worst enemy of Russia',[27] perhaps in this case also identifying his own persona with Russia to an extent. For sure, critics of Martens such as Schirren also had their own national aspirations and policies in mind. However, the aspect relevant for us lies somewhere else: the extensive treaty series by Martens reveals that he indeed saw international law primarily as evolving deals between the European great powers. As history evolved, old treaties would be set aside, and new ones would emerge instead. The strong and powerful European states might just become even stronger and more powerful in the process: a kind of survival of the fittest (or, rather, biggest) in the Darwinian sense. This transactional vision of international law and treaties was favourable for the European great powers, which would, even with occasional backlashes (such as the Treaty of Paris for Russia in 1856), win most

[25] E R Voronin (ed) *Prakticheskoe mezhdunarodnoe pravo i diplomatia F.F.Martensa, . . .*, 2023, 477.
[26] Carl Schirren, *Zur Geschichte des Nordischen Krieges. Rezensionen*, Walter G Mühlau, 1913, 125–206.
[27] E R Voronin (ed) *Prakticheskoe mezhdunarodnoe pravo i diplomatia F.F.Martensa, . . .*, 2023, 396.

of the time, as they would always be able to count on their superior military power, population, and resources. Using treaties, these empires might just keep expanding, as if by natural laws of history. This was imperialist international law which structurally favoured the stronger parties, empires, at least in its highly dynamic concept of treaties.

Its 1870 self-liberation from the stipulations of the Paris Peace Treaty of 1856 was not the only occasion when the Russian Empire used the *clausula rebus sic stantibus* argument in the late nineteenth century. The other example was Russia's unilateral termination of the free port status of Batumi (Batum) on 23 June 1886. Article 59 of the Berlin treaty of 1 (13) July 1878 had ceded Batumi from the Ottoman Empire to Russia but also envisaged free port (*porto franco*) status for the city,[28] which is nowadays part of Georgia. However, by a unilateral act, Russia brusquely ended this arrangement in 1886. Writing after the Second World War, Kozhevnikov argued—not very convincingly—that Article 59 had not been an 'imperative' but a 'facultative' obligation for Russia.[29] However, Russia's core argument was that the transit situation in the Caucasus had changed to the extent that outside powers could no longer expect to enjoy Batumi's free port status.[30]

At the end of the nineteenth century and during the early twentieth century, aggressive moves in violation of earlier treaties became increasingly popular among European powers, for example when the Austro-Hungarian Empire annexed Bosnia-Herzegovina in 1909, violating an earlier treaty stipulation. Some considered the proclamation of full independence of Bulgaria on 5 October 1908 to be a violation of Article 25 of the Berlin Treaty of 1878, in which Bulgaria's status was that of a vassal state of the Ottoman Empire.[31] International law literature before the outbreak of the First World War discussed Russia's Black Sea navy move of 1870 and its treaty law conceptual justification as a central and 'inspirational' precedent in this regard.[32] When Germany violated Belgium's neutrality at the beginning of the First World War in 1914, the ground had been prepared, as the practice to which the Russian Empire contributed significantly could be interpreted so that fundamental change of circumstances was indeed a legitimate option in international treaty law and practice in order to bypass earlier agreements and obligations. At least

[28] Kaufmann, *Das Wesen des Völkerrechts und die clausula* ..., 1911, 19–20.

[29] Kozhevnikov, *Russkoe gosudarstvo i mezhdunarodnoe pravo (do XX veka)*, 2006, 163.

[30] Ibid, 164.

[31] F N Kovalev, 'Korennoe izmenenie obstoyatel'stv (Doktrina i praktika), *SGP* No 3, 1970, 66–74 at 66–7.

[32] Kaufmann, *Das Wesen des Völkerrechts und die clausula* ..., 1911.

the great powers did just that, and they could refer to Russia in 1870 as a precedent. 'Those who are able to, are also free to' (*Wer kann, darf auch*), as the German international lawyer Erich Kaufmann (1880–1972) put it in the context of *clausula rebus sic stantibus*, just before the First World War.[33] In 1870, just as many times before and after, the Russian Empire could.

Martens: An International Lawyer of a Semi-peripheral Empire?

The role of Martens as tsarist Russia's foremost international lawyer goes beyond his theoretical–diplomatic views on international treaties and his position that such treaties can be 'terminated' (in reality, violated) when state interests demand it. Martens has become a symbol—and the most prominent representative—of an entire era in the Russian Empire's relationship with international law. However, there are divergent ways to understand his views, role, and impact, which to a large extent reflects how the Russian Empire's role in the era of Europe's empires has remained ambivalent in the historiography of international law.

In his account of the history of international law in countries such as Brazil, Argentina, Japan, China, Turkey, and Russia, Arnulf Becker Lorca has counted Martens among 'semi-peripheral international lawyers'.[34] Becker Lorca sees in the late nineteenth century 'non-Western nations and states and their lawyers [. . .] using international law to resist and in the process we will see them transforming international law'.[35] Becker Lorca also argues that 'throughout their writings, semi-peripheral internationalists pursued a distinctively non-European interpretation of the classical European law of nations [. . .] to advocate for a change in extant rules of international law and to justify the extension of the privileges of formal equality to their own states in their interaction with Western powers'.[36]

According to Becker Lorca, as a rule, semi-peripheral international lawyers argued against those 'Western' legal scholars who favoured an international legal order based on inequality.[37] He also makes a connection between the

[33] Ibid.
[34] Arnulf Becker Lorca, *Mestizo International Law. A Global Intellectual History 1842–1933*, CUP, 2014, 51, 125.
[35] Ibid, 15–16.
[36] Ibid, 50.
[37] Ibid, 60–1.

views of Martens and Russia's 'semi-peripheral' place in the world (economic) system—as 'Russia used international law internationally (vis-à-vis Western powers) to secure international relations based on sovereign equality'.[38] Becker Lorca further argues that 'Russia was not at the forefront of the 19th century expansion of European international law' and adds that 'to the extent that the world economic system did not consolidate around a division of labor and trade relations that favored Russian interests, 19th century Russia was semi-peripheral'.[39]

One can debate whether in economic terms the Russian Empire of the late nineteenth century was 'semi-peripheral' or not. For example, in the context of competing for hegemony over Persia, the (British) Imperial Bank of Persia and the (Russian) Discount and Loan Bank were both used for handing out politically motivated loans for the Persian Shah.[40] At the same time, Russia itself was heavily indebted, in particular to France, which made the loans look like a pyramid scheme, with Persia owing money to Russia and Russia itself owing even more money to France. In his study on the economic aspects of imperialism, the international lawyer Evgeny Pashukanis pointed out that by the end of the tsarist period, French and English capital had taken hold of the Russian Empire and, for example, Russia's initiative to build the Chinese Eastern Railway in Manchuria was funded by French capital.[41] Of course, Pashukanis framed pre-1917 Russian–West European economic relations in order to justify the Bolshevik decision not to repay tsarist-era loans.

However, when we talk about an international legal order based on equality, the question remains: is it apt to characterize the Russian Empire as 'semi-peripheral' when it systematically used international legal arguments to expand, both in Europe and in Asia, and competed with the British Empire for the title of territorially the biggest empire in the world? The Russian Empire of Martens' era systematically pursued territorial expansion and positioned itself as a *European* empire as against the Ottoman Empire and other Asian states. Therefore, Becker Lorca's concept of 'semi-peripherality', although otherwise an insightful one, does not in my view adequately capture Russia's role during late nineteenth–early twentieth-century European imperialism in international law.

[38] Ibid, 123.
[39] Ibid, 122.
[40] Firuz Kazemzadeh, *Russia and Britain in Persia, 1864–1914. A Study in Imperialism*, Yale UP, 1968, 302 et seq.
[41] E B Pashukanis, *Imperializm i kolonial'naia politika. Chast' pervaia: ekonomika imperializma. Kurs lektsii, chitannykh v I MGU*, Izdatel'stvo kommunistischeskoi akademii, 1928, 80.

One of the assumptions that Becker Lorca makes regarding the place of the Russian Empire in the history of international law is to think of Europe and the West as synonyms of sorts. Put differently, Becker Lorca posits that international law became an order of global geographical scope 'throughout the appropriation of the European legal tradition by non-Western legal scholars'.[42] But by the early twentieth century, Europe and the West were not synonyms; Russian elites often had a self-image of being both European *and* non-Western. Of course, there were elements of Russia's semi-peripherality *within Europe* while 'Europe' remained a contested concept in the Russian Empire, particularly after the lost Crimean War (1853–6). Martens even recounted in his diaries how in St Petersburg, because of their German names and family origins, he and foreign minister Nikolay Girs (1820–95) were often not considered genuinely 'Russian' enough by other people of influence, and how Tsar Alexander III repeatedly told his ministers that he did not care about Europe and would 'sneeze' at it, among other derisive comments.[43] There were indeed elements of cultural semi-peripherality and alienation in these Russian debates and realities.

I have not been able to find historical evidence for the following interpretation by Becker Lorca:

> However, as a consequence of the rise of positivism in European international law, the previous history of legal interactions between European, Russian and Ottoman powers was erased and Russian and Ottoman membership in the international community became contested. [. . .] Facing uncertainty about their membership in the European family of nations, and realizing the perils of possible exclusion, Russian and Ottoman officials sought to assimilate classical international law with an eye towards securing re-entry.[44]

One anecdotal example of how Russia was not excluded from European international law is that, from its foundation in 1873, Russian legal scholars were included in the membership of the *Institut de droit international*, with Count Vladimir Bezobrazov (1828–89),[45] Leonid Kamarovsky (1846–1912), and of course Martens as well. Regarding the topic of the Russian Empire's place in

[42] Becker Lorca, *Mestizo International Law*, 2014, 23. Cf. also 43 and 50–1.
[43] Voronin (ed) *Prakticheskoe mezhdunarodnoe pravo i diplomatia F.F.Martensa, . . .*, 2023, 89, 92, 105, 174, 534.
[44] Becker Lorca, *Mestizo International Law*, 2014, 119.
[45] See V M Koretski, 'Akademik V P Bezobrazov v Institute mezhdunarodnoga prava', *Soviet YBIL* 1973, 190–97.

European international law, we can listen to Martens himself. Writing from the perspective of the 1880s and seeing his own time already bridging natural law and legal positivism, Martens commented that, after 1721, no European question of great or small importance was decided without Russia.[46] He also observed that at the end of the eighteenth century, after Russia's successful wars against the Ottoman Empire and the partitions of Poland, St Petersburg became for a while a diplomatic hotspot where Europe's most important affairs were discussed and often decided.[47] Thus, in his time there was no uncertainty about Russia's continued membership in the European family of nations; even Russia's defeat in the Crimean War in 1856 did not change this, especially as St Petersburg recovered and expanded its positions quickly, at the latest after another successful war against the Ottoman Empire, in 1878.

However, Martens' Russia may indeed have been somewhat 'semi-peripheral' in its cultural–spiritual relationship with Europe and its international legal tradition(s). For example, at least before Martens, Russia's intellectual contribution to the discourse of international law did not correspond to the Russian Empire's political–military weight and its sometimes decisive role as one of the makers and guarantors of rules in European affairs. There were both West Europeans and Russians (such as Nikolay Yakovlevich Danilevsky, 1822–85) who emphatically did not consider Russia to be European. When the German philosopher Nietzsche spoke about the Russian Empire with admiration, juxtaposing it with the tradition of *Kleinstaaterei*—a system of small states; meant pejoratively—in Germany and Europe, it sounded as if the very essence of Great Russia was something other than that of Europe: genuinely imperial.[48] At the same time, Russia was decisively not 'semi-peripheral' as an imperialist power in the context of (European) international law, and in that sense its situation was not comparable to China, the Ottoman Empire, Brazil, and other non-European countries. Martens made much out of juxtaposing the 'civilized' Russian Empire particularly with the 'uncivilized' Ottoman Empire, but to an extent also with China. Thus, nineteenth-century Russia was not 'resisting the Europeans' or pushing for 'equality' with European/Western powers, or

[46] Martens, *Traité de droit international*, 1883, 138.

[47] Ibid, 147.

[48] Nietzche wrote: 'A sort of will, instinct, imperative, which cannot be otherwise than antiliberal to the point of wickedness: the will to tradition, to authority, to responsibility for centuries to come, to *solidarity* in long family lines forwards and backwards *in infinitum*. If this will is present, something is founded which resembes the *imperium Romanum*; or Russia, the *only* great nation to-day that has some lasting power and grit in her, that can bide her time, that can still promise something.—Russia the opposite of all wretched European petty-statism and neurasthenia.' Friedrich Nietzsche, The *Twilight of the Idols* or, *How to Philosophise with the Hammer*, translated by Anthony M Ludovici, Edinburgh: T N Foulis, 1911 (original German version 1888).

if so then only for imperial equality with the British Empire, its competitor in Asia. Martens argued systematically as a representative of Russia, as an East European, and a Eurasian—indeed, in this sense non-Western—empire which wanted to expand further, especially to the south and east, at the expense, in its own terminology, of 'half-civilized' and 'non-civilized' nations, such as the Ottoman Empire and China but also the Central Asian khanates and emirates. Moreover, Martens justified and legitimized the Russian Empire's historical conquests *within Europe*, especially regarding Poland, and expressed severe criticism against the by then already fashionable idea of self-determination of peoples, seeing what a danger this idea presented to the future of the Russian Empire, along with other European empires.

Becker Lorca observes correctly that some passages in Martens's textbook pay homage to the principle of equality of states.[49] For example, Martens argues that the status of 'great powers' is not rooted in international *law*, only in international politics.[50] At the same time, Martens considers congresses and conferences as 'organs' of the international community,[51] knowing—and describing—perfectly well what type of powers had played the leading role on such occasions: great powers, including Russia.

Moreover, Martens mildly criticized implementation of the principle of balance of power in seventeenth- and eighteenth-century European international law.[52] At the same time, against his contemporary critics of Russia—including Argentine's international lawyer Carlos Calvo (1824–1906)—he defended the Russian Empire's biggest acquisition in the European history of balance-of-power politics, namely the seizure of most of Poland in the late eighteenth century. Martens asserted that, by the time of writing, Poland was Russia's 'inalienable property'. According to Martens, after the Partitions of Poland and the Napoleonic wars, the other European powers gave Poland to the Russian Emperor Alexander I at the Congress of Vienna in 1815. Moreover, Martens argued that, whatever autonomy the Poles initially had, they lost it after their unsuccessful uprisings against the Russian Empire in 1831 and 1862.[53]

In the late eighteenth and throughout the nineteenth century, in Russian-annexed Poland, several major popular uprisings against Russian rule broke out and were violently suppressed by the Russian army. Alexander Suvorov (1729–1800), one of the most glorified tsarist Russian generals in history, was

[49] Becker Lorca, *Mestizo International Law*, 2014, 192.
[50] Martens, *Sovremennoe mezhdunarodnoe pravo tsivilizovannykh nardodov*, 1995, 382.
[51] Ibid, 297.
[52] Ibid, 165.
[53] Ibid, 314–16.

the suppressor of the Kosciucko-led uprising in 1794 in which thousands of Polish civilians were massacred by Russian troops after the Battle of Praga (a suburb of Warsaw). Later, other European powers, led by England, France, and Austria, protested the methods used by the Russian Empire when suppressing the January uprising of 1863 in Poland.[54] Thus, the question of the status of Poland was an important item in European public opinion in which Martens defended this significant imperial Russian acquisition.

On the level of general and emerging principles of international law, Martens criticized what he called 'the principle of nationality', which later became known as the right of peoples to self-determination.[55] Martens wrote on this in his textbook:

> Without denying the impact on international relations of nationality links and agreeing with the duties of every government to respect the rights and interests of all their subjects whatever their national origin and whatever national language they speak, we all the same cannot adhere to the view that the national composition of a State serves to secure order and law in the domain of international relations. Not to mention that the implementation of the principle of nationality should lead to a radical change of the political map of Europe and consequently inescapably cause international wars, we have no guarantee that the 'national States' formed will be imbued not only with an awareness of domestic unity but with respect for the legal order in their mutual relations, that they will recognize mutual rights and duties. To see a panacea in the principle of nationality for the settlement of all international difficulties seems to us to be an unfounded and dangerous conviction in its exceptional supremacy over all guiding ideas of our time. The principle of nationality, lacking a historical foundation, creates nothing stable, but is in a position to destroy much. If it were applied to Italy, it does not follow that it can be applied everywhere with benefit for peoples and with respect for inalienable requirements of truth and justice.[56]

This was the defence *par excellence* of the territorial integrity of the multinational Russian Empire, especially considering its eighteenth- and nineteenth-century European territorial acquisitions, which gave not a thought to the

[54] Grewe, *Epochen der Völkerrechtsgeschichte*, 1984, 578.

[55] Cf James Summers, *Peoples and International Law, 2nd revised edition*, Brill, 2014, 155 et seq.

[56] Martens, *Contemporary International Law of Civilized Peoples*, 2021, 117. (Martens, *Sovremennoe mezhdunarodnoe pravo tsivilizovannykh narodov*, 1995, 121; Martens, *Traité de droit international*, 1883, 196–7.)

nascent 'nationality principle'. As we shall see next, the scholarly and publicist activity of Martens was equally thought through vis-à-vis non-European peoples and territories, of whom the Russian Empire and its leading international lawyer certainly did not talk from the perspective of any equality.[57]

Martens as Russia's Colonialist International Lawyer

At the end of the nineteenth century, whenever a current issue arose among the European great powers and Russia's interests were at stake, Martens wrote pertinent articles in the *Revue de droit international et de legislation comparée*, the leading international journal of his time. So now, we will go through key messages in these articles, as they also well reflected Russia's imperial position vis-à-vis 'non-civilized' regions neighbouring Russia.

The context of Martens' first article in the *Revue* was the ongoing Russo–Turkish War (1877–8). This war led to a notable increase in the power of the Russian Empire, although Russia's initial territorial gains under the San Stefano Peace Treaty were later reduced in the Berlin Treaty, in which other European powers also participated under the leadership of the German Chancellor, Bismarck. Concerning the war of 1877–8, a lively debate arose in Europe about the legality of Russia's actions at the beginning of the war.[58] In his article in the *Revue*, Martens' main point was clear, though: Russia vis-à-vis Turkey was 'representative of the European concert, a champion of justice and international law'.[59] Martens argued that Russia had conducted a purely humanitarian intervention to defend its fellow Orthodox Christians under Ottoman rule, and it had done so in the name of 'the whole of Europe'.[60] According to Martens, the right to conduct this intervention against Turkey belonged to the whole Concert of Europe but—in the absence of interest in intervening from other European powers—Russia was also entitled to intervene alone, and it did so 'in the name of the highest interests of humanity and civilization'.[61]

[57] See for further details L Mälksoo, 'The Legacy of F F Martens and the Shadow of Colonialism', *Chinese JIL* Vol 21, 2022, 55–77.

[58] Skordos, *Südosteuropa und das moderne Völkerrecht. Eine transregionale und globale Geschichte im 19. und 20. Jahrhundert*, 2021, 106 et seq, 125–30. See also Thomas Erskine Holland, *A Lecture on the Treaty Relations of Russia and Turkey from 1774 to 1853, delivered at Oxford on April 28, 1877*, London: Macmillan & Co, 1877 and Serge Goriaïnov, *La question d'Orient à la veille du Traité de Berlin (1870–1876), avec une introduction par Boris Nolde*, Institut d'études slaves, 1948.

[59] F Martens, 'Étude historique sur la politique russe dans la question d'Orient', *RDILC* 1877, 51.

[60] Ibid, 57, 66.

[61] Ibid, 65.

These arguments involved a long backstory, first in the Peace Treaty of Küçuk-Kaynarca (1774) between the Ottomans and the Russian Empire which made Russia—at least in its own interpretation—the sole protective power of Orthodox Christians in the Ottoman Empire.[62] In the Paris Peace Treaty of 1856, this right was in principle 'collectivized' in Europe, but with the war of 1877–8 Russia de facto again took the matter into its own hands. With the sea battle of Navarino (1827), the Russian Empire gained a victory over the Ottoman navy, an event which has sometimes been considered to be one of the first humanitarian interventions (as its justification was to help the Greek insurgents).[63] However, it remained debatable in international law doctrine whether humanitarian intervention had become part of international law.[64] Nevertheless, in political terms, Russia and Martens used the doctrine of humanitarian intervention quite successfully against the Ottoman Empire.

In 1879 Martens published another paper in the *Revue* on Russia and England in Central Asia.[65] His main goal was to avert an open military clash there between the two countries, particularly in Afghanistan, where the English had gained the upper hand, and which bordered on the former Central Asian khanates of Khiva—which Russia had conquered in 1873, making it a vassal state—and Kokand, which Russia annexed in 1876. Martens argued that both the Russians and the English were charged by divine providence with civilizing the savage peoples of Central Asia.[66] Martens addressed the 'perverted instincts of the Asiatic hordes'[67] and pointed out the 'ignorance, cruelty and anarchy of the fanatical Uzbeks'.[68] The main point of Martens's article was to say that Russia and England, rather than going against each other in Central Asia, should operate there together as civilized—and civilizing—powers. The interests of Russia and England in Central Asia were one and the same.[69] Martens also explained why a war between England and Russia over Central Asia would not be a good idea: it would only further encourage the less civilized peoples of Asia. For example, should England win, this could only happen militarily thanks to recruits from India; however, Martens warned that victory would embolden the Indians and give them confidence to eventually turn against their own masters, the

[62] Skordos, *Südosteuropa und das moderne Völkerrecht*, 2021, 63, 75; Hendrik Simon, *A Century of Anarchy? War, Normativity, and the Birth of Modern International Order*, OUP, 2024, 229 *et seq.*

[63] Skordos, ibid, 70 et seq.

[64] Skordos, ibid, 73. See also Fabian Klose, *In the Cause of Humanity. A History of Humanitarian Intervention in the Long Nineteenth Century*, CUP, 2021.

[65] F Martens, 'La Russie et l'Angleterre dans l'Asie centrale', *RDILC* 1879, 227.

[66] Ibid, 229.

[67] Ibid, 232.

[68] Ibid, 255.

[69] Ibid, 301.

English.[70] This was a classic colonial discourse in European international law and there was no real difference in the justification for British rule in India and its influence in Afghanistan, as opposed to Russia's expansion in Central Asia.

Another article by Martens in the *Revue*, from 1882, concerned the relations and conflict between Russia and China, in the context of China's sudden refusal to ratify the Treaty of Livadia of 1879, which the Chinese envoy had signed at St Petersburg.[71] According to Martens, China's actions against Russia were in a way directed against all civilized/European nations and had China started and even won a war against Russia, this would inevitably have meant that all other Europeans would have been expelled from China as well.[72] Going through the history of Russian–Chinese relations—and especially the treaties of Nerchinsk (1689), Kyakhta (1727), and Kouldja (1851)—Martens concluded that one could not 'judge the Chinese based on the moral ideas and processes of civilized nations'.[73] Martens then proceeded to assert that the institute of consular jurisdiction in China was an 'absolute necessity' until Chinese laws were radically changed.[74] In contextualizing the Treaty of Livadia, Martens observed that international law could not be applied in an unlimited fashion towards the Chinese.[75] In 'civilized Europe', obligations that were taken upon oneself had to be kept—but, according to Martens, this was not the case in Asia and China. Moreover, a common interest bound all European civilized nations, including Russia, in China, 'to be true representatives of a superior civilization and of an intellectual and moral culture that engenders more benefits than blind submission to the precepts of Confucius'.[76]

However, another interesting aspect appears in Martens's discourse about Russia, China, and international law, in that—so Martens argued—Russia had been a friendlier, gentler neighbour and civilizer to China than the European maritime empires Britain and France.[77] For example, unlike West European empires, Russia had historically agreed to subject its citizens visiting China to Chinese jurisdiction. Martens argued that the conflict between Russia and China was essentially a result of how China had been treated by European 'civilized powers' other than Russia.[78] Indeed, certain differences did exist between

[70] Ibid, 298.
[71] F Martens, 'Le conflit entre la Russie et la Chine, ses origines, son développement, et sa portée universelle', *RDILC* 1880, 513, 582.
[72] Ibid, 515.
[73] Ibid, 539.
[74] Ibid, 594.
[75] Ibid, 616.
[76] Ibid, 619.
[77] Ibid, 597, 611.
[78] Ibid, 611.

British and French colonial approaches vis-à-vis China on the one hand, and Russian approaches on the other. While Britain in particular was pushing for the opening of Chinese treaty ports, Russia used the same momentum to annex Chinese territory. The 1879 Livadia treaty crisis itself was a crisis regarding the Chinese territory of Ili, which Russia had previously occupied.[79] Before that, the Tientsin treaty of 1858, signed between China and Britain after Britain's threats of war, had revised and extended previously granted European privileges and increased the number of treaty ports.[80] However, Russia's own priority was not open ports in China but expansion of territory. For several centuries, the border between the Russian and Chinese empires had been fixed by the treaty of Nerchinsk (1689). In the Far East, near the Amur River, this border had been much less favourable to imperial Russia than the border fixed by the Treaty of Aigun in 1858. Furthermore, with the Treaty of Beijing, concluded in 1860, Russia made gains on the Ussuri river and reached the Pacific Ocean where nowadays the city of Vladivostok (meaning in Russian: 'rule the East') is located. China lost further territories with the protocol of Chunguchak (Tarbagatai) in 1864, which dealt with the border in Central Asia. Overall, with these treaties the Russian Empire gained more than 1.7 million square kilometres.[81] Later, during the era of Nikita Khrushchev in the Soviet Union and Mao Zedong in the PRC, the PRC complained that these treaties were unequal, and the borders had consequently to be revised or compensated between the two socialist nations. Needless to say, Moscow rejected this assertion.[82]

With the St Petersburg treaty of 1881, the Russians further gained more than 40,000 square kilometres in Central Asia, in the Ili valley region.[83] Moreover, in 1895 England and Russia concluded a treaty in which they determined their mutual spheres of interest in the Pamir region. In that way, the Southeastern border of today's Tajikistan was established without China's participation and the Chinese Empire lost its control over the Pamirs. In 1911 Russia pushed the border further—in the treaty of Tsitsihar, between Russia's Aigun and Mongolia (then part of China)—compared to the earlier treaty of Kiakhta of 1727.

[79] See Immanuel CY Hsü, *The Ili Crisis: A Study of Sino-Russian Diplomacy*, Oxford: Clarendon Press, 1965.
[80] Becker Lorca, *Mestizo International Law*, 2014, 86.
[81] Horst Pommerening, *Der chinesisch-sowjetische Grenzkonflikt. Das Erbe der ungleichen Verträge*, Walter Verlag, 1968, 137.
[82] See further L Mälksoo, 'The Empires: China, Russia and the Soviet Union in the History of International Law', in: Ignacio de la Rasilla, Jiangyu Wang, Congyan Cai (eds) *Histories of International Law in China. All Under Heaven?* OUP, 2026.
[83] Pommerening, *Der chinesisch-sowjetische Grenzkonflikt. Das Erbe der ungleichen Verträge* 1968, 144.

The imperial interests of Russia—and Martens—were global. To return to the publicist activity of Martens as the leading Russian imperial international lawyer of the late tsarist era, another conflict of interest concerned Egypt. Instead of the British–French condominium against the backdrop of Egypt's formal suzerainty under the Ottoman Empire, Martens suggested the format of international (European) administration which would also have given the Russian Empire a share in the governance of Egypt.[84] Martens concluded that a compromise between the European powers was needed to reflect their 'historical mission which is to represent true European and Christian civilization in the lands of the East'.[85]

Martens's final article on colonial issues published in the *Revue* concerned the famous Berlin (Congo) conference of 1884–5.[86] Martens defended the main direction of the Berlin conference decisions on Africa, arguing that the Berlin Act established conditions in favour of the commerce of Europe and America which had to 'favor the progress of European culture in the dark continent'.[87] Moreover, Martens endorsed the political initiatives of the Belgian King Leopold in the Congo:

> It is beyond doubt that thanks to the generosity and political genius of King Leopold, the Free State of Congo will be endowed with a regime that will entirely conform to the requirements of European culture.[88]

What his Congo conference article in the *Revue* did not reveal explicitly was that Martens had also been influential in terms of formulating the Russian foreign ministry's legal–political positions for the conference in Berlin. On 26 October 1884, Martens wrote in his diary:

> In the Ministry, they think that the Berlin Conference concerns only Africa. But they completely forget that the same principles that the Conference will propose for the occupation of lands not yet occupied by civilized countries will afterwards probably also be applied in Asia and other parts of the world. Our [Russia's] future will be in Asia, where we will have to build markets for our goods, and not in Europe. In the Pacific Ocean, we must occupy islands

[84] F Martens, 'La question égyptienne et le droit international', *RDILC* 1882, 355, 392.
[85] Ibid, 400.
[86] F Martens, 'La conference de Congo à Berlin et la politique coloniale des États modernes', *RDILC* 1886, 113, 244.
[87] Ibid, 260.
[88] Ibid, 268.

> and lands that have not yet come under the sovereignty of civilized governments. And still the Emperor thinks that the question of occupation does not concern Russia at all![89]

On 29 October 1884, Martens indicated in his diary that he had prepared the Russian Foreign Affairs Ministry's legal memorandum for the purposes of the Berlin conference. In the diary entry for 1 November 1884, he was particularly proud of the way he had managed to influence the attitudes of the Russian foreign minister Nikolay Girs (1820–95):

> Without self-congratulation I must say that my memorandum opened the eyes of everybody in the Ministry as to the importance of the Berlin Conference. [. . .] Yesterday I wrote to Girs once more a long letter on the Berlin Conference in which I proposed to him the following thought. It is known that the Belgian King Leopold II gave a push to the question of settling Europeans on the banks of the Congo and inside Africa. To that end he sacrificed 17 million francs from his own means. For this reason, during the opening meeting of the Berlin Conference decency requires recognition of this great service by King Leopold in support of spreading the fruits of European civilization in Africa. Russia is not interested in African colonies and because of that she may take upon herself the initiative to propose to the Conference to pay homage to the generous activity of Leopold II in Africa.
>
> Girs had only one doubt: does the Belgian King not have any kind of commercial goals and interests in supporting the *Association africaine*?[90] I completely calmed him down, stating convincingly that the King does not have and may not have any interests of such a kind.[91]

Martens's enthusiasm about the Belgian King Leopold's personal project in the Congo was soon rewarded—the King appointed him a member of the Supreme Council of the Congo Free State which had been proclaimed on 25 May 1885. The Supreme Council was composed of two parts, the Court of Cassation and the Court of Appeal. The three foreigners in the Supreme Council—Thomas Barclay, Alphonse Rivier, and Martens—were confirmed in this position by

[89] Arkhiv Vneshnei Politiki Rossiiskoi Imperii (AVPRI), Moscow, Martens diaries, Fond No 340, opis no 787; E R Voronin (ed) *Prakticheskoe mezhdunarodnoe pravo i diplomatia F. F. Martensa* , 2023, 37.

[90] What was meant was the *Association internationale africaine* which the Belgian king Leopold II had founded in 1876 in Brussels, and the main task of which was to organize scientific expeditions in Central Africa.

[91] E R Voronin (ed) *Prakticheskoe mezhdunarodnoe pravo i diplomatia F. F. Martensa*, 2023, 38.

Leopold II on 21 August 1889. The Belgian colonial encyclopedia indicates that Martens remained in this position until his death in 1909.[92]

In his capacity as a member of the Free State's Supreme Council, Martens also published a memorandum exploring the nature of sovereignty that the Congo Free State arguably enjoyed.[93] Up until its annexation by Belgium in 1908, the Congo Free State was run as a personal dominion of the Belgian King Leopold II. The Berlin Act of 1885 left unresolved certain debatable questions regarding the limits of sovereignty of the Congo Free State, and it was now Martens's task to tie up the loose ends in terms of constitutional and international law. The main point of Martens's memorandum was that, in terms of its sovereign rights and authority, the Congo Free State was like any other sovereign state, with the exception of free navigation on the river Congo and its tributaries as well as prohibition of monopolies.[94] This narrative was not much interested in what had happened on the ground in the Congo during King Leopold's rule, especially the numerous crimes committed there in the name of profit and European civilization.[95]

Martens argued that the Congo Free State had not given up any rights of exploitation of natural resources on its territory. This state was the owner of the entire territory and the government could profit from its property, inter alia with concessions for payment. Thus, the main idea of the memorandum was to justify the fact that the main profits from the Congo Free State, whether directly or through concessions, must go to King Leopold II as sovereign. Private investors and foreign nations had to recognize who the new sovereign was and pay their dues accordingly. The point was also that—thanks to the perspective advocated by Martens, namely that King Leopold was a civilized ruler and the Congo Free State 'a normal state'—the rest of the 'civilized world' need not pay extra attention to what was going on there. In other words, Martens's legal memorandum offered *carte blanche* to King Leopold's interests and economic policies in the Congo. Moreover, it has been pointed out that Leopold succeeded only through a specifically international tactic to gain sovereignty over Congo.[96] Hence, his engagement of Martens from the Russian Empire was part of this successful internationalizing tactic.

[92] J-M Jadot, 'Martens de, Frédéric', in: *Bibliographie Coloniale Belge*, T. IV (1955), col 574–9 at 575.

[93] F de Martens, *État indépendant du Congo. Mémoire sur les droits dominiaux de l'état indépendant du Congo*, Bruxelles: Hachez, Novembre 1892.

[94] Ibid, 4.

[95] See Adam Hohschild, *King Leopold's Ghost: A Story of Greed, Terror, and Heroism in Colonial Africa*, Macmillan, 1998; D Van Reybrouck, *Congo. The Epic History of a People*, translated from the Dutch by S Garrett, Fourth Estate, 2014, 57 *et seq*; Éric Vuillard, *Congo*, Actes Sud, 2012.

[96] Carl Schmitt, *Der Nomos der Erde im Völkerrecht des Jus Publicum Europaeum*, 5th edn, Duncker & Humblot, 2011, 197.

At the same time, Russia as a 'civilized' Empire working together with other 'civilized' (West European) empires to divide and rule the world—and as constantly appears in Martens's international legal discourse—was to an extent also a deceptive façade. In his recently published diaries, Martens did not have to pretend and could write as he really thought about his own Russian Empire, himself, and the world. As a Lutheran with Baltic German as well as ethnic Estonian origins,[97] he complained about the limits to freedom of religion in Russia and saw in it 'proof of the ugly and barbaric state of the internal life of modern Russia'.[98] His comparison of internal life in France and Russia did not turn out to be in any way flattering for Russia.[99] Martens pointed out that Emperor Nicholas II knew perfectly well that, under his rule, individuals could be arrested and held for months and even years without a court judgment, under administrative supervision.[100] Moreover, at the First Hague Peace Conference Martens was unhappy about the secretive style of Staal, president of the Russian delegation:

> It's terribly amusing that people keep secrets at the end of the nineteenth century—and in a free country. We can ban everything, persecute and destroy everything and everyone. Not here in Holland.[101]

In 1894 Martens—who in his textbook had warned of the 'principle of nationality'—criticized the domestic imperial policies of Emperor Alexander III concerning the minority peoples of the Empire:

> I cannot at all sympathize with the internal policy of the late Sovereign [i.e., Alexander III], which was extremely destructive precisely for the unity of Russia. The systematic persecution of Jews, Finns and Baltic Germans significantly increased the centrifugal tendencies within the Empire.[102]

Nevertheless, at the best moments of his career as the Russian Empire's leading international lawyer, Martens enjoyed far more access and visibility than one might typically expect of international law professors and their publications:

[97] According to the Estonian novelist and lawyer Jaan Kross (1920–2007) in *Professor Martens' Departure. A Novel*, translated by Anselm Hollo, The New Press, 1994.
[98] E R Voronin (ed) *Prakticheskoe mezhdunarodnoe pravo i diplomatia F. F. Martensa*, 2023, 170.
[99] Ibid, 175.
[100] Ibid, 485.
[101] Ibid, 344.
[102] Ibid, 199. With sympathy for Finland, see also 490.

> Today I was received by the Emperor to present him with the twelfth volume of my 'Collected Treaties'. The Emperor was cordially gracious. I allowed myself to express the idea that we do not need to make haste with our activities in Asia. Our strength lies in the state of things, and Asia must belong to us.[103]

Martens was not the only Russian international lawyer during the late tsarist period who looked at international law from the imperial perspective and bearing in mind imperial interests, although he was by far the best known. For example, Vladimir Hrabar (1865–1956) wrote about the equality of states in international law after small states, led by the Brazilian Ruy Barbosa (1849–1923), clashed with the European great powers at the Second Hague Peace Conference in 1907. Hrabar advocated clearer and more realistic recognition in international law that there could not be full equality between the great powers and smaller states.[104] Imperial needs and realities were shaping Russian scholarship of international law in other ways, too. Even then, Kiev's professor of international law Vasily Andreyevich Nezabitovsky (1824–1883) and later also Tartu's (Yur'ev's) constitutional law professor Léon Challandes (Lev Adamirovich Shalland) (1868–1919) were discussing the nature of state territory in international legal theory,[105] a theme which is of course particularly interesting for empires preoccupied with their own vast territory, and which continued to interest Soviet scholars in the twentieth century and Russian legal scholars beyond.[106]

Imperialist Practices, Protectorates, and Spheres of Interest

In the late nineteenth century, the Russian Empire fully participated in the imperialist and colonialist practice of European international law, including acquiring territories by treaties. Acquiring some territories took decades and even centuries. For example, in Kazakhstan the first such treaty had been

[103] Ibid, 268.

[104] Vladimir Hrabar, 'Nachalo ravenstva gosudarstv v sovremennom mezhdunarodnom prave', in: *Izvestia Ministerstva Inostrannykh Del*, Tipografia V O Kirshbauma, 1912, 32 et seq (Later also published in French as V Hrabar, *La crise actuelle du principe de l'égalité juridique des états*, 1914).

[105] V A Nezabitovsky, *Uchenie publitsistov o mezhgosudarstvennom vladenii*, Kiev, 1862; L A Challandes, *Iuridicheskaya priroda terrotorial'noga verkhovenstva. Istoriko-dogmaticheskoe issledovanie*, Tom 1, Tip. Trenke i Fyuzno, 1903.

[106] See, eg, Yuri G Barsegov, *Territoria v mezhdunarodnom prave*, Gosudarstvennoe izdatel'stvo iuridicheskoi literatury, 1958; Boris M Klimenko, *Gosudarstvennaya territoria. Voprosy teorii i praktiki mezhdunarodnogo prava*, Mezhdunarodnye otnoshenia, 1974; Viatcheslav A Batyr, *Mezhdunarodnoe territorial'noe pravo*, Mezhdunarodnye otnoshenia, 2021.

signed on 10 October 1731 when the Russian representative Aleksei Ivanovich Tevkelev signed a treaty with Abū'l-Khair Khan (1693–1748) who was leader of the Kazakh Little jüz[107] in present-day western and central Kazakhstan. But the process of annexing the whole territory of today's Kazakhstan was completed only in the 1860s.[108] The Soviet legal scholar M A Sarsembaev of Kazakh State University estimated that the treaty between Abū'l-Khair Khan and the Russian Empress Anna Ivanovna (represented by Tevkelev) must be considered an international treaty which was voluntary and not forced upon the Kazakhs.[109] It would be interesting to learn more about whether contemporary Kazakh historians share this viewpoint, and how Kazakhstan's unification with Russia in the eighteenth and nineteenth centuries is interpreted today.

As already indicated, Russia also used the institute of protectorates in its territorial expansion and imperial encounters. In 1868, a Russian protectorate was established over the Emirate of Bukhara and, in 1873, over the Khanate of Khiva, both in Central Asia.[110] Both protectorates were also mentioned in Russian constitutional law treatises of the late tsarist period.[111] Russian official ideology on this is noteworthy (and the more elaborate international legal views of Martens, cited above, directly reflected this state ideology). On 21 November 1864, foreign minister Gorchakov explained it in a circular dispatch to Russian diplomatic representatives abroad:

> The position of Russia in Central Asia is that of all civilized States which are brought into contact with half-savage, nomad populations, possessing no fixed social organization. In such cases it always happens that the more civilized State is forced, in the interests of the security of its frontier and its commercial relations, to exercise a certain ascendancy over those whom their turbulent and unsettled character make most undesirable neighbors. [. . .] It is a peculiarity of Asiatics to respect nothing but visible and palpable force.[112]

[107] Jüz (or Juz) were structural divisions within the Kazakh community dating back to post-Mongol times. See Didar Kassymova, Zhanat Kundakbayeva, Ustina Markus, *Historical Dictionary of Kazakhstan*, Lanham: The Scarecrow Press, 2012, 129 et seq.

[108] M A Sarsembaev, 'Dobrovol'noe prisoedinenie Kazahstana k Rossii: mezhdunarodno-pravovye aspekty', *SGP* No 12, 1982, 85–8 at 86.

[109] Ibid, 86–7.

[110] Korovin, *Sovremennoe . . .*, 1926, 40.

[111] See, eg, L A Challandes, *Russkoe gosudarstvennoe pravo*, Tip Schnakenburga, 1908, 25.

[112] Cited in Seymour Becker, *Russia's Protectorates in Central Asia: Bukhara and Khiva, 1865–1924*, Harvard UP, 1968, 18.

In 1864, Gorchakov compared this Russian expansion to that of the US (in the West), France (in North Africa), the Netherlands and Britain (in India) and considered it motivated less by ambition than by necessity.[113]

Establishing a protectorate could be a delicate matter and often ended up with salami tactics being pursued. Russia's 1868 treaty with Bukhara hid Article One in a secret supplement, which declared that the emir of Bukhara would pay a war indemnity 'as a sign of his sincere desire to live in friendship with the Russian Empire and to acquire the protection of His Imperial Majesty the Great Emperor of All the Russians'.[114] On 28 September 1873, a new treaty was concluded with Bukhara. Whereas the Khivan treaty established a Russian protectorate over that country by depriving the Khan of control of Khiva's foreign relations, the Bukharan treaty preserved the formal sovereignty of the emir's country.[115] However, from 1895, when Russia undertook control and protection of the Bukharan–Afghan frontier, Bukhara may be regarded as a de facto Russian protectorate.[116]

In 1873, Russia took over Khiva: Article 1 of the Russo–Khivan treaty of 12 August 1873 reduced Khiva to the legal status of a Russian protectorate. The Khan declared himself the 'obedient servant' of the Russian Emperor and renounced his right to conduct foreign relations:

> Saiyid Muhammad Rahim Bohadur Khan acknowledges himself to be the obedient servant of the Emperor of All the Russians. He renounces the right to maintain direct and friendly relations with neighboring rulers and khans and to conclude with them any commercial or other treaties; he will not undertake any military actions against them without the knowledge and permission of the supreme Russian authority in Central Asia.[117]

Article 2 settled the problem of the Russo–Khivan boundary, giving extensive territories to Russia (for example, the eastern Caspian shore). Besides a number of valuable commercial privileges, Russia gained control of Khiva's external affairs and of navigation on the Amu-Darya River. Russian subjects were granted special legal status, while the abolition of slavery in Khiva was also made as a legal commitment to Russia.[118] Writing in 1882, Martens

[113] Emanuel Sarkisyanz, 'Russian Imperialism Reconsidered', in: Taras Hunczak (ed) *Russian Imperialism from Ivan the Great to the Revolution*, Rutgers UP, 1974, 45–81 at 49.
[114] Becker, *Russia's Protectorates in Central Asia*, 1968, 42.
[115] Ibid, 77.
[116] Ibid, 154.
[117] Ibid, 316.
[118] Ibid, 75–6.

explained that the Caspian Sea had already become 'a Russian sea' after conclusion of the treaty of Turkmenchay with Persia in 1828.[119] As for Khiva, Martens highlighted the fact that, in its civilizing mission, Russia had made efforts to stop the slave trade in Central Asia.[120] However, from the perspective of Russia's advances in Khiva and Kokand, Britain—as Russia's rival empire in the region—pointed out that the Russian government had given pledges not to move further militarily or annex further territories, pledges that were violated in the process.[121] In some cases protectorates were also annexed. Between 1868 and 1875 Kokand was politically Russia's favourite among the Central Asian khanates but in February 1876 Kokand was annexed to Russian Turkestan as the Fergana Oblast.[122]

Similarities between Russian and Western colonial practices and events were manifest not only in form but also in abuses. In the Caucasus, imperial Russia's conquest of Circassia was particularly bloody and ended with the expulsion of the Circassians to the Ottoman Empire in 1864. Sarkisyanz observes that the massacres of the Yomud Turkomans—ordered by Konstantin von Kaufman, the first Governor-General of Russian Turkestan in 1873—and the massacre of the Tekke Turkomans under General Mikhail Skobelev in 1881 accorded with contemporary 'pacification' practices in the colonial territories of Western powers.[123] For example, on 24 January 1881, the Russians stormed the fortress of Geok-Teppe. Thousands of Tekke Turkomans fled into the desert pursued by Cossack cavalry. In addition to 6500 bodies found in the fortress, 8000 fugitives were caught and hacked to death by Russian soldiers; in contrast, only 59 Russians were killed. Firuz Kazemzadeh, the Iranian historian of Central Asia, concludes: 'Thus was civilization introduced to the Turkomans.'[124] In 1898, in the Andijan uprising, some 1500 local armed men attacked Russian forces in a fortification which was formerly part of the Khanate of Kokand. Commenting on this event, a Soviet legal scholar maintained that it was organized by a 'nationalist clique' with the purpose of separating Uzbekistan from Russia and bringing it to dependence from the Ottoman Empire.[125] Later, a

[119] Martens, *Traité de droit international*, 1883, 496.
[120] Ibid, 346, 433.
[121] Firuz Kazemzadeh, *Russia and Britain in Persia, 1864–1914. A Study in Imperialism*, Yale UP, 1968, 26, 36.
[122] Becker, *Russia's Protectorates in Central Asia: Bukhara and Khiva, 1865-1924*, 1968, 90.
[123] Emanuel Sarkisyanz, 'Russian Imperialism Reconsidered', in: Taras Hunczak (ed) *Russian Imperialism from Ivan the Great to the Revolution*, Rutgers UP, 1974, 63.
[124] Kazemzadeh, *Russia and Britain in Persia, 1864–1914. A Study in Imperialism*, 1968, 76.
[125] Kh P Vakhidov, 'Politicheskie vzgliady prosvetitelei narodov Srednei Azii vtoroi poloviny XIX. v', *SGP* No 7, 1955, 100–8 at 101.

vast Central Asian rebellion took place against Russian settlers in 1916.[126] In sum, the Russian Empire's encounters in Central Asia were quite typical of the violence of other European colonial empires in their overseas territories.

In the final decades of the Russian Empire, territorial deals and encounters in Asia increasingly involved other European colonial empires, which had expanded simultaneously. For example, on 27 February 1895, Britain and Russia signed an agreement in London defining 'the Spheres of Influence of the two Countries in the Region of the Pamirs'.[127] In St Petersburg on 31 August 1907, Britain and Russia signed a convention on Persia, Afghanistan, and Tibet. Although the preamble referred to the 'integrity and independence of Persia', the treaty carved Persia into three spheres of influence. The northern, and largest, was reserved for Russia. In addition, there were British and neutral spheres.[128] During the decade before the Russian revolutions of 1917, the Russian Empire regularly intervened in the political and economic matters of Persia,[129] for example in 1907 against the Persian Constitutional Revolution.[130] It is of particular interest that Soviet scholars of international law, especially during the interwar period, critically pointed out such facts of tsarist imperialism without inhibition. The Persian–Soviet treaty of friendship of 26 February 1921 also reads as a condemnation of such earlier tsarist policies, for example Article 8 paragraph 1:

> Federal Russia finally renounces the economic policy pursued in the East by the tsarist Government, which consisted in lending money to the Persian Government, not with a view to the economic development of the country, but rather for purposes of political subjugation.[131]

To give another example—based on the interwar narrative of the Soviet international lawyer Evgeny Korovin—Japan and tsarist Russia had four predominantly secret treaties: 1907, 1910, 1912, and 1916.[132] We should note that the

[126] Aminat Chokobaeva, Cloé Drieu, Alexander Morrison (eds), *The Central Asian Revolt of 1916. A Collapsing Empire in the Age of War and Revolution*, Manchester UP, 2019.

[127] Becker, *Russia's Protectorates in Central Asia: Bukhara and Khiva, 1865-1924*, 157.

[128] Kazemzadeh, *Russia and Britain in Persia, 1864–1914. A Study in Imperialism*, 1968, 498–9; Sardari, *Un chapitre de l'histoire diplomatique de l'Iran*, 1941, 148 et seq.

[129] Sardari, ibid, 161 et seq.

[130] M Rapoport, 'Sushchnost sovremennogo mezhdunarodnoga prava', *SGP* No 5–6, 1940, 137–53 at 137.

[131] Persia and the Russian Socialist Federal Soviet Republic, Treaty of Friendship, signed at Moscow on 26 February 1921, LNTS 1922, 400–13.

[132] Evgeny A Korovin, *Iaponia i mezhdunarodnoe pravo*, Sotsekgiz, 1936, 48–52. For a Western discussion, see Ernest Batson Price, *The Russo-Japanese Treaties of 1907–1916 Concerning Manchuria and Mongolia*, Baltimore: The Johns Hopkins Press, 1933.

treaties were concluded immediately after the Portsmouth Peace Treaty which ended the Russo-Japanese war of 1904–1905. In the 1907 treaty (Izvolsky-Motono), the secret part of the treaty stipulated that Manchuria was divided into two spheres of influence: the northern part to Russia and the southern part to Japan. Russia recognized Japan's special interests in Korea, while Japan recognized Russia's interests in Outer Mongolia. The 1910 secret treaty went a step further and—building on the previous spheres of interest— 'allowed' Russia to take all necessary measures there. The 1912 secret treaty (Motono-Sazonov) was concluded after the 1911 revolution in China. Again, special interests of both powers in Manchuria and Mongolia were reiterated, but now Inner Mongolia was also divided into two spheres of influence. Furthermore, on 3 July 1916 two treaties were concluded in St Petersburg, one public, the other secret. The secret treaty stipulated that both countries did not want to see any third foreign states in China and would act together against them. In the words of the Soviet international lawyer Evgeny Korovin, the whole of China was now the object of an imperialist treaty between tsarist Russia and imperial Japan.[133]

Finally, it is also relevant to see how the Russian Empire's territorial composition was dealt with in imperial constitutional law and legal literature on the subject. To start with, Russian constitutional law was somewhat scant, but following the 1905 revolution, on 26 April 1906, the Russian Basic Law was adopted. Its Article 1 declared the Russian state to be unitary and indivisible. However, when for example Baron Boris Nolde (1876–1948), in the imperial capital St Petersburg, discussed the constitutional law of the Russian Empire, the great majority of his attention went to the history of autonomy as well as autonomy claims in the Western border territories of Russia.[134] For Baron Nolde, the Russian Basic Law implied clearly: neither the Emperor not the state duma could allow any Russian territory to secede. However, annexing new territories was constitutionally acceptable because adding new territories would not have negatively affected the state unity of the Russian Empire.[135] When the Russian emperors had given privileges while conquering or annexing places such as the Ukraine, the Baltic provinces, Georgia, or Finland, these were 'never regarded as eternal or unchangeable norms'.[136] This attitude went hand in hand with Martens's view—already discussed—of the changeability of international

[133] Ibid, 53.
[134] Boris Nolde, *Ocherki po russkomu gosudarstvennomu pravu*, Tipografia PRAVDA, 1911.
[135] Ibid, 251.
[136] Ibid, 279.

treaties as well. Nolde described how initially, when Ukraine was made part of the Russian Empire after 1654, it maintained its autonomy, with its own state organs, budget, and laws.[137] However, from the time of Tsar Peter I, the Russian authorities started to curb Ukraine's autonomy, especially in the context of rebellions and wars such as the Great Nordic War, in which the Ukrainian hetman Mazepa sided with Sweden. In the time of Empress Catherine II, the elimination of Ukraine's autonomy within the Russian Empire was completed.[138] In the Baltic provinces, too, there had been a treaty (or agreement) about privileges and autonomy which Peter the Great concluded with the Baltic German Noble Corporations (in German: *Ritterschaften*) in 1710; not an international agreement, because the organizations of the Baltic German Barons had not been subjects of international law, but still a binding agreement. Nevertheless, at the end of the nineteenth century, Tsar Alexander III liquidated this agreement or quasi treaty-based autonomy in the Baltic provinces—another case of using *clausula rebus sic stantibus* by the Russian Empire, this time domestically. Thus Nolde concluded that the history of the Baltic provinces in the nineteenth century was a steady process of replacing local law with the central laws of the Russian Empire.[139] In other words, in the mind of Baron Nolde, writing in 1911, the Russian Empire was on its way to becoming at least constitutionally more unitary. However, it was not long before the First World War and the changes that it brought about shook the foundations of the status quo in the Russian Empire.

Mandelstam in Paris in 1919: the Liberal Swansong of the Old Russian Empire in International Law

In terms of international legal arguments, the symbolic swansong of the old Russian Empire had already been heard after Tsar Nicholas II abdicated in March (February according to the old Russian calendar) 1917 and the Bolsheviks had killed him together with his family in Yekaterinburg on 17 July 1918. The period between March and November 1917 was a very interesting time in Russia's international transformation, when the provisional government tried to introduce reforms that took into account demands for autonomy

[137] The French translation of Nolde's history of Ukrainian engagement with and liquidated autonomy in the Russian Empire is: Boris Nolde, *L'Ukraine sous le protectorat russe. Traduit du russe par Maurice Gehri*, Payot, 1915.

[138] Nolde, *Ocherki po russkomu gosudarstvennomu pravu* , 1911, 322–9.

[139] Ibid, 409.

of the peoples of the Empire.[140] For example, ethnic Estonians—who had historically been split between the two provinces of Estonia and Livonia—were now organized to live in a single united province, for which purpose the northern part of the province of Livonia was attached to Estonia. This was already a Russian Empire without an Emperor: the short-lived Russian republic *qua* Empire.

In 1917, during the regime of the Russian provisional government, the head of the legal department of the Russian MFA was Andrei Nikolaevich (André) Mandelstam (1869–1949), an international lawyer educated in the imperial capital, St Petersburg, inter alia by Martens.[141] In 1893, Mandelstam started to work at the Ministry of Foreign Affairs of the Russian Empire. Academically, he specialized initially in private international law and in 1900 at St Petersburg University defended his master's thesis on the Hague conference and the codification of international private law, Martens being one of the two opponents.[142] When the Bolsheviks came to power in Russia, Mandelstam escaped first to Constantinople and then to Paris. When the Paris Peace Conference convened in 1919, Mandelstam was already living in Paris, and in the context of the peace conference, he wrote a memorandum on whether and how the principle of self-determination of peoples—which had famously been proclaimed by US President Woodrow Wilson—should be applied to Russia.[143] Mandelstam's short answer was that, except for Poland—to which statehood had been promised in Wilson's fourteen points and which by 1919 had already been recognized de facto by the Western allies—no other territory should be allowed to secede from Russia based on the right of peoples to self-determination. For example, Mandelstam maintained:

> It seems to us that the absolute independence of Latvia, Lithuania and Estonia gravely endangers the vital interests of Russia and, consequently, creates an international situation which is most dangerous for permanent peace.[144]

[140] See S L Ronin, 'Konstitutsionnye proekty Vremennogo pravitel'stva', *SGP* No 4, 1947, 45–53 and William E Pomeranz, *Law and the Russian State. Russia's Legal Evolution from Peter the Great to Vladimir Putin*, Bloomsbury Academic, 2019, 68 et seq.

[141] S V Ivanenko, *Sankt-peterburgskaya shkola mezhdunarodnoga prava. Mesto i rol' sankt-peterburgskogo universiteta, ego uchenykh i vypusknikov v stanovlenii i razvitii nauki i praktiki mezhdunarodnoga prava. Chast' pervaya 1720–1920-e gg*, Iuridicheskii tsentr, 2019, 266. See also Artur Simonyan, 'Russia's Counter-revolutionary International law in the Scholarship of Boris Mirkine-Guetzévitch', *EJIL* No 35, 2024, 797–804.

[142] Ivanenko, ibid, 267.

[143] André Mandelstam, *Mémoire sur la délimitation des Droits de'l État et de la Nation d'après la doctrine du Président Wilson*, Paris: Imprimerie Polyglotte Hugonis, 1919.

[144] Ibid, 25.

Mandelstam elaborated that US President Wilson may not have meant the 'absolute' right of peoples to self-determination because this would mean not only secession but also that a polity could in principle choose to live outside the community of nations.[145] Following the school of Martens on this issue, Mandelstam emphasized that one had to distinguish normatively between different situations. The first case was trusteeship of civilized peoples over non-civilized ones or those with 'rudimentary civilization' such as, Mandelstam wrote, the Senegalese, the Moroccans, the Kyrgyz, the Bashkirs, and others. Mandelstam maintained that they did not deserve the same political regime as, for example, the civilized Poles, the Yugoslavs, the Czechoslovaks, or the Finns.[146] These nations were ready neither for independence nor even for autonomy. It was in the interests of those peoples themselves that a more civilized nation should exercise trusteeship over their affairs, asserted Mandelstam.

Furthermore, Mandelstam added that the other situation had until recently been possible, too: that a non-civilized people would exercise power over civilized ones, as had been the case with the Ottoman Empire over peoples which were 'infinitely superior' to it: the Greeks, the Arabs, the Armenians, the Syrians.[147] Again like Martens, Mandelstam revealed his particularly negative attitude towards the Ottoman Empire. He had been a Russian diplomat there during the First World War and later also wrote about the massacres of the Armenians in the Ottoman Empire.[148]

The third option, Mandelstam posited, was when civilized peoples exercised power over other (usually smaller) civilized nations, as in the case of the Austro-Hungarian and Russian Empires. But, according to Mandelstam, these two former empires nevertheless deserved entirely different solutions after the First World War, as far as the right of peoples to self-determination was concerned.[149] In Russia, he argued, there were many peoples with 'rudimentary civilization' such as the Kyrgyz, the Bashkirs, the Buryats, the Kalmyks, the Tartars, the Voguls (Mansi), the Ostiaques (Khanty), the Mordva, the Cheremiss (Mari), the Cherkess, the Lesgines, and the other 'tribes' of the Caucasus, among others. Their level of development did not merit autonomy

[145] Ibid, 26.
[146] Ibid, 29.
[147] Ibid, 30.
[148] See André Mandelstam, *Le sort de l'empire Ottoman*, Paris: Librairie Payot & Co, 1917; André N Mandelstam, *La Société des Nations et les Puissances devant le Problème Arménien*, Paris: A Pedone, 1926.
[149] Mandelstam, *Mémoire sur la délimitation des Droits de'l État et de la Nation d'après la doctrine du Président Wilson* , 1919, 33.

but trusteeship in the name of the international community—but of course provided by the Russian state.[150]

Then there were peoples with high levels of education and sense of nationhood but who did not yet (or any more) enjoy autonomy in the Russian Empire. The Poles deserved independence but not within the borders claimed by 'Polish imperialism'.[151] Mandelstam argued further that Russia's loss of Finland would involve the gravest consequences for Russia and, in fact, for Finland itself as well, because of Finland's inevitable economic feebleness.[152] On Estonia, Mandelstam argued at length with Kaarel Robert Pusta (1883–1964), a member of the Estonian diplomatic delegation in Paris and later Estonia's foreign minister and member of the *Institut de droit international*, over their mission to achieve recognition for the Republic of Estonia.[153] Mandelstam's argument was that whatever the Estonians wanted to achieve politically and economically, they could achieve in a federal Russia under the supervision of the League of Nations. In any case, full separation of Estonia would go against the vital interests of the Russian people.[154] Lithuania, too, should stay with future democratic Russia, argued Mandelstam.[155]

Concerning Latvia's independence claims, just as Mandelstam rejected the arguments of Pusta, Estonia's diplomat in Paris, he similarly rejected the plea for independence by Latvia's diplomat Zigfrīds Anna Meierovcs (1887–1925), whose arguments, in Mandelstam's view, had 'neither juridical nor political value'.[156] The secession of the Baltic provinces of Estonia and Latvia would have grave consequences for Russia's national security.[157]

Even more consequential was Mandelstam's analysis as to why Ukraine should not be allowed to separate from Russia:

> If we rise above the struggles of the moment, if we consider the permanent interests, the eternal ideals of the two peoples, it becomes clear that a complete separation can only occur to the detriment of either of the two. [. . .] There is no need for a long demonstration to prove that the independence of Ukraine is equivalent to the death of Great Russia. A glance at the map is

[150] Ibid, 37.
[151] Ibid, 38.
[152] Ibid, 44–6.
[153] In January 1921, the leading European powers gave collective recognition *de jure* to the Baltic States.
[154] Ibid, 52.
[155] Ibid, 63.
[156] Ibid, 55.
[157] Ibid, 56–7.

> enough. [. . .] The League of Nations could not grant Ukraine this complete separation unless it denied Russia the right to life.[158]

Writing in Paris in 1919, Mandelstam concluded that the situation in the former Russian Empire differed 'radically' from the former Austro-Hungarian Empire,[159] although he failed to specify wherein lay this radical difference. Martens too had argued in 1882 that even if the principle of nationality worked for Italy, this did not mean it was necessary or desirable elsewhere (read: in Russia). Whereas in 1882 Martens's general argument against self-determination of peoples had, somewhat nebulously, been the 'inalienable requirements of truth and justice',[160] Mandelstam in his 1919 memorandum before the 'civilized world's' diplomatic community resorted in his closing argument to the special qualities of the Russian soul and literature:

> But the Russian people have their own soul, the Russian soul, the soul of Tolstoy, of Pushkin, of Lermontov, of Vladimir Solovev, of Gogol, of Dostoevsky, of Turgenev.[161]

One could assume that this soul was so special that the Empire was a necessity and secessions were undesirable. This quote also fits well with the post-2022 debates on whether and how Russian philosophy and literature have historically also contributed to and expressed Russian imperialism (or colonialism), and how often people are unaware of the imperialist views which several of these great writers exhibited. Ukraine under Russian military attack even adopted a law on decolonization concerning symbols of Russian culture in Ukraine. Mandelstam's argument demonstrates that at least the 'soft power' which radiated from the names of these famous writers was also used in the context of international legal arguments and diplomacy, to defend the Empire.

André Mandelstam later became one of the first proponents of human rights in international law—the rapporteur of the Institut de Droit International's (IDI) report on human rights in its 1929 New York session, as an international human rights proclamation a predecessor of the Universal Declaration

158 Ibid, 73–6.
159 Ibid, 77.
160 Martens, *Contemporary International Law of Civilized Nations*, 2021, 117. (Martens, *Sovremennoe mezhdunarodnoe pravo tsivilizovannykh narodov*, 1995, 121; Martens, *Traité de droit international*, 1883, 196–7.)
161 Mandelstam, *Mémoire sur la délimitation des Droits de'l État et de la Nation d'après la doctrine du Président Wilson* , 1919, 80.

of Human Rights.[162] The Soviet scholar Evgeny Korovin took note of the fact that in 1921, at the IDI, Mandelstam propagated recognition of the individual in international law, in order to obtain international legal status for Russian 'counter-revolutionary emigrants'.[163] Mandelstam's opposition to the independence of the Baltic States in 1919 did not prevent him from later becoming Lithuania's legal agent in the *Panevežys–Saldutiskis Railway* Case at the PCIJ, in which judgment was issued on 28 February 1939.[164] The other exiled Russian constitutional and private international law scholar, Baron Boris Nolde, represented Estonia in this case.

In our context, the overall impression of Mandelstam's views was that human rights were entirely compatible with the idea(l) of the integrity of the Russian Empire as well as the hierarchy of peoples based on their perceived 'civilization'. Indeed, in his understanding, a liberal empire may even have been the most trusted provider of human rights. As an imperial internationalist, Martens had already indicated in 1882 that rising self-determination claims meant trouble for the Empire. Having lost his homeland, and with the Bolsheviks in power in Russia in 1919, Mandelstam still faithfully continued in this imperial Russian tradition, resisting with his memorandum secessions from Russia.

Nevertheless, another question which international lawyers such as Martens and Mandelstam must still have asked themselves—even if not in public—was: how realistic was a 'liberal Empire' in Russia? The imperial mindset ran very deep and there seemed to be no alternative among leading 'bourgeois' Russian lawyers, as indeed was also shown in the international legal views of the Russian community in exile after 1917. For example, writing from exile in Prague in 1923, Mikhail Arturovich Tsimmerman (1887–1935) narrated how the First World War had been a clash of European empires, including the Russian Empire. However, at least in its German-sponsored Brest-Litovsk treaty version of March 1918, Tsimmerman posited that application of the right of peoples to self-determination (only) to the Russian Empire had been 'completely artificial and unilateral'.[165] Tsimmerman himself had been a prisoner of

[162] Helmut Philipp Aust, 'From Diplomat to Academic Activist: André Mandelstam and the History of Human Rights', *EJIL* Vol 25, 2014, 1105–21; Dzovinar Kévonian, 'André Mandelstam and the Internationalization of Human Rights (1869–1949)', in Pamela Slotte and Miia Halme-Tuomisaari (eds), *Revisiting the Origins of Human Rights*, CUP, 2015, 239–66.

[163] E A Korovin, *Sovremennoe mezhdunarodnoe publichnoe pravo*, Moscow/Leningrad: Gosudarstvennoe izdatel'stvo, 1926, 21.

[164] *Panevežys-Saldutiskis Railway*, PCIJ Series A/B. No 76, Judgment of 28.02.1939.

[165] M A Tsimmerman, *Ocherki novoga mezhdunarodnoga prava. Posobie k lektsiam*, Plamia, 1923, 127.

war of the German Empire during the First World War and had been an officer in the White Army resisting the Bolsheviks in southern Russia in 1918–20.[166] Extensively discussing the post-First World War peace treaties in Europe, Tsimmerman focused on the major peace treaties such as the Versailles and Saint Germain peace treaties of 1919, as well as the League of Nations, leaving the Soviet peace treaties with those states which had separated from Russia in 1920 completely out of his analysis, as if he did not recognize them, even though the emergence of new 'small states' out of European empires was the very subject of his book. Even contemporary Russian historians in exile who otherwise recognize, for example, the illegality of the Soviet occupation of the Baltic States in 1940, such as Andrey Borisovich Zubov (b 1952), argue that the fact that secessionist border states like Estonia concluded peace treaties with the Russian Bolsheviks in 1920 was a 'moral mistake'.[167] However, as the views of Mandelstam also reveal, the Russian 'White' movement was not endorsing secessions from the Russian Empire.

At the end of the day, the question remains whether—compared to the Russian Bolsheviks, to whom we turn next—imperial legal scholars such as André Mandelstam were just more principled and honest in resisting attempts to secede from the Russian Empire. In their view, no territory was permitted to leave the Russian Empire, nor were they willing to make even tactical compromises.

[166] S V Ivanenko, *Sankt-peterburgskaya shkola mezhdunarodnoga prava. Mesto i rol' sankt-peterburgskogo universiteta, ego uchenykh i vypusknikov v stanovlenii i razvitii nauki i praktiki mezhdunarodnoga prava. Chast' pervaya 1720–1920-e gg*, Iuridicheskii tsentr, 2019, 322–3.

[167] Jaanus Piirsalu, 'Ajaloolane Andrei Zubov: Tartu rahu bolševikega oli Eesti moraalne viga', Diplomaatia, February 2020, https://diplomaatia.ee/ajaloolane-andrei-zubov-tartu-rahu-bolsevikega-oli-eesti-moraalne-viga/.

4

From Soviet Russia to the Soviet Union: The Interwar Period and the Second World War

Taking a Distance from Tsarist Russia

During the First World War, Russia's Bolsheviks heavily criticized the war as 'imperialist' and made the point that workers across borders had no need for or interest in this war—that the war was being waged in the interests of capitalists. This was one of their main political slogans when paving the way towards power in Russia. They also criticized the tsarist government and again in 1917 the Provisional Government, initially highlighting breaks rather than continuities with their policies and with their way of seeing the world, including in aspects relevant for international law. On coming to power in November 1917, the Bolsheviks issued manifestos such as the Decree on Peace (8 November 1917), the Declaration of the Rights of the Peoples of Russia (15 November 1917) and the Appeal to the Muslims of Russia and the East (3 December 1917), which in their rhetoric stood for a world without annexations, endorsed the right of peoples to self-determination up to the point of the right to separate from Russia, and supported the equality of peoples with different cultural backgrounds, European or non-European, Christian or not. The Bolsheviks understood themselves as fiercely 'anti-imperialist', a self-understanding that remained central for Soviet discourse until the very end of the Soviet Union in 1991. However, this does not mean that the earlier discourse of 'civilized' and 'uncivilized' states was replaced overnight—during the interwar period at least, Soviet legal scholars writing on international and constitutional law occasionally still resorted to distinctions between 'civilized', 'semicivilized', and 'uncivilized' nations,[1] just as—for example—their Russian 'bourgeois' colleague André Mandelstam had done in Paris in 1919.

[1] EA Korovin, *Sovremennoe mezhdunarodnoe publichnoe pravo*, Moscow/Leningrad: Gosudarstvennoe izdatel'stvo, 1926, 7; N. Cheliapov, 'Partia i natsional'nyi vopros', SGIRP, No 5–6, 1930, 101–21 at 103.

Russia, the Soviet Union, and Imperial Continuity in International Law. Lauri Mälksoo, Oxford University Press.
 DOI: 10.1093/9780198955962.003.0004

These new understandings also manifested themselves in concrete policies relevant for international law. For example, when the Bolsheviks accessed the archives of the Russian Ministry of Foreign Affairs, they made public a whole list of (more than a hundred) secret treaties which Russia had concluded with Britain, France, Japan, and other powers both during and before the First World War.[2] Nikolay Grigorevich Markin (1893–1918)—a revolutionary naval officer and agent of Trotsky, the Soviet commissar for foreign affairs—played a distinct role in the process, securing the texts of the secret treaties and helping to make them public. These treaties included designs for further territorial expansion by Russia and its treaty partners: treaties with Britain and France regarding the territories of the Ottoman Empire (Russia was promised Constantinople as a prize for the Allies' expected common victory in the First World War) and agreements with Japan on the partition of Manchuria and other territories in China. Publishing these agreements involving previous Russian governments had a great propaganda effect and made the point that the Bolsheviks had in mind a quite different understanding of Russia's national interest than the traditional diplomats of the Romanov Empire and the 1917 Provisional Government.

However, the most immediate situation to tackle was the war itself. In March 1918, the Soviet government signed treaties with the Central Powers—led by imperial Germany—at Brest-Litovsk, ending the war on the Eastern front.[3] With these treaties, the Soviet government approved significant territorial losses in favour of Germany. A separate Treaty of Brest-Litovsk was concluded between Soviet Russia and Ukraine, which had emerged, supported by imperial Germany, as a new state in the territory of the former Russian Empire. This also meant that Soviet Russia recognized Ukraine's independence. However, there was a significant nuance—a twist, even: on 4 (17) December 1917, Soviet Russia had also recognized the 'independence' of *Soviet* Ukraine.[4] At least two parallel and competing ideas existed of what Ukraine was meant to be: a pro-Soviet Russian Ukraine or a Ukraine aiming at genuine separation from Russia (but at the same time, geopolitically, also aligned to imperial Germany). As we shall see next, this competition of parallel claims to self-determination—one dependent on, the other antagonistic to, Soviet Russia—arose in most of

[2] See M P Iroshnikov, A O Chubarian, *Tainoe stanovitsia iavnym. Ob izdanii sekretnykh dogovorov tsarskogo i vremennogo pravitel'stv*, Nauka, 1970.

[3] See Borislav Chernev, *Twilight of Empire: The Brest-Litovsk Conference and the Remaking of East-Central Europe, 1917–1918*, University of Toronto Press, 2017.

[4] S M Ravin, 'Istoricheskii opyt sovetskogo federalizma', *SGP* 1957, No 11, 74–85 at 79. See also B M Babii, 'Obrazovanie Ukrainskogo Sovetskogo sotsialisticheskogo gosudarstva', *SGP* No 3, 1958, 43–53.

the border territories of the former Empire. Soviet Russia appropriated self-determination claims in these secessionist territories to label national self-determination and even statehood as a status which was not meant to denote a genuine transfer of sovereignty from (Soviet) Russia.

In November 1918 a revolution broke out in Germany as well, and on 13 November the Soviet government annulled the Brest-Litovsk Peace Treaties with Germany, the other Central Powers, and Ukraine. The Treaty of Brest-Litovsk—the first Soviet experience in treaty-making under militarily unfavourable conditions and in contradiction to earlier Tsarist Russian commitment to the allies that a separate peace with the enemies will not be concluded—deeply influenced Soviet thinking about treaties, especially politically important treaties. In Soviet scholarship on international law, in any discussion on the law of treaties, it became a standard trope to point out that the Soviet government had every right and legitimacy to annul the Brest-Litovsk Treaty in November 1918. A somewhat trickier question was exactly why or on what legal–philosophical basis this was so. Lenin's explanation had been that Soviet Russia 'traded territory' (parts of the former Russian Empire) 'to win time', to consolidate the contested Bolshevik regime in Russia. From the Bolshevik comments, it appeared that they saw the Brest-Litovsk treaties and their concessions to Germany and the other Central Powers—as well as an independent national Ukraine—as tactical, not final. In terms of the balance of power, the Brest-Litovsk treaties were snapshots of the status quo. The Bolshevik expectation was that the communist revolution would soon break out in Central and Western Europe, when everything would fundamentally change in any case.

Reconciling Revolutionary Imperialism with Self-determination Claims in the Former Russian Empire

When we think of what imperialism means or how it might be perceived by other states or populations struggling for self-determination and statehood, then it is of interest to observe that although Soviet Russia defined itself as a fiercely 'anti-imperialist' power, it also wrote into its first constitution of 10 July 1918 that its aim was the victory of socialism in all countries.[5] If imperialism means expansion, then Soviet Russia's disregard for national borders in the

[5] E Korovin, *Mezhdunardonoe pravo perekhodnoga vremeni*, Moscow/Petrograd: Gosudarstvennoe izdatel'stvo, 1923, 15.

name of world revolution was also perceived as expansionist and in that sense quasi-imperialist, at least in the Central and East European states bordering Russia and by 'bourgeois' political forces who did not share Bolshevik aims. Peter Kleist, a German scholar writing in 1934, called the Soviet approach 'revolutionary imperialism'.[6] Jean-Yves Calvez, a French legal scholar, wrote in 1953 that the Soviet state—if it still was a state—was by vocation a 'world republic' and by definition an international state.[7] One of Lenin's last wishes was that the Soviet Union would extend further and in his commemorative speech of 26 January 1924 after Lenin's death, Stalin promised to do exactly that.[8]

Internationalist transboundary sentiments were also present in the works of early Soviet international law scholars. As Evgeny Korovin, the first important Soviet international lawyer, put it in 1923:

> The international proletariat was always a faithful ally of Soviet Russia. More than once, during the years of its ordeals, with warm and brotherly calls, Russia appealed to them over the heads of bourgeois governments.[9]

Korovin also pointed out that while the institute of nationality existed in international law, Soviet Russia treated persecuted communists in foreign countries in principle as if they were its own nationals; state borders were insignificant in terms of this class relationship.[10] The neighboring powers in Europe and elsewhere perceived this approach by a rhetorically fiercely 'anti-imperialist' power as interventionist and expansionist in its own way.

Besides Ukraine already mentioned above, the Bolsheviks were soon confronted with independence declarations by national political movements in territories of the former Empire. For example, Finland proclaimed independence on 6 December 1917. Soviet Russia recognized Finland as a state on 18 (31) December18 1917.[11] However, civil war later broke out in Finland and the borders with Russia needed to be determined; the Finnish–Soviet Peace Treaty of Dorpat (Tartu) was concluded on 14 October 1920.

For territories occupied by imperial German forces in 1917–18 such as Lithuania, Latvia, and Estonia, the chance to establish their statehood de facto

[6] Peter Kleist, *Die völkerrechtliche Anerkennung Sowjetrußlands*, Ost-Europa-Verlag, 1934, 77.

[7] Jean-Yves Calvez, *Droit international et souveraineté en URSS. L'évolution de l'idéologie juridique soviétique depuis la Révolution d'Octobre*, Librairie Armand Colin, 1953, 63.

[8] Ibid, 55.

[9] E A Korovin, *Mezhdunardonoe pravo perekhodnoga vremeni*, Gosudarstvennoe izdatel'stvo, 1923, 33.

[10] Ibid, 31.

[11] S M Ravin, 'Istoricheskii opyt sovetskogo federalizma', *SGP* 1957, No 11, 74–85 at 79.

only came when Germany had signed the armistice treaty at Compiègne in November 1918. Based on the conditions of the armistice, the German army had to withdraw from the former Russian Empire's occupied territories. In most territories in which secessionist political movements had proclaimed independent states—Estonia, Latvia, Ukraine, among others—the Soviets responded by proclaiming parallel *Soviet* republics of the same titular nation or increased their military pressure if those republics had already been proclaimed sooner than the Soviet proclamations. For example, although the 'bourgeois' Republic of Estonia had been proclaimed in Tallinn on 24 February 1918, Narva in November 1918 saw the Soviets proclaim the Workers' Republic (Commune) of Estonia, which the Soviet Russian government in Moscow promptly recognized as an independent state on 7 December 1918. War broke out between Soviet Russia and the emerging 'bourgeois' Republic of Estonia and lasted more than a year. Only after the 'bourgeois' forces prevailed militarily in what Estonia came to see as its War of Independence did Soviet Russia recognize the Republic of Estonia as a matter of law (but also the 'bourgeois' government), in the Peace Treaty of Tartu (the Estonian–Soviet Russian peace treaty) of 2 February 1920.

On 22 December 1918 Soviet Russia recognized Latvia and Lithuania, and on 4 February 1919 Byelorussia, as independent states—but again with the same caveat that it was the Soviet-proclaimed formations that were recognized. However, in Latvia and Lithuania the 'bourgeois' governments prevailed as well, and Soviet Russia recognized the Republics of Latvia and Lithuania *de jure* in 1920. In Byelorussia the Soviet government prevailed and so it was reintegrated in the same political space as Soviet Russia.

From the moment of their creation, the national Soviet republics and formations worked closely together with the Soviet Russian government and received 'military aid' from it, although in fact they were in important ways part of the Soviet Russian government. In the words of the Soviet legal scholar S M Ravin, discussing the history of the Soviet federation: 'The friendship of the Soviet peoples and their state connections strengthened under the conditions of civil war.'[12] The Soviet legal scholar B Levin, writing on the occasion of the fortieth anniversary of the Estonian workers' commune, wrote that the commune testified to the emergence of the first forms of international legal assistance between socialist republics, being based on the principles of proletarian internationalism.[13] Other Soviet legal scholars commented that, once

[12] Ibid, 80.
[13] B I Levin, 'Sorokoletie Estliandskoi trudovoi kommuny', *SGP* No 11, 1958, 19–26 at 19.

the Soviet government had recognized Soviet Estonia, Latvia, and Lithuania in December 1918, 'close cooperation was established between them and Soviet Russia in the fight against counterrevolution and foreign intervention'.[14] One scholar from Byelorussia maintained that a key feature of the foreign policy of Soviet Byelorussia before the formation of the USSR was that it was 'carried out under the leadership of the Communist Party, in brotherly union with the Russian SFSR, on the basis of mutual help from all Soviet republics'.[15] Professor O I Chistyakov of Moscow State University summed the situation up in the following fashion:

> Thus on the ruins of the former Russian Empire emerged new independent socialist states. However, the creation of independent Soviet republics did not mean their separation from Russia. To the contrary, its consequence was the unification of the Byelorussian, Latvian, Azerbaijani and other peoples with the Russian people and all other peoples of the Russian Federation at a new, higher level.[16]

Christyakov also explained how, before the formation of the Soviet Union, other—non-Russian—'independent' Soviet republics outsourced some key functions of their government to Moscow (the new capital of Soviet Russia, instead of St Petersburg):

> Federal relations between the independent Soviet republics were at that time quite unique. Their characteristic feature was that all independent Soviet republics recognized as common and federal the organs of power and administration of the Russian RSFSR. In that way, the highest organs and law of the Russian Federation featured simultaneously in a double role: they served the Russian RSFSR itself and at the same time the common needs of the federal association of independent Soviet republics.[17]

The so-called national Soviet republics worked closely together with Soviet Russia; especially in military matters (the Red Army), no genuine distinction existed between them and the Soviet Russian centre.

[14] G Ya Kliava, V O Miller, 'Slavnoe dvadsatiletie pribaltiiskikh sovetskikh respublik', *SGP* 1960, No 7, 11–21 at 11.
[15] S V Vikharev, 'Soyuznaya respublika kak sub'ekt mezhdunarodnoga prava', *SGP* No 6, 1960, 65–73 at 68.
[16] O I Chistiakov, 'RSFSR i obrazovanie Soyuza SSR', *SGP* No 11, 1972, 3–9 at 7.
[17] Ibid, 7.

Some years later, on 30 December 1922, the republics in which the Soviets had prevailed were all also formally merged with Soviet Russia into one state, the Soviet Union. The main insight in this context is that the Soviet Russian government rhetorically supported the right of peoples to self-determination 'up to the point of separation from Russia' but in practice this was more a fiction or an act of 'doing things by words', as it could only be independence of *a certain kind* acceptable to the Russian Bolsheviks. Soviet Russia recognized the 'independence' of other Soviet republics, although dominated over them militarily and exercized otherwise control over them. At the same time, in the territory of the former tsarist Empire, the Red Army fought against 'bourgeois' forces who genuinely wanted to separate from Russia. Thus, a principled difference in perspective emerged: what the nationalist 'bourgeois' republics saw as their wars of national liberation from (Soviet) Russia, Soviet Russia and local communists framed as class wars in the territory of the former Russian Empire. It is also important to keep in mind that the struggle over the future of the territories of the former Empire was not merely based on ethnicity. The Soviet Russian leadership included a significant number of prominent individuals representing non-Russian ethnicities. For example, the first Minister of Justice (and notable Soviet legal theoretician), Pēteris Stučka (1865–1932),[18] was ethnic Latvian by origin. In that sense, there was something genuinely internationalist in the new revolutionary government of Russia, or the continuity of the Empire in a new form.

The same story repeated itself in other border areas of the former Russian Empire, where nationalist 'bourgeois' formations were struggling for power against Soviet Bolshevik formations militarily supported by Soviet Russia. After the Second World War, when the Soviet Union was at its peak level of self-confidence, Soviet legal scholars looked back at the years after the 1917 October Revolution and spoke frankly about the non pro-Soviet Russian self-determination claims in the former Empire:

> History demonstrated that Armenia, Georgia and Azerbaijan separating from Soviet Russia depended entirely on foreign states. It is enough to say that the very act of the proclamation of independence of Georgia, Azerbaijan and Armenia in May 1918 was to a significant extent dictated by Germany and Turkey.[19]

[18] See, eg, Petr I Stucka, *Die revolutionäre Rolle von Recht und Staat—Theorie 1*, Übersetzung und Einleitung von Norbert Reich, Frankfurt: Suhrkamp Verlag, 1969.

[19] A Z Begiyan, 'Obrazovanie sovetskikh respublik Zakavkazia—torzhestvo leninskoi natsional'noi politiki i printsipov gosudarstvennoga suvereniteta', *SGP* No 2, 1961, 48–58 at 49.

Sometimes the unit of self-determination was not so obvious at the beginning, at least from the perspective of Soviet policy. For example, in February 1919 the Lithuanian–Byelorussian Soviet Republic was proclaimed but it soon dissolved in July 1919, also because most of Lithuania at the time was already controlled by the Polish army.[20] Then the Byelorussian Soviet Republic was proclaimed instead, as a 'bourgeois' government had effectively established itself in Lithuania. The Byelorussian Soviet Republic was proclaimed as a counterproject to the 'bourgeois' National Republic of Byelorussia, which was proclaimed in March 1918 and, according to Soviet legal scholars, was 'under the influence of the Germans' and proclaimed by 'enemies of the Byelorussian people'.[21] The National Republic of Byelorussia soon had to retreat as the Soviets consolidated their power and Moscow restored its influence.

Soviet Use of Treaties in the Space of the Empire

One interesting aspect of Soviet state practice in the early years was the somewhat liberal use of the institution of 'treaties' in the space of the Empire. Concluding a treaty seems to indicate that the other party is a subject of international law. Indeed, early Soviet Russia had no problem with this association being invoked in various situations in the territory of the former Empire. Moreover, Soviet Russia wanted to encourage this association: the former Russian Empire had now become a territory of various sovereign—but Soviet—entities which concluded treaties with each other on a formally equal basis. Later, during the final decade of the Soviet period, legal scholars from increasingly frustrated non-Russian Soviet republics—such as Levan Aleksidze from Georgia—started to emphasize that the Soviet Union was created through treaty by genuinely sovereign republics. Aleksidze rejected the view of some Soviet constitutionalists from Moscow that even in the period 1918–22 the bond between various Soviet republics with Soviet Russia was that of confederation rather than federation.[22] By the early 1980s, this historical debate was already a proxy debate about conditions in the Soviet Union and whether other Soviet republics were 'equal' to or dominated by Russia. In contemporary Western scholarship, for example, Professor Kaj Hobér of Uppsala University

[20] V A Krutalevich, 'Stanovlenie natsional'noi gosudarstvennosti belorusskoga naroda', *SGP* No 12, 1967, 49–57 at 52.

[21] L A Rudzitsky, V A Dorogin, 'Obrazovanie Belorusskoi SSR', *SGP* No 4, 1957, 12–19 at 16.

[22] L A Aleksidze, 'Znachenie obrazovania SSSR dlia obespechenia mira i mezhdunarodnoga pravoporiadka', *Soviet YBIL* 1982, 11–28 at 16.

has supported the view that before 1922 Soviet republics were indeed sovereign states and treaties between them were international treaties.[23]

When Soviet Russia concluded 'treaties' with other Soviet formations in the territory of the former Russian Empire, the agenda was to maintain and strengthen close ties with Soviet Russia rather than endorse a genuine secession. The treaties also reflected Soviet Russia's balance of power with national Bolshevik forces. In this sense, we can speak of a certain specific Soviet Russian appropriation of the language of national self-determination, the format of international treaties, and formal attributes of the sovereignty of non-Russian Soviet republics, all while substantive ties with Soviet Russia were maintained and over time strengthened. It was a compromise of power: places in the imperial periphery were recognized as 'national' and nominally even 'sovereign' but Soviet Russia got to maintain very close substantive ties with these other Soviet territories, exercising military–political control. It was more of a legal–theoretical fiction to say that Soviet Russia also developed federal relations with the USSR,[24] as Soviet scholars postulated; in terms of power, both were entangled. These aspects seem important to highlight considering the opinion—sometimes expressed in Western academic literature—that Lenin's concept of self-determination was more far-reaching and *genuine* ('up to the point of separation from Russia') than, for example, the designs of US President Woodrow Wilson for the empires defeated in Europe and the Middle East during the First World War.[25] Looking at actual Soviet practice, it is doubtful whether Soviet Russian readiness to support the self-determination of non-Russian peoples was ever genuine in the sense of accepting their full and unconditional secession.

Reimagining Soviet Russia's Political Relations in the East

In light of troubles with 'bourgeois' liberal aspirations to national self-determination, particularly at the former Empire's western borders, Soviet Russia increasingly turned its attention eastwards. After the Bolshevik Revolution, non-Bolshevik state formations emerged, for example Kokand

[23] Kaj Hobér, *The Perestroika Era and International Law*, Edward Elgar Publishing, 2024, 173.

[24] O I Chistiakov, 'Razvitie federativnykh otnoshenii mezhdu USSR i RSFSR (1917–1922 gg)', *SGP* No 2, 1954, 14–25.

[25] See, eg, Bill Bowring, 'The Soviets and the Right to Self-Determination of the Colonized. Contradictions of Soviet Diplomacy and Foreign Policy in the Era of Decolonization', in: Jochen von Bernstoff, Philipp Dann (eds) *The Battle for International Law. South–North Perspectives on the Decolonization Era*, OUP, 2019, 404–25 at 410.

Autonomy (or Turkestan Autonomy); albeit this existed only from November 1917 to February 1918. Later, during the Soviet period, the history of such formations was written by the winners: the Bolsheviks. For example, writing in 1948, the Soviet legal scholar Radzhapov characterized Kokand Autonomy in the following way:

> The bourgeois 'Kokand Autonomy' government like other 'national' bourgeois governments in border regions was anti-people, counterrevolutionary, and set for itself the goal of tearing Turkestan away from Soviet Russia.[26]

On May 1, 1918, Turkestan was declared an autonomous 'republic' within Soviet Russia. Moreover, the Bolsheviks came to power in the former tsarist protectorates of Bukhara and Khiva (by then renamed Khorezm, according to the ancient name of Khiva) and Soviet Russia concluded 'union' treaties with these workers' republics, at the same time recognizing their statehood and 'independence'. The 'union' treaty with the Khorezm Soviet National Republic was concluded on 13 September 1920 and the treaty with the Bukhara Soviet National Republic on 20 March 1921.[27] In the Treaty of Alliance with Khorezm, the Soviet government

> unconditionally recognizes the complete independence of the Khorezm Soviet People's Republic, with all the consequences stemming from such recognition. For the realization of the slogans for which the Russian workers are fighting, the RSFSR renounces for all time all those rights which were established by former Russian governments with respect to the Republic of Khorezm.[28]

The Soviet Russian–Bukharan Treaty of Alliance of 20 March 1921 recognized Bukhara as 'completely independent'[29] and referred to the two countries' 'common struggle and unification of forces against the imperialist world bourgeoisie'.[30] These territories, which had been Russian protectorates during the imperial period, were now recognized as new workers' states but also

[26] S Radzhapov, 'Etapy razvitia sovetskogo gosudarstvennogo stroya v Srednei Azii', *SGP* No 11, 1948, 61–67 at 62.
[27] E A Korovin, *Sovremennoe mezhdunarodnoe publichnoe pravo*, Moscow/Leningrad: Gosudarstvennoe izdatel'stvo, 1926, 40.
[28] Cited in Jan F Triska, Robert M Slusser, *The Law, Theory, and Policy of Soviet Treaties*, Stanford UP, 1962, 201.
[29] Ibid, 201.
[30] Korovin, *Mezhdunarodnoe pravo perekhodnoga vremeni*, 1923, 14.

'in alliance' with Soviet Russia. According to the treaties, Soviet Russia represented the two republics in their international relations.[31] But this was not so different from what the tsarist-era concept of protectorate implied, even though rhetoric had changed, of course. During the 1960s, a wave of scholarship in the Soviet Union characterized the marriage of self-determination and Sovietization in Central Asia in the early 1920s:

> Soviet Russia took part in the closest way in forming and strengthening Soviet republics in the national border territories, providing them necessary help.[32]

Some years after the union treaties with Bukhara and Khorezm, these Central Asian polities were formally made part of the Soviet Union, and their territories were reorganized in 1924 according to Soviet nationality policies and concepts. It was during these years and based on Bolshevik decisions that Kazakhstan, Uzbekistan, Turkmenistan, Tajikistan, and Kyrgyzstan were born as Soviet republics. In May 1925, the Uzbek SSR—which at that time included the Tajik ASSR, as well as the Turkmen SSR—'voluntarily entered the Soviet Union, where they became sovereign members of the Union with equal rights', as the Soviet legal scholar A Gordienko put it in 1967.[33] Here was a strong element of revolutionary nation-making, and even the names of whole nations or nationalities could acquire new meanings over time: for example, Kazakhs had also been called Kyrgyz in the early twentieth century.[34] Again, alternative ideas to the Soviet understandings of self-determination existed: for example, some political forces promoted the idea of a united Turkic republic in Central Asia. The Soviet communist dismissal of this idea was unequivocal:

> This proposal was artificial and did not reflect the reality on the ground as in Central Asia, one Turkic nation never existed.[35]

[31] Radzhapov, 'Etapy razvitia sovetskogo gosudarstvennogo stroya v Srednei Azii', 1948, 64.

[32] Sh Z Urazaev, 'Rol' RSFSR v sozdanii sovetskoi gosudarstvennoi deyatel'nosti narodov Srednei Azii (1917–1922 gg), *SGP* 1964, No 6, 106–11 at 111.

[33] A A Gordienko, 'Samoopredelenie narodov i obrazovanie sovetskoi natsionalnoi gosudarstvennosti v Srednei Azii', *SGP* No 5, 1967, 76–84 at 84.

[34] Gordienko, ibid, 80. See also G S Sapargaliev, M A Binder, 'Razvitie sovetskoi natsional'noi gosudarstvennosti kazakhskogo naroda', *SGP* No 9, 1970, 24–31 at 25.

[35] Gordienko, 82.

Nevertheless, some Western authors characterized Soviet national policies in Central Asia as the age-old imperial approach of 'divide and conquer'.[36]

1920–1 Peace Treaties at the Western Border of the Empire and Their Aftermath

In republics where the 'bourgeois' nationalist forces prevailed in military conflict with Soviet Russia and the local Bolsheviks (which the narrative of the Soviet government and Soviet legal scholars critically presented as these same 'bourgeois' forces having been helped by outside powers such as Britain and France), Soviet Russia concluded peace treaties with those republics in 1920, as well as in March 1921 with Poland (the Peace of Riga).[37] Finland and Poland had a unique constitutional history in the Russian Empire, which may explain why the Soviet Russian peace treaties with these states did not include an explicit reference to the right of peoples to self-determination as a ground for their secession. At the same time, the 1920 Soviet Russian peace treaties with the Republics of Estonia, Latvia, Lithuania, and Georgia included precisely this reference as the Soviet acknowledgment of the principle based on which these republics separated from Russia 'voluntarily and for ever', as the text of the treaties expressed it.[38] Later, the Soviet narrative presented these peace treaties as a generous gift by Soviet Russia which 'gave' independence to these new smaller new republics.[39] However, it is important to keep in mind that in all of these republics 'bourgeois' independence was achieved only after military conflict with Soviet Russia. Several early Soviet international lawyers highlighted their disagreement with the way some 'bourgeois' territories separated from Russia. For example, Korovin wrote in 1923 about the post-revolutionary military conflicts and civil war:

> The Entente tried—by the hand of Kolchak, Yudenich, Miller, Wrangel, Poland and the Baltic vassals—to strangle the world hearth of revolution.[40]

[36] Ibid, 76 (Referring to Aleksander G Park, *Bolshevism in Turkestan 1917–1927*, Columbia UP, 1957).

[37] See P N Ol'shansky, *Rizhskii dogovor i razvitie sovetsko-pol'skikh otnoshenii*, Nauka, 1974.

[38] See, eg, Art II of the Peace Treaty of Tartu between Soviet Russia and the Republic of Estonia, February 2, 1920, http://www.worldlii.org/int/other/LNTSer/1922/92.html.

[39] See, eg, I Levin, 'Natsional'nyi vopros v Evrope i ugroza voiny', *SGP* 1934, No 4, 14–29 at 17.

[40] Korovin, *Mezhdunarodnoe pravo perekhodnoga vremeni*, Gosudarstvennoe izdatel'stvo, 1923, 59.

At the Genoa diplomatic conference on 20 April 1922, the Soviet Russian delegation presented a memorandum according to which, because of the First World War, 'the Russian people lost huge territories which were important for its state development'.[41] These comments did not demonstrate genuine reconciliation with secessions from Russia.[42] In several aspects, Soviet Russian legal scholars also added a certain conditionality to their interpretation of Soviet peace treaties with 'bourgeois' republics such as Poland and Estonia. They emphasized that when Poland was (re-)born as a state and received recognition as a matter of law—at the Versailles Peace Treaty of 1919 but especially in the 1921 Soviet Russian–Polish Peace Treaty of Riga— of borders which included sizeable Ukrainian, Byelorussian, and Jewish minorities, it was in the context of Warsaw respecting the rights of those minorities. However, Soviet legal scholars early on complained that the Polish government had 'systematically' violated those minority rights.[43] Second, Soviet internationalists referred to the conditionally formulated mention of future 'permanent neutrality' in the Peace Treaty of Tartu with Estonia (Article V), suggesting that for Estonia the pursuit of treaty-based neutrality as mentioned in the peace treaty with Soviet Russia constituted a *pactum de contrahendo*: a binding legal instrument under international law.[44] In September 1939, when the Soviet Union demanded that its military bases be established in the territories of the three Baltic States, its negotiators inter alia argued that the Baltic States had not managed to remain properly 'neutral' when the Second World War broke out. The Baltic States had declared themselves neutral at the beginning of the Second World War, but their neutrality was not treaty-based and in that sense not permanent. Regarding some other neighbours, especially Afghanistan, during the interwar period the Soviet Union managed to arrange it that the state concerned accepted neutral status. For example, on 24 June 1931, the Treaty of Neutrality and Mutual Non-Aggression was concluded between Afghanistan and the Soviet Union; it was extended in 1955, by which time both states were members of the UN.[45]

41 LA Modzhoryan, 'Identichnost, nepreryvnost i pravopreemstvo sub'ektov mezhdunarodnogo prava', *SGP* 1959 No 9, 61–70 at 65.

42 On 1 August 2014, when unveiling a monument in Moscow celebrating the Russians who fought in the First World War, President Vladimir Putin said that victory in the First World War was 'stolen from our country. It was stolen by those who called for the defeat of their homeland and army, who sowed division inside Russia and sought only power for themselves, betraying the national interests.' See President of Russia, 'Unveiling of a Monument to World War I Heroes', 1 August 2014, http://en.kremlin.ru/events/president/news/page/627.

43 E A Korovin, *Sovremennoe mezhdunarodnoe publichnoe pravo*, .Gosudarstvennoe izdatel'stvo, 1926, 56; I Levin, 'Dogovory o zashchite prav natsional'nykh menshinstv', *SGP* No 6, 1934, 63–6.

44 E A Korovin, *Sovremennoe mezhdunarodnoe publichnoe pravo*, 1926, 59.

45 V N Durdenevsky, 'Neitralitet v sisteme kollektivnoi bezopasnosti', *SGP* 1957, No 8, 81–91 at 85.

Short Life of Soviet Treaties in Former Russian Imperial Space

As we have seen, Soviet Russian treaties with other Soviet republics in the territory of the former Russian Empire highlighted close cooperation with Soviet Russia, especially in military matters and in terms of common communist party politics. These treaties were designed to facilitate reintegration of national Soviet republics with Soviet Russia, which concluded treaties of alliance with the following Soviet republics: Azerbaijan (30 September 1920), Ukraine (29 December 1920), Byelorussia (16 January 1921), Armenia (2 December 1920), Bukhara (4 March 1921), Khorezm (13 September 1920), and the Far Eastern Republic (14 May 1920). A protocol of 22 February 1922 entrusted the RSFSR with representing all these republics at the Genoa Conference.[46] During the Cold War, Triska and Slusser, the leading Western researchers of Soviet treaties, came to the following conclusion:

> These treaties, which resembled in form international treaties but were in fact closer to constitutional than international law, were agreements concluded for the purpose of furthering the Communist revolution territorially.[47]

One of the foremost Soviet authorities on international treaty law, Anatoly Talalaev, described the fate of Russia's treaties with the Far Eastern Republic: by November 1922, the Far Eastern Republic had fulfilled its historical role as a bulwark 'against imperialist aggression by Japan in the Far East' and 'liquidated itself'; it was integrated into the Russian RSFSR on 15 November 1922 and earlier treaties were terminated.[48]

Soviet Russian treaties with new neighbouring 'bourgeois' republics proclaimed Soviet recognition of self-determination and nationhood separate from Soviet Russia 'for ever'. However, the story of the Soviet Russian peace treaty with the (Menshevik-led) Democratic Republic of Georgia proved a sobering one. Professor Levan Aleksidze of Tbilisi University—who was one of the most prominent Soviet international lawyers from non-Russian republics and who in the 1960s had published on the history of Georgian–Russian

[46] Jan F Triska, Robert M Slusser, *The Law, Theory, and Policy of Soviet Treaties*, Stanford UP, 1962, 206.

[47] Ibid, 206.

[48] A N Talalaev, *Pravo mezhdunarodnykh dogovorov. Tom 2. Deistvie i primenenie dogovorov. Dogovory s uchastiem mezhdunarodnykh organizatsii*, Zertsalo, 2011 (Originally, Mezhdunarodnye otnoshenia, 1985), 173. On the history of the Far Eastern Republic, see Ivan Sablin, *The Rise and Fall of Russia's Far Eastern Republic, 1905–1922. Nationalisms, Imperialisms, and Regionalisms in and after the Russian Empire*, Routledge, 2019.

treaties—was among the legal scholars who, in the early 1990s, analysed the circumstances of how the Soviet government was established in Georgia, in violation of the Soviet Russian–Georgian peace treaty. Aleksidze co-authored a Georgian governmental report on the takeover of the Georgian Democratic Republic by Soviet Russia in 1921.[49]

The story itself was the following. On 26 May 1918, the National Council of Georgia proclaimed the independence of Georgia. On 7 May 1920, Soviet Russia concluded a peace treaty with the Democratic Republic of Georgia, which also implied Soviet Russia's recognition of Georgia's independence as a matter of law, based on the right of peoples to self-determination (as in a previous Soviet Russian treaty with the Republic of Estonia). The Georgian–Soviet Russian treaty also had a 'secret supplement' in which the government of Georgia pledged not to create any obstacles to communist propaganda and activities in the country. However, in one of the first academic monographs on international law in the Soviet Union, published in 1923, the Soviet Russian international lawyer Evgeny Korovin made public the content of this 'secret supplement'.[50] In 1920 and 1921, Georgia's independence was recognized by Germany, Belgium, France, Great Britain, Italy, Japan, Poland, Austria, Romania, Luxembourg, and Mexico. The Democratic Republic of Georgia was in the process of becoming a member of the League of Nations in Geneva. However, on 25 February 1921, the Soviet Army entered the Georgian capital Tbilisi and established control over Georgia. Military operations in Georgia ended in the second half of March 1921 and the government of the Democratic Republic of Georgia was forced into exile.[51] Thus, at the end of the day the solemn treaty between Georgia and Soviet Russia concluded on 7 May 1920, with references to self-determination and recognizing the independence of the Democratic Republic of Georgia, meant little, as within less than a year from conclusion of the treaty the Soviet Russian military took control of Georgia anyway, and the Bolsheviks Sovietized Georgia. What mattered was the actual and changing balance of forces, not solemn promises in a treaty. On the level of principles, too, Korovin, in his 1923 treatise on international law, postulated that international law had always been based on the balance of power.[52] Later,

[49] 'Zakliuchenie Kommissii po voprosam politicheskoi i pravovoi otsenki narushenia Dogovora mezhdu Gruziei i Sovetskoi Rossiei ot 7 maia 1920 goda', 18.11.1989, in: Levan Aleksidze, *International Law and Georgia (From Antiquity to Present)*. Selected Papers Published in 1957–2012, Ivane Javakhishvili Tbilisi State University, 2012, 715–30.

[50] Korovin, *Mezhdunarodnoe pravo perekhodnoga vremeni*, 1923, 32.

[51] Levan Aleksidze, *International Law and Georgia (From Antiquity to Present). Selected Papers Published in 1957–2012*, Ivane Javakhishvili Tbilisi State University, 2012, 727.

[52] Korovin, *Mezhdunarodnoe pravo perekhodnoga vremeni.*, 1923, 9.

the Soviet Georgian legal scholar V Parkosadze admitted that suppressing the Menshevik-led Democratic Republic of Georgia had not been an easy task:

> In Georgia, crushing the bourgeois–landowners' state apparatus, both at the center as well as in the provinces, happened in quite complicated conditions because the influence of Menshevik and petty bourgeois elements was still quite strong.[53]

In Armenia,[54] the main competitor of the Bolsheviks was the national party of Dashnaktsuyun, colloquially known as the Dashnaks. In February 1921 they seized power in Armenia but, in the words of a Soviet Armenian legal scholar:

> The Red Army defended the independence of not only the Russian people but also of other peoples of Russia. [. . .] The Russian people and its Red Army gave brotherly assistance to Armenia. With the help of the Red Army, on 2 April 1921 Soviet power was restored in the capital of Armenia.[55]

On 12 March 1922, a union treaty was signed, and the Transcaucasian Federal Union of Soviet Socialist Republics was formed between Georgia, Armenia, and Azerbaijan. This 'federation within a federation' lasted for fourteen years until a new Soviet constitution was adopted in December 1936 and the three Caucasian republics independently became federal units of the USSR.[56]

Territorial Rights: Emphasizing State Continuity with Tsarist Russia

Soviet Russia tried to keep as much of tsarist territory as possible, but not all territory could be kept. Poland, Finland, Estonia, Latvia, and Lithuania separated from Russia in 1917–19; in other places, Moscow was able to halt separation (Ukraine, Georgia, Byelorussia, and elsewhere). In this context, it also became a subject of debate whether Soviet Russia (and, since the end of

[53] V V Parkosadze, 'Iz istorii sozdania i razvitia sovetskoi gosudarstvennosti v Gruzii', *SGP* 1967, No 1, 82–7 at 82.

[54] See on the proclamation of Armenia's statehood: Gegam Petrosyan, *Zakavkaz'e v diplomaticheskikh peripetiakh: stanovlenie armianskoi nezavisimoi gosudarstvennosti (fevral' 1917- iun' 1918 gg.)*, Izdatel'stvo EGU, 2019.

[55] A Z Begiyan, 'Velikii Oktiabr i sozdanie sovetskoi armianskoi gosudarstvennosti', *SGP* No 7, 1967, 3–9 at 5–6.

[56] V V Parkosadze, 'Zakavkazskaya federatsia i ee rol' v razvitii natsionalnoi gosudarstvennosti narodov Zakavkazia', *SGP* No 12, 1972, 66–72 at 67, 72.

1922, the Soviet Union) had maintained state continuity with tsarist Russia or whether the old Empire had come to an end. Some of the Soviet policies seemed so radically different both from tsarist Russia as well as other capitalist countries that some foreign legal scholars even assumed that Russia's state continuity had been broken; they postulated that the Soviet Union was a new, revolutionary state.[57]

Besides nationalization policies in Soviet Russia (the liquidation of private property on land and means of production), the Soviet government also announced that it would not pay back the loans of tsarist Russia and the provisional government as these had arguably been made in the interests of Russia's previous ruling classes but also with the purpose of keeping the Russian Empire fighting the Central Powers in the First World War. Before the First World War, France in particular and French citizens individually had made loans on a massive scale to Russia, France's ally. The Soviet Russian decision not to repay this money was a heavy financial blow to many lenders. It was also considered illegal according to the traditional rules of state succession in international law in Europe, as even a radical change of government was not recognized as an acceptable excuse to default on payments regarding previous foreign loans. In addition, when concluding treaties with its neighbors, new and old, Soviet Russia annulled previous debts owed to it: for example, Article V paragraph 3 of the Soviet Russian–Turkish Treaty of 16 March 1921, concluded in Moscow, proclaimed:

> The Government of the RSFSR hereby declares, in particular, that it considers Turkey free from any monetary or other obligations originating from any international pacts concluded between Turkey and the tsarist government.

The peace treaties with Estonia, Latvia, and Lithuania, concluded in 1920, also stated that these new nations were not responsible for any parts of the tsarist Russian debt. France was not happy about this way of getting rid of tsarist-era debt and in 1922 attempted to collect a portion of it from the Baltic States directly, via rules of state succession.[58] Elements of this kind in state practice initially indicated that Soviet Russia wanted to break with state continuity with the Russian Empire and even refused state succession on what classical international law would otherwise have mandated, especially succession of loans by previous governments.

[57] Peter Kleist, *Die völkerrechtliche Anerkennung Sowjetrußlands*, Ost-Europa-Verlag, 1934, 16, 80.
[58] E Korovin, *Sovremennoe mezhdunarodnoe publichnoe pravo*, 1926, 34.

However, in relations with other powers and especially concerning questions of a territorial nature, it was soon clear beyond doubt that Soviet Russia asserted continuity of rights with the Russian Empire. Where the Russian Empire had been involved in a treaty-based solution to certain territorial situations and had acquired certain rights or at least a place at the decision-making table, and then after 1917 foreign powers attempted to regulate the same issue without the Soviet Russian government (initially not recognized by the Western powers), the Soviets protested and complained that Russia's historical rights had been violated. This was a pattern which played out in multiple different circumstances.

For example, in 1920 states gathered in Paris and decided on the sovereignty and regime of the Spitzbergen (Svalbard) islands: sovereignty went to Norway. On 12 February 1920 the Soviet government protested that it had played no part in these deliberations, even though the Russian Empire had been involved in regulation of the area in 1872.[59] The Soviet government protested that it would not allow 'under any circumstance that its international relations should be disposed of by others without its approval'.[60] The same logic applied to the situation concerning the neutrality of Aaland Islands, where a treaty concerning their neutrality was made between France, Britain, and Russia (1856). In 1921, Germany, Denmark, Estonia, Finland, France, Britain, Italy, Latvia, Sweden, and Poland concluded a new treaty on the same topic.[61] On 28 June 1920, the Soviet Russian government protested tits lack of inclusion as the matter also concerned Russia's tsarist-era treaty rights:

> There is no treaty stipulation based on which the sovereignty of the Russian republic over the Aaland Islands would have ceased to exist. For that reason, no decision concerning these islands will be effective if the Russian government was not invited to participate in it.[62]

The situation with the River Niemen (Nemunas) belonged to the same category. The international status of the River Nemunas was established by Article 14 of the acts of the Congress of Vienna, inter alia carrying the signature of the Russian Empire's representative. In August 1922, the Soviet government announced that it would not allow any decision on the question of the River

[59] R V Dekanozov, 'Demilitarizatsia i neitralizatsia Spitsbergena', *Soviet YBIL* 1966/7, 181–94 at 182.
[60] I S Peretersky, 'Znachenie mezhdunarodnoga dogovora dlia tret'ego (ne zakliuchivshego etot dogovor) gosudarstva', *SGP* No 4, 1957, 71–80 at 75.
[61] Korovin, *Sovremennoe mezhdunarodnoe publichnoe pravo*, 1926, 60.
[62] Peretersky, 'Znachenie mezhdunarodnoga dogovora dlia tret'ego . . .', 1957, 75.

Niemen without its participation and 'in any case will consider non-binding for itself all kinds of agreements made to the detriment of the legal rights of the Soviet government'.[63]

In the same way, in 1922 the Soviet government protested when the Washington conference discussed the question of the Chinese Eastern Railway in Manchuria but Soviet Russia was not invited nor otherwise formally part of the resolution, even though the railway had been built with funds from the Russian Empire. Similarly, on 2 September 1926 the Soviet government protested that Spain had not invited it to the revision conference of the 1906 Algeciras Act. Russian participation in 1906 would have given an equal right to participation in 1926 as well, so the Soviet government argued. As a consequence, the Soviet government reserved for itself the right not to recognize any result of the revision conference arrived at without its participation.[64] In its relations with Romania, the interwar Soviet Union also argued for the continuity of rights based on the Constantinople convention of 1881, concerning regulation of the use of the River Danube.[65]

These cases were at least partly about the Soviet government's desire to achieve the international recognition that it initially lacked. At the same time, these examples also demonstrate that Soviet Russia and the Soviet Union proceeded from an assumption of continuity of rights with tsarist Russia, especially in territorial matters. However, territorial issues were key in terms of the survival of the Empire. Only in terms of tsarist Russian debts which the Soviet government refused to pay was there a strong Soviet claim to a break in continuity of Russian obligations. Soviet legal scholars later came up with various theories and justifications as to why the Soviet Union was the same state as the Russian Empire, as a subject of international law—but yet at the same time need not be responsible for tsarist-era debts.

In certain territorial and self-determination questions concerning the former Russian Empire, the issue remained unresolved, as Soviet Russia and later the Soviet Union did not recognize territorial changes undertaken without its approval. In 1812, by the Treaty of Bucharest, the Russian Empire had annexed Bessarabia, part of a former protectorate of the Ottoman Empire: Moldova. In January 1918, Romania annexed Bessarabia, but until 1940, when the Soviet Union seized this territory back, the Soviet government did not

[63] Ibid, 75–6.

[64] Ibid, 76.

[65] M A Lebedev, 'Nekotorye voprosy pol'zovania inostrannoi territoriei v sovremennom mezhdunarodnom prave', *Soviet YBIL* 1981, 282–7 at 287 (Also referring to P G Fandikov, *Mezhdunarodno-pravovoi rezhim Dunaya*, Moscow: Gosyurizdat, 1955).

recognize Bessarabia as part of Romania. Soviet legal scholars later asserted that Bessarabia had been 'an inseparable part of Soviet Russia, connected with it through a shared historical fate'.[66] The Soviets argued that self-determination did not apply here as the Romanian and Moldovan languages were similar but not identical; they promoted the idea that the Moldovans were an ethnicity separate from the Romanians and ordered that the 'Moldovan' language be written not in the Latin alphabet but in the Russian alphabet, *kirillitsa*. Because of the territorial dispute over Bessarabia, the Soviet Russian legal discourse in the 1930s portrayed Romania (a nation much smaller in size than Russia) as another 'imperialist' state. However, according to the Soviet scholar I Levin, Romania's was an 'imperialism' which was not able to act independently but rather carried out the tasks given to it by bigger imperialist powers.[67]

During the Genoa Economic and Financial Conference of April and May 1922—its first major encounter with the capitalist world—Soviet Russia presented credentials from eight other Soviet national republics (Ukraine, Byelorussia, Georgia, Armenia, Azerbaijan, Bukhara, Khorezm, and the Far Eastern Republic) as well as its own.[68] However, their constitutional relationship with Soviet Russia was soon about to change. On 30 December 1922 the union treaty forming the Soviet Union was concluded by Soviet Russia, Soviet Ukraine, Soviet Byelorussia, and Soviet Transcaucasia.

Combating Imperialism Abroad and Keeping the Empire Safe at Home

It is interesting to follow how understandings of self-determination and sovereignty under the conditions of federalism evolved in Soviet constitutional and international legal thought. For example, I Levin, writing in the journal *Sovetskoe gosudarstvo i pravo* in 1934, postulated that socialism would eventually lead to the merger of all separate nations into one humankind—but would do so through 'dialectical development', because first there would be a temporary blossoming of national cultures.[69] Levin postulated that national cultures would die, but only after exhausting their potential. Under the conditions

[66] P V Voronin, A A Karlov, 'Sozdanie moldavskoi sovetskoi natsional'noi gosudarstvennosti', *SGP* No 6, 1967, 12–20 at 14.
[67] I Levin, 'Natsional'nyi vopros v Rumynii', SGRP 1931, No 10-12, 186–209 at 189.
[68] Peter Alfons Steiniger, *Oktoberrevolution und Völkerrecht: eine populärwissenschaftliche Studie*, Berlin: Staatsverlag der Deutschen Demokratischen Republik, 1967, 13.
[69] I Levin, 'Srednyaya Azia—primer konsolidatsii natsii v usloviakh diktatury proletariata', *SGP* No 6, 1934, 74–82 at 74.

of capitalism, the manifestation of self-determination was to establish a separate nation state; under the conditions of socialist revolution, the manifestation of self-determination was to create a federation. Levin maintained:

> Thanks to it (i.e., the federation which it creates -L.M.), only socialism is capable of resolving the question of nations and nationhood, not destroying the common economic territory in the process and avoiding political and economic Balkanization. [. . .] The proletariat decisively rejects all nationalist metaphysics of the nation, which has now become the ideological and political weapon of fascism. The question of nations and nationhood at this stage is completely subjugated to the tasks of the revolution.[70]

Another Soviet legal scholar, Mikhail Yakovlevich Rapoport (1889–1969),[71] who worked at Leningrad State University, expressed the same thought in 1940, when he wrote after the conclusion of the Nazi–Soviet non-aggression pact that recognition of the right of peoples to self-determination constitutes 'as is well known, only a part of the general question of the proletarian revolution'.[72] What was really meant is that by that time little remained of the right of peoples to self-determination in Soviet practice and thinking, at least in the 'bourgeois' sense of the concept.

With great publicity, Soviet Russia also renounced earlier 'unequal treaties' with neighbouring nations in Asia: the 'uncivilized' peoples of Martens and also of André Mandelstam. This was one of the most visible changes and differences in Soviet foreign legal policy compared to the tsarist Empire. New treaties were concluded, for example with Afghanistan, Persia, and Turkey as well as with China and Mongolia. During the Soviet period, these treaties were extensively referred to and celebrated as manifestations of progressive principles which the Russian Bolsheviks introduced towards Russia's neighbours in the 'East'.[73] During the Cold War, these treaties were interpreted in the West to the effect that their main goal was to replace British influence in these

[70] Ibid, 76.

[71] On his biography, see https://bioslovhist.spbu.ru/person/3627-rapoport-rappoport-mihail-akovlevic.html.

[72] M Rapoport, 'Sushchnost sovremennogo mezhdunarodnoga prava', *SGP* No 5–6, 1940, 137–53 at 142.

[73] See, eg, N V Zakharova, 'Otkaz Sovetskogo gosudarstva ot dogovorov tsarskoi Rossii, narushavshikh prava narodov vostochnykh stran', *Soviet YBIL* 1962, 126–36; K A Adzharov, 'V I Lenin i pervye dogovory Sovetskogo gosudarstva so stranami Vostoka', *Soviet YBIL* 1969, 58–68; Kaforov Zaver Murad ogly, 'Mezhdunarodno-pravovoe znachenie dogovora o druzhbe mezhdu RSFSR i Afghanistanom', *Soviet YBIL* 1982, 302–15; A N Mikhailov, 'Iz istorii sovetsko-turetskikh mezhdunarodno-pravovykh otnoshenii (k 60-letiu Sovetsko-turetskogo dogovora 1921 g)', *Soviet YBIL*, 1982, 307–15.

territories with Soviet influence.[74] In the preamble to the treaty between Soviet Russia and Atatürk's Turkey, signed in Moscow on 16 March 1921, both states referred to 'their solidarity in the struggle against imperialism'. The Western powers had at the time not yet recognized either the Soviet Russian or the Turkish governments as a matter of law. The historian Samuel J Hurst argues that these conventions were an extension of Lenin's argument that socialists and anti-colonial nationalists shared an anti-imperialist cause.[75]

Based on early Soviet practice in international law, what can be concluded regarding imperialism? Some authors argue that the Soviet Russian (as well as Mexican) revolutions became an inspiration in anti-imperialist struggles elsewhere:

> The two revolutions represented the possibility of radical social and economic change at the national level, created legal systems that survived for many decades, inspired transnational movements striving against imperialism and for social revolution, decisively changed international relations, and motivated international legal innovators to create new forms, principles, and institutions.[76]

However, paradoxically—as the Soviet Russian case demonstrates—a nation, while able to inspire transnational movements striving against imperialism, at the same time can itself continue to be imperialist, at least from the perspective of its own neighbours and formerly suppressed peoples.

With some nations, such as China, disputes emerged during the interwar period over whether the Russian Bolsheviks were willing to change their actual policies based on their proclaimed progressive principles (for example, on the question of the Eastern Chinese Railway in Manchuria).[77] The new treaties condemned the tsarist inequalities of the past but themselves still also contained elements which were not reciprocal, especially in security matters. For example, the Persian–Soviet Russian Treaty of Friendship of 26 February 1921 contained a list of condemnations of tsarist Russian policies; indeed, Soviet

[74] Jan F Triska, Robert M Slusser, *The Law, Theory, and Policy of Soviet Treaties*, Stanford UP, 1962, 204.

[75] Samuel J Hirst, *Against the Liberal Order. The Soviet Union, Turkey, and Statist Internationalism, 1919–1939*, OUP, 2024, 32.

[76] Kathryn Greenman, Anne Orford, Anna Saunders, Ntina Tzouvala, 'International Law and Revolution: 1917 and Beyond', in: Kathryn Greenman et al (the same eds) *Revolutions in International Law: The Legacies of 1917*, CUP, 2021, 2.

[77] See further Chiang Kai-shek, *Soviet Russia in China. A Summing Up at Seventy*, Taipei: China Publishing Company, 1969, 62–71; E B Pashukanis, *Ocherki po mezhdunarodnomu pravu*, Sovetskoe zakonodatel'stvo, 1935, 52–3.

legal scholars liked to emphasize how progressive this was.[78] However, some of the treaty's security-related articles put limitations on Persian sovereignty, for example Article 6:

> If a third Party should attempt to carry out a policy of usurpation by means of armed intervention in Persia, or if that Power should desire to use Persian territory as a base for operations against Russia, or if a Foreign Power should threaten the frontiers of Federal Russia or those of its Allies, and if the Persian Government should not be able to put a stop to this menace after having been once called upon to do so by Russia, Russia shall have the right to advance her troops into the Persian interior for the purpose of carrying out the military operations necessary for its defense. Russia undertakes, however, to withdraw her troops from Persian territory as soon as the danger has been removed.[79]

As a sidenote, Persia—or Iran, as the country has been known since 1935—played an important role in the life of the Soviet international lawyer Fedor Kozhevnikov, who from late 1934 to January 1937 was the Soviet trade representative in Tehran.[80] Based on Article 6, cited above, the Soviet Union occupied Northern Iran from 25 August 1941, after Nazi Germany invaded the USSR in June 1941.[81] In a coordinated action, the other part of Iran was occupied by the United Kingdom; both nations had already agreed on spheres of influence in Persia before the First World War. Thus, the early Bolshevik treaties played a significant role in practice and proved useful for the Soviet Union even twenty years later. The Iranian government formally denounced the 1921 agreement in March 1959, referring to its clauses such as Article 6. One reason was that at the end of the Second World War, the Soviet Union was in no hurry to remove its forces from Iran, and in 1946 the United Nations had to ask the USSR to withdraw them from Iran's territory.[82]

Soviet Russia's proclaimed support for self-determination has continued to fascinate scholars. Professor Bill Bowring of Birkbeck College has taken a

[78] See, eg, E A Korovin, 'K voprosu o roli narodnykh mass v razvitii mezhdunarodnoga prava', *SGP* No 3, 1956, 50–60 at 52.

[79] Persia and the Russian Socialist Federal Soviet Republic, Treaty of Friendship, signed at Moscow on February 26 1921, LNTS 1922, 400–13. See also Art 7 regarding the Caspian Sea.

[80] F I Kozhevnikov, 'Iz zapisok diplomata', in: AN Vylegzhanin, Yu M Kolosov, E S Krivchikova (eds), *Rossiia i mezhdunarodnoe pravo. Materialy mezhdunarodnoi konferentsii, poskhviachennoi 100-letiu F. I. Kozhevnikova, 15.10.2004*, Moscow: Izdatel'stvo 'MGIMO-Universitet', 2006, 7–13.

[81] Sergey Monin, '"Delo s Iranom deistvitel'no vyshlo neplokho"', *MZh* No 8, 2011, https://interaffairs.ru/jauthor/material/518.

[82] Jan F Triska, Robert M Slusser, *The Law, Theory, and Policy of Soviet Treaties*, Stanford UP, 1962, 137.

somewhat favourable position on the Soviet role in establishing the right of peoples to self-determination under international law. Bowring argues that the USSR played a leading role in the emergence of the right of peoples to self-determination, 'in the teeth of fierce resistance from the great colonial powers'.[83] Bowring further argues that, for Lenin at least, self-determination was not a mere slogan, but a principle he put into practice with immediate effect within the former Russian Empire following the Bolshevik Revolution.[84] In that sense, Bowring considers it unjust and incorrect when the role of Soviet Russia or the Soviet Union is diminished when the emergence of the right of peoples to self-determination in international law is discussed, as seems to be the case in a leading monograph on the history of self-determination by Jörg Fisch.[85] However, Bowring nevertheless also admits that the Soviet position on self-determination was still also 'contradictory' and even 'hypocritical'.[86] A closer historical reading of the Soviet practice of self-determination after 1917, as offered here, suggests that one should indeed be critical of Lenin's and the Soviet approach to self-determination: the Bolsheviks did not conceive of it as acceptance of genuine secession from the Russian Empire. To verbally support the right of peoples to self-determination, for example in treaties, and yet fight militarily to keep or bring the former tsarist Empire's territories together was a novel tactic by the new, revolutionary rulers of the Empire.

[83] Bill Bowring, 'The Soviets and the Right to Self-Determination of the Colonized. Contradictions of Soviet Diplomacy and Foreign Policy in the Era of Decolonization', Jochen von Bernstorff, Philipp Dann (eds) *The Battle for International Law. South–North Perspectives on the Decolonization Era*, OUP, 2019, 404–25 at 404.

[84] Ibid, 410.

[85] Jörg Fisch, *The Right of Self-Determination of Peoples. The Domestication of an Illusion*, Translated by Anita Mage, CUP, 2015.

[86] Bowring, 'The Soviets and the Right to Self-Determination of the Colonized . . . , 2019, 404, 411, 425.

5
Interwar Soviet International Law Scholars and the Buildup to the Nazi–Soviet Pact of 1939

One of the best-known music pieces of the Soviet period is 'Time, Forward!' by Georgy Sviridov, the main melody of which was also used for the Soviet TV evening news programme Vremya. But how much did the Soviets want to bring international law forward, compared to the earlier Russian imperial period? In the following, we will explore what the two leading Soviet international law scholars of the interwar period—Evgeny Korovin and Evgeny Pashukanis—wrote about matters related to the transformation of the Russian Empire, the state identity of Soviet Russia and the Soviet Union, and conditions of termination of treaties. The assumption here is that their views on international law also reflected the *Zeitgeist* of interwar Soviet Russia and the Soviet Union.

Imperialism-related Themes in the Work of Evgeny Korovin

The first Soviet legal scholar to write about international law in a way that also became accessible in other countries was Evgeny Korovin (1892–1964). His 1923 book *International Law of the Transition Period* was translated into German and became quite well known, at least in Europe, also because of its main message: the book declared an end to common international law with capitalist countries.

Writing in 1923, Korovin postulated that Soviet Russia was 'encircled' by imperialist powers,[1] and defined the phenomenon of imperialism in the following way:

[1] E A Korovin, *Mezhdunardonoe pravo perekhodnoga vremeni*, Moscow/Petrograd: Gosudarstvennoe izdatel'stvo, 1923, 6.

Russia, the Soviet Union, and Imperial Continuity in International Law. Lauri Mälksoo, Oxford University Press.
 DOI: 10.1093/9780198955962.003.0005

> Imperialism as the newest stage of capitalist development, with its unstoppable expansion (*Drang nach . . .*), the conquest of colonies, markets, oligarchy of financial capital, monopoly of international trusts, with its ideology of *Weltstaat* (world state) and world trust, with all the stages which lead to it (spheres of influence, colonial and postcolonial division of the world, great power concert) is in its essence hostile to international law.[2]

Korovin also maintained in his 1923 text that in terms of international legal subjecthood, Soviet Russia was the same state as the old Russian Empire:

> [O]ne does not need to be a qualified legal scholar to understand that the 'state of Russia' has not existed since 1917 and does not need recognition of its existence in anything new or factual or juridical.[3]

In Korovin's early Soviet Russian narrative began the trope that military intervention was a vicious thing in the hands of capitalist imperialist states whereas in the hands of 'progressive' states such as Soviet Russia, it was a tool for progress:

> The utter disapproval of Russian workers to every kind of interventionist campaign by the Entente does not amount to a rejection of intervention as a method of class struggle, but rather a rejection and judgment of (Entente) intervention alone. In circumstances that are well known, intervention may become the greatest weapon of progress, a surgical incision, facilitating the labor pains of a new world, but in the hands of the Entente is a synonym for utter retrogression.[4]

In this understanding, for example, the Soviet Russian reconquest of independent Georgia in 1921 had apparently been nothing other than a 'surgical incision' in the name of historical progress and world revolution. Korovin developed his views further in his textbook on international law published in 1926.[5] An intriguing assessment of the beginning of this book is that international law is no longer seen as universal; Korovin calls it 'contemporary European–American international law'.[6] He sees among Soviet republics an

[2] Ibid, 10.
[3] Ibid, 20.
[4] Ibid, 59–60.
[5] E A Korovin, *Sovremennoe mezhdunarodnoe publichnoe pravo*, Moscow/Leningrad: Gosudarstvennoe izdatel'stvo, 1926.
[6] Ibid, 3.

alternative international law emerging, an inter-Soviet law or the 'federation law of the new expanded Soviet Union'.[7] The point was that—just as the Soviet Russian constitution of 1918 suggested—the Soviet Union could expand further. In our context of exploring the Russian and Soviet relationship with imperialism and colonialism, what is also interesting is that Korovin takes an intermediary position on the colonial question. Because why, in his view, is international law not universal?

Korovin writes:

> In any case the fact remains indisputable that full international communication between any states, for example West European democracies and Eastern despotisms where the whole of societal life is based on the Shariah, is unattainable and cannot be achieved in any other way but at the price of any of the contracting parties changing their internal character. Such states, only partially participating in the international communication of the European type, include Persia, Afghanistan, Siam, China, Morocco, etc.[8]

Thus, in Korovin's early Soviet Russian interpretation, inequalities between states were due not only to the imperialist attitude of the capitalist states but also to their cultural–developmental differences. However, Korovin is also critical and sarcastic about Western colonial countries:

> The colonial history of practically any imperialist state teaches us that half-savage people may, even sometimes successfully, oppose and make agreements with cultured predators and the state machine serving them.[9]

In 1926, Korovin also further elaborated his views on the issue of state continuity between the Russian Empire and Soviet Russia. Korovin argued that it was settled that the Russian Soviet Federative Socialist Republic was the continuator state of the Russian Empire, the same state as tsarist Russia in international law:

> In the international legal sense the RSFSR is the same legal subject as the Russian Empire: this is the answer in predominant theory and practice. [. . .] Its borders were considerably diminished, its internal order changed

[7] Ibid, 7–8.
[8] Ibid, 7.
[9] Ibid, 20.

> fundamentally [. . .] but the Russian state as a subject of international rights and obligations has remained unchanged.[10]

The aspect which brought about a certain change in Korovin's view was the formation of the Soviet Union on 30 November 1922. The reason why the Soviet Union could be considered as a new state, in Korovin's view (even though he admitted that many considered *the Soviet Union* and not just Soviet Russia, which formed part of it, as the continuator state of the Russian Empire), was that the union treaty of 30 November 1922 specified that joining the Soviet Union was open to all socialist Soviet republics, both those existing and those that might emerge in the future.[11] Thus, Korovin's theory of distinguishing between Soviet Russia and the Soviet Union in terms of state identity enabled keeping the door open for the Soviet Union's further expansion, beyond the borders of the former Russian Empire and without direct association with the Russian Empire's pre-1917 past.

Having suggested that the Russian Empire and the Soviet Union were not the same state as subjects of international law (though Soviet Russia was identical to the tsarist Empire), Korovin immediately added a reservation to this statement, namely that the Russian Empire and the Soviet Union still had much in common:

> Does it mean that there is no state succession at all between Russia and the Soviet Union? Not at all, as the RSFSR is a participant in establishing the new union state—the successor to the Russian Empire—as a consequence of which the USSR succeeds the latter so to speak at the second level.[12]

In Korovin's interpretation, Soviet Russia was the state continuator of tsarist Russia and the Soviet Union was its state successor: a complex analytical construction.

What Korovin also brought to Soviet discourse on international law in 1926 was a different kind of realism than that, for example, which Martens had expressed in his public writings. Martens was a realist, too, in the sense that for him international agreements were a result of the balance of power, wars, and the determination and negotiating skills of emperors, their foreign ministers, and their diplomats. However, the realism of Korovin as a Marxist scholar

[10] Ibid, 29.
[11] Ibid, 30.
[12] Ibid, 30.

was more structural, about the nature of the international community. For example, Korovin did not want to downplay the fact that, in the history of international law, European empires had often talked about the equality of states whereas in reality, in several epochs—including, in Korovin's view, during his own early League of Nations era—the great powers dominated small states.[13] Another example: the institution of permanent neutrality in international law was, in Korovin's view, a restriction of the sovereignty of neutral states, achieved in the interest of the great powers, which wanted a buffer zone between them.[14]

Concerning treaties and the Russian imperial legacy of the events of 1870, the end of the neutrality of the Black Sea and the London declaration of 1871, Korovin maintained in 1926 that it was possible to terminate treaties unilaterally when circumstances changed fundamentally (*clausula rebus sic stantibus*).[15] He also wrote a separate article on this issue, using *clausula rebus sic stantibus* to justify the Soviet government's decision not to repay Tsarist-era debts.[16]

In other words, in this regard nothing had changed in early Soviet legal views compared to the late tsarist approach (Martens). Korovin simply mentioned well-known cases from state practice such as the tsarist Russian ones on Black Sea neutrality and the free port status of Batumi, but also how in 1919 China repudiated earlier coercive treaties with the Russian Empire, namely those concluded in 1913 and 1915.[17]

Korovin rationalized *clausula rebus sic stantibus* in the following way:

> Under the reservation of unchanged circumstances, this situation is conditionally expressed—is indisputable for international phenomena—that at some moments in history the vital interests of the participants appear so much stronger than legal obligations taken upon oneself earlier, which imperiously tilts them towards the first rather than the second. [. . .] Also in the international sphere there is a situation in which one legal order is replaced by another which differs qualitatively and in underlying principles. [. . .] This inevitably involves annihilation of all those legal relations based on a

[13] Ibid, 46.
[14] Ibid, 56.
[15] Ibid, 95.
[16] E A Korovin, 'Ogovorka *rebus sic stantibus* v mezhdunarodnoi praktike RSFSR', *Sovetskoe pravo*, No 3 (6), 1923. Cited in A N Talalaev, *Pravo mezhdunarodnykh dogovorov. Tom 2. Deistvie i primenenie dogovorov. Dogovory s uchastiem mezhdunarodnykh organizatsii*, Zertsalo, 2011 (Original: Mezhdunarodnye otnoshenia, 1985).
[17] Korovin, *Sovremennoe mezhdunarodnoe publichnoe pravo*, 1926, 95.

precondition of the social unity or identities of the social edifice of the treaty partners.[18]

As examples, Korovin, writing in 1926, gave the Soviet Russian 1917 publication of and refusal to implement Tsarist-era secret treaties as well as the Soviet annulment of the Brest-Litovsk Peace Treaty with imperial Germany in November 1918, concluded in March of the same year.[19] In a later work on imperial Japan and international law, Korovin reminded his readers of what Bismarck had apparently once said about international treaties: most treaties are like agreements between the horse and the rider.[20] This was meant mostly as an ironic criticism of other, imperialist states in history and the present—but if indeed this is what international agreements represented for imperialist states, how could the Soviet Union have practised a fundamentally different approach to treaties?

To wrap up on the interwar views of Korovin, he was in favour of state continuity between the Russian Empire and Soviet Russia, and the main reason why, in 1926, he suggested that the Soviet Union should be treated as the successor state to the Empire was the initial Soviet hope that more states would become socialist and then join the Soviet Union, a new federation which would expand further than the Russian Empire ever reached. Second, Korovin—also based on Soviet practice—supported the notion of terminating treaties because of a fundamental change in circumstances: another important continuity with tsarist Russian international law doctrine, particularly that of Martens.

Interlude: Taracouzio and Looking at the Soviet Practice of International Law from the US

What was known about and thought of Soviet international law doctrine in the West? One work which dealt with this topic explicitly was written in the US by a former officer in the White Army during the Russian civil war, Timofei Andreevich Tarakus-Taracuzio (also: Tarakusev), or, as he became known in the US, Timothy Taracouzio (1897–1958), a scholar with Georgian roots.[21] He wrote his book on the Soviet Union and international law at

[18] Ibid, 95.
[19] Ibid, 95.
[20] Korovin, *Iaponia i mezhdunardnoe pravo*, Sotsekgiz, 1936, 54.
[21] T A Taracouzio, *The Soviet Union and International Law. A Study based on the Legislation, Treaties and Foreign Relations of the Union of Socialist Soviet Republics*, The Macmillan Company, 1935.

Harvard University and later became head of the Russian division of the Naval Intelligence School in Washington, DC. Taracouzio emphasized the historical and ideological newness of the Soviet regime but did not really examine the question how much of old Russian ideas about international law the Soviets built on and continued with. He was more a chronicler of early Soviet practice of international law but did not attempt to put Soviet theoretical views on international law into a historical or comparative perspective. Although his book was published in New York in 1935, the manuscript was apparently completed earlier: for example, Taracouzio's narrative was still based on the assumption that the Soviet Union was not a member of the League of Nations,[22] even though it had become a member of the League in 1934. On international treaties, Taracouzio observed correctly that under the principle of *rebus sic stantibus* the Soviet authorities consider their social revolution as sufficient justification for denouncing treaties entered into by the tsarist government of Russia.[23] But Taracouzio had nothing to say or predict in terms of what one could expect of Soviet behaviour in terms of adherence to *Soviet* treaties, even though there was already enough material to be discussed—both in practice as well as in the writings of international lawyers such as Korovin—so that by 1939 the question had become one of the central issues in European politics. Taracouzio also at least implicitly assumed that the old Russian Empire ended as a state in 1917; in its stead, several successor states came later, including—but not only—the Soviet Union.[24] However, interpretations of the international legal subjecthood of Soviet Russia and the Soviet Union had already taken a different turn in the Soviet Union.

Evgeny Pashukanis and Empire

Another important Soviet international law author during the interwar period was Evgeny Pashukanis (1891–1937), who among other things criticized some of Korovin's views quite forcefully.[25] It was an interesting characteristic in the interwar Soviet international law scene that Pashukanis attacked Korovin and,

[22] Ibid, 291.
[23] Ibid, 250.
[24] Ibid, 24.
[25] E Pashukanis, *Ocherki po mezhdunarodnomu pravu*, Sovetskoe zakonodatel'stvo, 1935; reprinted with foreword by Theodor Schweisfurth as E B Pašukanis, *Umrisse des Völkerrechts*, Berlin Verlag, 1971, 191, Pashukanis writes about Korovin: 'The conclusion is quite strange for an author who wants to be considered a Marxist.'

in turn, Andrey Vyshinsky ferociously attacked Pashukanis, who had already been executed by the Soviet government in 1937.[26] Rivalries among leading Soviet international and public lawyers also mirrored rivalries and changing power relations in the Soviet political leadership, in particular the Stalinist Great Terror.

Pashukanis has received considerable attention as a Marxist theoretician of law,[27] and has been considered 'perhaps the most important Marxist legal theorist' and a 'key reference point'.[28] During the later years of the Cold War, interest in him revived among Soviet legal scholars.[29] However, his main work on international law (1935) has not been easily accessible in the West: it was republished in Berlin in 1971, but still only in Russian, and even this reprinted volume is rare and not accessible through most libraries.[30] Only Pashukanis's Soviet encyclopedia entry on international law from 1926 has been translated and referred to more widely in Western scholarly literature.[31] In the encyclopedia entry, Pashukanis gave an ultra-realist account of the essence of international law between capitalist states, though in this text he had very little to say in terms of how revolutionary countries like Soviet Russia would do it better. According to Pashukanis, the basic trait of imperialism was that the interaction between capitalist states was a constant struggle: 'every exchange is the continuation of an armed conflict and the prelude to the next.'[32] International organizations and institutions—even commissions for the management of treaty rivers such as the Rhine and the Danube—historically merely reflected which states were on top and when. Just as Korovin had done in the 1920s, Pashukanis observed that international law existed only to the extent that there was a balance of power:

[26] See A Vyshinsky, 'Osnovnye zadachi nauki sovetskogo sotsialisticheskogo prava', *Sovetskoe gosudarstvo* No 4, 1938, 4–5 at 36–9.

[27] China Miéville, *Between Equal Rights. A Marxist Theory of International Law*, Brill, 2005; Michael Head, *Evgeny Pashukanis: A Critical Reappraisal*, Routledge, 2008; Cosmin Cercel, Gian-Giacomo Fusco, Przemyslaw Tacik (eds), *Legal Form. Pashukanis and the Marxist Critique of Law*, Routledge, 2025.

[28] Robert Know, 'Marxist Approaches to International Law', in: Anne Orford and Florian Hoffmann with Martin Clark (eds) *The Oxford Handbook of the Theory of International Law*, OUP, 2016, 306–26 at 315.

[29] D B Levin, 'Pashukanis kak iurist-mezhdunarodnik', *SGP* No 9, 1981, 96–103; L Ya Gintsburg, 'Protiv spekuliatsii imenem sovetskogo uchenoga-iurista', *SGP* No 3, 1973, 102–8.

[30] E Pashukanis, *Ocherki po mezhdunarodnomu pravu*, Moscow, 1935.

[31] E Pashukanis, 'Mezhdunarodnoe pravo', in: Entsiklopedia gosudarstva i prava, Izdatel'stvo kommunisticheskoi akademii,1926, vol 2, 858–74, republished in: Piers Beirne, Robert Sharlet (eds) *Pashukanis: Selected Writings on Marxism and Law*, Translated by Peter B Maggs, Academic Press, 1980, 168–82.

[32] Ibid, 169.

> No matter how eloquently the existence of international law is proved, the fact remains of the absence of an organizational force which could coerce a state with the same ease as a state coerces an individual person. The only real guarantee that relationships between bourgeois states (and in the transitional period with states of another class type) will remain on the basis of equivalent exchange, i.e. on a legal basis (on the basis of mutual recognition of subjects), is a real balance of forces. Within the limits set by a given balance of forces, separate questions may be decided by compromises and by exchange, i.e. on the basis of law. [. . .] In critical periods, when the balance of forces has fluctuated seriously, when 'vital interests' or even the very existence of a state are on the agenda, the fate of the norms of international law becomes extremely problematic.[33]

For Pashukanis, bourgeois liberal idealism about international law was basically a lie and a smokescreen for actual power relationships:

> Open denial of international law is politically unprofitable for the bourgeoisie since it exposes them to the masses and thus hinders preparations for new wars. It is much more profitable for the imperialists to act in the guise of pacifism as the champions of international law.[34]

However, it implicitly followed that since the international community of (capitalist) states was so rotten and aggressive, and international law as supported by the 'imperialists' such a lie, then the only socialist country in the world—the Soviet Union—had to play along. In his lengthier 1935 work on international law, Pashukanis further developed his radically sceptical ideas. If, for Martens, international law and treaties had been an expression of competition among the European great powers, then additionally Pashukanis emphasized the class component in the struggle between powers:

> Questions of domestic and foreign policy that are resolved by the actual balance of class forces will be resolved by sharpened class struggle. Anyone who denies it is either lying to himself or, as happens more often, is trying to lie to others. Not a single juridical formula, no matter how ostentatiously it may be proclaimed or confirmed, stands outside the actual balance of powers that lie behind it. So, for example, we take well into account that not a single treaty on

[33] Ibid, 1926, 179.
[34] Ibid, 1926, 180.

> non-aggression, neutrality, and the like, concluded by the Soviet Union with capitalist countries, in itself guarantees non-use of force against us.[35]

But in these conditions, could *capitalist* states rely on treaties with the Soviet Union? Furthermore, for Pashukanis, it followed that

> One should not regard international law as outside politics. In an epoch of imperialism, international law is one of the forms, one of the means, with the help of which imperialist States struggle among themselves, and ensure the division of spoils, namely territory and unrestrained profit.[36]

In this light, Pashukanis also saw the history of Soviet Russia, which had to hand over Russian imperial territories in 1918–20:

> It is true that the proletarian state in capitalist encirclement must sometimes carry out the politics of compromises, i.e. temporary concessions, necessary to ensure and strengthen its existence. [. . .] The amounts of concessions are determined by the specific balance of power. At the time of Brest, the Soviet republic had to make big sacrifices, 'to give up' space [. . .] in order to gain time. These times have long passed. Now the balance of power is completely different. Now our international position is formulated by the formula of comrade Stalin: 'We don't want foreign land. But our own land, not an inch of our land will we give to anyone.'[37]

Thus, it implicitly followed that Soviet Russian territorial concessions in the peace treaties of 1920–1 were temporary, due to the unfavourable balance of power at the time. Because what really was 'foreign land' and 'our land' from the Soviet Russian perspective, after such temporary compromises had been made at the expense of former tsarist territory? Furthermore, Pashukanis highlighted the thought of Stalin that a state had to be strong in order to survive in the international community; or, in the words of Stalin: 'In our time, they do not take into consideration the weak; only the strong are taken into consideration.'[38]

So, for Pashukanis, international law as such was characterized by the following specific features: extreme instability and weak enforcement in practice;

[35] Pahsukanis, *Ocherki po mezdhunarodnomu pravu*, Sovetskoe zakonodatel'stvo, 1935, 5–6.
[36] Ibid, 9.
[37] Ibid, 18.
[38] E Pashukanis, 'Vstuplenie SSSR v Ligu natsii', *SGP* No 6, 1934, 23–8 at 22.

when stronger states violate international law against weaker states, this usually goes unpunished. Moreover, international legal disputes often do not reach a final settlement.[39]

Pashukanis laid out how, since 1917, Soviet Russia had ostentatiously proclaimed that it would terminate all unequal relations in the East. However, what this meant in practice often remained contested. Pashukanis recounted how in 1929 'Chinese militarists' violated the treaty on the mutual administration of the Chinese Eastern Railway, to which the Red Army was forced to give a military response. For Pashukanis, the Soviets wanted only respect for the treaty with China, which foresaw common administration of the railway. Nevertheless, on 23 March 1935 the Soviets sold their rights to the Chinese Eastern Railway (in Manchuria) to the Japanese, for 140 million yen, of which one-third was paid in cash and the rest in goods.[40] Based on publications in the journal *Sovetskoe gosudarstvo i pravo*, differences with China over the administration of the Chinese Eastern Railway preoccupied Soviet legal scholars quite intensely.[41] Perhaps this was also because the differences with the Republic of China revealed that foreign policy was not so simple and Manichaean as declaring the tsarist government 'imperialist' and the Soviet government as being against imperialism.

In 1934, the Soviet Union became a member of the League of Nations. However, Pashukanis also warned that this in no way meant that the Soviet Union was responsible for the League's past decisions. 'The USSR especially has no responsibility for the Versailles Peace and other peace treaties signed without its participation', Pashukanis explained,[42] echoing views already expressed in Soviet foreign policy. However, the peace treaties in the Versailles system were inevitably intertwined with Soviet treaties as well; for example, Soviet Russia had agreed on its border with Poland in the Peace Treaty of Riga of 18 March 1921 and although this did not concern Poland's Western border, it still implied recognition of Poland in its existing borders, which in turn was also a result of the Versailles Peace Treaty. At the same time, on 28 October 1920 the League of Nations (also suggesting this to be valid 'for Russia' as well) had approved the allocation of Bessarabia as part of Romania. The interwar Soviet Union did not recognize these 1920 borders with Romania and Pashukanis's assessment of this border delimitation was disapproving:

[39] Pashukanis, *Ocherki po mezhdunarodnomu pravu.*, 1935, 22.
[40] Ibid, 53–6.
[41] N Terentyev, 'KVZhD', *SGP* 1933, No 4, 88–96; I Trainin, 'Imperializm na Dal'nem Vostoke i SSSR', *SGP* 1932, No 7–8, 147–68.
[42] Pashukanis, *Ocherki po mezhdunarodnomu pravu,* 1935, 62.

> Thus, a sovereign state without its approval received a 'deputy' and thus imposed upon, in this way a commission was proposed to carry out border demarcation 'on site', i.e., on territory under not only juridical but also factual Soviet rule .[43]

During the interwar period, several Soviet legal scholars protested over Romania's control of Bessarabia, reflecting the fact that the Soviet government did not recognize that sovereignty over Bessarabia had officially passed to Romania.[44]

In 1919 in Paris, the Russian emigrant André Mandelstam had considered many of Russia's nationalities not ready for any kind of self-determination or independent statehood, both culturally and in terms of civilization. Pashukanis and other Soviet international lawyers chose different language to address this issue. 'After the October Revolution, the Bolshevik party adopts the principle of federation of Soviet republics as one of the means to resolve the national question', whereby 'every republic may at any moment in time return full sovereignty to itself on the international legal plane'.[45] However, according to Pashukanis, a number of Soviet peoples were still backward, and this now had to be confronted within the Soviet Union, through Soviet politics:

> The proletariat is not satisfied with formal equality but is struggling against survival of the inequality which exists between backward and advanced peoples. In the Soviet Union, we help the workers of more backward ethnic groups to build their culture, to build their Soviet statehood.[46]

In other words, the *mission civilisatrice* still continued, but in Soviet style, as some peoples in the Soviet Union continued to be more advanced than others, presumably first and foremost the Russians.

We now come to the question in Pashukanis's treatise on international law which has been of interest to us throughout this study: what is the nature of international treaties, and can a state unilaterally free itself from its treaty obligations? On this question, Pashukanis writes:

> In reality the force of an international treaty is determined by certain material interests and the forces standing behind those interests. A treaty is operational

[43] Ibid, 126.
[44] I Levin, 'Natsional'nyi vopros v Rumynii', SGRP 1931, No 10–12, 180–209.
[45] Pashukanis, *Ocherki*, 93–4.
[46] Ibid, 192.

> and binding as long as those interests and forces are present. No state has ever signed a treaty if it does not have an interest in it or if some kind of power does not force it. [...] Therefore each international treaty—as long as it reflects the existing interests of the parties and is dictated by them, and as long as it reflects the political situation of existing power—constitutes a long-term design for known relations.[47]

In this perspective, full continuity exists with the Tsarist-era views of Martens on Martens; a continuity between the tsarist and Soviet flexible and realist approaches to international treaties according to which treaties cannot be much more than a reflection of the balance of power at the time of their signing. As leading Soviet international lawyers, both Korovin and Pashukanis held the view that at least the Soviet state—as the first ever proletarian state—could terminate treaties unilaterally, and that *clausula rebus sic stantibus* reflected the reality of international legal practice.

Pashukanis then cites further historical examples regarding violation of earlier treaties in the context of *clausula rebus sic stantibus.* In his view, among such cases were the proclamation of the independence of Bulgaria in 1908 and Italy switching alliances during the First World War (1915), as well as France's choice to stop making payments for its military debt to the US (1932).[48] Based on these examples and earlier practice, Pashukanis concludes:

> In that way even bourgeois internationalists are forced to recognize the existence of historical events that destroy the force of any international treaty. [...] One can say that a state born out of revolution has an enhanced right to terminate treaties which were concluded with respect to the earlier existing social structure. It is exactly on such positions that the Soviet government stood and still stands.[49]

Pashukanis then applied these general views generously to the Soviet Union's existing treaties with the capitalist world. For example, although the Soviet Union had become a member of the League of Nations in 1934—which meant that the League's Covenant had become binding on it, too—Pashukanis wrote in 1935 that 'the USSR knows very well the limited importance of the articles of the Covenant of the League of Nations'.[50] In the earlier revolutionary years,

[47] Ibid, 155.
[48] Ibid, 160–1.
[49] Ibid, 161.
[50] Ibid, 184.

Lenin had called the League of Nations an 'organization of international robbers'.[51] In the Soviet perception, this was also because—as one German socialist international lawyer from the GDR put it—in 1920–1, the League of Nations acted as an 'organized center of intervention against the Soviet state'.[52] When the Soviet Union joined the League of Nations in 1934, the Soviet foreign minister Maxim Litvinov (1876–1951) made it clear in his country's official statements in Geneva that the League of Nations system entailed elements of which the Soviet Union would not have approved if it had been able to negotiate the foundations of the organization in 1919: the mandate system for former colonies of empires defeated in the First World War (Article 22 of the Covenant) as well as the legal possibility to go to war under Articles 12–15 of the Covenant. Litvinov also criticized the fact that racial equality was not recognized in Article 23 of the Covenant.[53]

Pashukanis' explanation of why and under what conditions the USSR joined the League of Nations was cynical:

> It is clear to the workers of the USSR and the whole world that when the Soviet government decided to respond positively to the invitation to join the League of Nations, then this is not because of a change in our principled attitude towards the League, but because the specific international legal situation changed.[54]

On treaty commitments, it was clear from the approaches of Korovin and Pashukanis—as two leading interwar Soviet international lawyers—that the Soviet Union would abandon the principle of *pacta sunt servanda* in geopolitically critical conditions. Soviet treaty practice since 1939 has reflected this explicitly.

The 1939 Nazi–Soviet Pact as a Manifestation of Soviet Imperialism

On 23 August 1939, Nazi Germany and the Soviet Union concluded a non-aggression pact. This had a secret protocol according to which six smaller

[51] E Pashukanis, 'Vstuplenie SSSR v Ligu natsii', *SGP* No 6, 1934, 23–8 at 23.

[52] Peter Alfons Steiniger, *Oktoberrevolution und Völkerrecht: eine populärwissenschaftliche Studie*, Staatsverlag der Deutschen Demokratischen Republik, 1967, 125.

[53] Pashukanis, *Vstuplenie* SSSR v Ligu natsii', 1934, 27. See further M M Litvinov, *Vneshniaya politika SSSR. Rechi i zayavlenia 1927–1935*, Gosudarstvennoe sotsial'no-ekonomicheskoe izdatel'stvo, 1935, 77 et seq.

[54] Pashukanis, *Vstuplenie* SSSR v Ligu natsii', 1934, 24.

states, situated between or near them in Central and Eastern Europe and born towards the end of the First World War were allocated to spheres of influence between the two powers, with the guarantee of non-intervention by the other party. Colloquially, this agreement is also called the Molotov–Ribbentrop Pact, the Nazi–Soviet Pact and sometimes also the Hitler–Stalin Pact. The idea and initiative for the secret protocol and division of the spheres of influence was Stalin's. However, Hitler, due to his own imperialist and revisionist plans for Germany, especially his plan to attack Poland, went along with it.[55] Based on Soviet assurances achieved by this agreement, on 1 September 1939 Germany attacked Poland militarily and later, after the Polish army and population had already suffered heavy losses against the Germans, the Soviet Union moved in on 17 September 1939, occupying and annexing Soviet-allocated territories in Eastern Poland.[56] The Soviets waited to invade until they thought they could argue that the Polish state no longer existed—a characterization with which the Polish government in exile vehemently disagreed. Three days after Germany invaded Poland, German foreign minister Ribbentrop inquired of the Soviets what they were waiting for; they, too, should seize their agreed prey in Poland.[57] However, the reason for the Soviet delay was that the Soviet Union could now argue that Poland had already 'collapsed' and the extent of the Soviet Union's involvement was limited to 'liberating' Ukrainians and Byelorussians in Eastern Poland. Nevertheless, Soviet campaign against Poland was a real war; the Red Army lost 737 dead and 1,862 wounded, or 2,599 casualties.[58] The two powers, Nazi Germany and the Soviet Union, even held a common military parade in Brest-Litovsk as a symbolic reminder of the place where the two powers had left off with their bilateral treaty-making and allocation of territories in March 1918. Later, on 28 September 1939, in another secret protocol, the two powers changed aspects of their spheres of influence so that Lithuania was allocated from the German to the Soviet sphere of influence, while Germany received additional territories in Poland.

The 1939 Nazi–Soviet pact was born out of both Nazi and Soviet rejection of the Versailles system. As early as 1922, Soviet revolutionary and Comintern activist Karl Radek (1885–1939) had written that one of the goals of the Versailles Peace Treaty had been 'the destruction of Russia as a great power'.[59] Vyacheslav

[55] Claudia Weber, *Der Pakt. Hitler, Stalin und die Geschichte einer mörderischen Allianz*, München: CH Beck, 2019, 65–7.

[56] See further Roger Moorhouse, *Poland 1939. The Outbreak of World War II*, Basic Books, 2020.

[57] Weber, *Der Pakt*, 2019, 81.

[58] Sean McMeekin, *Stalin's War*, Penguin Books, 2021, 101.

[59] K B Radek, *Likvidatsia Versal'skogo mira: doklad IV Kongressu Kommunistischeskogo Internatsionala*, Petrograd: Izdanie Kommunisticheskogo Internatsionala, 1922, 21.

Molotov (1890–1986), the Soviet foreign minister whose signature is on the Nazi–Soviet pact, even called Poland 'a bastard of the Versailles treaty'.[60]

With the Nazi–Soviet non-aggression pact, Hitler's Germany ensured that when it seized Poland by military force, it would not also face a war with the Soviet Union. But why was this secret agreement interesting and important for the Stalin-led Soviet Union? Later, Russian foreign policy apologists explained that the pact was necessary in order to postpone the inevitable German aggression against the Soviet Union and to gain strategic depth for the military defence of Moscow and Leningrad in case of a future Nazi German attack. At the same time, the secret agreement of August 1939 also followed a highly specific Russian/Soviet imperial logic: to take back as much as possible from what used to be the territory of the Russian Empire until 1917. True, regarding the main object of prey, Poland, the line of the Nazi–Soviet pact largely followed the Curzon line of 1919, as proposed by the British foreign minister as to where the ethnic Soviet–Polish border should run.[61] During the war between Soviet Russia and Poland (1919–21), the Red Army almost reached Warsaw, but after the Polish 'miracle on the Vistula' the fortunes of war turned, and Poland achieved for itself more favourable borders than the Curzon line and fixed them in the Soviet–Polish Riga Peace Treaty of 18 March 1921.

From the Soviet side, the 23 August 1939 Nazi–Soviet secret agreement was a demonstration of two key international legal ideas in Soviet thinking and practice—first, that the Soviet Union still saw itself as a continuator state of the Russian Empire as far as territory was concerned; second, that the Soviet Union understood treaties such that if the geopolitical interests of the proletarian state so demanded, previous treaties could be violated.

The territories affected by the secret protocols had formed the basis for historical German–Russian territorial deals, especially the three partitions of Poland in the eighteenth century, which remained effective until 1918. Besides its part of Poland, what the Soviet Union asked for in the secret protocols was freedom of action in the territory of the old Russian Empire: Finland, Estonia, Latvia, Lithuania, and Bessarabia. The only place where the Soviet Union was willing to 'lose out' compared to the former territory of the Russian Empire was the territory of Poland itself. For example, since the late eighteenth century, the Warsaw region had belonged to the Russian Empire, whereas now, based on the secret protocols, it was allocated to the Nazi German 'sphere of influence'.

[60] Weber, *Der Pakt*, 2019, 50.
[61] Ibid, 93, 98, 216.

We know already from the Melian dialogue of Thucydides that if an empire can expand and gain territory without war, then it will prefer to do so. And so, for the Soviet Union too, the first move in its sphere of influence was to present ultimatums to the governments concerned and ask for establishment of military bases in their territory. The three Baltic States gave in to these Soviet demands and so, in autumn 1939, Soviet military bases were established in Estonia, Latvia, and Lithuania, with Soviet guarantees of preservation of state sovereignty. Finland refused to give in to the Soviet demands for military bases and territorial concessions, so the Soviet Union started a war against Finland on 30 November 1939 (the Winter War). Because of the Soviet attack against Finland and the Soviet refusal to engage in the dispute resolution mechanism foreseen in the Covenant of the League of Nations, the Soviet Union was expelled from the League as an aggressor state on 15 December 1939. However, the Indian Marxist international law scholar B. S. Chimni has still criticized the expulsion of the Soviet Union from the League of Nations as "selective"; in contrast, Italy had not been expelled after its aggression against Abessinia.[62]

In June 1940, Moscow presented ultimatums to the governments of the three Baltic republics, demanding a complete overhaul of their governments. When the ultimatums were accepted, the Soviet Union militarily occupied the three states, Sovietized them, and not long afterwards, in August 1940, annexed all three. In terms of the Soviet discourse, one noteworthy testimony from this time is what was recorded by Vincas Krėvė-Mickevičius (1882–1954), a famous writer in Lithuania who was appointed head of the 'people's government of Lithuania' on 24 June 1940. The value of his testimony can also be critically challenged because he had himself collaborated with the Soviet power in 1940 and gave his testimony during the Nazi German occupation of Lithuania during the Second World War. But what he said as testimony fits a Soviet pattern and seems plausible. Krėvė-Mickevičius met with the Soviet foreign minister Molotov in Moscow on 30 June 1940 to discuss the next steps regarding the future of Sovietized Lithuania. During their conversation, Molotov expressed the opinion that the Russian tsars had aimed to reach the coasts of the Baltic Sea since the reign of Ivan the Terrible, but did not do so for their own personal desires but because the needs of development of the Russian state and nation demanded it; it was no different now, in 1940.[63] This is quite a succinct expression of the continuity in tsarist and Soviet imperial(ist) identities. In

[62] B S Chimni, 'Inclusion and Exclusion in International Organizations', in: Jan Klabbers (ed) *The Cambridge Companion to International Organizations Law*, CUP, 2022, 76–97 at 87.

[63] Boris Meissner, *Die Sowjetunion, die baltischen Staaten und das Völkerrecht*, Verlag für Politik und Wirtschaft, 1956, 82 (With specific references to the original testimony indicated).

addition, Molotov explained to Krėvė-Mickevičius in the same conversation that small peoples would disappear anyway, small states would be integrated into the Soviet Union, and the Soviet system would determine the future of Europe.[64] In his programmatic speech at the Supreme Council of the Soviet Union, Molotov complained that the 1939 pacts of mutual assistance had not led to 'rapprochement' with the Baltic States due to their bourgeois governments and, making the case for annexation of the Sovietized Baltic republics, emphasized the importance of control over the Baltic Sea ports.[65]

During their treaty-based alliance, which lasted almost two years, Germany and the Soviet Union at several times had divergent interpretations of their mutual obligations to each other. For example, the Soviet Union considered it a violation of the Pact when Germany concluded a transit treaty with Finland, which belonged to the Soviet sphere of influence according to the non-aggression pact. Germany was taken aback when, in June 1940, the Soviet Union demanded—and took from Romania—not only Bessarabia but also Northern Bukovina, with the city of Chernivtsi in contemporary Ukraine (Cernăuți in Romanian).[66] On 12–13 November 1940, while visiting Berlin, the Soviet foreign minister Molotov experienced a bombing raid by the British air force but also brought with him Stalin's wish and specification that the Soviet Union also considered parts of the Danube river, especially the Danube delta, as within its sphere of influence.[67] From the perspective of the Soviet Union, the Danube proved quite important in the post-Second World War history of international law, so we will return to this topic and Soviet legal foreign policy on the region in the next chapter. As the Soviet Union's treaty allies, Germany's military representation even attended the 1 May 1941 military parade in Moscow, less than two months before Hitler's Germany attacked the Soviet Union.

The German historian Claudia Weber has argued that, in terms of its actual impact, the Nazi–Soviet pact with its secret protocols was one of the most important treaties of the twentieth century.[68] This must have been the case because during the Nuremberg trials in 1945 the issue of the Nazi–Soviet non-aggression pact and its secret protocols was the single most important issue or red line for the Soviets, in that they were not willing to surrender

[64] Cited in Weber, *Der Pakt*, 2019, 177.
[65] V M Molotov, 'Vneshnyaya politika Sovetskoga Soyza. Doklad na zasedanii VII Sessii Verkhovnoga Soveta SSSR', 1.08.1940, *SGP* No 8–9, 1940, 3–4.
[66] Weber, *Der Pakt*, 2019, 189.
[67] Ibid, 189.
[68] Ibid, 71.

control over drafting the judgment.[69] At the same time, the 1939 pact has often been underestimated and bypassed when telling the story of the impact on international law of the Soviet Union and the socialist revolution. For example, a relatively recent and otherwise highly interesting study of this very topic hardly mentions the secret protocols of the pact,[70] even though highlighting that outside Europe, the Soviet Union was a model in terms of anti-imperialist struggles. However, the consequence of the pact was that in 1939–40, the Soviet Union violated the sovereignty and/or borders of six member states of the League of Nations, namely Poland, Finland, Estonia, Latvia, Lithuania, and Romania. The pact does not fit in the model according to which imperialism is defined primarily through capitalism; nor does it support a convenient reduction—at least in Eastern and Central Europe—that the Second World War was in simplistic terms a struggle between a 'good' alliance and a 'bad' one. The alliance between great powers in 1939–41 was different from the alliance 1941–45.

An additional aspect of the 1939 Nazi–Soviet pact was what it revealed about the Soviet attitude towards international treaties. The Soviet foreign policy approach in 1939 fittingly mirrored what leading Soviet international lawyers such as Korovin and Pashukanis had consistently argued during the 1920s and 1930s, namely that treaties could be violated when the interests of the proletarian state so demanded. Throughout the 1920s and 1930s, with respect to its border states, the Soviet Union initiated and took upon itself a whole range of treaty obligations, which it violated with the conclusion of the Molotov–Ribbentrop Pact. In 1928 the Soviet Union was not invited to Paris when states adopted the Briand–Kellogg Pact in which they renounced war 'as an instrument of national policy in their relations with one another' (Article 1).[71] However, Moscow proposed the same pact—which had been an example of 'imperialist pacifism', as Usenko later called it—[72] to its neighbours, with the result that the so-called Litvinov convention was concluded in 1929, signed by the Soviet Union and its 'bourgeois' border states. Furthermore, in 1933, at the initiative of Soviet foreign minister Maxim Litvinov, a treaty defining aggression was signed in London by the Soviet Union and its border states—a

[69] Francine Hirsch, *Soviet Judgment at Nuremberg. A New History of the International Military Tribunal after World War II*, OUP, 2020, 104–5.

[70] Kathryn Greenman, Anne Orford, Anna Saunders, Ntina Tzouvala (eds) *Revolutions in International Law: The Legacies of 1917*, CUP, 2021.

[71] See further Oona A Hathaway, Scott J Shapiro, *The Internationalists. How a Radical Plan to Outlaw War Remade the World*, New York: Simon & Schuster, 2017.

[72] E T Usenko, 'Printsip demokraticheskogo mira—naibolee obshchaya osnova sovremennogo mezhdunarodnoga prava', *Soviet YBIL* 1973, 13–42 at 26.

treaty that listed several specific activities defined as aggression. However, in June 1940, the Soviet Union violated this treaty towards the Baltic States, for example by conducting a naval blockade against Estonia. The Soviet Union had also concluded bilateral non-aggression pacts with its border states in the West. Finally, by joining the League of Nations in 1934, the Soviet Union was bound by the Covenant of the League of Nations towards its fellow League of Nations members. Before being replaced as Soviet foreign minister by Molotov, Maxim Litvinov also advocated in the League of Nations that aggressors should be held accountable.[73] The volte-face of concluding a non-aggression pact with secret protocols with Germany in 1939 demonstrated how treaty obligations and the underlying principle of international treaty law, *pacta sunt servanda*, were entirely subordinated to the expansionist–revisionist agenda of the Soviet Union. Quite characteristic was what Soviet foreign minister Molotov wrote on 17 September 1939 to Grzybowski, the Polish minister in Moscow:

> The Polish–German war has made apparent the internal bankruptcy of the Polish state. During ten days of military operations Poland has lost all of its industrial regions and its cultural centres. Warsaw no longer exists as the capital of Poland. The Polish government has fallen and shows no sign of life. This means that the Polish state and its government have ceased in fact to exist. Likewise the treaties concluded by the USSR and Poland have lost force. Poland, left to itself and without leadership, has been turned into a convenient field for any eventuality and unexpected occurrence, which could create a threat for the USSR. Therefore, having been neutral up to now, the Soviet government can no longer be neutral to these facts.[74]

How to relate to Soviet European conquests in 1939–40 after the Soviet Union had become an ally against Nazi Germany caused some considerable headaches in London and Washington, as Moscow demanded recognition of its conquests.[75] The issue was on the table—but at the same time was not resolved unequivocally—at the Soviet–US–UK Crimea (Yalta) conference in February 1945.

[73] M Litvinov, *Protiv agressii*, OGIZ, 1938, 58 et seq.
[74] Jan F Triska, Robert M Slusser, *The Law, Theory, and Policy of Soviet Treaties*, Stanford UP, 1962, 155.
[75] See Kaarel Piirimäe, *Roosevelt, Churchill, and the Baltic Question: Allied Relations during the Second World War*, Palgrave Macmillan, 2014.

How did Soviet international lawyers deal with the 1939 Nazi–Soviet non-aggression pact and the territorial consequences of its aftermath? In their influential post-Second World War Soviet textbook on international law, Vsevolod Durdenevsky (1899–1963) and Sergey Krylov (1888–1958) resolved it by 'correcting' history just somewhat: in their narrative of what happened in international law during the Second World War, they offered a list of twenty-six European 'sovereign states' as of 1 September 1939. The three Baltic States and League of Nations members of Estonia, Latvia, and Lithuania were not mentioned;[76] by 1947 they had disappeared, not just from the world political map but also from the Soviet narrative of interwar European political history.

Durdenevsky enjoyed influence as an international lawyer. Having been educated as a lawyer during the tsarist period (graduating from Moscow University in 1911), he became a professor at the same university in 1922. From 1944 to 1961, he worked in the treaty law department of the Soviet foreign ministry and in the Soviet delegation attended the Potsdam conference, the Paris peace conference, the Belgrade conference on the regime of the Danube, and others. His fellow textbook author Krylov was a graduate of St Petersburg University from the same year, 1911. He worked as a professor of international law at MGIMO University in Moscow but, just like Durdenevsky, also worked as an expert in the Soviet foreign ministry. Krylov became the first Soviet judge at the ICJ (1946–52) and a member of the ILC in the period 1953–6.[77]

Durdenevsky also looked back at the change of Soviet borders during the Second World War in an article dedicated to the topic in 1947.[78] He acknowledged that the question of territory was the most important question in state succession and supported the view that the tsarist Empire ended as a state or, rather, was 'replaced' in 1917 by a higher type of state in terms of a new social–economic formation.[79] Durdenevsky explained the territorial gains which the Soviet Union made in the Second World War, inter alia in Poland:

> [In 1921] The Polish military dictatorship of Pilsudski succeeded, with the help of Western great powers, in conquering Western Ukraine and

[76] V N Durdenevsky, S B Krylov (eds), *Mezhdunarodnoe pravo*, Moscow: Iuridicheskoe izdatel'stvo ministerstva iustitsii SSSR, 1947, 117.

[77] S V Bakhin (ed) *Rossiiskaya assotsiatsia mezhdunarodnoga prava. 1957–2007. Biografichesky slovar'*, St Peterburg: Izdatel'ski Dom Sankt-Peterburgskoga gosudarstvennogo universiteta, 2007, 85–6, 142–3.

[78] V N Durdenevsky, 'Sovetskaya territoria v aktakh mezhdunarodnoga prava za 30 let (1917–1947 gg)', *SGP* No 12, 1947, 58–65.

[79] Ibid, 58.

> Byelorussia, violating the most obvious ethnographic borders ('the Curzon line'). Aiming for peace for the sake of recovery [. . .] the Soviet republics made territorial concessions, at the same time stipulating minority rights in Poland; the Poland of Pans ignored these rights, systematically violating the Riga treaty.[80]

Durdenevsky also had justifications for other Soviet territorial gains, for example in Bessarabia:

> In 1918, the Romanian boyars seized Bessarabia, obtaining approval of the annexation of Bessarabia from England, France, Italy, and Japan in Paris on October 28, 1920, and hoped to achieve recognition of this fact from the Soviets. However, the Soviet people and government did not recognize the seizure or the Paris protocol.[81]

The Soviets also annexed the Republic of Tannu Tuva at the border with Mongolia:

> In October 1943, the Tuva national republic—where a considerable part of the population consists of Russian emigrants from tsarist times (Old Believers who escaped persecution) voluntarily joined the Soviet Union and became part of the Russian SFSR as an autonomous oblast.[82]

Finally, Southern Sakhalin and the Kurile islands:

> The Crimean (Yalta) agreement of February 11, 1945 between the USSR, the USA, and the UK and which was published in February 1946, arranged the return of Southern Sakhalin to the USSR. The Portsmouth treaty of conquest fell apart. The historic rights of the peoples of the Soviet Union were restored not only in Sakhalin but also in the Kurile islands.[83]

Thus, by 1945, the Soviet Union had reclaimed several territories which had been part of the Russian Empire but also gained further territories which had never been part of the Russian Empire. When we read the views of Soviet

[80] Ibid, 62;.
[81] Ibid, 62.
[82] Ibid, 65.
[83] Ibid, 65.

interwar international lawyers such as Korovin and Pashukanis, we can see that none of this must have come as a big surprise: the possibility of territorial acquisitions through 'termination' of treaties and taking advantage of the new balance of power had been kept theoretically and doctrinally open in Soviet international legal publications.

6

The Cold War: Interpretations of Soviet State Identity, Federalism, and Self-Determination

At the end of the Second World War, the Soviet Union annexed territories which in the early twentieth century had formed part of the Russian Empire: Estonia, Latvia, Lithuania, parts of Western Belarus and Western Ukraine, and Southern Sakhalin. It also acquired territories which had not previously been part of the Russian Empire, such as Galicia (Lemberg/Lwów/Lvov/Lviv region) or parts of Germany's East Prussia (which became Soviet Russia's Kaliningrad oblast and which had been briefly under Russian occupation in the eighteenth century). Moscow also achieved a situation where the regimes in neighbouring countries in Central and Eastern Europe quickly came under its hegemonic control: Poland, the German Democratic Republic, Czechoslovakia, Hungary, Romania, and Bulgaria, as well as (elsewhere) Mongolia and other territories. The sovereignty of some European states which—or whose populations—had been at war with the Soviet Union during the Second World War emerged with 'strings attached' to their statehood, either de facto or as a matter of law: Finland (neutrality and certain restraints in foreign policy, even though Finland successfully managed to avoid a state socialist regime being established) and Austria (negotiated neutrality based on a treaty in 1955 which ended Soviet occupation).

In international legal theory, the new situation in the Soviet Union was reflected in several imperially inspired doctrines and discourses. These illustrate the main thesis of this book, namely that there was continuity between the two different formations of the Empire: tsarist Russia and the Soviet Union.

- The first of these was the doctrine of state continuity between the Russian Empire and the Soviet Union, although this came with interesting nuances and intra-Soviet debates.

Russia, the Soviet Union, and Imperial Continuity in International Law. Lauri Mälksoo, Oxford University Press.
 DOI: 10.1093/9780198955962.003.0006

- The second was how federalism was construed in the Soviet Union, claiming that both the Soviet Union and its constituent Soviet republics were sovereign states at the same time—a claim that did not hold up against the political facts on the ground regarding the Soviet republics.
- The third was the doctrine of how self-determination of peoples was promoted vis-à-vis the outside world (concerning other empires) and how it was construed domestically, within the Soviet Union itself.
- Fourth, another imperial continuity was the flexible Soviet approach to terminating inconvenient treaties.
- Fifth was the idea that at least since 1945 the Soviet Union was a 'great power' and generally that the world is divided into great powers and smaller states, with implications for international law and prerogatives for great powers.
- Sixth was the Soviet-promoted concept of peaceful coexistence, which critics have come to associate with the historical concept of the balance of power in international law.
- Seventh was the doctrine of socialist international law for dependent states, particularly in the Eastern bloc.

In the following we will examine the first three of these legal doctrines and thereafter, in the next chapter, turn to treaties, great power doctrines, balance of power, and socialist international law.

The Soviet Union's Continuity with the Russian Empire

The international lawyer who, after the Second World War, decisively shaped Soviet thinking on the question of the Soviet Union's state identity with tsarist Russia was Fedor Ivanovich Kozhevnikov, who later (1953) became the Soviet judge at the ICJ. In his publications, he wrote with adoration of Stalin's ideas from the perspective of international law,[1] so in this sense we can also think of Kozhevnikov as a Stalinist. Other prominent Soviet international lawyers at the time, such as Krylov—the first Soviet judge at the ICJ—were also preoccupied with what Stalin thought about international law.[2] However, Kozhevnikov's

[1] F I Kozhevnikov, 'I V Stalin ob osnavnykh printsipakh sovremennoga mezhdunarodnoga prava', *SGP* No 12, 1949, 95–109; F I Kozhevnikov, 'Nekotorye voprosy mezhdunarodnoga prava v svete truda I V Stalina, 'Marksizm i voprosy iazykoznania', *SGP* No 4, 1951, 25–36.

[2] See also for extensive reference to Stalin's thought in Serge Krylov, 'Les notions principales du droit des gens'. (La doctrine soviétique du droit international)', *RCADI* Vol 70, Martinus Nijhoff, 1947, 423 et seq.

main contribution to international law in the Soviet Union comprised two books published after the Second World War on the history and evolution of international law in pre- as well as post-1917 Russia.[3] Kozhevnikov's understanding of Russia's positive and progressive role in the history of international law was so exaggerated and one-sided that even his Soviet contemporary international lawyers—for example Evgeny Korovin—reproached him for having too uncritical an approach to tsarist Russia's accomplishments in international law.[4] In many ways, the debate about how to evaluate tsarist Russia's role in the history of international law was closely related to the debate on the question whether the Soviet Union was identical to the Russian Empire as a subject of international law. It was also a debate about the present day, as behind it lurked the question: how *Russian* should the Soviet Union be—or should it be openly recognized that it was? Kozhevnikov's history of international law in Russia always highlighted Russian imperial achievements. This imitated Stalin's approach in his famous toast to the Great Russian people on 24 May 1945, and the new—more openly pro-Russian—history policies adopted by the Soviet state during the Second World War.

However, here we are mainly interested in how Kozhevnikov shaped the debate on state identity and international legal personality in the Soviet Union. In his 1948 book *The Soviet State and International Law 1917–1944*, Kozhevnikov wrote that after the 1917 October Revolution, Russia became a 'Soviet socialist state, the great Soviet Union'.[5] To be as precise as possible, some of Kozhevnikov's statements on this subject need to be cited at length here:

> The Great socialist October Revolution in Russia creates a new state—a Soviet socialist state which in terms of its social class content was diametrically opposed to that which existed in Russia previously. In other words, in place of the old Russia emerges the new socialist Russia but this is nevertheless none other than old Russia. [. . .] In other words, the Great October socialist revolution does not create in the juridical sense a new subject of international law. Soviet Russia steps up as successor to the rights of old Russia. Any attempt to limit Soviet Russia in these rights—but even more so to deprive it of these rights—has invariably provoked its decisive protests. [. . .] What is the Soviet Union from the perspective that interests us? Undoubtedly, this is Russia, in

[3] F I Kozhevnikov, *Sovetskoe gosudarstvo i mezhdunarodnoe pravo 1917–1944 gg. (Opyt istoriko-pravovogo issledovania)*, Iuridicheskoe izdatel'stvo ministerstva iustitsii SSSR, 1948.

[4] E Korovin, 'Rossiya i mezhdunarodnoe pravo', *SGP* No 2, 1949, 65–6. See also S Mamulya's review of Kozhevnikov's book, ibid, 67–70.

[5] Kozhevnikov, *Sovetskoe gosudarstvo i mezhdunarodnoe pravo 1917–1944 gg*, 1948, 6.

> the form of the socialist Soviet state. This is no surprise as it is generally recognized that the Russian people are the leading force among all the peoples of our state. [. . .] In that way, Russia was, is, and will be.[6]

Upon closer reading of Kozhevnikov's ideas, what is noteworthy is that the Soviet Union is both a new state ('creates a new state') as well as an old one ('this is nevertheless none other than old Russia'). Two extremes are reconciled into a satisfactory whole: an expression of Soviet Marxist dialectics—reconciling contradictions—of which we will later present more examples. Moreover, Kozhevnikov speaks at the same time about state continuity as well as succession, flexibly blurring these two concepts of international law. Although Kozhevnikov became famous for emphasizing Soviet state identity with the Russian Empire, he later, in a co-authored text, had no problem in referring to the Soviet relationship with tsarist Russia as a case of 'state succession'.[7] This flexibility—or lack of concern with the precision of concepts—remains characteristic of Soviet and Russian treatment of issues of state continuity and succession, with the intended meaning that today's Russia is the same state as the Russia of the past, except in matters where Russia wants to avoid bearing the consequences of that sameness. For example, none of the Soviet advocates of state continuity (rather than state succession) acknowledged that the Soviet Union might also have been responsible for tsarist-era debts.

Because of this flexibility of approaches, the debate about the exact relationship between tsarist Russia and the Soviet Union was also one of the debates in the Soviet Union in which a certain diversity of opinion was accepted in legal scholarship. As discussed previously, in the 1920s Korovin tried to present the Soviet Union as something different from the Russian Empire, identifying only Soviet Russia (as the core of the Soviet Union) with the Russian Empire, also with the hope that other states might still become socialist and join the union in the future. In some ways, Kozhevnikov's strong views on Soviet continuity with imperial Russia were a response to earlier views by Soviet international law colleagues who emphasized the disruption of state continuity in 1917. Thus, in 1947 Vsevolod Durdenevsky—Kozhevnikov's international law colleague from Moscow, fellow Soviet diplomat, and international law adviser at the Soviet UN delegation—had written in an article in the journal *Sovetskoe*

[6] Ibid, 32–5.
[7] F I Kozhevnikov, I P Blishchenko, 'Sotsializm i sovremennoe mezhdunarodnoe pravo', *SGP* No 4, 1970, 88–95 at 90.

gosudarstvo i pravo that the history of international relations knew cases of termination of states.[8] Durdenevsky opined that the case of Russia after 1917 was one which involved a replacement with a new, higher type of state in terms of social-economic formation. A state that comes to an end hands over succession to the new state, the most important part of which is territory.[9] Durdenevsky's frequent co-author, Krylov, also wrote this in their common textbook on international law in 1947, when he discussed replacement of a state—consisting of one type of historical formation—with another type. In Krylov's view, one such case was France after the French Revolution of 1789, when the monarchist, absolutist, and feudal formation was replaced with the bourgeois state. Krylov added:

> Or another historical example, lucky for humanity, was tsarist Russia, a prison house of peoples. In this Russia the revolution overthrew tsarist power, and instead of tsarist Russia emerged a new state, a state of a new type: our great socialist Motherland.[10]

Kozhevnikov's strongly and emotionally expressed view that the Soviet Union as a subject of international law was the same state as tsarist Russia set the tone for Soviet debates during later decades, right up until the disintegration of the Soviet Union. Nevertheless, some Soviet legal scholars challenged it. In a monograph published in 1961, Mirza Mosesovich Avakov (1925–87) inclined more towards the state succession perspective.[11] Avakov was a Soviet veteran of the Second World War who lived and taught initially in Leningrad and Minsk. As a member of the delegations of the Byelorussian SSR and the Soviet Union, he attended several major international conferences in Vienna and elsewhere. During the later stage of his career, Avakov became Professor of International Law at the Diplomatic Academy of the Russian MFA in Moscow.[12]

The focus of Avakov's academic work was state succession in the context of a fundamental change in its 'social structure'.[13] He also critically claimed that

[8] V N Durdenevsky, 'Sovetskaya territoria v aktakh mezhdunarodnoga prava za 30 let (1917–1947 gg)', *SGP* No 12, 1947, 58–65 at 58.

[9] Ibid, 58.

[10] V N Durdenevsky, S B Krylov (eds) *Mezhdunarodnoe pravo*, Iuridicheskoe izdatel'stvo Ministerstva yustitsii SSSR, 1947, 153–4.

[11] Mirza M Avakov, *Pravopreemstvo Sovetskogo gosudarstva*, Gosudarstvennoe izdatel'stvo iuridicheskoi literatury, 1961.

[12] 'Avakov, Mirza Mosesovich', Russian Wikipedia article https://ru.wikipedia.org/wiki/%D0%90%D0%B2%D0%B0%D0%BA%D0%BE%D0%B2,_%D0%9C%D0%B8%D1%80%D0%B7%D0%B0_%D0%9C%D0%BE%D1%81%D0%B5%D1%81%D0%BE%D0%B2%D0%B8%D1%87 .

[13] Avakov, *Pravopreemstvo Sovetskogo gosudarstva*, 1961, 5.

bourgeois scholarship on issues of state continuity and succession was characterized by 'dogmatism, juridism, and analysis of the "pure" legal norm'.[14] This was apparently also a reference to the fact that international legal theory in the West had tried to keep the notions of state continuity and succession separate from each other and even construe them as conceptual opposites. Avakov's main thesis was that in 1917 the Russian proletariat liquidated the old, bourgeois state and created a new Soviet one.[15] Conceptually, these were cases of state succession where a new subject of international law emerged after a social revolution and then at least some rights and obligations of the old subject of international law would be transferred to the new one, even though the limits of that transfer would be determined 'by the class essence of the new state and the generally recognized norms of international law'.[16] Avakov agreed with Krylov's 1947 view—namely that the Soviet Union was a new state—and disagreed with Kozhevnikov's 1948 thesis on state continuity with tsarist Russia.[17] Whether or not to accept any tsarist Russian obligations depended on the 'sovereign will of the Soviet state'.[18] The theory of—and political demand for—continuity (that is, respect for tsarist-era obligations) for Soviet Russia and the Soviet Union was 'bourgeois, reactionary, and dogmatic'.[19] When a new subject of international law annulled the debts of the previous subject, this in no way stood in contradiction to international law.[20] On this issue, there was no disagreement between Soviet supporters of the two opposite theories: state continuity and state succession. Moreover, just like Kozhevnikov, Avakov of course agreed that Soviet territorial expansion during the Second World War had been a positive event, as the Soviet Union had finally received 'durable and just borders'.[21]

The reception of these two theories proves that Kozhevnikov's thesis eventually won more supporters among Soviet international lawyers. Lidiya Artemevna Modzhoryan (1911—96) agreed that the Soviet Union as a subject of international law was the same state as the Russian Empire yet at the same time was not obliged to honour certain of the Russian Empire's treaty or contractual obligations.[22]

[14] Ibid, 9.
[15] Ibid, 11.
[16] Ibid, 10.
[17] Ibid, 14–15.
[18] Ibid, 17.
[19] Ibid, 18–19.
[20] Ibid, 67.
[21] Ibid, 110.
[22] L A Modzhoryan, 'Identichnost, nepreryvnost i pravopreemstvo sub'ektov mezhdunarodnogo prava', *SGP* 1 No 9, 959, 61–70 at 63, 66.

Among the Soviet theorists of international law, perhaps the synergetic last word on the question belongs to Natalya Zakharova, whose academic work focused on the impact of social revolution on treaties and statehood. Her core ideas on this subject matter were initially expressed in her *Soviet Yearbook of International Law* article in 1960.[23] Zakharova observed correctly that, practically speaking, the two concepts did not differ so much, as the representatives of both concepts, for example Kozhevnikov and Avakov, still assigned to the Soviet Union the right to abandon previous Russian treaties while highlighting the Soviet Russian claim to the continuity of tsarist rights in territorial situations and prerogatives such as the Aaland and Spitzbergen islands. Nevertheless, according to Zakharova, the correct legal theory was that the Soviet Union continued the international legal personality of the Russian Empire.[24] At the same time, Zakharova asserted that the Soviet concept of state continuity in cases of fundamental changes to the structure of the state (social revolution) has 'nothing in common with the bourgeois theory of continuity', which assumed the continuity of treaties.[25] Thus, Zakharova admitted that Soviet legal scholars were using formally the same concepts as they had been developed in classical international law—mostly developed in Europe—but when needed, those same scholars construed those concepts in line with their own different, idiosyncratic meaning. For Soviet international lawyers, it was not an insurmountable problem to announce that a certain international legal concept meant something else for the Soviet Union and socialist states.

In her 1966 monograph on the topic, Zakharova expanded these ideas on state continuity further. Again, she started her analysis by observing that the Soviet scholars who disagreed on the question whether the Soviet Union was a new state (state succession) or continued the legal personality of tsarist Russia (state continuity) did not have any disagreement on the issue that, in the case of social revolution, a state such as Soviet Russia was entitled to abandon treaties concluded by the previous regime.[26] Nevertheless, Zakharova's main point was that social revolution did not change or terminate the subjecthood of a state in international law; therefore, there was no state succession or transfer of rights from one subject to another.[27] In particular, the revolution did not change Russia's territorial rights; in Soviet practice, continuity was simply assumed.[28]

[23] N V Zakharova, 'O mezhdunarodnoi pravosubyektnosti gosudarstva pri sotsial'noi revoliutsii (nekotorye voprosy pravopreemstva)', *Soviet YBIL* 1960, 157–66.
[24] Ibid, 160.
[25] Ibid, 160–1.
[26] N V Zakharova, *Vlianie sotsial'noi revoliutsii na silu mezhdunarodnogo dogovora*, Nauka, 1966, 4.
[27] Ibid, 8.
[28] Ibid, 118–19.

According to Zakharova, this also corresponded to the expectations of the Soviet people:

> The position of the Soviet government concerning the international legal subjecthood of Russia corresponded to the representation of the masses that Russia lives on as a country, as their motherland. [. . .] Neither juridical documents nor historical facts give any reasons to assert that because of the Great October Revolution the international legal subjecthood of Russia was interrupted.[29]
>
> It also mattered where in the Soviet Union one thought about these things. A Ya Esayan from Yerevan State University in Soviet Armenia emphasized that Soviet Russia was identical with Tsarist Russia but after 1917, the other Soviet republics became genuinely independent states and joined the union with Soviet Russia on a voluntary basis. In this sense at least, there could not have been full state identity between the Soviet Union as a whole and imperial Russia.[30] However, this view too proceeded from the reality that there was no significant differences between the territories of the two (except mainly for Poland and Finland which were now independent states). Esayan also followed Zakharova's concept that changes in the class structure of a state's governance do not destroy state continuity as such.[31]

No further noteworthy theoretical discussions took place on the subject of state identity in the legal scholarship of the Soviet Union. This explains why we can draw the conclusion that the Kozhevnikov–Zakharova position on the state continuity of the Soviet Union with tsarist Russia had been accepted as the predominant interpretation in the Soviet Union. The Russian Empire was the Soviet Union's past in international law. In terms of international legal subjecthood, for the Soviet Union state continuity with the Russian Empire was a legal fact. It was also a perception expressed in Western scholarship during the 1960s that the state continuity (rather than state succession) perspective had become dominant in the legal theory of the Soviet Union.[32] The political message and consequences of the state continuity doctrine were also significant within the Soviet Union—perhaps tsarist Russia was not such a

[29] Ibid, 120–1.

[30] A.Ya. Esayan, *Nekotorye voprosy teorii i istorii mezhdunarodnoga prava*, Erevan: Izdatel'stvo Yerevanskogo universiteta, 1977, 110-114, 123.

[31] Ibid, 143.

[32] Theodor Schweisfurth, *Der internationale Vertrag in der modernen sowjetischen Völkerrechtstheorie*, Verlag Wissenschaft und Politik, 1968, 321.

'prison house of peoples' (Lenin) after all if the Soviet Union controlled almost the same territory; it had been a progressive feature that all these peoples were brought together into one state by the Russian Empire.

When in 1978 the Vienna Convention on Succession of States in Respect of Treaties was adopted, with a 'clean slate' doctrine for newly independent states born out of colonization, Soviet legal scholars, including Mirza Avakov, suggested that this had also been the influence of Soviet Russia and the Soviet Union's decision not to honour Russia's tsarist-era debts.[33] We should note, however, that the Vienna Convention on Succession of States in Respect of Treaties has been ratified only by a modest number of states (currently not even thirty), and it is unlikely that any of its key controversial principles have become part of customary international law.

Soviet Federalism and the 'Sovereignty' of Soviet Republics

We have already seen how Marxist dialectics as a way of tackling and 'reconciling' contradictions was used in the case of state continuity in the Soviet Union. This enabled the simultaneous argument, namely that the Soviet Union preserved state continuity with the Russian Empire but was not responsible for the Russian Empire's debts or, generally, key parts of tsarist constitutional reality. Soviet scholarship often responded that it had its own, socialist doctrine which used the same concepts of classical international law (such as state continuity) but filled them with its own content, different from the 'bourgeois' doctrine of the West. At the end of the day, using this kind of dialectic says something profound about the Soviet Union—indeed, as Stalin had already stated on one occasion:

> This is the Marxist formula. Is it 'contradictory'? Yes, it is 'contradictory'. But this contradiction is Life, and completely reflects Marxist dialectic.[34]

Another doctrine where a similar dialectic was used concerned the status of Soviet republics in the Soviet Union. That is, Soviet legal scholars developed

[33] E D Beishembiev, 'Rapallskii dogovor i ego rol' v razvitii sovremennogo mezhdunarodnoga prava (k 60-letiu podpisania dogovora)', *Soviet YBIL* 1981, 270–6 at 275; M M Avakov, 'Pravopreemstvo gosudarstv v otnoshenii dogovorov (Venskaya konventsia OON 1978 g)', *SGP* No 12, 1979, 82–5 at 85; M M Boguslavsky, V V Tsybukov, 'Novaya kontseptsia o pravopreemstve gosudarstv', *SGP* No 3, 1984, 118–24.

[34] Cited in Anton Weiss-Wendt, *The Soviet Union and the Gutting of the UN Genocide Convention*, The University of Wisconsin Press, 2017, 41.

the theory that both the Soviet Union and the fifteen Soviet republics which formed part of it were sovereign states at the same time. From the comparative perspective, this was not entirely unprecedented: for example, the constitutional and international legal realities of the Holy Roman Empire of the German Nation and of the Austro-Hungarian Empire had been complex and contradictory.[35] The German lawyer Samuel von Pufendorf (1632–94) had even called the Holy Roman Empire 'an irregular body resembling a monster'.[36]

In parallel, there was a historical debate about the status of Soviet republics in the period 1918–22. While, for example, Levan Aleksidze from Georgia argued that the federation formed on 30 December 1922 was treaty-based and before that Soviet republics were fully independent states and only in confederation with Soviet Russia, some authors from Moscow, such as Lepeshkin, claimed the opposite, namely that even in 1918–22 ties between Russia and other Soviet republics were federal–constitutional, not based on international law.[37] Nikolay Aleksandrovich Ushakov (1918–2002), Soviet member of the ILC 1967–86, resolved the contradiction between the two factions of opinion with the help of Marxist dialectics:

> Apparently, both moments existed simultaneously in dialectical interconnectedness and in the final effect worked in one direction: in the direction of voluntary unification of Soviet republics in a united mighty Soviet Union.[38]

Ushakov emphasized that every Soviet republic in the Soviet Union was a sovereign state.[39] At the same time, he recalled the words of the Soviet leader after 1964, Leonid Ilyich Brezhnev: communists always saw the national question through the lens of the class struggle; the solution to this question must be subordinate to the interests of the revolution and socialism.[40] In other words, self-determination in terms of nationalism had to be subjugated to proletarian solidarity in the socialist federation. Because of the federalist solution, 'backward' border regions of the Russian Empire were turned into economically

[35] On sovereignty in the Austro-Hungarian Empire, see Natasha Wheatley, *Life and Death of States: Central Europe and the Transformation of Modern Sovereignty*, Princeton UP, 2023, 12, 57.

[36] Samuel Pufendorf, *De statu Imperii Germanici* (On the Constitution of the German Empire), 1667.

[37] L A Aleksidze, 'Znachenie obrazovania SSSR dlia obespechenia mira i mezhdunarodnoga pravoporiadka', *Soviet YBIL* 1982, 11–28; citing Lepeshkin, *Sovetskii federalizm*, Iuridichecheskaya literatura, 1977, 238.

[38] N A Ushakov, 'Mezhdunarodno-pravovye aspekty obrazovania Soyuza SSR', *Soviet YBIL* 1972, 11–24 at 13.

[39] Ibid, 19.

[40] Ibid, 12.

and culturally developed socialist republics.[41] Ushakov concluded his argument with another example of Marxist dialectics, turning a common-sense contradiction into a Soviet legal reality:

> The tendency of rapprochement of the peoples of socialist countries is unbreakably connected with the tendency of all-encompassing development of the peoples of those countries, with the strengthening of their sovereignty.[42]

In other words, by becoming more integrated, Soviet peoples strengthened their sovereignty. A further aspect in this apparent paradox was to say that while in 'bourgeois' federations, the units of federation could not be sovereign, the units of Soviet federation could be precisely that. An 'organic unity' linked the sovereignties of the Soviet Union and its constituent republics; furthermore, when the Soviet republics formed the Soviet Union in 1922, they 'not only maintained but significantly strengthened their sovereignty'.[43] The Soviet constitutional law scholar Manelis argued on this account:

> During the period of expanded construction of communism, a further strengthening is taking place in terms of the unity of the sovereignty of the USSR and the sovereignty of union republics. The objective foundation of this process is a new stage of development of interethnic relations characterized by further rapprochement of nations and their achieving full unity.[44]

In non-Russian union republics, the goal of such 'full unity' in the Soviet Union was often perceived as further Russification. However, for Manelis, sovereignty within the Soviet Union meant that 'national limitedness, national exclusivity' were alien in terms of the sovereignty of Soviet republics.[45]

Another Soviet constitutionalist, Shevtsov, maintained that the sovereignties of the union and the Soviet republics were complementary; a dialectical interconnectedness, harmony, and ultimately unity of these sovereignties existed.[46] The two Soviet sovereignties were not 'isolated' from each other.[47] At the same time, the Dean of the Faculty of Law of Tashkent State University

[41] Ibid, 19.
[42] Ibid, 22.
[43] B N Manelis, 'Edinstvo suvereniteta Soyuza SSR i suvereniteta soyuznykh respublik v period razvernutoga stroitel'stva kommunizma', *SGP* No 7, 1964, 17–26 at 17–18.
[44] Ibid, 20.
[45] Ibid, 20.
[46] V S Shevtsov, 'Suverenitet v Sovetskom soyuznom gosudarstve', *SGP* No 6, 1972, 49–58 at 50, 56.
[47] V S Shevtsov, 'Nekotorye problemy teorii Sovetskogo soyuznogo gosudarstva', *SGP* No 4, 1978, 25–34 at 34.

(Uzbek SSR) claimed that socialist federalism was intrinsically linked with the principle of equal rights of nations.[48] Marxist dialectics or scholasticism never really disappeared from the picture, though: for example, when a Soviet Kazakh constitutionalist argued that Soviet federalism and the sovereignty of Soviet republics remained an effective tool for the 'rapprochement and merger' of nations but also asserted that the rapprochement of Soviet socialist republics 'is far from yet meaning their merger'.[49] The Dean of the Faculty of Law of Rostov State University, K D Kormasova, argued that federalism was necessary in the Soviet Union to deal with the gap in terms of social, political, economic, and cultural development between the peoples of the USSR; it was a fact that some ethnic groups were in this regard more developed than others.[50] Kormasova was wary of 'nationalism', but in reality what she and other Soviet legal scholars from the imperial centre were confronted with were suppressed self-determination claims in non-Russian Soviet republics:

> Nationalism is a complicated phenomenon which has many shades and varieties. It does not always express itself in open form, and knows how to disguise itself. At the contemporary stage there are quite dangerous expressions of nationalism at the level of ideology. With its help, imperialist circles try to shake the political unity of peoples of the USSR, peoples of other socialist countries, and undermine socialist internationalism.[51]

At the same time, Kormasova was confident that 'migration processes' between the Soviet republics—that is, by which the percentage of native Russian speakers grew among the population of other Soviet republics—led to further 'internationalization' of the Soviet Union:

> Developing based on equal rights, national languages, especially Russian, have a benevolent effect on the progressive development of the process of internationalization of the spiritual life of socialist nations.[52]

[48] A A Agzamkhodzhaev, 'Sotsialisticheskii federalizm i printsip ravnopravia narodov', *SGP* No 12, 1972, 52–58.

[49] A Sh Tuganbaev, 'Razvitie natsional'noi gosudarstvennosti narodov Srednei Azii i Kazakhstana', *SGP* No 12, 1972, 59–65 at 64.

[50] K D Kormasova, 'Sovetskaya natsional'naya gosudarstvennost'—vazhnyi faktor internatsional'nogo edinstva narodov SSSR', *SGP* No 8, 1976, 12–8 at 16.

[51] Ibid, 17.

[52] Ibid, 18.

However, people in several Soviet republics—not least in the Soviet-occupied Baltic States—often perceived these tendencies in the Soviet Union as at a conscious state effort towards further Russification.

A wave of legal scholarship from each of the Soviet republics asserted that these were sovereign states—while at the same time accepting all those caveats, which were formulated by legal scholars in Moscow.[53] Because the Ukrainian and Byelorussian SSR were accepted as founding member states of the UN in 1945, the claim to sovereign status of the Soviet republics came particularly strongly from these republics, in terms of scholarship perhaps particularly from Byelorussia.[54] Soviet legal scholars were also acutely aware of a deep scepticism in the West as to whether the Soviet republics were 'sovereign' in any meaningful way; however, this was brushed away by citing the 'imperialism' of Western states.[55] Western critics of the official concept of the sovereignty of the Soviet republics were labelled 'falsifiers'.[56]

In the 1970s, Henn-Jüri Uibopuu (1929–2012), an Austrian international lawyer born in the interwar Republic of Estonia, argued that the Soviet theory of the sovereignty of Soviet republics was a 'fiction' directed more to the outside world because it offered an opportunity to potentially attract other countries to join the Soviet Union and save the face of its new constituent parts at the same time as they would not have to lose their sovereignty in the process.[57] According to Uibopuu, the Uzbek SSR in particular served as a Soviet showcase model for Asian and African states.[58] However, I would argue that even more important still was the Soviet domestic dimension, which was imperial and whose purpose was to mislead: that is, by asserting the legal theoretical 'sovereignty' of Soviet republics, the Soviet Russian imperial centre could

[53] See, eg, K N Nurbekov, 'Obrazovanie kirgizskoi suverennoi sovetskoi sotsialisticheskoi respubliki', *SGP* No 9, 1958, 43–50 at 43; G B Akbarov, 'Iz opyta osuschestvlenia mezhdunarodnykh sviazei Tadzhikskoi SSR', *Soviet YBIL* 1969, 309–14; A N Mikhailov, 'Uzbekskaya SSR—ravnopravnyi sub'ekt mezhdunarodnoga prava', *Soviet YBIL* 1972, 25–37 at 25; A Ya Yarmatov, 'Obrazovanie Turkmenskoi SSR i razvitie ee suverennykh prav', *SGP* No 10, 1974, 27–31 at 28.

[54] Yu P Brovkva, *Mezhdunarodnaya pravosub 'ektnost' BSSR*, Nauka i tekhnika, 1967; Yu P Brovkva, 'Soyuznaya Respublika—sub'ekt mezhdunarodnoga prava', *SGP* No 12, 1972, 36–42 at 42. Critically, see also Wolodymyr Sawchak, *The Status of the Ukrainian SSR in View of State and International Law*, London: Ukrainian Information Service, 1971.

[55] See, eg, S V Vikharev, 'Soyuznaya respublika kak sub'ekt mezhdunarodnoga prava', *SGP* No 6, 1960, 65–73 at 65.

[56] B L Manelis, 'Protiv burzhuaznoi fal'sifikatsii natsional'no-gosudarstvennogo ustroistva SSSR', *SGP* No 3, 1968, 57–66 at 62.

[57] Henn-Jüri Uibopuu, *Die Völkerrechtssubjektivität der Unionsrepubliken der UdSSR*, Springer-Verlag, Wien, 1975, 304–5.

[58] Ibid, 306. On 'showcasing' Soviet Uzbekistan and Central Asia more generally at this time, see also Akbar Rasulov, 'Central Asia as an Object of Orientalist Narratives in the Age of Bandung', in: Luis Eslava, Michael Fakhri, Vasuki Nesiah (eds) *Bandung, Global History, and International Law. Critical Pasts and Pending Futures*, CUP, 2017, 215–31.

claim that the periphery of non-Russian Soviet republics had already achieved self-determination, statehood, and sovereignty. They had no need to look for something that was already there, and the Empire would survive intact.

Self-Determination during the Cold War: Soviet Self-Representation Abroad and at Home

Soviet endorsement of the right of peoples to self-determination has been discussed in a monograph written by the German international lawyer Johannes Socher[59] so there is no need to repeat his detailed and highly relevant research findings here. Soviet legal scholars took pride in the fact that the USSR supported inclusion of the right of peoples to self-determination in the 1945 negotiations leading to adoption of the UN Charter as well as the 1966 UN human rights covenants in which self-determination occupies a prominent place in Article 1 of both covenants. The Soviet approach was, of course, that Russia had progressively resolved its imperial and self-determination issues in 1917 whereas the West had not; therefore, the Soviet Union actively supported decolonization efforts concerning the West European colonial empires.

However, at the Bandung conference of 1955, some governments of the non-communist 'Third World' states raised the sincerity of Soviet rhetoric towards issues of self-determination, empire, and colonialism. To start with, there was a certain disagreement in Bandung over what constituted 'colonialism' and 'imperialism'.[60] For example, at the plenary meeting in Bandung the representatives of Iraq, Iran, the Philippines, Turkey, and Pakistan uttered the accusation that Soviet communism was neocolonialism, while Ceylon (today's Sri Lanka) made a similar charge in the political committee.[61] Ceylon's prime minister Kotelawala commented that 'if we are united in our opposition to colonialism, should it not be our duty openly to declare our opposition to Soviet colonialism as much as to Western imperialism?'—an idea that drew some support in Bandung.[62]

[59] Johannes Socher, *Russia and the Right to Self-Determination in the Post-Soviet Space*, OUP, 2021.

[60] Luis Eslava, Michael Fakhri, Vasuki Nesiah (eds) *Bandung, Global History, and International Law. Critical Pasts and Pending Futures*, CUP, 2017, 21, 30.

[61] Chen Yifeng, 'Bandung, China, and the Making of World Order in East Asia', in: Luis Eslava, Michael Fakhri, Vasuki Nesiah (eds) *Bandung, Global History, and International Law. Critical Pasts and Pending Futures*, CUP, 2017, 177–95 at 186.

[62] Rose Parfitt, 'Newer is Truer', in: Eslava et al (eds), *Bandung, Global History, and International Law*, 2017, 51.

However, the outcome of the 'imperialism and colonialism' debate concerning the Soviet Union was less evident after Bandung. One social movement created as a direct result of the Bandung conference was the Afro-Asian People's Solidarity Organization (AAPSO). This created the Afro–Asian Writers' Conference, which held its inaugural meeting in 1958 in Tashkent, capital of the Uzbek SSR.[63] Soviet writers of course praised the 'spirit of Bandung'[64] and Soviet advances to Asian and African countries were based on the assumption that this was a meeting of likeminded nations, all struggling against (Western) imperialism and colonialism. However, from a realistic viewpoint it was also the expression of Bismarck's maxim that 'my enemy's enemy is my friend'. Soviet support to Afro–Asian liberation movements also demonstrates that no critics of empires are as motivated and dedicated as rival great (imperial) powers.

When the Colonial Independence Declaration of 1960 was prepared at the UNGA, the Soviet Union even demanded a binding date (the end of 1961) to be fixed for the abolition of colonialism. Johannes Socher points out the hypocrisy of the Soviet position:

> This championship of the termination of colonial rule based on self-determination was, of course, based on extreme hypocrisy: the Soviet Union could only support calls for 'national liberation' in Africa and Asia without risking its territorial integrity because it presented itself as a commonwealth of free and equal nations.[65]

In 1960, although many states at the UNGA identified the Soviet Union as a colonial power, references to geographical separation nevertheless dominated as an objective prerequisite (the so-called saltwater test). Geographical separation was one of the elements to determine which territories qualified as 'non-self-governing' in a UNGA resolution which defined the basic colonial unit.[66] In that sense, supporting and ensuring success for such a distinction at the UNGA was also a remarkable success of Soviet diplomacy; one that favoured the history and interests of the two Eurasian continental empires, especially Russia (the Soviet Union). Important in this regard was also the Soviet

[63] Eslava et al (eds), *Bandung, Global History, and International Law*, 2017, 12–3.

[64] See, eg, E Zhukov, 'Konferentsia stran Azii i Afriki v Bandunge i ee istoricheskoe znachenie', *MZh* No 5, 1955, 18–34; Peredovaya, 'Dukh Bandunga – znamenie natsionalnogo vozrozhdenia', *MZh* No 4, 1957, 9–14.

[65] Socher, *Russia and the Right to Self-Determination in the Post-Soviet Space*, 2021, 31.

[66] Ibid, 32..

leader Nikita Khruschev's speech at the UNGA on 23 September 1960. In his speech, Khruschev maintained forcefully that, in Russia, everything imperialist and colonialist came to an end with the Bolshevik revolution in 1917.[67] Khruschev's comments at the UNGA so aptly summarize the Soviet self-image and discourse about Russia's imperial history that they are worth quoting at greater length here:

> It may be said that it is easy for the Soviet Union to advocate liquidation of the colonial system, since the Soviet Union has no colonies. Yes, that is so. We have no colonies and no capital in other countries. But there was a time when many of the nationalities inhabiting our country suffered the bitter oppression of tsarism, of the landlord–bourgeois system. Conditions in remote areas of the tsarist Empire hardly differed from those of colonies because their populations were cruelly exploited by the autocracy, by capitalism. Whereas the autocracy looked upon the peoples of Central Asia and Transcaucasia, and other nationalities inhabiting the Russian Empire, as a source of profit, after the October Revolution, when these peoples obtained complete freedom, they quickly improved their economic, cultural, and social condition.
>
> Let us take, for example, the Soviet Republics of Central Asia. Today, Kazakhstan, Uzbekistan, Kirghizia, Turkmenistan, Tadzhikstan—all the sister republics of Central Asia—have been transformed from backward colonies of tsarist Russia into advanced, industrially developed socialist republics.[68]

Khruschev continued in similar vein:

> In the borderlands of Russia, the tsarist Government pursued an essentially colonialist policy which differed little from what can be observed today in colonial countries: Uzbeks, Kazakhs, Tadzhiks and other non-Russian nationalities were scornfully called 'aliens'. They were not considered human beings and were ruthlessly exploited. National differences, hatred and dissension were fomented between these nationalities, and the tsarist Empire was held together only by bayonets and oppression. When the peoples of Central Asia and Transcaucasia were given their national freedom and equal rights

[67] UNGA, 15th session, Official records, 869th plenary meeting, 23.09.1960, Speech by Mr Khrushchev, Chairman of the Council of Ministers of the Union of Soviet Socialist Republics, 68–84, paras 192–3.
[68] Ibid, paras 192–3.

> with the other peoples of Russia, they showed their capabilities in the development of their national economy and culture.
>
> Did the development of our country suffer by granting to the peoples the right of independence and self-determination? Is there strife and enmity between nationalities in our multi-national country or a disintegration of the State? No, there is nothing of the sort, nor can there be.[69]

This was the Soviet self-image. However, upon critical examination of Soviet history and reality, questions remained. In this context, Socher's conclusion on the Soviet approach to the right of peoples to self-determination is pertinent:

> While the Soviet Union may therefore rightly be called one of the strongest and most aggressive supporters of self-determination *outside* its own sphere of influence in the context of decolonization specifically [. . .] Soviet doctrine on self-determination played a second, highly contradictory and—one might say perverted—role *inside* the Eastern bloc.[70]

Here I would add: not only in the Eastern bloc generally but—equally importantly—also inside the Soviet Union itself. When we contrast what Soviet leaders and diplomats said abroad and how self-determination issues were presented at home, in the Soviet Union, then it appears that these were two different worlds; indeed, presented differently in the same Soviet law journals. Again, examples can be drawn from the leading Soviet journal of public law, *Sovetskoe gosudarstvo i pravo*, which naturally enough included a condemnation of Western colonialism,[71] while at the same time the patronizing imperialist tone about non-Russian peoples of the Soviet Union also persistently came through in discussions on implementing self-determination within the Soviet Union.

Soviet Russian legal scholars emphasized that the initial heavy blow to the system of colonialism had already been delivered by Russia's October

[69] Ibid, paras 207–8.

[70] Socher, ibid, 35.

[71] See, eg, I D Levin, 'Rabstvo vo vladeniakh imperializma', *SGP* No 10, 1951, 55–63; L A Modzhoryan, 'Bor'ba demokraticheskogo lageria za natsional'nuyu nezavisimost' i natsional'nyi suverenitet', *SGP* No 1, 1953, 52–65; G V Sharmazanashvili, 'Kolonial'naya voina – gruboe narushenie mezhdunarodnoga prava', *SGP* 1957, No 10, 55–61; Yu A Yudin, 'Nekotorye problemy stanovlenia natsional'noi gosudarstvennosti v nezavisimykh stranakh Afriki', *SGP* No 2, 1961, 35–47; D B Levin, 'Printsip samoopredelenia natsii i likvidatsia kolonializma', *SGP* No 8, 1962, 90–9; D I Baratashvili, 'Natsional'no-osvoboditel'noe dvizhenie i razvitie mezhdunarodnoga prava', *SGP* No 9, 1967, 69–75. The same discourse was also visible in the *Soviet Yearbook of International Law*, see, eg, L A Modzhoryan, 'Raspad kolonial'noi sistemy imperializma i Organizatsia Ob'edenennykh Natsii', *Soviet YBIL* 1960, 121–43.

Revolution in 1917.[72] Lev Matveevich Entin (b. 1928), at that time an associate professor at the University of Stalinabad (today's Dushanbe), criticized Western approaches to decolonization, arguing that it was a 'pseudo democratic disguise' by Western colonial powers when they pretended that decolonization was of a voluntary nature and started to extend political rights to the population in colonies.[73] Yuri Adol'fovich Yudin (1926–2000), who headed Soviet legal studies of African countries, criticized constitutional reforms carried out by the colonial powers in Africa along with constitutions thus adopted, with the apparent purpose of actually slowing down the process of decolonization in Africa.[74] Yet Soviet diplomacy at the UN and legal scholars writing in the Soviet Union were unanimous that decolonization was necessary in order to implement self-determination.[75] Discussing the important 1960 UNGA session—in which the programmatic Khruschev speech already cited was delivered—Soviet legal scholars condemned Canadian Prime Minister John Diefenbaker (1895–1979) who declared at the UN that the USSR, too, was a colonial country because of the situation of peoples there who were not ethnic Russian.[76] Much later, when the UNGA had adopted (1974) the Charter of Economic Rights and Obligations of States, expressing ideas about the new international economic order from the Third World perspective, Grigory Tunkin with a co-author argued that the principles proclaimed in the Charter did not yet have the quality of international law but also pointed out that the main obstacle for their maturation into international law was imperialism with its intrinsic tendency to exploit less developed nations.[77] These Soviet positions of course implied that imperialism equalled Western imperialism.

At the same time, in narratives with respect to Soviet peoples, it was common in the Soviet Union, especially during the decolonization period in the West, to emphasize the leading role of the Russian people in the historical processes which covered the evolution from tsarist Russia to the Soviet Union. For example, G T Taymanov wrote about Soviet Kazakhstan as follows:

[72] S V Molodtsov, 'Raspad sistemy kolonializma i ego vlianie na mezhdunarodnoe pravo', *SGP* 1956, No 5, 79–6 at 79.

[73] L M Entin, 'O reaktsionnoi suschnosti burzhuaznykh iuridicheskikh teorii dekolonizatsii', *SGP* No 5, 1959, 108–15 at 111, 114.

[74] Yu A Yudin, 'Natsional'no-osvoboditel'naya bor'ba narodov Afriki i manevry imperialistov', *SGP* No 6, 1959, 112–23 at 113, 123.

[75] See, eg, D B Levin, 'Printsip samoopredelenia natsii i likvidatsia kolonializma', *SGP* No 8, 1962, 90–99.

[76] R A Tuzmukhamedov, A L Larionov, 'Napadki na printsip samoopredelenia narodov i natsii', *SGP* No 10, 1963, 132–136 at 132.

[77] G I Tunkin, V M Shishkin, 'O mezhunarodno-pravovykh printsipakh novoga mezhdunarodnoga ekonomicheskoga poriadka', *SGP* No 9, 1980, 88–96 at 96.

> All peoples living in our homeland saw their liberation in the unification with the Great Russian people which organized and rallied them to fight against tsarist autocracy and foreign invaders. [. . .] The voluntary unification of Kazakhstan with Russia, which was completed by the mid-nineteenth century, had a tremendous progressive meaning. Thanks to accession to Russia, Kazakhstan avoided enslavement by Central Asian feudal states behind whose back stood the most aggressive great power during that period: England.[78]

Taymanov concluded with the already familiar Soviet dialectic on sovereignty: the voluntary entry of the Kazakh SSR to the Soviet Union is 'one of the brightest expressions of its sovereignty'.[79]

Another legal scholar, Kh P Vakhidov from Tashkent (Uzbekistan), argued the following:

> In the 1880s, Central Asia was finally united with Russia. By its objective consequences, the fact of unification of Central Asia with Russia was a deeply progressive event, determining the fate of the peoples of Central Asia. [. . .] A lasting union between the workers of Central Asia with the Great Russian people took shape. The Russian people helped the peoples of Central Asia to liberate themselves from social and national repression.[80]

The very same Soviet legal scholar postulated further that establishing tight economic and cultural connections with Russia was in Central Asia's own interest because Russia 'stood incomparably higher in the economic and cultural sense'.[81] In contemporary conditions, too, argued the same scholar, the Central Asian peoples could 'lean on brotherly help from the Great Russian people'.[82] Another Soviet legal scholar, Sh Z Urazaev, emphasized the 'enormous role of the Soviet federation in ensuring necessary help in the social–economic, cultural, and constitutional development of small nations on the part of a more developed and stronger nation'.[83] Urazaev emphasized that

[78] G T Taimanov, 'Kazakhskaya SSR v Sovetskom mnogonatsional'nom gosudarstve', *SGP* No 4, 1954, 27–38 at 28.
[79] Ibid, at 31.
[80] Kh P Vakhidov, 'Politicheskie vzgliady prosvetitelei narodov Srednei Azii vtoroi poloviny XIX. v', *SGP* No 7, 1955, 100–8 at 100.
[81] Ibid, at 100.
[82] Ibid, at 108.
[83] Sh Z Urazaev, 'Rol' RSFSR v sozdanii sovetskoi gosudarstvennoi deyatel'nosti narodov Srednei Azii (1917–1922 gg)', *SGP* No 6, 1964, 106–11 at 106.

Soviet Russia showed intense involvement and interest in the constitutional reorganization of 'border regions' and provided them with 'necessary help' in the process.[84] At the same time, other authors emphasized that the political reorganization of Central Asia in the Soviet Union was all bottom-up and expressed the will of their peoples.[85]

Another Soviet legal scholar, M Fedorov, explained how Yakutia, with 'decisive brotherly help from Russians and other Soviet nations' managed to achieve socialism, 'bypassing the capitalist stage of development'.[86] His colleague, V A Zibarev from Tomsk, discussed the situation with the peoples of the Russian Arctic regions and referred to their 'utter backwardness' historically.[87] The fact that the Soviet Union organized these peoples in national territories within the Russian RSFSR testified to the fact that they now enjoyed sovereignty, the right to self-determination, and political equality,[88] added Zibarev before concluding:

> The historical experience of the peoples of the North completely refutes fabrications by neo-colonizers about the impossibility of peoples who are developmentally retarded to have their own state existence. The development of the peoples of the North proved the possibility of creation of national statehood.[89]

What these examples reveal is that in the Soviet Union quite a widespread effort was made in domestic Soviet legal discourse to convince Soviet citizens—and especially legal specialists—that self-determination had been achieved for everyone under the leadership of the Russian people. What this discourse helped to ensure was that, compared to tsarist Russia, during the 1950s and 1960s the Soviet Union would not lose any territory because of self-determination claims in the style of Western colonies. The tone of Soviet discourse on the right of peoples to self-determination was very different regarding the Soviet Union itself, on the one hand, and the outside world (the former West European empires), on the other. How to relate to Russia's imperial legacy even strained relations in the Soviet dissident movement where

[84] Ibid, 111.
[85] A A Gordienko, 'Samoopredelenie narodov i obrazovanie sovetskoi natsional'noi gosudarstvennosti v Srednei Azii', *SGP* No 5, 1967, 76–84 at 83.
[86] M M Fedorov, 'V I Lenin i avtonomia Iakutii', *SGP* No 4, 1972, 122–5 at 125.
[87] V A Zibarev, 'Natsional'no-gosudarstvennoe stroitel'stvo u narodov Severa', *SGP* No 12, 1972, 81–7 at 81–2.
[88] Ibid, 85–6.
[89] Ibid, 87.

the critical approaches differed in Moscow on the one hand and in the Baltic republics and Ukraine on the other.[90] Dissidents in the latter demanded the recognition that in terms of rights, the root of evil in the Soviet Union was not communism or authoritarianism as such but the uninterrupted legacy of Russian imperialism.

[90] Benjamin Nathans, *To the Success of Our Hopeless Cause. The Many Lives of the Soviet Dissident Movement,* Princeton University Press, 2024, 513-4.

7

The Cold War: Soviet Views on Treaties, Peaceful Coexistence, and Socialist International Law as Imperial Doctrines

The imperial doctrines to be examined in the following concern Soviet post-1945 views on treaties (especially possibilities for their termination), peaceful coexistence, the great power status of the Soviet Union, and socialist international law.

Treaty Law and *Clausula Rebus Sic Stantibus*

As discussed in this book in the context of both tsarist Russia and the interwar Soviet Union, questions of the validity and termination of treaties have been central for the solution of Russia's imperial status and territorial issues. In the Second World War, the Soviet Union expanded territorially and, on several occasions, the price for this was Soviet violations of previous treaties. In December 1939, the Soviet Union was—as we have seen—expelled from the League of Nations, essentially because of its violation of the League of Nations Covenant vis-à-vis Finland (and its refusal to undergo the dispute settlement mechanism foreseen in the Covenant). The question also arose of the context in which, in 1945, the Soviet Union terminated its earlier (1941) pact of non-aggression and neutrality with Japan. This meant that Soviet international lawyers had to somehow make sense of all this contradictory practice, of which contemporaries were keenly aware, even if in the Soviet Union they did not definitively know about important aspects such as the secret protocols of the Nazi–Soviet non-aggression pact.

Following the execution of Evgeny Pashukanis in 1937, the leading Soviet international lawyer was Andrey Yanuarevich Vyshinsky (1883–1954). Vyshinsky was another example of how expertise and authority in legal academia was combined with high positions in the Soviet government: he started

Russia, the Soviet Union, and Imperial Continuity in International Law. Lauri Mälksoo, Oxford University Press.
 DOI: 10.1093/9780198955962.003.0007

out as a prosecutor in the Stalinist show trials during the 1930s and later became Soviet foreign minister in 1949, after Molotov fell out of favour with Stalin. At the end of the 1940s, Vyshinsky coedited the *Diplomatic Dictionary*, which explained as follows about termination of treaties. First, more than 40 per cent of treaties contained a termination clause:

> However, in recent times the opinion is widespread that even when such a special clause is not present, denunciation is always possible. Several cases of unilateral termination of a treaty have occurred in practice on the basis of a radical change in the international situation.[1]

Reading between the lines, it was unambiguously clear that much of the relevant practice also happened to be Russian and Soviet practice before and during World War II. Another article in the *Diplomatic Dictionary* which dealt with the fate of the Soviet–Polish Riga Peace Treaty of 18 March 1921 stated:

> [It] was operational until September 17, 1939 when—in connection with the collapse of the Polish state—the Soviet government annulled all treaties and agreements which had been concluded with Poland. Western Ukraine and Western Byelorussia, in correspondence with the will of the population of these oblasts, joined the USSR.[2]

In the aftermath of the Second World War, the leading Soviet international lawyer specializing in the law of treaties was Vladimir Mikhailovich Shurshalov (1913–90), whose work as an international law scholar took him to the State Institute of Law in Moscow as well as to the Peoples' Friendship University in Moscow as a professor and, towards the end of his life, to the Diplomatic Academy.[3] What Shurshalov had to offer was a copy of the tsarist-era (Martens') doctrine of the indispensability of *clausula rebus sic stantibus*, with a Marxist–Leninist emphasis on economic factors. Shurshalov explained:

> Notwithstanding the specifics of international relations, the reality and validity of the norms of international law as well as these or other stipulations in international treaties depend in the result on the economic conditions that gave birth to them. From this viewpoint, only international treaties that

[1] A Y Vyshinsky (ed) *Diplomaticheskii slovar*, Vol II, article 'Mezhdunarodnye dogovory', Moscow: Gosudarstvennoe izdatel'stvo politicheskoi literatury, 1950, 138.
[2] Ibid, 511 (Article 'Rizhskii mirnyi dogovor 1921').
[3] See http://intlaw.rudn.ru/history-in-faces/shurshalov/.

> correspond to objective conditions are real and effective. A treaty that is contrived will be changed by life as something alien to it, not corresponding to its needs. The failure of these or other international plans, agreements, or unions is often explained precisely by the fact that they appear to be built on subjective wishes, without consideration for the actual needs and relations of life. [. . .] Whatever the deadline of a treaty, its implementation will stop in practice if the objective conditions which preceded it cease to exist, since as a rule the scope and purpose of a treaty reflect the changing needs of international life. On the other hand, the duration of treaties serves as a yardstick of their actual correspondence to international life. This has first order importance for understanding the nature of *clausula rebus sic stantibus*. 'Eternal' treaties last no longer than those concrete international relations which they are called upon to regulate. When those relations change drastically, international treaties—notwithstanding their 'eternality'—will stop being applied and become a matter of history. When the connection between an international treaty with the needs of international life is violated, external guarantee [of the treaty] turns into a mere formality.[4]

The classic Soviet example was the annulment of the Brest-Litovsk Peace Treaty in November 1918, some seven months after it was signed. Shurshalov explained that this particular treaty was a fine example of the impact of political conditions on the validity of international treaties. In the words of Shurshalov: 'as the Brest-Litovsk treaty was built on a deplorable political foundation, it could not create a legal basis for peaceful relations between Soviet Russia and Germany.'[5]

The argumentation in Shurshalov's monograph on the validity of treaties climaxed when the author offered a list of situations in which treaties were, in his interpretation, not valid under international law. This read like a list covering almost all significant foreign policy acts of the US and other Western states after the Second World War. According to Shurshalov, the following were invalid:

- International treaties violating the peace and security of nations and which had an aggressive character: the Washington treaty which established NATO could serve as an example.[6]

[4] V M Shurshalov, *Osnovania deistvitel'nosti mezhdunarodnykh dogovorov*, Izdatel'stvo akademii nauk SSSR, Moscow, 1957, 12–14.
[5] Ibid, 36.
[6] Ibid, 148.

- Treaties violating the principle of peaceful coexistence of all states, notwithstanding their social structure, such as treaties discriminating against socialist countries in trade.[7]
- Treaties undermining the territorial integrity of a certain state, such as certain territorial stipulations in the US–Japan 'peace treaty' (quotation marks by Shurshalov) which created a special status for Okinawa; also the US treaty with the Kuomintang-led Republic of China.[8]
- Treaties violating the sovereignty of states, such as the agreement establishing US military bases in the UK.[9]
- Treaties that justified intervention in the domestic affairs of other states such as the 1954 Manila pact and again the 1954 US–Kuomintang China (Taiwan) treaty.[10]
- Treaties violating equality and mutual benefit, such as unequal treaties with China, as well as the US Marshall plan.[11]
- Treaties violating earlier recognized obligations and thus the principle of *pacta sunt servanda* being not valid. For example, at the Potsdam conference in 1945 it had been agreed that the victorious allies would decide on the future of Germany together, but now the Western Allies had decided to violate this obligation towards the Soviet Union. The fact of the UK and France having concluded the Paris agreements (with the Federal Republic of Germany) had at the same time gravely violated their obligations based on the Anglo–Soviet and Franco–Soviet treaties from the Second World War, Shurshalov concluded.[12]

Thus, according to Shurshalov, many important (Western) treaties were, in his view, void and invalid. His concept of international treaties was not entirely consequential as he seemed to measure Soviet and Western—especially US—treaty situations with a different yardstick.

Based on the interwar writings of Pashukanis and the post-Second World War views of Vyshinsky and Shurshalov, we can say that Soviet views on the use of *clausula rebus sic stantibus* were extensive and highly permissive, especially regarding the Soviet Union, which was seen as a state with a new social structure and which was therefore allowed to unilaterally terminate previous

[7] Ibid, 149.
[8] Ibid, 149.
[9] Ibid, 150
[10] Ibid, 151.
[11] Ibid, 153.
[12] Ibid, 153–4.

treaties. Even when *clausula rebus sic stantibus* was not explicitly mentioned, its justificatory essence in discussions on treaty law usually came through. Thus in 1954 the Soviet ICJ judge, Fedor Kozhevnikov, opined that the conclusion of the Nazi–Soviet non-aggression pact of 23 August 1939 had been 'striking evidence of the wisdom of Soviet foreign policy in those historical conditions'.[13]

Writing in 1968, the German scholar Theodor Schweisfurth commented that, in recognizing the doctrine of *clausula rebus sic stantibus*, Soviet doctrine was in essence no different from Western international law doctrines.[14] Nevertheless, even if the doctrine of *clausula rebus sic stantibus* had not disappeared from Western doctrines of international law, by the mid-twentieth century[15] it was not so systemic and blatant as in Soviet doctrine and practice of international law. The primacy of *pacta sunt servanda* was still usually emphasized in Western approaches to treaty law because without it an international treaty cannot be more than that described in the perspective of Martens: a snapshot of the balance of power at any given moment of time. It is difficult to find leading Western international lawyers by the 1950s who would have defended *clausula rebus sic stantibus* so extensively as, for example, Shurshalov (or Vyshinsky), or who would have justified Soviet treaty violations with such commitment as Kozhevnikov. Moreover, when we look at Soviet practice of treaties as well, we see that Pashukanis interpreted and Shurshalov—already based on the experience of Soviet policy in the Second World War—reflected Soviet practice quite adequately. This is how Soviet practice regarding treaties had been, especially in the early years of the Second World War (1939–40). In his analysis of the Soviet approach to treaties, Schweisfurth was primarily looking at the Soviet doctrine of international treaties, though without examining the intrinsic links of these views with Soviet treaty practice and foreign policy needs. In discussions about *pacta sunt servanda* and *clausula rebus sic stantibus*, context was everything. Before and after the Second World War, strong support for *clausula rebus sic stantibus* (Pashukanis, Vyshinsky, and Shurshalov) either paved the way for or justified Soviet territorial aggrandizement, forcible return of the territories of the Russian Empire, and beyond.

Soviet international lawyers also justified Soviet termination of the Soviet–Japanese neutrality treaty on 5 April 1945. The treaty had been concluded on 13 April 1941, that is, during the period when the Nazi–Soviet non-aggression

[13] F I Kozhevnikov, 'Nekotorye voprosy teorii i praktiki mezhdunarodnoga dogovora', *SGP* No 2, 1954, 62–76 at 68.

[14] Schweisfurth, *Der international Vertrag . . .*, 1968, 326.

[15] See also, eg, Wilfried Schaumann, 'Clausula rebus sic stantibus', in: Hans-Jürgen Schlochauer (ed) *Wörterbuch des Völkerrechts, Erster Band*, de Gruyter, 1960, 289–91 at 290.

pact was in force. Galina explained that during the Second World War, Japan's cooperation with Nazi Germany became more intense; a new situation emerged compared to the moment when the Soviet pact with Japan was concluded.[16] This was never a convincing explanation because in 1941 cooperation between Nazi Germany and imperial Japan had already been very close; but at the same time, throughout the Second World War, Japan still avoided attacking the Soviet Union militarily. The Soviet entry into the war against Japan in September 1945 was based on decisions made by Soviet, US, and UK leaders at the Yalta conference in February 1945; this also set the termination of the Soviet–Japanese neutrality treaty of 1941.

Nevertheless, at some point during the Cold War, Soviet international law doctrine abandoned the previous extensive *clausula rebus sic stantibus* justification and, if it favoured termination of a treaty, instead referred to violation by the treaty partner instead; this was seen as a legally stronger basis.[17] Talalaev made the point that Martens, Korovin, Shurshalov, and other earlier Russian and Soviet legal scholars had been wrong to emphasize *clausula rebus sic stantibus* so strongly.[18] *Pacta sunt servanda* was increasingly emphasized when the Soviet leadership started to feel that it was necessary—although increasingly difficult—to maintain the geopolitical status quo in Europe rather than expand further territorially. For example, after the Paris treaties were concluded on 23 October 1954 with the Federal Republic of Germany and the latter was militarily integrated into NATO, Soviet international lawyers and commentators started to invoke the principle of *pacta sunt servanda*.[19] The argument was that—with the 1945 agreements of Yalta and Potsdam as well as in bilateral UK–Soviet and Franco–Soviet treaties—Soviet treaty partners in the West had been obliged to decide matters related to the future of Germany *together* with the Soviet Union. Thus, Soviet legal scholars argued that 'militarizing' the Federal Republic of Germany (FRG) was a violation of previous agreements with the Soviet Union and simply integrating the FRG into the West without Soviet approval was a violation of international treaties.[20] Soviet

[16] A Galina, 'Problema neitraliteta v sovremennom mezhdunarodnom prave', *Soviet YBIL* 1958, 200–29 at 213–4.

[17] Kazimierz Grzybowski, *Soviet Public International Law. Doctrines and Diplomatic Practice*, Leyden: A. W. Sijthoff, 1970, 441. See also A N Talalaev, 'Prekrashchenie mezhdunarodnykh dogovorov v istorii i praktike sovetskogo gosudarstva', *Soviet YBIL* 1959, 144–57.

[18] A N Talalaev, *Pravo mezhdunarodnykh dogovorov. Tom 2. Deistvie i primenenie dogovorov. Dogovory s uchastiem mezhdunarodnykh organizatsii*, Zertsalo, 2011 (Originally, Mezhdunarodnye otnoshenia, 1985), 217.

[19] Kommentator, 'Parizhskie soglashenia—ugroza bezopasnosti Evropy', *MZh* No 2, 1954, 15–28 at 26; G I Tunkin, 'Parizhskie soglashenia i mezhdunarodnoe pravo', *SGP* No 2, 1955, 13–22.

[20] V Durdenevsky, S Krylov, 'Narushenie imperialisticheskimi gosudarstvami printsipa sobliudenia mezhdunarodnykh dogovorov', *MZh* No 2, 1955, 64–71.

legal scholars also asserted that the 1945 Yalta and Potsdam territorial and geopolitical agreements had been international treaties, even though some of them were made in oral form and were not subject to ratification.[21]

The tandem of Durdenevsky and Krylov claimed that all major Russian rulers—Vladimir Momomakh, Ivan the Terrible, Peter the Great, Catherine the Great—had strongly supported the principle of *pacta sunt servanda.*[22] At the same time, while Durdenevsky and Krylov invoked the principle of *pacta sunt servanda* (also referring to a *Pravda* newspaper editorial of 16 February 1947 which had spoken about the importance of honouring treaties), they also indicated that this underlying principle did not apply to several types of treaties: unequal treaties, treaties imposed on weaker states, and those which ignored the sovereign rights of one party.[23] Specifically, *pacta sunt servanda* did not apply in November 1918 when Soviet Russia annulled the Brest-Litovsk Peace Treaty with Germany.[24] It was also clear in this narrative that the Soviet Union would decide itself to which treaties *pacta sunt servanda* applied and to which not. Almost simultaneously, the same views on this subject were offered by Fedor Kozhevnikov (who at that time was already a judge at the ICJ).[25] That said, the volte-face in favour of *pacta sunt servanda* in parts of Soviet international law theory was completed only—and notably—with the important condition that the principle did not apply to treaties which the Soviet Union had unilaterally terminated.

However, the coexistence of views supporting extensive *clausula rebus sic stantibus* (Shurshalov) and respect for *pacta sunt servanda* in Soviet international law publications in the 1950s demonstrates a certain level of flexibility and freedom to adopt contradictory positions and theories; of course, so long as one did not contradict Soviet *raison d'état* and the government's specific positions on international issues. The Soviet international law experts' choice as to whether to support strong *pacta sunt servanda* or extensive *clausula rebus sic stantibus* was not centrally coordinated; yet the predominant views each decade corresponded to the country's geopolitical situation and needs. However, the more time passed from Soviet violations of treaties during the Second World War and the more the Soviets started to worry about the sustainability of their hegemony in Central and Eastern Europe, the greater the

[21] For US views, see Herbert W Briggs, 'The Leaders' Agreement of Yalta', *AJIL* Vol 40, 1946, 376–83; Stephen C Y Pan, 'Legal Aspects of the Yalta Agreement', *AJIL* Vol 46, 1952, 40–59.

[22] Durdenevsky, Krylov, 'Narushenie imperialisticheskimi gosudarstvami, 1955, 65.

[23] Ibid, 66.

[24] Ibid, 66.

[25] F I Kozhevnikov, 'Nekotorye voprosy teorii i praktiki mezhdunarodnoga dogovora', *SGP* No 2, 1954, 62–76, at 62.

tendency to advocate for a stronger principle of *pacta sunt servanda* and dismiss the earlier favourite *clausula rebus sic stantibus*, forgetting that Soviet policy was based on a completely flexible approach to treaties when the Soviet Union (re-)gained territories in 1939–45.

During the Cold War, the dominant Western view on Soviet treaty law and practice was not very favourable.[26] Jan F Triska and Robert M Slusser, working at the Hoover Institute of Stanford University, observed that the Soviet theory of treaties was 'absolutely dependent' on state practice.[27] Their conclusion on Soviet treaty law and practice was the following:

> Can the Soviet leaders be trusted to honor the commitments they voluntarily assume in international treaties? Basing one's answer to this question on the past behavior of the Soviet leaders, one would have to say that the chances that they can be trusted are distinctly poor. Furthermore, the more important the subject of a given treaty and the more directly it is related to Soviet long-term objectives, the better are the chances of the Soviet Union's honoring the treaty. [. . .] The Soviet discipline of international law performs a subservient and supporting function in the formulation of Soviet foreign policy, and there is no reason to think that it will soon acquire a more influential position. Soviet international law specialists have repeatedly demonstrated that they are able to provide promptly and efficiently a defense for any action taken by the Soviet leaders in the field of foreign policy, no matter how crude a violation of [. . .] international law. [. . .] For the reasons stated, we believe that there are no factors in Soviet treaty theory, law or policy that constitute a guarantee that the USSR will honor its commitments under a given treaty.[28]

During the United Nations Conference on the Law of Treaties in Vienna (1968–9) the classic question of the proper relationship between the principle of *pacta sunt servanda* and *clausula rebus sic stantibus* was of course one of the central strategic issues to be resolved in the codification.[29] Commenting on this process, Talalaev repeated the official Soviet statement at the Vienna conference and pointed out that, at the conference, some states such as the

[26] See eg Laurence W Beilenson, *The Treaty Trap. A History of the Performance of Political Treaties by the United States and European Nations.* A Foreign Policy Research Institute Book, Public Affairs Press, 1969, 190.

[27] Jan F Triska, Robert M Slusser, *The Law, Theory, and Policy of Soviet Treaties*, Stanford UP, 1962, 27, 36.

[28] Ibid, 397–9.

[29] See Shabtai Rosenne, *A Guide to the Legislative History of the Vienna Convention*, A W Sijthoff, 1970, 286 et seq.

US, Italy, Turkey, and Chile had taken the principle of *pacta sunt servanda* 'to the extreme'.[30] The Soviet delegate in Vienna emphasized that 'historical facts and the reality of international life' were such that, under the auspices of *pacta sunt servanda*, some states demand respect for treaties which were treaties in name only.[31] Throughout history there had been predatory and forced treaties which facilitated colonial conquest and aggression.[32] During the diplomatic conference in Vienna, the Soviet Union supported the principle of *pacta sunt servanda* but the Soviet delegation also emphasized that this principle only applied to 'legal' (*pravomernye*) treaties; the unequal treaties covered by Western imperialist countries were not covered by it.[33] This seemed like a big change from Russia's and the Soviet Union's earlier support for *clausula rebus sic stantibus* but in practice the result was not so different from the Soviet perspective.

However, Soviet practice during the Second World War had been much more strongly based on *clausula rebus sic stantibus* than authorized by the Vienna codification: Article 62 of the Vienna Convention on the Law of Treaties. During the Second World War, the Soviet Union violated several treaties and then claimed they were no longer valid.

Apart from the strategic question how to relate to *pacta sunt servanda*, Soviet diplomacy at the Vienna conference was active on the issue of universal participation in treaties, criticizing that Western states were willing to unduly restrict access to certain (regional) multilateral treaties.[34] In reality, the debate about the 'universality of treaties' was a proxy debate for expanding UN membership to socialist states such as the GDR, the PRC, and socialist Vietnam.[35]

During the late Soviet period in the 1970s and 1980s, it became mainstream in Soviet scholarship of international law to support *pacta sunt servanda* and dismiss *clausula rebus sic stantibus* as a manifestation of bourgeois abuses.[36] Within the Soviet Union, where access to information was tightly controlled, many people were not even aware of the treaty-related circumstances by which

[30] A N Talalaev, 'Nekotorye voprosy teorii mezhdunarodnogo dogovora na venskoy konferentsii OON', *Soviet YBIL* 1970, 112–27.
[31] Ibid, 121.
[32] Ibid.
[33] A N Talalaev, *Venskaya konventsia o prave mezhdunarodnykh dogovorov. Kommentarii*, Iuridischekaya literatura, 1997, 174; A N Talalaev, *Pravo mezhdunarodnykh dogovorov. Tom 1. Obshchie voprosy*, Zertsalo, 2011 (Originally, Mezhdunarodnye otnoshenia, 1980), 63–7.
[34] I I Lukashuk, 'Nekotorye voprosy kodifikatsii i progressivnogo razvitia prava mezhdunarodnykh dogovorov', *Soviet YBIL* 1966/7, 51–71 at 64–5.
[35] A N Talalaev, *Pravo mezhdunarodnykh dogovorov. Tom 1. Obshie voprosy*, Zertsalo, 2011 (Original: Mezhdunarodnye otnoshenia, 1980), 52.
[36] See, eg, O I Tiunov, 'Printsip dobrosovestnogo sobliudenia mezhdunarodnykh obiazatel'stv i doktrina *rebus sic stantibus*', *Soviet YBIL* 1978, 101–12 at 106.

the Soviet Union expanded its territory during the Second World War, or how Soviet international lawyers such as Pashukanis anticipated treaty violations. This new Soviet literature favouring *pacta sunt servanda* often neglected the fact that leading imperial Russian and Soviet legal scholars had in the past supported extensive use of *clausula rebus sic stantibus* when the needs of the Russian or Soviet state required a major revision of the status quo, and that they were themselves writing in a state which was already enjoying a new, post-Second World War territorial status quo.

Great Powers and Small States

A further imperially inspired doctrine which the Soviet Union used, especially during the early stages of the Cold War era, was to emphasize that it was a 'great power' (*velikaya derzhava*) in the context of international law and the United Nations, as a founding nation of the UN and permanent member of the UN Security Council.[37] The Korean War (1950–3) also brought to light the veto power of permanent members due to the controversial Security Council voting in which a resolution on Korea was adopted without Soviet participation (as the Soviet delegation boycotted the Council's meeting over the question which government was entitled to represent China). Soviet scholarly *opinio juris* was unanimous: the 'unanimity of the great powers' was a foundational constitutional principle at the UN and thus sacrosanct.[38] This view was consistently defended in the decades that followed beyond the Korean War.[39] The UN Charter acknowledged that the great powers played a 'special role'.[40] Ushakov used Marxist dialectics to explain the importance of the principle of unanimity of great powers: while not contradicting the principle of sovereign equality at the UN, the principle of unanimity of great powers was one of the most important means of implementing and strengthening the principle of

[37] See Serge Krylov, 'Les notions principales du droit des gens' (La doctrine soviétique du droit international)', *RCADI* Vol 70, Martinus Nijhoff, 1947, 173.

[38] S Borisov, 'Neudavshaiasya ataka protiv printsipa edinoglasia velikikh derzhav v Sovete Bezopasnosti', *SGP* No 6, 1950, 51–8; S V Molodtsov, 'Pravilo edinoglasia postoyannykh chlenov Soveta Bezopasnosti—nezyblemaya osnova OON', *SGP* No 7, 1953, 44–57.

[39] F I Kozhevnikov, A P Movchan, 'Ustav OON—voplyushenie obshepriznannykh printsipov mezhdunarodnoga prava', *SGP* 1955, No 6, 3–7 at 4; S Borisov, 'Protiv proektov peresmotra Ustava OON', *SGP* 1955, No 6, 92–8 at 98; G I Morozov, 'O novykh planakh revizii Ustava OON', *SGP* No 5, 1959, 116–24 at 122; N A Ushakov, 'O narushenii protsedury golosovania v Sovete Bezopasnosti OON', *SGP* No 1, 1960, 89–97 at 89, 97.

[40] N A Ushakov, 'K voprosu o prave "veto" v organizatsii ob'edenennykh natsii', *Soviet YBIL* 1959, 212–28 at 213.

sovereign equality.[41] During the later stages of the Cold War, the phrase 'unity of the great powers' faded away in Soviet doctrine to an extent, but principled defence of the veto power of permanent members of the UN Security Council remained.[42]

In the history of international law, the idea that the 'great powers' played a special role had often been present but it was understood as a political reality or principle, not a legal one. However, after the Second World War, Soviet international lawyers—including Grigory Tunkin—started to emphasize that this was now anchored in international law, and smaller states had to accept key agreements between great powers as well.[43]

However, the Soviet discourse on 'great powers' was more widespread and systemic than just in the context of the UN; it was more like a lens through which to see the international community. Thus, Soviet authors would highlight that the USSR was also a 'great sea power'[44] and point out that the most challenging disputes were those between great powers.[45] Moreover, Soviet legal scholars would also mean it as a sincere recognition of other nations considered friendly, such as in statements that China or India are 'great powers'.[46] But it could also mean a warning and criticism of rivals, for example—when relations between the USSR and the PRC had already turned sour—when saying that the PRC had turned itself into a 'mighty militarist great power'.[47]

The great power doctrine had many implications, including in the context of the law of the sea. For example, Soviet claims against the backdrop of traditional understandings of internal waters were extensive. These claims also constituted vivid examples of state continuity between the Russian Empire of the tsars and the Soviet Union. To illustrate, when the Soviet Union made extensive claims, the argument was usually based on tsarist-era explorations, adoption, or legal acts. For example, the question of rights over the Arctic seas and islands became highly topical in the Soviet Union as early as the 1920s.[48] At the end of the Stalin era, Vyshnepolsky argued that all seas in the Russian Arctic sector—the Kara, Laptev, East Siberian, and Chukchi Seas (the latter

41 Ibid, at 220.

42 V N Fedorov, 'Kritika nekotorykh planov peresmotra Ustava OON', *SGP* No 4, 1973, 85–91 at 88.

43 See Kazimierz Grzybowski, *Soviet Public International Law. Doctrines and Diplomatic Practice*, Leyden: A W Sijthoff, 1970, 81.

44 S Vyshnepolsky, 'Svoboda morei v epokhu imperializma', *SGP* No 1, 1949, 13–25 at 13.

45 O V Bogdanov, 'Peregovory—osnovnoe sredstvo mirnogo uregulirovania mezhdunarodnykh raznoglasii', *SGP* No 7, 1957, 71–80 at 79.

46 I Kurdov, 'Velikaya derzhava kitaiskogo naroda', *MZh* 1954, No 2, 81–99; V Avarin, 'India—velikaya derzhava', *MZh* No 2, 1956, 16–24.

47 L M Gudoshnikov, 'O politicheskom rezhime v Kitae', *SGP* No 3, 1982, 111–18 at 118.

48 See, eg, W L Lakhtine, *Prava na severnye poliarnye prostranstva* (Rights over the Arctic Regions), Izdanie litizdata Narodnoga Komissariata po Inostrannym Delam, 1928.

within the limits of the Soviet polar sector)—had to be recognized as Soviet internal waters and therefore closed seas and areas of Soviet sovereignty.[49] His argument was that Tsar Ivan Grozny had already regarded the Arctic seas as 'our land'[50] and that Russian legal acts had been issued such an *ukaz* of Tsar Boris Godunov in 1619 regarding the Kara Sea.[51] Another reason why, according to Vyshnepolsky, sovereignty over the Arctic seas had to belong to the Soviet Union was that they were seas of a special kind, *sui generis*.[52] Moreover, the Northeast Passage was never an international waterway, either juridically or de facto.[53] These claims were based on the sectoral theory according to which the Soviet Union would claim unusually extensive sovereignty in the Arctic seas, as an exception to the generally accepted treaty or customary rules of the law of the sea.

Another example concerned the Peter the Great Gulf, the largest gulf in the Sea of Japan, near Vladivostok. On 21 July 1957, the Soviet Union declared that for historical reasons Peter the Great Gulf constituted Soviet internal waters.[54] The US, Great Britain, and Japan protested this claim and designation. The argumentation of Soviet international lawyers focused inter alia on a Russian legal act of 1901, 'Rules for the production of marine fisheries in the territorial waters of the Amur Governorate General'.[55] The Soviet legal scholar Romanov argued that this was a case of state succession, in that the Soviet Union simply inherited tsarist Russia's rights in the Peter the Great Gulf.[56] In our own time, too, in the twenty-first century, Russian international lawyers—referring to state practice—claim that Peter the Great Gulf is Russian historical waters.[57]

The notion of great powers also implied a sense of great power rivalry, which always had a spatial dimension. As the Soviet Union established its hegemony over Central and Eastern Europe after the Second World War, it promoted the idea that the rules of navigation on the Danube River were in need of revision by the riparian states.[58] The result was a diplomatic conference in Belgrade which resulted in the signature of the Convention regarding the

[49] S A Vyshnepolsky, 'K probleme pravovoga rezhima Arkticheskoi oblasti', *SGP* No 7, 1952, 36–45 at 45.
[50] Ibid, 38.
[51] Ibid, 39.
[52] Ibid, 40.
[53] Ibid, 43.
[54] A Nikolaev, 'O zalive Petra Velikogo', *MZh* No 2, 1958, 50–7 at 50.
[55] Ibid, 53; V A Romanov, 'Zaliv Petra Velikogo—vnutrennie vody Sovetskogo Soyuza', *SGP* No 5, 1958, 47–55 at 48.
[56] Romanov, 'Zaliv Petra Velikogo', 1958, 50.
[57] Vyacheslav A Batyr, *Mezhdunarodnoe territorial'noe pravo*, Mezhdunarodnye otnoshenia, 2021, 77.
[58] V N Durdenevsky, 'Dogovornyi rezhim Dunaya', *SGP* 1946, No 2, 68–73 at 73.

regime of Navigation on the Danube on 18 August 1948. This convention replaced the Convention instituting the Definitive Statute of the Danube which was signed at Paris on 23 July 1921. The main difference was that powers such as France, the UK, Belgium, Italy, and Greece—who had been co-signatories of the 1921 Convention and had seats at the table on management of Danube River matters—were now excluded. In preparation for the Belgrade conference, France, the UK, and the US raised the argument of acquired rights but, for example, the foreign minister of socialist Hungary, Erik Molnár (1894–1966), rejected these claims, arguing that so-called acquired rights based on previous conventions were enjoyed by the great powers at the expense of small riparian states, with the purpose of bringing the Danube under control of imperialist policies and influences.[59] The Soviet foreign minister, Andrey Vyshinsky, also attacked the earlier 1921 Convention by pointing out that Soviet Russia had not been a signatory state, even though the Russian Empire used to have a say in regulation of Danube issues in the treaties of 1856 and 1883.[60] Thus, we can once again see here that the state continuity claim and the attack on British and French 'acquired rights' in a way meant restoration of Russia's imperial rights of access and participation, while elbowing out other, Western 'great powers'. In principle, free navigation was ensured in both the 1921 and 1948 conventions, but in terms of access to and management of the river there were also changes in terms of who was in charge. Symbolically it also mattered that the he first language of the original of the 1948 Convention was Russian.

This is also how various great power doctrines related to each other: changes in the balance of power in favour of the Soviet Union by the end of the Second World War had to be reflected in treaties. However, Soviet attempts did not always successfully invoke *clausula rebus sic stantibus* in geopolitically sensitive territorial issues. For example, towards the end of the Second World War, the Soviet Union failed in its proposals to Norway to revise the 1920 Spitzbergen (Svalbard) treaty, while Turkey did not agree to revise the 1936 Montreux Convention regulating navigation in the Turkish straits: the Bosporus and the Dardanelles.[61] The new balance of power also had its limits and sometimes resistance to Soviet pressure proved successful.

[59] A Ya Vyshinsky, 'Dunaiskaya konferentsia i nekotorye voprosy mezhdunarodnoga prava', *SGP* 1948, No 11, 16–25 at 17.

[60] Pierre Hentgès, 'Dunaiskaya konferentsia kak konets 'priobretennym pravam', *SGP* No 2, 1949, 47–52 at 51 (Originally published in *Democratie nouvelle* 1948 No 9, 480–483).

[61] Erlend M Leonhardsen, 'Pride and Perseverance: Strategic Use of Rebus Sic Stantibus in Russian Foreign Policy 1870–1950', 63 *German YBIL* 2020, 581–620 at 604–15.

The opposite of the great powers in Soviet discussions about international law were 'smaller states'. These were not defined strictly but the concept was a rather broad one, apparently encompassing most states which were not great powers. In Soviet narratives of international law, 'small and weak states' or 'peoples' (*malye i slabye gosudarstva; narody*) needed protection and deserved full rights in the international community.[62] They were in constant danger of being abused by large capitalist states such as the US which would not treat them equally.[63] At the same time, the Soviet Union, led by Soviet Russia, had gathered 'small and weak' peoples under its wing. Of course, no contradiction was seen in the fact that, at the same time, the Soviet Union was also promoting special rights and prerogatives for the 'great powers'. However, a certain warning to small states could be found in the Soviet literature on international law: they should consider neutrality instead of joining military blocs adversarial to the communist countries led by the Soviet Union.[64] For example, Durdenevsky and Osnitskaya made the point that, for small states in Europe and elsewhere, neutrality was a way of ensuring their independence.[65] Soviet international law scholarship was generally quite preoccupied with the institution of neutrality in international law and related historical precedents, not only in Europe but also, for example, in Afghanistan, as the Soviet Union preferred states that were not part of the Soviet-led alliance to stay at least neutral.[66] However, when citing the neutrality of Switzerland as a positive example, one could ask whether neutrality of this kind would also have been stable—in the immediate geographical neighbourhood of the Russian Empire and the Soviet Union—for states which had in the past seceded from Russia or on whose territory wars involving Russia were carried out (Although general Suvorov also had a Swiss campaign in 1799.)

[62] See, eg, G. F. Kalinkin, 'Malye gosudarstva—polnopravnye sub'ekty mezhdunarodnoga prava', *SGP* No 2, 1973, 75–80; Kamo Adibekovich Manukyan, *Printsip ravnopravia gosudarstv v mezhdunarodnom prave*, Izdatel'stvo erevanskogo universiteta, 1975.

[63] See, eg, E A Korovin, 'Proletarskii internatsionalizm i mezhdunarodnoe pravo', *Soviet YBIL* 1958, Moscow, 1959, 50–73 at 56; G Tunkin, 'XXVI s'ezd KPSS i dal'neishee razvitie sovetskoi nauki mezhdunarodnoga prava', *Soviet YBIL* 1981, 12–25 at 16; Yuri G Barsegov, *Territoria v mezhdunarodnom prave*, Gosudarstvennoe izdatelstvo yuridicheskoi literatury, 1958, 6.

[64] N Pavlovsky, 'Malye strany i NATO', *MZh* No 12, 1961, 88–92; A Stepanov, 'Malye strany pered alternativoi', *MZh* No 4, 1965, 49–56.

[65] V N Durdenevsky, G A Osnitskaya, 'Neitralitet i atomnoe oruzhie', *SGP* No 2, 1960, 101–5 at 102.

[66] See, eg, K A Baginyan, 'Postoyannyi neitralitet, pravo na samooboronu i sistema regionalizma v svete Ustava OON', *SGP* 1956, No 6, 102–9; V N Durdenevsky, 'Neitralitet v sisteme kollektivnoi bezopasnosti', *SGP* 1957, No 8, 81–91; S Malolin, 'O politike neitraliteta v Shvetsii', *MZh* No 9, 1955, 84–91; O Afanasyeva, 'K istorii shveitsarskogo neitraliteta', *MZh* No 1, 1956, 78–84; D Mel'nikov, 'Problema neitraliteta i sovremennoe mezhdunarodnoe polozhenie', *MZh* No 2, 1956, 72–80; E Korovin, 'Problema neitraliteta na sovremennom etape', *MZh* No 3, 1958, 48–54; V Volgin, '150 let shveitsarskogo neitraliteta', *MZh* No 11, 1965, 70–3; E L Borodulin, 'K voprosu o statuse postoyannogo neitraliteta', *Soviet YBIL* 1966/7, 195–202.

Peaceful Coexistence, Balance of Power, and *Jus Ad Bellum* Issues

One of the most popular Soviet slogans during the Cold War in the context of international law was 'peaceful coexistence'.[67] This was also an example of successful migration of ideas, because India and China included 'peaceful co-existence' in the preamble to their April 1954 bilateral treaty, as one of the five principles (*Panch Shila*),[68] and a year later it was included in the outcome of the Bandung conference. However, the exact contours and implications of this principle were not always clear. In the ways it was expressed in the countless interaction points of international law and politics, the Soviet concept of peaceful coexistence had different political connotations in different contexts and times.[69] In our context of investigating the imperial and great power background of Soviet interpretations of international law, some Western criticisms of this principle are also of interest. Namely, Boris Meissner (1915–2003), a West German expert on Soviet Union and international law, highlighted the connection between peaceful coexistence and *Realpolitik*, making the point that substantively it was surprisingly like the age-old European legal–political principle of the balance of power (*iustum potentiae aequilibrium*).[70] The rationale for this view was also that peaceful coexistence assumed acceptance of the territorial status quo, which was seen as acceptance of Soviet hegemony in Eastern and Central Europe.[71]

Interwar Soviet legal scholars such as Evgeny Pashukanis had asserted that balance of power lay behind treaties and generally backed observance of international law.[72] However, after the Second World War, the balance of power as a historical concept was already associated with the 'evil' power politics of imperialist states, which Soviet legal scholars Natalya Zakharova and

[67] See Georgi Zadorozhny, *Peaceful Coexistence. Contemporary International Law of Peaceful Coexistence*, Progress Publishers, 1968 and in other socialist countries Miroslav Potočny, Stanislav Myslil, *Legal Principles of Peaceful Co-Existence*, Translated from Czech by Dr Zdeněk Červenka, Státni pedagogické nakladatelství, 1968. For recent discussion of this principle, see also Kaj Hobér, *The Perestroika Era and International Law*, Edward Elgar Publishing, 2024, 42 et seq.

[68] Henn-Jüri Uibopuu, *Die sowjetische Doktrin der friedlichen Koexistenz als Völkerrechtsproblem*, Verlag Notring, 1971, 237.

[69] Earlier discussions of the principle include Edward McWhinney, '"Peaceful Coexistence" and Soviet–Western International Law', *AJIL* 1962 Vol 56, 951–70 at 970; Edward McWhinney, *'Peaceful Coexistence' and Soviet-Western International Law*, A W Sijthoff, 1964; Bernard Dutoit, *Coexistence et droit international a la lumière de la doctrine soviétique*, A. Pedone, 1966.

[70] Boris Meissner, 'Das Wesen und der Geltungsbereich des Völkerrechts', in: Reinhart Maurach, Boris Meissner (Hg) *Völkerrecht un Ost und West*, Stuttgart: W Kohlhammer Verlag, 1967, 9–38 at 24.

[71] Cf E V Korovin, 'Ustav OON i mirnoe sosuschestvovanie', *Soviet YBIL* 1960, 28–57 at 42.

[72] E Pashukanis, 'Mezhdunarodnoe pravo', from: Entsiklopedia gosudarstva i prava, Moscow: Izdatel'stvo kommunisticheskoi akademii,1926, vol 2, 858–74, republished in: Piers Beirne, Robert Sharlet (eds) *Pashukanis: Selected Writings on Marxism and Law*, Translated by Peter B Maggs, Academic Press, 1980, 168–82 at 179.

Yuri Barsegov assumed that the Soviet Union had nothing to do with.[73] They maintained that, after the Second World War, the balance of power was already directed against the Soviet Union and that several Western authors had postulated that such a balance could be achieved in the alliance and cooperation of small states against a great power such as the Soviet Union.[74] Zakharova also argued that capitalist states favoured balance of power arrangements because Western security organizations such as NATO were of a closed nature; socialist states were not allowed to join them.[75]

Even more linked to the old balance of power than the principle of peaceful coexistence—the exact normative meaning of which remained somewhat nebulous—was a principle which the Soviet Union and Soviet legal scholars started to raise from the 1970s onwards, namely the principle of 'equal security' (*odinakovaya bezopasnost'*; *ravnaya bezopasnost'*).[76] According to Malinin, it meant that no party was entitled to receive one-sided advantages in terms of ensuring its security; it meant, literally, preservation of parity or balance between powers.[77] During the late 1970s, other Soviet legal scholars also emphasized the importance of this parity or balance in international law.[78] Titov, discussing the idea of creating a nuclear-free zone in Northern Europe, potentially including parts of Soviet territory, maintained that any implementation of such an idea should take 'balance of power' as its basis.[79] So in practice, although on the surface Soviet discourse on international law sounded solidly idealist and revolutionary, the age-old realist balance-of-power thinking never disappeared from among its foundational ideas—even when the concept of balance of power appeared under the guise of different labels.

A key element in ensuring the balance of power was regulation of the use of military force (*jus ad bellum*). During the interwar period, Soviet international lawyers had promoted the right of intervention by the USSR as a state of and for the proletariat, whereas after the Second World War—as a consequence of which the USSR could satisfy its territorial and hegemonic appetite—the Soviet approach to *jus ad bellum* became much more restrictive. Soviet

[73] N V Zakharova, I Yu Barsegov, 'O tak nazyvaemoi teorii 'ravnovesia sil', *Soviet YBIL* 1959, 272–82.
[74] Ibid, 278.
[75] N V Zakharova, 'O poniatii i suschnosti kollektivnoi bezopasnosti', *SGP* No 8, 1958, 47–54 at 53.
[76] S A Malinin, 'Aktual'nye problemy mezhdunarodnoi bezopasnosti v svete reshenii XXVI syezda KPSS', *Soviet YBIL* 1981, 26–41 at 30; L A Ivanashchenko, 'Printsip ravnoi bezopasnosti storon i ego znachenie dlia sovremennogo mezhdunarodnoga prava', *Soviet YBIL* 1976, 57–68.
[77] Malinin, ibid, 30.
[78] S A Malinin, 'Aktual'nye problemy mezhdunarodnoy bezopasnosti v svete reshenii XXVI syezda KPSS', *Soviet YBIL* 1981, 26–41 at 30.
[79] V G Titov, 'K voprosu sozdania beziadernoi zony na severe Evropy', *Soviet YBIL* 1981, 81–3 at 89–91.

international lawyers were against expanding the right to self-defence and, as a rule, favoured the narrowest interpretation of when military force could be used (self-defence only if an armed attack occurred or with UN Security Council authorization).[80] However, wars of national liberation against imperialist states were considered both legal and legitimate.[81]

As we will see in the next section, according to the Soviet approach, these rules and considerations did not apply to relations between the Soviet Union and other socialist countries. The Soviets also interpreted the right to carry out military intervention by invitation[82] extensively, especially justifying Soviet military intervention in Afghanistan after 1979. Although the UNGA condemned the Soviet invasion of Afghanistan, in Soviet legal narratives the US and other Western states which supported the Afghan mujahedeen fighters were acting illegally under international law.[83]

During the 1970s, a special dimension of non-use of force was Soviet interest in promoting the aspect of the inviolability of borders;[84] this became a key component of the Helsinki Accords (1975) and thus part of international law, at least within Europe.[85] As early as during the 1960s, Secretary-General Nikita Khruschev had proposed concluding a treaty which would have highlighted the illegality of the use of force for changing state borders.[86] At the 25th Soviet Communist Party Congress in 1976, the Soviet Union made a proposal to conclude a new universal treaty on the non-use of force, referring to the existence of nuclear weapons in the world as a new circumstance compared to the time of adoption of the UN Charter in 1945.[87]

[80] E I Skakunov, 'Nekotorye aspekty doktrinal'nogo tolkovania instituta samooborony', *Soviet YBIL* 1971, 259–65 at 259; V I Menzhinsky, 'Ustav OON i printsip neprimenenia sily', *Soviet YBIL* 1973, 82–99 at 92–3; V T Bulanenkov, Yu D Il'in, 'K razrabotke mezhdunarodno-pravovoga opredelenia agressii', *SGP* No 2, 1974, 78–83.

[81] G V Sharmazanashvili, 'Kolonial'naya voina—gruboe narushenie mezhdunarodnoga prava', *SGP* 1957, No 10, 55–61 at 60.

[82] On this, see generally Georg Nolte, *Eingreifen auf Einladung. Zur völkerrechtlichen Zulässigkeit des Einsatzes fremder Truppen im internen Konflikt auf Einladung der Regierung*, Springer, 1999.

[83] R A Tuzmukhamedov, 'Afghanskaya revoliutsia i mezhdunarodnoe pravo', *SGP* No 4, 1984, 85–92 at 85–6.

[84] L I Volova, 'Mezhdunarodno-pravovoi printsip territorialnoi neprikosnovennosti i nerushimost' granits evropeiskih gosudarstv', *Soviet YBIL* 1974, 126–39.

[85] I P Blishchenko, 'Zakliuchitel'nyi akt Soveshania po bezopasnosti i sotrudnichestvu v Evrope – dal'neishee razvitie mezhdunarodnoga prava', *SGP* No 12, 1976, 82–90 at 84–5; Ya A Grigelionis, 'Printsip nerushimosti granits v mezhdunarodnom prave', *Soviet YBIL* 1981, 55–70 at 63, 68; V I Menzhinsky, 'Printsipy mira, bezopasnosti i sotrudnichestva (K 10-i godovshine Khelsinkskoga soveshania), *SGP* No 8, 1985, 89–95 at 92.

[86] S Molodtsov, 'Granitsy i pravo', *MZh* No 4, 1964, 9–17 at 9; D Mel'nikov, 'Nezyblemost' evropeiskikh granits', *MZh* No 9, 1966, 10–18.

[87] V I Menzhinsky, 'XXV siezd KPSS i printsip neprimenenia sily v mezhdunarodnykh otnosheniakh', *SGP* No 2, 1977, 106–14 at 111; N N Ulyanova, 'Vazhnaya mera povyshenia neprimenenia sily (k voprosu o zakliuchenii Vsemirnogo dogovora o neprimenenii sily', *Soviet YBIL* 1981, 41–55 at 45.

Peaceful coexistence and balance of power were also directly related to nuclear weapons in the sense of who had them and who did not. After the Soviet Union managed to acquire nuclear weapons in 1949, it continued to promote disarmament and a ban on nuclear tests, and even nuclear weapons as such.[88] According to Soviet diplomatic proposals, the use of nuclear weapons had to be banned altogether; or the Soviet Union and the Warsaw Pact countries—though the Soviet Union was the only nuclear state in the group—pledged not to be the first to use nuclear weapons in a military conflict.[89] However, the Soviet Union's rivals also regarded these proposals against the backdrop of Soviet proposals in the 1930s for complete disarmament—in other words, acknowledging the propagandistic element to them.

On 14 December 1979 the UNGA adopted—on a Soviet initiative—a resolution entitled 'Inadmissibility of the policy of hegemonism in international relations' in which states (at page 5) inter alia resolutely condemned 'imperialism, colonialism and neo-colonialism'. At the same time, the document also reflected Sino-Soviet rivalries and the so-called Sino-Soviet split during the Cold War, from 1960 onwards. Initially, relations between the PRC and the USSR had been filled with mutual admiration and praise, for example when the Treaty of Friendship was concluded between Mao and Stalin in 1950.[90] However, as time went on, the debate about the history of the mutual border—but especially on the nuclear status of the PRC and the leadership claims of the Soviet Union in the socialist bloc—for a while turned the two biggest socialist countries into one another's biggest critics. The Soviet Union and the People's Republic of China started to accuse each other of hegemonism.[91] The PRC constitution of 1975 even declared the aim of fighting against imperialism and 'social-imperialism', which meant the Soviet Union.[92] In contrast, Soviet legal

[88] Editorial, 'Postavit' yadernoe oruzhie vne zakona', *MZh* No 5, 1957, 3–7; V Kirillov, 'Narody zhdut soglashenia o prekrashenii iadernykh ispytanii', *MZh* No 12, 1959, 36–41; O V Bogdanov, 'Sovetskii plan vseobchego razoruzhenia i mezhdunarodnoe pravo', *SGP*, No 2, 1960, 46–56; M Lvov, 'Atomnuyu bombu—vne zakona!', *MZh* No 1, 1965, 12–21.

[89] O V Bogdanov, 'Otkaz ot primenenia iadernogo oruzhia—trebovanie vremeni', *SGP* No 7, 1977, 132–8 at 133; O V Bogdanov, 'Otkaz SSSR ot primenenia pervym iadernogo oruzhia v mezhdunarodnom prave', *SGP* No 4, 1983, 89–96; Anonymous, 'Mezhdunarodno-pravovye problemy polnoga zapreshchenia ispytanii iadernogo oruzhia', *SGP* No 11, 1986, 80–5.

[90] A Astrakhansky, 'Nerushimaya druzhba velikikh narodov', *MZh* 1955 No 2, 47–55; N Shmigol', 'Dogovor velikoi druzhby', *MZh* No 2, 1959, 82–5.

[91] On the Soviet side, see, eg, G Apalin, 'Maoizm—rezerv imperialisticheskoi reaktsii', *MZh* No 7, 1969, 27–36; A B Kozyrev, 'Politika gegemonizma—ugroza miru i mezhdunarodnomu pravoporiadku', *SGP* No 4, 1982, 85–93 at 86, 92.

[92] L M Gudoshnikov, 'Antinarodnaya konstitutsionnaya deklaratsia maoistov', *SGP* No 2, 1976, 95–102 at 100. The next PRC constitution (adopted on 5 March 1978) was still characterized by Gudoshnikov as being informed by the spirit of Chinese 'chauvinism and hegemonism': see L M Gudoshnikov, 'Tretia konstitutsia KNR', *SGP* No 1, 1979, 34–9 at 39.

scholars argued that PRC policies at the time in the UN 'denied international law' and in particular worked against Soviet proposals for disarmament.[93] Mirroring what the Chinese communists stated and noticed about the Soviet Union, Soviet legal scholars wrote that the PRC was discriminating against non-ethnic Chinese peoples in the PRC.[94] The Soviet Union (and Soviet legal scholars) also promoted the idea of collective security in Asia, which the PRC criticized as directed primarily against it,[95] and criticized states such as Japan and the US for their policies of rapprochement with the PRC.[96]

The Soviet conflict with the PRC also spoiled the prospects for success of socialist international law which would have encompassed all socialist states during the Cold War. It fundamentally challenged the Marxist–Leninist proposition that relations between socialist countries were on a qualitatively different level. Moreover, Soviet international law theoreticians did not have a good answer to this conflict-ridden reality, which was there for everyone to see. When Soviet international lawyers published a six-volume showcase treatise on international law with its last volume dedicated specifically to socialist international law, all they could do with respect to the PRC was to criticize Maoist policies.[97] Nevertheless, as we will see next, the Soviet Union demonstrated the real-life consequences of socialist international law—particularly decisively in Central Europe.

Socialist International Law

A special Soviet hegemonic doctrine was 'socialist international law'.[98] While in principle Soviet legal scholars wanted it to be applied throughout the socialist or socialist-leaning world—for example, also in Mongolia and Cuba—[99]its

[93] G Apalin, F Liev, 'Pekin: kurs na podryv mezhdunarodnoga pravoporyadka', *SGP* No 12, 1977, 76–84 at 76.

[94] L M Gudoshnikov, 'Velikoderzhavnyi shovimizm rukovodstva KNR v voprosakh natsional'no-gosudarstvennogo stroitel'stva', *SGP* No 9, 1973, 92–100 at 100.

[95] R A Tuzmukhamedov, 'Kollektivnaya bezopasnost' v Azii i mezhdunarodnoe pravo', *SGP* No 4, 1974, 99–105 at 101.

[96] M V Demchenko, 'Dogovor, popustitelstvuyushi agressoru', *SGP* No 7, 1979, 121–8 at 128; A Kemov, 'Sodeistvie vooruzheniu Kitaya - protivopravno', *SGP* No 2, 1980, 57–65 at 60–1.

[97] F I Kozhevnikov, V M Koretski, D B Levin, G I Tunkin, N A Ushakov, V M Chikvadze, V M Shurshalov (eds), *Kurs mezhdunarodnoga prava v shesti tomakh. Tom VI. Mezhdunarodnoe pravo v otnosheniakh mezhdu sotsialisticheskimi gosudarstvami*, Nauka, 1973, 12–14, 33, 64, 69–70, 235.

[98] See generally V M Shurshalov (ed), *Mezhdunarodno-pravovye formy sotrudnichestva sotsialisticheskikh gosudarstv*, Izdatel'stvo Akademii nauk SSSR, 1962 and G M Velyaminov, *Sotsialisticheskaya integratsia i mezhdunarodnoe pravo*, Mezhdunarodnye otnoshenia, 1982.

[99] M I Lazarev, 'Revoliutsennaya Kuba i mezhdunarodnoe pravo', *SGP* No 7, 1966, 70–7 at 76.

main area of application was Central and Eastern Europe. Among its most visible effects was that it was used to justify Soviet military interventions in Hungary (1956) and Czechoslovakia (1968). In 1956, this theory was based on interpretations of the Soviet government's declaration of 30 October 1956 which justified the intervention in Hungary on the basis of 'proletarian internationalism'.[100] The UNGA and Western organizations also became involved and Soviet intervention against Hungary was condemned as a violation of international law.[101] However, at least in their domestic discourse, leading Soviet international lawyers presented a narrative that it had been imperialist states which had violated international law in Hungary, by supporting the 'counterrevolutionary rebellion'.[102]

The first *Soviet Yearbook of International Law* was published just after the Soviet intervention in Hungary, and the main point of Evgeny Korovin's article on 'Proletarian Internationalism and International Law' was to justify that intervention.[103] According to Korovin, a new type of international relations had emerged among the socialist states,[104] where—so went Korovin's narrative—no antagonistic controversies arose, nor was there any place for fighting or animosity:[105] a somewhat surprising assertion after Soviet military suppression of the Hungarian uprising. Korovin continued that the main point of socialist international law was that, among socialist states, established concepts of international law—sovereignty, equality, non-intervention, and the like—acquired a new content, a new quality. For example, concerning the principle of equality of states, this meant that the equality of socialist states radically differed from the 'equality' between imperialist and smaller states, postulated Korovin.[106] An example of the equality between socialist nations was the Soviet–Hungarian declaration of 28 March 1957—adopted after Soviet military suppression of the revolution—which, in the spirit of socialist internationalism, was concerned with the 'welfare of workers in both countries'.[107] Korovin maintained:

[100] N P Farbegov, 'O edinstve sotsialisticheskikh gosudarstv i svoeobrazii ikh politicheskikh form', *SGP* No 6, 1957, 40–51 at 50–1.

[101] See *Hungarian Situation and the Rule of Law*, International Commission of Legal Scholars, 1957, 9–13; KA Baginyan, 'Printsip nevmeshatel'stva i Ustav OON', No 6, *SGP* 1957, 62–70 at 68.

[102] F I Kozhevnikov (ed) *Mezhdunarodnoe pravo*, Moscow: Gosudarstvennoe izdatel'stvo yuridicheskoi literatury, 1957, 16.

[103] E A Korovin, 'Protelarskii internatsionalizm i mezhdunarodnoe pravo', *Soviet YBIL* 1958, 50–73.

[104] Ibid, 53.

[105] Ibid, 55.

[106] Ibid, 56.

[107] Ibid, 56.

> Exactly because of this goal and in the interests of the socialist camp as a whole, the Soviet Union offered and offers to Hungary comprehensive economic and other help so that the Hungarian people could as quickly as possible overcome the consequences of the counterrevolutionary mutiny and pursue the path of further material and cultural advancement.[108]

Moreover, just as the principle of equality of states meant something else for socialist states, the same was the case with sovereignty generally. For example, the Soviet–Albanian declaration of 17 April 1957 emphasized that 'only in the commonwealth of socialist states' did Albania 'for the first time in its history' acquire and enjoy full national sovereignty. Moreover, this statement about the centrality of exercising sovereignty together, in a commonwealth, was true for all socialist states.[109] In the words of Korovin, again referring to dialectics:

> What is genuinely beneficial for a socialist state is always beneficial also to the whole socialist camp. What is beneficial to the whole socialist camp is unconditionally beneficial to every country which forms a part of it.[110]

For Korovin, the final conclusion of the Hungarian 'mutiny' was that the attempt by the 'renegade' Hungarian leader Imre Nagy (1896–1958) to turn Hungary away from the Warsaw Pact—which was founded in 1955—and declare Hungary neutral was futile: 'not a single socialist state can expect its security to be ensured by proclaiming its neutrality.'[111]

Sebastian Gehrig has highlighted Korovin's writings on socialist international law and argues that Korovin concentrated on technocratic and economic cooperation as examples of an emerging socialist international legal system.[112] Gehrig thus sees strong similarities between the Soviet doctrine of socialist international law and Western functionalist scholars on regional integration. However, to the extent that Korovin's writings also justified Soviet military intervention in the commonwealth of socialist states, the essence of socialist international law was not merely technocratic but was also geopolitical: based on the resolution to use force within the socialist commonwealth, if necessary.

108 Ibid, 56.
109 Ibid, 58.
110 Ibid, 58–9.
111 Ibid, 65.
112 Sebastian Gehrig, 'A Socialist Legal Universalism? Cold War Struggles over International Law', in: Raluca Grosescu, Ned Richardson-Little (eds) *Socialism and International Law. The Cold War and Its Legacies*, OUP, 2025, 17–43 at 28.

Another article reacting to the Hungarian events of 1956 was by Grigory Tunkin, who argued that when relations between socialist and capitalist states were governed by the overarching principle of peaceful coexistence, then between socialist states such an overarching principle was different—proletarian internationalism.[113] It all boiled down to the understanding of the right of peoples to self-determination. Indeed, the following further passage from Tunkin in many ways sums up the Soviet imperialist approach to international law at the time:

> The principle of proletarian internationalism is dialectically connected with other postulates of Marxist–Leninist theory and first of all with the principle of self-determination of nations. [. . .] In contrast to bourgeois nationalists, conflating the right to self-determination with secession, with fragmentation of a centralized state into small state units, Marxism–Leninism sees the internal dialectical connection between the principle of self-determination of peoples and the principle of proletarian internationalism. V I Lenin indicated that it is impermissible to confuse the question of the right of a nation to secede freely from the question whether to do so makes sense in this or another moment for each specific nation. Recognition and protection of the right of peoples to self-determination does not at all exclude the struggle for unification of the proletariat of various nations, for the unification of socialist states. Between these principles exists dialectical unity.[114]

As already exemplified earlier, the dialectical method was an important tool in Soviet approaches to international law, a way to overcome apparent contradictions and even offend against common logic. We will return to more of these examples later.

During negotiations in January 1948, Stalin clashed with Yugoslav negotiators over how to shape relations in the socialist bloc and what rights the USSR would have over its socialist satellites.[115] In his 1959 article, Tunkin criticized Yugoslavian 'revisionists' such as the Union of Yugoslavian Communists, who argued that between socialist states, too, relations should be based on general—not particular—socialist international law.[116] It was commonly

[113] G I Tunkin, 'Novyi tip mezhdunarodnykh otnoshenii i mezhdunarodnoe pravo', *SGP* No 1, 1959, 81–94 at 88.
[114] Ibid, 89.
[115] Arno Trültzsch, *Sozialismus und Blockfreiheit. Der Beitrag Jugoslawiens zum Völkerrecht 1948–1980/91*, Wallstein Verlag, 2021, 124.
[116] Tunkin, ibid, 86, 93.

a view in Soviet publications at the time that the Yugoslavs had not understood the principle of proletarian internationalism correctly.[117] Later, when Albania sided with Mao's PRC, Soviet authors also criticized the Albanian leadership for not having correctly understood the essence of proletarian internationalism.[118]

Furthermore, in his 1959 article Tunkin highlighted the importance of prioritizing socialist international law in relations between socialist countries:

> To argue that relations between socialist countries must be regulated only by principles of general international law means denying the different class character of relations among socialist countries, sliding onto the rails of non-partisanship, sliding into the swamp of bourgeois normativism.[119]

A Soviet legal scholar who took an interest in issues of socialist international law was Evgeny Trofimovich Usenko (1918–2010). Usenko postulated that, in general international law, the key principle was peaceful coexistence, whereas in socialist international law it was proletarian internationalism. This meant that all key concepts of general international law acquired a new meaning for relations among socialist states: for example, the principle of non-use of force did not even exist between socialist countries as 'it lacked any foundation' between them.[120] The mistake made in 1956 by the Hungarian leader—the 'right-wing revisionist'—Imre Nagy was to look at his country's status only through the prism of 'petty bourgeois nationalism' and equality of states, without considering the aspect of proletarian internationalism between the Soviet Union and Hungary.[121] Usenko wrote on these issues regularly, for example highlighting in 1970 that state sovereignty was important for socialist nations but not in terms of the survival of nationalism or national limitedness.[122] Usenko's core interpretations of socialist international law remained the same over the Soviet period; only the troublesome cases which he warned about changed: when writing in the early 1960s, these were Hungary in 1956

[117] T Timofeev, 'O nekotorykh voprosakh proletarskogo internatsionalizma', *MZh* No 5, 1957, 41–51 at 47.

[118] N Vinnitsky, A Arkadyev, 'Komu na ruku raskolnicheskaya deyatel'nost' albanskikh rukovditelei', *MZh* No 2, 1962, 76–81.

[119] Tunkin, ibid, 94.

[120] E T Usenko, 'Mezhdunarodnoe pravo v vzaimootnosheniakh sotsialisticheskikh gosudarstv', *Soviet YBIL* 1966/7, 30–50 at 42.

[121] Ibid, 38.

[122] E T Usenko, 'Mezhdunarodnopravovye problemy sotsialisticheskoi ekonomicheskoi integratsii', *Soviet YBIL* 1970, 13–28 at 18.

and the Yugoslavian 'revisionists',[123] then later, in the early 1980s, Poland with its anti-Soviet *Solidarność* popular movement.[124]

Grigory Tunkin, too, regularly returned to the themes of socialist international law, in anticipation of events in Czechoslovakia as well as after the Prague Spring was suppressed in August 1968 by the Soviet Union and its Warsaw Pact allies. Tunkin argued that capitalist and socialist states had a different concept of self-determination: while the first created nation states as an expression of self-determination, the socialist concept was based on the brotherhood of nations and their unification.[125] Tunkin justified the August 1968 Soviet-led military intervention against Czechoslovakia based on the principles of socialist internationalism.[126] This time, one of Tukin's main lines of defence was a citation from Lenin, namely:

> The purpose of socialism is not the destruction of humankind in small states and any kind of isolation of nations, but their rapprochement and their merger.[127]

At the same time, Tunkin observed that imperialism was kindling nationalism in the socialist commonwealth as well, as the events in Czechoslovakia in 1968 demonstrated.[128] The main point, according to Tunkin, was that in the socialist commonwealth the principles of sovereignty, equality of states, and non-intervention in domestic affairs were subordinated to the higher principle of socialist internationalism which, however, 'in no way means denying or belittling the national aspect in these relations'.[129] The socialist principles of respect for sovereignty, equal rights, and non-intervention differ qualitatively from the principles of general international law bearing the same name; in socialist international law these principles are present to 'strengthen and develop the brotherly commonwealth of socialist countries'.[130] Here, Tunkin relied on another citation from Lenin which supported his understanding of socialist international law:

[123] E T Usenko, 'Osnovnye mezhdunarodno-pravovye printsipy sotrudnichestva sotsialistichesikh gosudarstv', *SGP* No 3, 1961, 16–29 at 19.
[124] E T Usenko, 'Mezhdunarodno-pravovye problemy rashirenia i uglublenia sotrudnichestva sotsialisticheskikh gosudarstv', *Soviet YBIL* 1982, 28–40 at 29, 32.
[125] G I Tunkin, 'Bor'ba dvukh kontseptsii v mezhdunarodnom prave', *SGP* No 11, 1967, 140–9 at 145.
[126] G I Tunkin, 'V I Lenin i printsipy otnoshenii mezhdu sotsialisticheskimi gosudarstvami', *Soviet YBIL* 1969, 16–32.
[127] Tunkin, ibid, 23; citing Lenin, *Polnoe sobranie sochinenii*, vol 27, 256.
[128] Tunkin, ibid, 24–5.
[129] Tunkin, ibid, 25–6.
[130] Tunkin, ibid, 26.

> V I Lenin, formulating the Marxist concept of the self-determination of peoples, decisively dissociated himself from the bourgeois concept of this principle, with its purpose of creating the 'nation state'. Lenin emphasized that the principle of self-determination of peoples in its Marxist understanding is a means for the rapprochement of nations. [. . .] 'We demand,' wrote Lenin, 'the right of secession of suppressed peoples not because we dream of economic fragmentation or of the ideal of small states, but on the contrary, because we want large states and rapprochement, even merger of nations but on a genuinely democratic, genuinely internationalist basis which is unthinkable without freedom to secede.[131]

Tunkin concluded that the understanding of sovereignty in socialist international law meant that countries faithful to socialism were obliged to intervene and defend socialist sovereignty elsewhere, along the lines of proletarian internationalism, just as five socialist states led by the Soviet Union had done so militarily in Czechoslovakia in August 1968. This was the foundation of a new type of international law—'the socialist international law of the future'.[132] Nevertheless, for some reason Tunkin was later still sometimes superficially seen in the West as someone who represented a 'retreat from ideology towards greater objectivity' in Soviet scholarship of international law.[133]

A further specific phenomenon of socialist international law consisted in bilateral treaties between the Soviet Union and other socialist states: treaties which—according to Soviet lawyers—formed a 'system'.[134] Soviet legal scholars emphasized that these treaties were meant to defend socialism and its achievements.[135] Saltanov referred to the preamble of the Soviet–Czechoslovak Treaty of Friendship of 6 May 1970, proclaiming that 'the support, strengthening and defense of socialist achievements which have been gained at the price of heroic efforts and self-denying work of both peoples, remains the common international debt to socialist countries'.[136] As this example demonstrates, such treaties were sometimes also renegotiated—or, rather, imposed—right after Soviet intervention, again asserting the principle of proletarian internationalism. At the same time, in the West—for example in the Federal Republic of

[131] Tunkin, ibid, 26; citing Lenin, *Polnoe sobranie sochinenii*, vol 27, 68.
[132] Tunkin, ibid, 27.
[133] Karl-Heinz Ziegler, *Völkerrechtsgeschichte. Ein Studienbuch*, C H Beck, 1994, 291.
[134] A S Bakhov, 'Formy politicheskogo sotrudnichestva evropeiskikh sotsialisticheskikh gosudarstv', *SGP* No 3, 1972, 74–8 at 82.
[135] N V Zakharova, 'Dvustoronnie dogovory o druzhbe, sotrudnichestve i vzaimopomoshi sotsialisticheskikh gosudarstv', *SGP* No 2, 1962, 80–91 at 81.
[136] V S Saltanov, 'Dvustoronnie dogovory sotsialisticheskikh gosudarstv o druzhbe, sotrudnichestve i vzaimnoi pomoshi i ikh mezhdunarodno-pravovoe znachenie', *Soviet YBIL* 1971, 80–95 at 85.

Germany—several legal scholars criticized these Soviet treaties as imposed and generally as expressions of Soviet hegemony and 'structural violence' in Central Europe.[137] Reflecting the geopolitical situation in Central Europe during the Cold War, these bilateral treaties were defended all the more by the international lawyers of the GDR.[138] Besides classic bilateral treaties between states, Meissner also drew attention to agreements between the communist parties of socialist states, agreements in which the Soviet Communist Party's (and thus also the Soviet Union's) leading role was expressed explicitly and which were of a quasi-international legal character.[139]

Over the last decades of the Cold War, the focus of Soviet international lawyers in the context of socialist international law was mainly on two international organizations created in the Soviet bloc, one dealing with the economy (the COMECON Council of Mutual Assistance)[140] and the other with security (the Warsaw Pact).[141] Soviet legal scholars emphasized that—unlike in the capitalist world—the organizations of the socialist commonwealth were based on the complete equality of bigger and smaller states: every member state had the same number of votes.[142] This fact did not change much in the Western perception that, de facto, the Soviet role in these organizations of socialist states—and beyond these organizations in Central and Eastern Europe—was hegemonic.[143] Writing during the Nazi period in Germany

[137] See, eg, Willi Schwanitz, *Die hegemoniale Vertragspolitik. Militärpolitik und Völkerrecht*, Berlin Verlag, 1983, 14.

[138] H Kröger, 'Oktyabrskaya revoliutsia, mezhdunarodnoe pravo i 'bonnskaya vostochnaya politika'', *SGP* No 12, 1967, 102–10 at 109.

[139] Boris Meissner, 'Das Wesen und der Geltungsbereich des Völkerrechts', in: Reinhart Maurach, Boris Meissner (Hg) *Völkerrecht un Ost und West*, Stuttgart: W Kohlhammer Verlag, 1967, 9–38 at 38.

[140] P A Tokareva, 'Mezhdunarodnaya ekonomicheskaya organizatsia novoga tipa', *SGP* 1959, No 2, 104–11; M D Kudryashov, V I Morozov, 'Ustav Soveta Ekomomicheskoi Vzaimopomoshi—pravovoe vyrazhenie ekonomicheskogo sotrudnichestva novoga tipa', *SGP* No 10, 1960, 22–30; V I Morozov, 'Pravovye aspekty deyatel'nosti organov Soveta ekonomicheskoi vzaimopomoshi', *SGP* No 10, 1961, 146–54; E T Usenko, 'Sotrudnichestvo stran-chlenov SEV i sotsialisticheskii internatsionalizm', *SGP* No 4, 1970, 79–87; E T Usenko, 'Pravovye aspekty kompleksnoi programmy sotsialisticheskoi eskonomicheskoi integratsii', *SGP* No 7, 1973, 63–72; M M Boguslavsky, 'Pravovye voprosy nauchno-tekhnicheskoi integratsii stran-chlenov SEV', *SGP* No 9, 1977, 117–24; K Bekher, V V Fomin, 'Perestroika mezhdunarodnykh ekonomicheskikh otnoshenii i strany sotsialisticheskoga sodruzhestva', *SGP* No 10, 1977, 107–114; E A Usenko, 'O dogovornoi kompetentsii SEV', *SGP* No 6, 1979, 98–106; E T Usenko, 'Sovet ekonomischeskoi vzaimopomoshi—sub'ekt mezhdunarodnoga prava', *Soviet YBIL* 1979, 11–44; I I Lukashuk, 'Normotvorcheskaya deyatel'nost' SEV', *Soviet YBIL* 1980, 29–53; G M Velyaminov, 'Soglasovannye predlozhenia i dogovorennosti—pravovye akty v ramkakh SEV', *SGP* No 11, 1990, 107–15.

[141] A S Bakhov, 'Varshavskii dogovor kak faktor mezhdunarodnoy bezopasnosti', *Soviet YBIL* 1980,12–28.

[142] P A Tokareva, 'Stanovlenie sistemy mezhdunarodnykh organizatsii sotsialisticheskikh gosudarstv', *SGP* No 10, 1967, 64–72 at 72; N Fadeev, 'SEV - sotrudnichestvo ravnopravnykh natsii', No 4, 1967, 8–16.

[143] Boris Meissner, 'Das Wesen und der Geltungsbereich des Völkerrechts', in: Reinhart Maurach, Boris Meissner (Hg) *Völkerrecht un Ost und West*, W Kohlhammer Verlag, 1967, 9–38 at 37; Theodor

but before the Second World War, the international lawyer Heinrich Triepel (1868–1946) had argued that dominant powers tended to establish direct empire over nations whom they considered less developed and whom they therefore wanted to further 'educate', whereas with nations who were considered by and large equal in development, the most common form of domination was hegemony.[144] For Triepel, hegemony was one of the forms in which imperialist politics found its expression.[145] During the Cold War, the understanding in West German scholarship was that Soviet practice in Central Europe corresponded to the phenomenon of hegemony as earlier elaborated by Triepel.[146]

Soviet practices demonstrate that unequal relations in bilateral treaties were skilfully balanced by highlighting formal equality in regional organizations of socialist states. In the words of the German historian Arno Trültzsch, Soviet theory in this regard was power politics clothed in an international legal facade[147] and was meant to justify Soviet hegemony.[148] In the West, the predominant view of socialist international law—and, as its military component was colloquially called from the late 1960s, the Brezhnev doctrine—was that its tenets were not compatible with general international law, including the UN Charter.[149] Theodor Schweisfurth concluded that the interventionism of socialist international law recalled not only the international-law *Großraum* theory of the Nazi German legal theoretician Carl Schmitt (1888–1985) but also the Russian tsarist approach during the nineteenth-century Holy Alliance, when the Russian Empire intervened militarily in Central Europe in order to combat revolutions and prevent certain political reforms.[150] However, writing in the Federal Republic of Germany, Schweisfurth also saw striking similarities between the Soviet interventionist doctrine and similar US doctrines as applied, for example, in Guatemala (1954), Cuba (1960), and the Dominican Republic (1965)—thus establishing similar concepts and interventionist

Schweisfurth, *Sozialistiches Völkerrecht? Darstellung—Analyse— Wertung der sowjetmarxistischen Theorie vom Völkerrecht 'neuen Typs'*, Berlin: Springer, 1979, 481.

144 Heinrich Triepel, *Die Hegemonie. Ein Buch von führenden Staaten*, W Kohlhammer, 1938, 147–8.
145 Ibid, 189.
146 Schweisfurth, *Sozialistisches Völkerrecht?*, 1979, 480.
147 Arno Trültzsch, *Sozialismus und Blockfreiheit. Der Beitrag Jugoslawiens zum Völkerrecht 1948–1980/91*, Wallstein Verlag, 2021, 94.
148 Ibid, 88–9.
149 Boris Meissner, 'Das Wesen und der Geltungsbereich des Völkerrechts', in: Reinhart Maurach, Boris Meissner (Hg) *Völkerrecht un Ost und West*, Stuttgart: W Kohlhammer Verlag, 1967, 9–38 at 35–8; John Norton Moore, Robert F Turner, *International Law and the Brezhnev Doctrine*, University Press of America, 1987.
150 Schweisfurth, *Sozialistisches Völkerrecht?*, 1979, 569.

justifications between the two competing superpowers of the Cold War era.[151] In their writings, both Schmitt and Triepel were fascinated by US imperialism in international law: another indication that the harshest critics of empires are their rivals. Of course, during the Cold War the Federal Republic of Germany was not a rival to the US but rather a state dependent on the latter both militarily and politically.

Kaj Hobér has argued that Soviet military intervention in Afghanistan in 1979 also had a direct connection with the 'Brezhnev doctrine' and demonstrates that, even after adoption of the Helsinki Accords in 1975, the Soviet leaders did not abandon this hegemonic doctrine.[152] However, the Soviet leadership used a mixture of justifications for Afghanistan (especially including intervention by invitation), and it can also be argued that the Helsinki Accords were meant for the regulation of European matters, not Afghanistan.

Increasing Faith in International Law?

The US legal scholar Boris Mamlyuk argues that the Soviets showed 'increasing faith' in international law over the course of the Cold War.[153] Mamlyuk highlights that the Soviets felt they had not received what they thought they had been promised by the Western Allies during the Second World War. American officials leaked copies of the original text of the secret protocols of the Nazi–Soviet Non-Aggression Pact of 23 August 1939—which they had received from the German archives—to the Western media and the German defence lawyers at the Nuremberg trials,[154] which, according to Mamlyuk, contributed to the Soviet 'crisis of faith' regarding international law:

> The mainstream historical narrative posits that after facing numerous betrayals at the hands of Western powers, including the Molotov–Ribbentrop Pact, the Allies' delay in opening the Western front, and breach of the abovementioned 'gentlemen's agreements' at Nuremberg, the Soviets had a crisis of faith.[155]

[151] Schwisfurth, ibid, 559. For the same point, see also Jens Hacker, *Die Intervention in Theorie und Praxis*, in: Reinhart Maurach, Boris Meissner (Hg) *Völkerrecht un Ost und West*, W Kohlhammer Verlag, 1967, 154–77 at 175.

[152] Kaj Hobér, *The Perestroika Era and International Law*, Edward Elgar Publishing, 2024, 85.

[153] Boris N Mamlyuk, 'The Cold War in Soviet International Legal Discourse', in: Matthew Craven, Sundhja Pahuja, Gerry Simpson (eds) *International Law and the Cold War*, CUP, 2020, 339–75 at 365.

[154] Francine Hirsch, *Soviet Judgment at Nuremberg. A New History of the International Military Tribunal after World War II*, OUP, 2020.

[155] Mamlyuk, 'The Cold War', 354.

In the same context, Mamlyuk also refers to Soviet 'traumatic international law encounters'.[156] This narrative accommodates the Soviet imperial historical perspective because what is seen as a relevant 'trauma' lies primarily not in the 1939 Nazi–Soviet division of Eastern Europe but in US officials making it public in 1945, thus disappointing the Soviet Union and disturbing its preferred narratives.

To an extent, we can see 'increasing faith' in the way the Soviet doctrine of international law flips from strong support of *clausula rebus sic stantibus* to *pacta sunt servanda* or from support of revolutionary interventions to advocacy of a strict prohibition of use of force in international law. However, these changes were related to Soviet conquests in the Second World War, and the country's territorial saturation as a result. A formerly revisionist power challenging the status quo became a keen guardian of its possessions. Nevertheless, as demonstrated in this chapter, Soviet doctrines of international law during the Cold War were to an important extent shaped by Soviet imperialist thought.

[156] Ibid, 374.

8

From Perestroika to Putin's Russia: Swinging Back to the Imperial Concept of International Law

Many years have passed since the dissolution of the Soviet Union in December 1991. Nevertheless, what particularly interests us is the transformations of mentality and discourses in post-Soviet Russian international law. In the post-Soviet space, the Russian–Georgian war of 2008, Russia's annexation of Crimea in 2014, and in particular its full-scale military invasion of Ukraine since 2022 have been transformative events. But what mindsets and mentalities in Russian international legal discourses prepared the ground for the country's aggression against Ukraine?

The Perestroika era was a time of revelations in the Soviet Union. Suddenly it was possible to question everything that had been the governmentally mandated or favoured truth in Soviet international and constitutional legal discourses. Soviet citizens could finally learn the historical truth about Soviet policies at the beginning of the Second World War—for example, that the Soviet Union had committed aggression against Finland in late 1939 and had executed some 22,000 Polish officers—prisoners of war—in 1940 at Katyn and other locations in the Soviet Union.[1] In December 1989, the Soviet parliament declared the secret protocols of the Nazi–Soviet non-aggression pact of 23 August 1939 null and void from the very beginning. At a meeting between the Warsaw Pact members in Moscow on 4 December 1989, the 1968 invasion of Czechoslovakia was declared illegal.[2] However, while many in the West celebrated Gorbachev's new policies in international law as a grand and peaceful gesture, a remarkable act of goodwill from Moscow, many citizens in Central and Eastern Europe understood it as an end to either an illegal situation or

[1] MI Semiryaga, 'Asimmetrichnaya voina. K 50-letiu okonchania sovetsko-finliandskoi voiny (1939–1940 gg)', *SGP* No 4, 1990, 116–23; MI Semiryaga, 'Prestuplenie v Katyni', *SGP* No 12, 1990, 110–18 and 1991 No 1, 91–102.

[2] Kaj Hobér, *The Perestroika Era and International Law*, Edward Elgar Publishing, 2024, 81.

Russia, the Soviet Union, and Imperial Continuity in International Law. Lauri Mälksoo, Oxford University Press.
 DOI: 10.1093/9780198955962.003.0008

one which did not correspond to their peoples' preferences. What is so heroic about ending an illegal situation which should never have materialized in the first place?

In the following, I have organized the discussion around the following keywords, which were already central in earlier chapter(s) concerning the Soviet Union: federalism; continuity versus state succession; ideas about Russia's great-power status; treaties; and *pacta sunt servanda* versus *clausula rebus sic stantibus.*

Federalist Ideas, Self-Determination, and International Law

Post-Soviet Russia has been developing in much the same way as the Soviet Union in the 1920s: initially, federalist ideas were celebrated and even anchored in 'treaties'; but soon the centralizing vision of statehood gathered itself and restored the imperial, unitary vision of Russia.

Struggling against the centrifugal process during the last years of the Soviet Union, Soviet legal scholars who wanted to maintain the territorial integrity of the state suggested going back to the drawing board, arguing that the Soviet Union should be preserved but under new, more democratic conditions. For example, in 1990 three Soviet Russian lawyers proposed:

> The Communist Party of the Soviet Union considers that—for the sake of the interests of the peoples themselves and bearing in mind worldwide tendencies towards integration—it is important to preserve the integrity of the union as a multinational state. This year we already need to work out a new treaty on the union of the republics as sovereign socialist states, based on a strictly voluntary nature, mutual benefit, and freedom of national self-determination.[3]

The only problem with this approach and promise was that it had already been tried, but not with lasting success: in 1922, the Soviet Union was formally based on a treaty but—while the sovereignty of the constituents was emphasized—over time the rights of the constituent parts of the union vanished to the extent that the concept of the 'sovereignty of union republics' remained a mere fiction, upheld by the Soviet government and legal scholarship. In response, two Armenian legal scholars wrote in the same journal, *Sovetskoe gosudarstvo i*

[3] BS Krylov, IN Kuznetsov, NA Mikhaleva, 'Kontseptsia Soyuznogo dogovora', *SGP* No 10, 1990, 3–12 at 3.

pravo, in 1990: 'If nowadays someone tries to speak of the development, the expansion of sovereignty, of the Soviet republics, then it transforms into a game of words because in reality [Soviet] republics never enjoyed sovereignty.'[4]

Some years later, the US legal scholar Jeffrey Kahn put it even more radically: the USSR was a 'federal facade that barely masked the most centralized state in modern history'.[5]

To understand the disintegration of the Soviet Union and the emergence of the post-Soviet Russian Federation and other post-Soviet states, it is important to keep in mind that the decision-makers of that era had in mind as a key reference point the transformation of the Russian Empire in 1917–22 through Soviet Russia and other Soviet republics to the Soviet Union. Just as in 1922 the Soviet Union was founded on—and the core Empire preserved thanks to—a treaty, now it was again meant to be about renewal of treaty relations. The failed *coup d'état* of part of the Soviet leadership in August 1991 was about preserving the Soviet Union as a unitary state. The coup was organized to prevent the forthcoming signing of the new union treaty between the Gorbachev-led Soviet government in Moscow and the Soviet republics, which would have changed the nature of the Soviet Union from federation to confederation. With the failure of the coup, secession of the former Soviet republics went ahead regardless, so that in December 1991 they became formally independent states. The three Baltic States—which maintained that they had been illegally occupied and annexed by the Soviet Union since 1940—restored their statehood in August 1991.

When the Soviet Union dissolved in December 1991 and the Commonwealth of Independent States (CIS) was created, Russian international lawyers started to ponder the legal nature of the CIS. Writing in 1994, Grechko and Shinkaretskaya observed that the second session of the interparliamentary assembly of the CIS in December 1992 decided to examine the question 'of the development of confederation relations between the participants of the Commonwealth' in the coming years.[6] But what did this formulation mean? Grechko and Shinkaretskaya pointed out that, in the Soviet Union, the notion of 'confederation' had significantly changed over time. The *Great Soviet Encyclopedia* of 1973 defined confederation as a 'permanent union of sovereign states'. However, Soviet textbooks, the *Great Soviet Encyclopedia*, and the *Diplomatic Dictionary* published in the 1980s started to refer to 'confederation'

[4] LM Karapetyan, GM Khachatryan, 'Suverenitet narodov v mnogonatsional'nom gosudarstve', *SGP* 1990 No 11, 3–14 at 5.
[5] Jeffrey Kahn, *Federalism, Democratization, and the Rule of Law in Russia*, OUP, 2002, 1.
[6] LV Grechko, GG Shinkaretskaya, 'Poniatie konferedatsii i SNG', *Moscow JIL* 1994, 61–73 at 61.

as a 'form of government' (*forma gosudarstvennogo ustroistva*) between sovereign states. Grechko and Shinkaretskaya suggested that this modification to the Soviet encyclopedia became a gamechanger since 'form of government' can only mean 'form of state'.[7] The two authors concluded that 'from the beginning', the CIS was therefore a confederation—that is, a 'form of state'.[8] Thus, again, as during the Soviet period, a legal–political problem was resolved by assigning a different meaning to a concept, because, traditionally, 'confederation' means a union of sovereign states. Again, this was done in support of centripetal forces in the Empire. According to this logic, former Soviet republics could not become independent of Russia even after declaring independence and becoming member states of the UN, as long as they were part of the new confederation (CIS).

In the 1990s, the newly established *Moscow Journal of International Law* became one of the platforms for the defence of the Empire and pushback against further disintegration of the Russian Federation. The key theme for the Russian Federation after the dissolution of the Soviet Union was federalism. Russian international and constitutional law journals in the 1990s were filled with articles criticizing separatism in regions, their authors worried about the further dissolution of the Russian Federation. Writing in 1995, Andrei Aleksandrovich Gromyko-Piradov (b 1966) concluded: 'We can say that to preserve Russia as an integral and indivisible state, it is necessary to clear the "mine" laid in 1917 by the October Revolution, which proclaimed the idea of "national self-determination"'.[9]

Much later, when justifying the annexation of Crimea and the war against Ukraine, Putin used the same metaphor of a 'mine' which the Bolsheviks arguably laid under the edifice of the Russian Empire in and after 1917, with rhetoric supporting the right of peoples to self-determination.

The main contested point remained as to whether the post-1991 Russian Federation itself was based on constitution or treaty. Scholars writing in Russia's international and constitutional law journals vehemently defended the idea that the Russian Federation was based on a constitution, not on a treaty or treaties.[10] Nevertheless, on 31 March 1992 the Federation Treaty was signed by the Russian government and the regions, a treaty that acknowledged republican 'sovereignty' and their right to self-determination. Technically, the

[7] Ibid, 62.
[8] Ibid, 72.
[9] AA Gromyko-Piradov, 'Suverenitet i konflikty v Rossii v pervoi polovine 1990-kh godov', *Moscow JIL* No 4, 1995, 52–63 at 61.
[10] GV Degtev, 'Federalizm v sovremennoi Rossii', *Moscow JIL*, 2001, 82.

Federation Treaty consisted of three separate treaties and two protocols.[11] Tartarstan and Chechnya, the two regions of the Russian Federation with the most advanced sovereignty claims at the time, refused to sign the Federation Treaty because, for them, it did not go far enough. Tartarstan also held a referendum in which 61.3 per cent favoured Tartarstan as a 'sovereign state'.[12] For regional political elites, a 'treaty-constitutional' approach for the Russian Federation meant not federation but a loose confederation of sovereign states; in contrast, federal elites held the reverse view, namely that the Federation was a free-standing sovereign entity that did not need justification from its member-units.[13] Regional political elites were also relying on President Yeltsin's initial statement that regions could take 'as much sovereignty as they could swallow'.

In 1993, when a new Russian Constitution was drafted, key commitments made to the Russian republics and regions in the Federation Treaty of 31 March 1992—commitments both symbolic and practical, such as power-sharing—were unilaterally repealed by Moscow.[14] Here is a clear historical parallel with how the 1922 treaty of the establishment of the Soviet Union was essentially pushed into irrelevance and oblivion when the imperial centre reestablished control over the Soviet republics, which remained 'sovereign states' only formally. The tsarist Empire, too, unilaterally eviscerated the autonomy of Ukraine in the eighteenth century as well as Finland and the Baltic provinces in the late nineteenth century.

During the 1990s, several bilateral 'treaties' were also concluded between Moscow and the ethnic republics of the Russian Federation such as Tartarstan, Kabardino-Balkaria, and Baskhortostan. For example, the Treaty on the Demarcation of Objects of Jurisdiction and the Mutual Delegation of Powers Between the Bodies of State Power of the Russian Federation and the Republic of Tartarstan was signed on 15 February 1994. At least the Tartar side led the treaty negotiations with Yeltsin's Russia with the understanding of Tartarstan's old statehood predating its conquest by Muscovy in the sixteenth century.[15] Tartarstan was described in the preamble of its treaty as 'a state united with the Russian Federation', less than the 'associated' status claimed in the republic's constitution—but still a remarkable statement of autonomy.[16] Altogether, forty-seven of the eighty-nine units of the Federation negotiated bilateral treaties

[11] Jeffrey Kahn, *Federalism, Democratization, and the Rule of Law in Russia*, OUP, 2002, 126.
[12] Ibid, 131–2.
[13] Ibid, 149.
[14] Ibid, 137–8.
[15] Ibid, 151.
[16] Ibid, 164.

with the federal government.[17] The last treaty between the Russian central government and a federal unit was signed on 16 June 1998.[18] Some started to call the period 1994–8 in the Russian Federation 'the parade of treaties' or 'parade of sovereignties'.[19] However, a gathering of dark clouds over these treaty republics was indicated when the Ministry of Justice of the Russian Federation announced in late 1996 that nineteen out of twenty-one republican constitutions violated the federal Constitution.[20]

Indeed, a key policy of President Putin was established—with strong help from the Russian Constitutional Court, which rejected claims of 'sovereignty' by the republics—[21] that eventually all such bilateral treaties would be terminated and phased out. The last such bilateral treaty—with Tartarstan—expired in 2017.[22] With some parallels (even though the Russian army never left the 'sovereign states' within the Russian Federation), this also echoes the experience of the Baltic States and Georgia as new states concluding treaties with Soviet Russia in 1920. In 1920, the sovereignty of the Baltic States and Georgia was proclaimed 'for ever', but Moscow unilaterally snatched it back from Georgia in 1921 and from the Baltic States (de facto even if not de jure) in 1940. For former parts of the Russian Empire, it is very difficult to negotiate a treaty on sovereignty and secession with Russia because—from the perspective of the rulers of Russia, whether Soviet or post-Soviet—such treaties primarily reflected the fluctuating balance of power and consequently could be repealed when the central government's power consolidated once again. Put differently, a sentiment exhausted from the Empire could over time easily turn into a mood nostalgic for the Empire. Caroline von Gall, a German constitutional law scholar, has concluded that in the Russian Federation the very purpose of federalism differs from Western models, as its essence in Russia is state unity rather than support of diversity and pluralism.[23]

A special post-Soviet situation is the 'union state' between the Russian Federation and Belarus. Unlike Chechnya and Tartarstan, Byelorussia (the previous official name of Belarus) was one of the leading Soviet republics, since 1945 a UN member state whose leader participated in a core group of Eastern

[17] Ibid, 150.
[18] Ibid, 159.
[19] Ibid, 168.
[20] Ibid, 173.
[21] Ibid, 249–50.
[22] See William E Pomeranz, *Law and the Russian State: Russia's Legal Evolution from Peter the Great to Vladimir Putin*, Bloomsbury, 2019, 163.
[23] Caroline von Gall, *Die Konzepte 'staatliche Einheit' und 'einheitliche Macht' in der russischen Theorie von Staat und Recht. Der Einfluss des Gemeinschaftsideals auf die russische Verfassungsentwicklung*, Duncker & Humblot, 2010, 292.

Slavic Soviet republics that liquidated the Soviet Union in December 1991; indeed, the very decision to dissolve the Soviet Union was made on the territory of Soviet Byelorussia. However, on 8 December 1999 the leaders of Russia and Belarus signed a treaty forming a 'union state' between the two 'sovereign states'.[24] From the beginning, Russian scholars such as Nadezhda Pastukhova played with the idea that the union state between Russia and Belarus was a unique confederation which had the potential to quickly become a federation, as both the Russian and Belarus peoples 'did not want the dissolution of the Soviet Union' and most of them 'perceive each other as one people'.[25]

Writing in 2001, Galina Georgievna Shinkaretskaya from the Institute of State and Law of the Russian Academy of Sciences, also a member of the international law council at the Russian Ministry of Foreign Affairs, reminded her readers that under the treaty concluded on 8 December 1999 unification had become an international legal obligation for both Russia and Belarus.[26] That is, unification was no longer an option: they were legally obliged to do so. Another legal scholar, NA Mikhaleva, added that unification between the two states would mean 'the highest form of integration between two sovereign states'.[27] Mixing international legal analysis and geopolitical argumentation, Sergey Nikolaevich Baburin (b 1959), a legal scholar and politician (including one presidential candidacy), suggested that unification of Russia and Belarus was a symbol of the 'awakening' of the Empire, and that the Russian Federation could not be restricted to the constraints of a nation state.[28]

Writing in 2012, Dmitriev and Mironov argued that the union treaty between Russia and Belarus foresees 'a state of the confederate type'—an unconventional definition of 'confederation', already familiar to us—but specified that in history a confederation was usually only a temporary phenomenon. Either the union dissolves as a confederation into separate sovereign states or it becomes a genuine federation so that, for example, the Republic of Belarus could join the Russian Federation as a republic with special status, or its six oblasts could join.[29] Before President Putin used the territory of Belarus to attack Ukraine in February 2022, some Russian legal scholars also highlighted

[24] See, eg, Nadezhda Pastukhova, *Soyuz Rossii i Belorussii: istoria, nastoyashchee, perspektivy*, Kniga i biznes, 2000, 57–8.

[25] Ibid, 42–3.

[26] GG Shinkaretskaya, 'Soyuznoe gosudarstvo Belorussii i Rossii', *GP* 2001 No 4, 84–8 at 88.

[27] NA Mikhaleva, 'Pravovye problemy sozdania soyuznogo gosudarstva Rossii i Belarusi', *GP* 2002 No 6, 14–21 at 14.

[28] Sergey N Baburin, *Mir imperii. Territoria gosudarstva i mirovoi poryadok*, St Petersburg: Izdatel'stvo R Aslanova 'Iuridiceshki tsentr Press', 2005, 550 et seq.

[29] Yu A Dmitriev, VO Mironov, 'Netipichnaya forma gosudarstvennogo ustroistva', *GP* 2012 No 7, 82–91 at 86.

the importance of the neutrality of Belarus, a constitutional aspiration at the time.[30] However, as a consequence of the constitutional referendum held in Belarus on 27 February 2022, the article according to which Belarus was pursuing the status of a neutral state was removed from the constitution of the country.

The inner-Russian discussion on the meaning of the right of peoples to self-determination continued in the post-Soviet Russian Federation. Writing in 2004, Mamonov maintained that the international legal principle of the right of peoples to self-determination was not applicable to the Russian Federation, 'because it covers nations who are living in territories which are colonies'.[31] Instead, what was needed was to 'work out the politics of protectionism with respect to the state-forming ethnos and adopt a special federal solution for this problem'.[32] Thus, times had changed so that according to this author, at that time, after the dissolution of the Soviet Union and with the 'parade of sovereignties' in the Russian Federation, these were already ethnic Russians who needed special measures and governmental protection.[33]

The academic legal discourse on ethnic minorities in the Russian Federation can still resemble patronizing discourses already familiar during the Soviet era. The common theme is that, historically, joining the Russian Empire was good for other ethnicities—especially for the minority indigenous peoples. Writing in 2004, Yakovlev concluded that the unification of Yakutia with Russia 'had a progressive meaning as it corresponded with the formation of the centralized, multinational Russian state'.[34] Furthermore, Yakovlev argued: 'The arrival of the Russians and establishment of the jurisdiction of Russian legislation helped to direct the development of societal relations of the Yakutians in a civilized legal channel. Yakutia became part of a strong, mighty, civilized state'.[35]

The same pattern of thought, though in a more generalized way, comes up in a 2005 *Gosudarstvo i pravo* article by Tikhomirov:

> The Russian geopolitical tradition is not determined by the classic motives of colonization and exploitation but with the inevitable and urgent need to

[30] Olga I Chupris, Elena S Smirnova, 'Neitralitet respubliki Belarus kak iuridicheskaya norma', *Moscow JIL* No 4, 2017, 107–15.

[31] VV Mamonov, 'Gosudarstvennyi suverenitet i territorial'naya tselostnost' – glavnye printsipy sovremennoi rossiiskoi gosudarstvennosti', *GP* 2004 No 4, 5–12 at 5.

[32] Ibid, 12.

[33] Ibid.

[34] N M Yakovlev, 'Znachenie progressivnogo rossiiskogo zakonodatel'stva dlia Iakutii posle ee prisoedinenya k Rossii', *GP* 2004 No 10, 92–9 at 92.

[35] Ibid, 99.

> protect small peoples and in creating the best conditions for prosperity in the framework of a united Muscovite state.[36]

In other words, there has been a continuity of legal–political legitimation of Russia as a multinational state and—at least historically—an empire. Such statements are not different from what was discussed about the history of the Russian Empire in Soviet constitutional and international law literature, especially in the leading journal *Sovetskoe gosudarstvo i pravo* during the 1960s–80s. Incidentally, such analyses usually do not problematize the fact that Russia's regions such as Yakutia are among the richest in natural resources.

State Continuity or Succession?

Putin's Russia solved the dilemma—of state continuity with or succession to the Soviet Union— with a unique constitutional compromise which suggested that the Russian Federation is both: it is the same state as the Soviet Union, but at the same time not the same state. When the Russian Constitution was amended by the 'all-Russian vote' on 1 July 2022, one change among others was the addition of Article 67.1, paragraph 1 according to which:

> the Russian Federation is the state successor of the USSR on its territory and also state successor (continuator)[37] of the USSR in terms of membership in international organizations and their organs, membership in international treaties, and also when foreseen with international treaties with respect to actions and obligations of the USSR beyond Russian borders.

What is remarkable about this constitutional statement is how it uses the concepts of state succession (правопреемство) and continuity (правопродолжательство; also континуитет) essentially as describing one and the same state: today's Russian Federation. The reason for this is that, on the one hand, the Russian Federation in its state practice has emphasized that it has continued the rights and personhood of the USSR, especially on the UN Security Council; while on the other, in post-Soviet Russian scholarship of international law, disagreements have arisen about whether state continuity or

[36] Yu A Tikhomirov, 'Geopoliticheskie imperativy bezopasnosti rossiiskogo gosudarstva', *GP* 2005 No 1, 80–87 at 81.

[37] Russian: *pravopreemnik (pravoprodolzhatel).*

state succession is the right concept to use, in other words whether the Russian Federation is, as a subject of international law, the same state as the USSR or not. Both concepts have been used interchangeably. Stanislav Valentinovich Chernichenko (1935–2021), one of the leading international law academics in post-Soviet Russia, criticized the simultaneous use in Russia of both concepts—state continuity and state succession—to characterize the international legal status of the post-1991 Russian Federation.[38] Chernichenko favoured the concept of state continuity, just as the Russian MFA has claimed it in the UN Security Council and elsewhere in state practice.[39]

However, Russian scholarly opinions have been more diverse. Some examples of how the concept of 'state succession' has continued to be favoured by Russian international lawyers—at least besides 'state continuity' with the Soviet Union—are the following. In an article in the *Moscow Journal of International Law*, Galina Shinkaretskaya discussed the problem of state succession and the borders of the Russian Federation,[40] observing that after the dissolution of the Soviet Union the population in several post-Soviet states found the borders between Soviet republics unjust.[41] Although the guiding principles of the formation of former Soviet—now national—republics had been ethnic, some of these territories—since December 1991 outside the control of Moscow—were still up to 100 per cent inhabited by ethnic Russians:

> On the psychological level interrepublican borders were not perceived as borders between states [. . .] Thus, neglect of the most important principle of international law—the principle of sovereignty of the people—led to the emergence of borders which create obstacles to normal interstate cooperation.[42]

Again speaking of the 'sovereignty of the *people*' (as 'one of the most important principles of international law'), in her analysis Shinkaretskaya demonstrated the flexibility of basic international legal concepts. She asserted that post-Soviet borders between the former constituent republics of the Soviet Union needed a different approach from that by which the Soviet border had been dealt with. Additionally, Article 5 of the CIS agreement enshrined the

[38] Stanislav V Chernichenko, *Teoria mezhdunarodnoga prava*, Vol II, NIMP, 1999, 58–87.
[39] Ibid.
[40] GG Shinkaretskaya, 'Problemy pravopreemstva i granitsy Rossiiskoi Federatsii', *Moscow JIL* No 4, 1995, 84–105.
[41] Ibid, 88.
[42] Ibid.

obligation to guarantee 'openness of borders', freedom of movement of citizens, and transfer of information in the framework of the CIS.[43] Moreover, Shinkaretskaya pointed out that the succession of borders, according to international legal opinion, was not always absolutely certain.[44] What is more, she also opined that as Russia declared itself 'sovereign' from the Soviet Union, the Russian Federation as a subject of international law was identical with the Russian Soviet Federative Socialist Republic (SFSR); with respect to the Soviet Union, the new Russian Federation was only a state successor, like the remaining fourteen ex-Soviet republics.[45] When the heads of state of the CIS decided that the Russian Federation would continue membership of the Soviet Union at the UN and in other international organizations, this was—according to Shinkaretskaya—an expression of agreement by other successors of the Soviet Union, namely that the Russian Federation 'succeeded' to Soviet positions in these organizations.[46] Shinkaretskaya further observed:

> The case of inheriting the borders of the USSR and the lines of administrative division drawn by the Soviet authorities, when not colonies, but republics that were previously equal in rights, became sovereign states, is still unique. But the mechanism for inheriting borders is the same as in Latin America in the last century and in Africa in the middle of this century. [...] Thus, *uti possidetis* is not an independent legal principle and acquires a legal character, becoming part of the broader principle of the inviolability of borders. [...] The situation is much more complicated with that part of the borders which, before the collapse of the USSR, was the border between the union republics. Neither the population nor the leadership of the CIS countries and Russia perceive this part as a 'real' state border, which in the perception of the Soviet people should always be 'locked'. The appearance of such a border between groups of the population that traditionally lived the same life is perceived as an injustice. The concept of justice plays a greater role in the problem of boundaries than in any other area. No border will be stable if the people living on both sides do not consider the border to be fair. In the case of the borders of independent states—the former republics of the USSR—a solution can only be fair if it makes the presence of the border almost invisible, that is, it preserves the status quo as much as possible.[47]

[43] Ibid.
[44] Ibid, 91.
[45] Ibid, 97.
[46] Ibid, 97.
[47] Ibid, 100–1.

In other words, what Shinkaretskaya proposed was that although international legal principles of state succession applied to the dissolution of the Soviet Union and its borders, the borders between Soviet republics should not have become 'real' (guarded, 'locked', and so on) borders as this would be 'unjust'. Soon, with respect to Georgia since 2008 and Ukraine since 2014, revision of these Soviet-era borders became official Russian policy.

Other Russian international lawyers came to differently nuanced conclusions regarding the issue of state identity (continuity) and state succession. Georgi Velyaminov made the point that although the territory of the Russian state ('in the broad sense') had changed and its socio-political system changed twice, its international personality was invariably preserved.[48] Where this sounds like state continuity (identity), Velyaminov qualifies the situation further by calling it 'partial succession' instead: 'In relation to the RSFSR, one can speak of nothing more than "partial succession", but not of a complete change of international personality and "full succession".'[49]

This assessment reflects Soviet Russian policy after 1917, namely that it accepted some earlier treaties and rejected others. Furthermore, in November 1996, France and the Russian Federation reached an agreement on the symbolic repayment by Russia of previous, tsarist-era debts.[50] Velyaminov concluded that the post-Soviet Russian Federation remained a 'state successor' to the Russian Empire, the Russian SFSR, and the Soviet Union.[51] Petr Kremnev, another international law scholar from Moscow, has expressed doubts as to whether state continuity is the right term for characterizing the Russian Federation's post-1991 status.[52] Kremnev concluded that the Belovezhe agreements which ended the Soviet Union in December 1991 were both unconstitutional and illegal under international law, as they "violated the right of peoples to self-determination". Those Soviet people who wanted to continue living in one state had the right to do so—a right which was illegally ignored, argues Kremnev.[53]

Putting together both the concepts of 'state succession' (Shinkaretskaya, Velyaminov, Kremnev) and 'state continuity' (Chernichenko)—as did the Russian constitutional amendment of 1 July 2020—created the necessary flexibility for the Russian Federation. This is not a solution for legal purists but

[48] GM Velyaminov, 'Pravopreemstvo mezhdu Rossiiskoi Federatsii i Rossiiskoi imperii, mezhdunarodnye i vnutrennye aspekty', *Moscow JIL* No 3, 1998, 22–6 at 23.

[49] Ibid, 23.

[50] Ibid, 24.

[51] Ibid, 25.

[52] Petr P Kremnev, *Raspad SSSR: mezhdunarodno-pravovye problemy*, Zertsalo-M, 2005, 241–2.

[53] Ibid, 229–30.

in this way the Russian Federation can continue what it wants to continue and at the same time discontinue what it wants to discontinue. No faction of domestic international lawyer–experts is neglected or dismissed either. This flexibility in the use of concepts is a Russian imperial continuity with which we have already become familiar based on the earlier debate, namely whether the Soviet Union was a continuator state of the Russian Empire. This also epitomizes the continuity of the Soviet tradition of dialectical thinking and 're-solving' contradictions by 'reconciling' apparently contradictory concepts and positions.[54] Besides declarations of state continuity, 'state succession' also continues to be a popular classification in Russian scholarship of international law after the constitutional amendments of 1 July 2020.[55] However, in the end a certain revisionist claim to state continuity tends to prevail in the Russian legal-political argumentation. For example, in May 2025, Anton Kobyakov, an advisor of President Putin, announced at the St Petersburg Legal Forum that in 1991 the Soviet Union was not dissolved in a constitutionally proper way, and that therefore it continues to exist legally, and the war in Ukraine is not international but 'a domestic process'.[56]

Clausula rebus sic stantibus

One of this book's leitmotifs has been use of the *clausula rebus sic stantibus* argument in justifying Russian and Soviet conquests and in geopolitical changes. A general debate revolves around whether this argument has experienced a certain renaissance in international legal practice, compared to the restrictive formulation of the Vienna Convention on the Law of Treaties of 1969.[57] In the Russian Federation, this argument has been reused to justify seizure or—as it is seen in Russia—'return' of originally Russian imperial territories. In 2014, Russia annexed Crimea, violating its previous treaty commitments such as the 1994 Budapest memorandum and the 2003 border treaty with Ukraine. Was there any way to justify the Russian annexation in the context of international law, beyond a reference to the right of Crimea's Russian speakers

[54] In Western scholarship, see further also Guido Acquaviva, 'Russia as the State Continuing the Legal Personality of the USSR—An Inquiry into State Identity or Succession', *JHIL* No 23, 2019, 310–53.

[55] See, eg, Aleksandr N Savenkov, *Niurnberg. Prigovor vo imia mira*, Prospekt, 2022, 23.

[56] The Insider, 'Sovetnik Putina zayavil, shto "SSSR yuridicheskyi prozolzhaet sushchestvovat'", a voina s Ukrainoi—"vnutrennii protsess", 21.05.2025, https://theins.ru/news/281461?fbclid=IwY2xjawKa1NtleHRuA2FlbQIxMABicmlkETFOamwwMTJzdkR1dEp1V2E5AR5oAH0DB0WK7jp_k8lfZua5nHCulLhyOslK9AzlsQzZoyXOwqy8YZSpKKmATg_aem_ocCrFXH1t5tnUgWU0TgGqQ.

[57] See Julian Kulaga, 'A Renaissance of the Doctrine of *Rebus Sic Stantibus*?', *ICLQ* No 89, 2020, 477–97.

to self-determination? In 2014, one of the most experienced Russian international lawyers, Georgi Velyaminov, tackled this question in an article in the journal *Gosudarstvo i pravo*, the successor of *Sovetskoe gosudarstvo i pravo*. Velyaminov argues that although Crimea had been handed over from the Russian Soviet Federalist Socialist Republic (SFSR) to the Ukrainian SSR in 1954 'unconstitutionally', this did not matter from an international law perspective as, in the Budapest memorandum of 1994, Russia had indeed implicitly recognized Crimea as part of Ukraine.[58] However, Velyaminov further argues that the assurance given by Russia to Ukraine was not given absolutely and forever but only in the context of the Treaty on Nonproliferation of Nuclear Weapons.[59] Thus, at the end of his argumentation, Velyaminov draws his legal trump card—the good old principle of *clausula rebus sic stantibus*, already so familiar to us from tsarist Russian and Soviet history. According to Velyaminov, the Budapest memorandum was concluded under the circumstances prevailing in 1994—but those circumstances, order, and legality no longer existed in Ukraine in 2014.[60] In the same article published in 2014, Velyaminov, himself a Soviet Second World War veteran, also advocated for preventive military strikes against Ukraine: 'The experience of World War II and the Munich "policy of appeasement" regarding aggressive fascism which preceded it demonstrates that defense must be preventive. One need not wait until [the enemy] gathers forces for an open attack.'[61]

This psychology and guidance for action is exactly what President Putin expressed and implemented on 24 February 2022.

Other Russian international lawyers also justified Russia's violation of treaties concluded with Ukraine in the 1990s. International lawyers Voronin, Kulebyakin, and Nikolaev admitted the existence of these treaties between Russia and Ukraine fixing the border of 1991 but pointed out that few had bothered to ask whether they were in correspondence with an imperative norm in international law (*jus cogens*), namely the right of peoples to self-determination.[62] In their view, enforcing the right of peoples to self-determination is not aggression; after all, Russia's border with Ukraine was fixed against the backdrop of the 1997 Treaty on Friendship, Cooperation and Partnership—which Ukraine was no longer honouring since Maidan.[63]

[58] GM Velyaminov, 'Vossoedinenye Kryma s Rossiei: pravovoi rakurs', *GP* No 9, 2014, 12–18 at 13.
[59] Ibid, 16.
[60] Ibid, 16.
[61] Ibid, 17.
[62] ER Voronin, VN Kulebyakin, AV Nikolaev, 'Gosudarstvennyi perevorot v Kieve v fevral'e 2014.g: mezhdunarodno-pravovye otsenki i posledstvia', *Moscow JIL* No 1, 2015, 11–28 at 13.
[63] Ibid, 17, 22.

In its essence, this is the same argument on treaties presented by the Russian Empire in 1870 regarding its navy in the Black Sea region and, as this book has demonstrated, on which Russia and the Soviet Union have since repeatedly relied. It is only that nowadays, the argument of *jus cogens* can additionally be used on such occasions—but in a way showing how the argument of 'self-determination of peoples' goes back and forth in Russian history, at one time justifying secessions from Russia, and then at another justifying annexations by Russia. According to its recent uses in the Russian Federation, self-determination of peoples does not apply as a ground for secession in non-colonial situations where the political aspirations of arguably non-Russian ethnicities in the Russian Federation are concerned (for example, Chechnya and Tartarstan). However, it does apply concerning the rights of ethnic Russians or native Russian speakers living compactly outside the Russian Federation in other ex-Soviet republics (such as Crimea and the Donbas). Behind this paradox lies the principle of 'might makes right' and the idea that great powers formulate and guarantee international law according to their interests and preferences.

Because reference to *clausula rebus sic stantibus* and unilateral termination or violation of treaties seems such a constant in Russian and Soviet history, researchers have also asked where it originates from. The semiotician Yuri Mikhailovich Lotman (1922–93) traced it back to deeper structural cultural differences in the Middle Ages, when Western Europe developed a 'chivalrous' contractual culture and ancient Rus developed a culture of what Lotman called 'submission'.[64] Lotman postulated:

> In imbuing the concept of government with religious sentiment, social psychology of this type demands from society that it transfer its entire semiosis onto the tsar, who becomes a symbolic figure, a kind of living icon. The remaining members of society are left with behavior having zero semioticity; only purely practical activity is required of them.[65]

Russian and Soviet proclivity for the use of *clausula rebus sic stantibus* regarding treaties in international law also reflects how Russia as a country and society has experienced constitutional law in its history, that established rules

[64] Yuri Lotman, 'The Contract and Self-Surrender as Archetypal Models of Culture', in: Marek Tamm (ed) *Juri Lotman—Culture, Memory and History. Essays in Cultural Semiotics*, Translated from the Russian by Brian James Baer, Palgrave Macmillan, 2019, 49–66 at 52–3.

[65] Ibid, 57.

were volatile and in the end, notwithstanding occasional formal constitutional assurances, the tsarist-centralized model of governance prevailed.

Russia as a Great Power, Balance of Power, and the Defence of History

The predominant doctrine of international law during the Putin era can be described as realism. During the late 1980s one of the Soviet Union's most promising international lawyers, Rein Müllerson (b 1944), advocated for the revival of balance of power as a foundation for international law, writing in the context of Russia's justifications for annexing Crimea.[66] This is a contrast to some Soviet scholars who formally rejected balance of power as too 'bourgeois' and imperialist a doctrine,[67] even though, as we demonstrated above, parts of the Soviet doctrine of international law accepted the importance of balance of power under various labels. The problem with this kind of realism based on balance of power is that it tends to make international law a mere figleaf for great-power interests. One of Russia's contemporary leading international relations experts, Dmitri Trenin (b 1955), writes that international relations are based on force, not on law.[68] This had, even earlier, led to changes of discourse in Russian understandings of international law. When—during the Soviet area—in Soviet legal discourse 'small states' deserved equality and needed Soviet protection from US imperialism, now—based on Russia's post-Soviet experience—they had become problematic, such as when Lukashuk observed that small states could behave irresponsibly and exhibit the 'psychology of the weak'.[69] Making a similar point, Müllerson criticized tendencies of 'anarchophilia' which are promoted with the principle of self-determination in the international community.[70]

Just as during the Soviet period, one area in which the revival of great-power thinking is clearly evident is the international law of the sea and maritime claims. The tradition of the Vyshnepolsky article of 1954 lives on: recently,

[66] Rein Müllerson, *Dawn of a New Order: Geopolitics and the Clash of Ideologies*, IB Tauris, 2017, 154–61.

[67] NV Zakharova, I Yu Barsegov, 'O tak nazyvaemoi teorii 'ravnovesia sil', *Soviet YBIL* 1959, 272–82.

[68] Dmitri Trenin *Novyi balans sil. Rossiia v poiskakh vneshnepoliticheskogo ravnovesia*, Alpina Publisher, 2021, 25, 53.

[69] II Lukashuk, *Mezhdunarodnoe pravo. Obschchaya chast*, 2nd edn, Beck, 2001, 323.

[70] R Müllerson, *Dawn of a New Order: Geopolitics and the Clash of Ideologies*, IB Tauris, 2017, 151.

extensive claims to historical waters have again been presented in international law scholarship in Russia.[71]

Russia's Eurasianist integration project has also been linked to great-power needs and aspirations. The most pertinent examples are regional organizations in post-Soviet Eurasia, for example the Commonwealth of Independent States. To illustrate, Yuri Ilyich Skuratov (b 1952) writes that a key role in the project belongs to Russian culture and language.[72] He postulates that Eurasian integration is about positioning Russia as a superpower, as a first-order centre of world influence, as a great power.[73]

Finally, history remains contested by the example of the 1939 Nazi–Soviet non-aggression pact and its appraisals in Russian legal academia. Grigory Serafimovich Starodubtsev (b 1954) suggests that we need to separate the fully normal, usual, and legal non-aggression pact itself from the secret protocols, which remain controversial.[74] Writing in 2015, Starodubtsev argues that when the Soviet parliament declared the secret protocols of the pact void in 1989, this was not preceded by serious research; the matter of the secret protocols still needs further study instead of rushing to conclusions.[75] The current editor-in-chief of the journal *Gosudarstvo i pravo* and member of the Russian Academy of Sciences, Aleksandr Nikolaevich Savenkov (b 1961), has gone further by arguing that the December 1989 resolution of the Soviet parliament to declare the secret protocols of the Nazi–Soviet pact of 1939 void and illegal was itself 'legally invalid and illegal'.[76] There is little in terms of reasoning behind this claim by Savenkov, except that 'the decision on this question was already taken by the international military tribunal at Nuremberg'.[77] This is also a good example of why any continuity with previous decisions of the Russian and Soviet states needs to remain flexible: a Soviet decision from 1989 does not have to be binding on today's Russia or its advocates of international legal history policy.

[71] Ivan S Zhudro, 'Evoliutsia mezhdunarodno-pravovoga rezhima Severnogo Ledovitoga okeana i natsional'nye interesy Rossii', *Moscow JIL* No 2, 2016, 63–80 at 73, 77; NA Mincheva, 'Karskoe more v mezhdunarodno-pravovoi politike Rossii', *Moscow JIL* No 3, 2023, 41–51 at 47, 49; VV Gavrilov, RM Nurimbetov, 'Istoricheskie prava gosudarstv na morskie akvatorii i pravovoi status Okhotskoga moria', *Moscow JIL* No 4, 2022, 44–55 at 52, 54.

[72] Yu M Skuratov, 'Evraziiskaya paradigma Rossii i nekotorye problemy integratsii na prostranstve Sodruzhestva Nezavisimykh Gosudarstv (SNG), *GP* No 2, 2015, 89–95 at 91.

[73] Ibid, 91, 95.

[74] GS Starodubtsev, 'Protivodeistvie falsifikatsii otechestvennoi mezhdunarodno–pravovoi istorii', in: BM Ashavskiy, AA Moiseev (eds) *Sovremennoe mezhdunarodnoe pravo. Teoria i praktika. Liber Amicorum v chest' Stanislava Chernichenko*, Prospekt, 2015, 353–61 at 355–9.

[75] Ibid, 359, 361.

[76] Aleksandr N Savenkov, *Niurnberg. Prigovor vo imya mira*, Moscow: Prospekt, 2022, 24.

[77] Ibid, 108.

The government of the Russian Federation has also maintained continuity with the Soviet discourse on imperialism and colonialism. For example, a press release from the Russian MFA of 5 December 2024 commented on the fact that on 4 December 2024 the United Nations General Assembly (UNGA) adopted a resolution titled Eradication of Colonialism in All Its Forms and Manifestations, which was drafted by the Group of Friends in Defense of the UN Charter 'with the guiding role of Russia.'[78] A total of 113 countries voted for it while 63 states abstained, with no UN member state voting against. The Russian official press release stated: 'The core of the abstaining group is made up of the former Western parent states, which bear the brunt of responsibility for centuries of colonial oppression of Asian, African and Latin American countries.'[79]

In debates at the UN, Ukraine, Poland, and the Baltic States criticized what they saw as the Russian government's 'hypocritical' position on this matter.[80]

[78] Russian MFA, Press release on the adoption of UNGA resolution on eradicating colonialism in all its forms and manifestations, 5.12.2024, https://mid.ru/en/foreign_policy/news/1985538/.

[79] Ibid.

[80] UN, 'Delegates Voice Concern over Procedural Aspects, Language of Resolution on Eradicating Colonialism as Fourth Committee Approves 24 Texts, Concluding General Debate', 17.10.2024, https://press.un.org/en/2024/gaspd810.doc.htm.

9
In Conclusion

The intended contribution of this book is that it shows in some detail how imperial and imperialist ideas, doctrines, and practices played out in the history of international law and legal discourse in the Russian Empire and the Soviet Union. This aspect has so far been somewhat neglected in parts of the international law literature even though extensive justificatory arguments based on international law have played an important role in the expansion and preservation of the Russian Empire and its transformation in the Soviet Union. International law and its concepts, often interpreted idiosyncratically (for example, assigning a new meaning to a legal–political concept), served as a pool for justificatory reasoning in favour of the Soviet Union. The Israeli international lawyer Eyal Benvenisti has argued that manipulating international law may be less sinister than completely ignoring it.[1] However, the opposite argument can also be made, because a 'great power' that openly ignores international law is in some ways more honest in its brutality whereas manipulation in bad faith may fool at least some people somewhere, as the impression is invoked that, well, at least the 'great power' somehow justified its action in terms of international law and still cares about it. But what if it does not? Here is where the arguably indeterminate nature of some international legal doctrines can also become a problem, especially for smaller states who cannot impose their understanding of international law by force.

Russian imperialism has been a major force in the history of international law. Even though—in the Soviet self-understanding—imperialism for Russia ended in 1917 with the end of capitalism, the picture which emerges in the present study is that the Soviets managed to prolong the life of the Russian Empire until at least 1991, extensively using international legal arguments and doctrines in support. In that sense, Russia was more successful in keeping its Empire than were the West European maritime empires: Russia's Empire lasted longer and, perhaps most importantly, many people and nations, especially

[1] Eyal Benvenisti, 'The Resilience of International Law in the Face of Empire', *Just Security*, 17.02.2025, https://www.justsecurity.org/107820/resilience-international-empire/.

Russia, the Soviet Union, and Imperial Continuity in International Law. Lauri Mälksoo, Oxford University Press.
 DOI: 10.1093/9780198955962.003.0009

outside the West, learned to dissociate Russia from the evils of imperialism, just as suggested by Lenin, Khrushchev, but also Pashukanis. Various camouflage and facilitating doctrines were used to prolong the life of the Empire, including the concept that Soviet republics were 'sovereign', even though substantively they lacked the characteristics of state sovereignty and were subjugated to the Russian centre. In terms of decolonization, what happened for West European empires in around 1960 happened for the Soviet Union only in 1991, although at the time not even primarily based on demands by the formerly colonized Central Asian peoples. What is more, since President Putin came to power in Russia, the Russian government has tried to push back and rehabilitate its Empire, including with the help of international legal arguments. Russia's aggression against Ukraine since 2014 and especially since 2022 demonstrates that Russian imperialism continues to be a major factor in international politics, a challenge for international law as traditionally understood because imperialist states often have an agenda for revision of the territorial *status quo*. Russia's predecessor, the Soviet Union, co-created the international law of 1945 from a position of military strength plus territorial gains in Europe and Asia; but, now that Russia's territory has diminished since 1991, the new Russia of Putin is attacking the very foundations of international law of 1945, at least from the perspective of smaller neighbouring states such as Ukraine.

This book has argued that it makes sense also to understand the Soviet period in Russia's history from both the imperial and the imperialist perspectives. When we understand imperialism as a desire to territorially expand and motivation to defend land seizures—facilitated by international legal arguments and justifications, as discussed in this book—then Lenin's concept of imperialism ('as the highest stage of capitalism') is inadequate. On too many occasions was Soviet rhetoric in contexts of international law fiercely 'anti-imperialist', in stark contrast to Soviet expansionist behaviour towards its neighbours. Moreover, Muscovy started to expand and in this sense was imperialist long before the arrival of capitalism.

A particular tool of international legal policies in Russia and the Soviet Union has been treaties. At least in territories which have aimed to break away from the Empire throughout history, Russia and the Soviet Union have favoured a flexible approach to treaties, based on which any agreement reflects the balance of power at any given moment. This means that such treaties are not very stable and can be reversed by Russia when circumstances are geopolitically ripe.

Another conclusion from this study is the continuity between imperial ideas and doctrines of international law in the Russian Empire, the Soviet Union, and often also Putin's Russian Federation. Soviet approaches to international law were studied quite extensively in the West during the Cold War but not all researchers saw the connection between the doctrines of tsarist Russia and the Soviet Union, especially regarding Russia's flexible thinking on treaties.

An imperial continuity links Russian, Soviet, and post-Soviet international law. Although previous doctrines and interpretations of international law have several times been rejected and transformed, nevertheless the key interest in preserving the territory of the Empire has usually remained paramount. Characteristically, Maxim Anatol'evich Isaev (1966–2021), a constitutional lawyer from MGIMO University, has written that tsarist Russia was not a 'prison house of peoples' (as Lenin claimed) but a 'family of peoples', a dynamic system which offered its population peace and constituted their world (міръ).[2] Unlike for early Soviet legal scholars and politicians, the Russian Empire is no longer something to be condemned and criticized; one can and should be proud of it, its grandeur and might. Apparently, this conviction has never disappeared, and has influenced generations of international lawyers in Russia and the Soviet Union.

Considering that the imperial—and repeatedly also imperialist—trajectory has been characteristic of Russian and Soviet international law traditions for some four hundred years, and that so far there has been very little critical confrontation of this history among the international law community in Russia, it would be too idealistic to expect that Russia's foundational imperial trajectory in its international legal approaches will quickly or easily fade away. Some first steps can be witnessed among Russian international lawyers and human rights defenders in exile. For example, when they endorsed punishment of the crime of aggression and war crimes committed in the war against Ukraine in their 2023 Brussels declaration, they concluded that 'this war became possible because previous grave crimes committed by Russia's leadership and military on its own soil and abroad went unpunished'.[3] While this view does not highlight an explicit connection with the history of imperialism in Russia, others make that link. Representatives of the Russian opposition currently living outside the Russian Federation such as the former chess world master Garry Kasparov have made the point that, in the future, it will be necessary for the Russian state and society to confront crimes committed in the past and the state's imperialist legacy.[4] Vladimir Kara-Murza considers it a cardinal mistake that critical engagement with Russia's past and its state crimes was not consequentially tackled

[2] Maxim A Isaev, 'K voprosu o mezhdunarodno-pravovom statuse Velikoga kniazhestva Finliandskogo', *Moscow JIL* No 2018, 33–43 at 35–6.

[3] The Brussels declaration, 9.06.2023, https://meduza.io/en/feature/2023/06/09/the-brussels-declaration.

[4] Garry Kasparov in social media (e.g. on X, 10.12.2024: 'we must confront Russia's imperial past').

in Russia during the 1990s, unlike in most other Central and East European states.[5] The Belarus opposition leader in exile, Sviatlana Tsikhanouskaya, has celebrated the memory of Kastus Kalinouski (1838–64), who 'led the 1863–1864 uprising against imperial oppression'.[6]

In his recent interpretation of constitutional evolution in Russia, the Australian constitutional law scholar William Partlett has argued that Russia is not historically fated to remain a centralized, authoritarian country, despite a long history of commitment to the centralized state.[7] Partlett suggests that in making this positive claim for a balanced constitution, Russians can learn from the reasoning and arguments of the tsarist-era liberal statist movement and thus have a suggestion for interaction with post-Putin Russia:

> This has implications for the international community as well. Those hoping to support Russian democratic reform will need to look beyond personal guarantees from a new Russian leader or the promise of more constitutional rights. Instead, they must seek to encourage deeper structural and normative constitutional changes that can allow Russia to finally break with its deeply held commitment to a centralised state.[8]

However, from the perspective of the history of international law and international legal ideas as represented in Russia and discussed in the present study, a direct connection also exists between the centralization of power and the Empire; the first facilitated and justified the second. Identities constructed around the Empire are apparently one of the main reasons why liberal and rights-based reforms have not been successful in Russia. As far as the tsarist-era liberal statist movement was concerned, we should also not forget the legacy of Martens and Mandelstam, who wanted to reform the Empire and make it 'liberal' while also keeping it territorially intact. Reluctance to let the Empire go may have been one of the key reasons why liberal constitutional reforms in Russia failed in the first place, both in 1917 and after 1991. Thus, the main question for post-Putin Russia's leaders and legal elites is not just whether they would be willing to give up a centralized state and take human rights seriously; perhaps even more crucial is whether Russia is willing to critically work on and abandon its imperial identity in international law.

[5] Oliver Bilger, 'Wir kennen Putin, wir wissen, was er tut', Die Welt, 9.12.2024, https://www.welt.de/politik/ausland/plus254781012/Wladimir-Kara-Mursa-Wir-kennen-Putin-wir-wissen-was-er-tut.html (Paper edition 8.12.2024, under a different title: 'Was in Russland passiert, betrifft jeden').

[6] Sviatlana Tsikhanouskaya, on X, 02.03.2025.

[7] William Partlett, *Why the Russian Constitution Matters. The Constitutional Dark Arts*, Hart, 2024, 178.

[8] Ibid, 179.

Bibliography

UN Normative Acts

UNGA Resolution ES 11/1, 2 March 2022
UNGA Resolution ES 11/4, 7 April 2022
UNSC Res. 2202 (2015)

Court Judgments

ICJ, Application of the International Convention for the Suppression of the Financing of Terrorism and of the International Convention on the Elimination of All Forms of Racial Discrimination (*Ukraine v Russian Federation*), Request for Indication of Provisional Measures, Order of 19 April 2017

Panevezys–Saldutiskis Railway, PCIJ Series A/B. No 76, Judgment of 28.02.1939

Russian Constitutional Court ruling, 02.10.2022, No 39-П/2022 Po delu o proverke konstitutsionnosti ne vstupivshego v silu mezhdunarodnogo dogovora mezhdu Rossiiskoi Federatsiei i Khersonskoi oblasti o prinyatii v Rossiiskuyu Federatsiu Khersonskoi oblasti i obrazovanii v sostave Rossiiskoi Federatsii novoga subyekta

Treaties

Persia and the Russian Socialist Federal Soviet Republic, Treaty of Friendship, signed at Moscow on 26 February 1921, LNTS 1922, 400–13

Peace Treaty of Tartu between Soviet Russia and the Republic of Estonia, 2 February 1920, http://www.worldlii.org/int/other/LNTSer/1922/92.html

Constitutions

1918 Soviet Russian Constitution, https://www.constituteproject.org/constitution/Russia_1918

Declarations

The Brussels Declaration, 9.06.2023, https://meduza.io/en/feature/2023/06/09/the-brussels-declaration

Books

Levan Aleksidze, *International Law and Georgia (From Antiquity to Present). Selected Papers Published in 1957–2012*, Ivane Javakhishvili Tbilisi State University, 2012

Antony Anghie, *Imperialism, Sovereignty, and the Making of International Law*, CUP, 2005

David Armitage (ed) *Theories of Empire, 1450–1800*, Ashgate, 1998

Andreas von Arnauld, Thomas Kleinlein, Nele Matz-Lück (eds) *German Yearbook of International Law*, Vol 66, Duncker & Humblot, 2023

M A Avakov, *Pravopreemstvo Sovetskogo gosudarstva* (State succession of the Soviet state), Moscow: Gosudarstvennoe izdatel'stvo yuridicheskoi literatury, 1961

Sergey N Baburin, *Mir imperii. Territoria gosudarstva i mirovoi poriadok* (The world of Empires. State territory and world order), Izdatel'stvo R Aslanova 'Iuridiceshki tsentr Press', 2005

S V Bakhin (ed) *Rossiiskaya assotsiatsia mezhdunarodnoga prava. 1957–2007. Biograficheski slovar'* (Russian Association of International Law. 1957–2007. Bibliographical dictionary), Izdatel'ski Dom Sankt-Peterburgskoga gosudarstvennogo universiteta, 2007

G M Barats, *Kritiko-sravnitel'nyi analiz dogovorov Rusi s Vizantiei: Vosstanovlenie teksta, perevod, kommentarii i sravnenie s drugimi pravovymi pamiatnikami, v chastnosti – s Russkoyu Pravdoyu*, (Critical-comparative analysis of the treaties of Rus' with Byzantium: Restoration of the text, translation and comparison with other legal memorials, especially with Russkaya Pravda), Tipografia 1-i Kievskoi Arteli Pechatnogo Dela Trekhsvyatitel'skaia No 5, 1910

Yuri G Barsegov, *Territoria v mezhdunarodnom prave* (Territory in international law), Gosudarstvennoe izdatel'stvo iuridicheskoy literatury, 1958

Ernest Batson Price, *The Russo-Japanese Treaties of 1907–1916 Concerning Manchuria and Mongolia*, The Johns Hopkins Press, 1933

Vyacheslav A Batyr, *Mezhdunarodnoe territorial'noe pravo* (International territorial law), Mezhdunarodnye otnoshenia, 2021

Seymour Becker, *Russia's Protectorates in Central Asia: Bukhara and Khiva, 1865–1924*, Harvard UP, 1968

Arnulf Becker Lorca, *Mestizo International Law. A Global Intellectual History 1842–1933*, CUP, 2014

Laurence W. Beilenson, *The Treaty Trap. A History of the Performance of Political Treaties by the United States and European Nations.* A Foreign Policy Research Institute Book, Washington: DC, Public Affairs Press, 1969

Lauren Benton, Lisa Ford, *Rage for Order. The British Empire and International Law, 1800–1850*, Harvard UP, 2018

Lev Berdnikov, *Jews in Service to the Tsar*, translated by Nora Seligman Favorov, Russian Information Services, 2009

Carl Bergbohm, *Die bewaffnete Neutralität 1780–1783. Eine Entwicklungsphase des Völkerrechts im Seekriege*, Puttkammer & Mühlbrecht, 1884

Yu P Brovkva, *Mezhdunarodnaya pravosub 'ektnost' BSSR* (International legal personality of the Byelorussian Soviet Socialist Republic) Nauka i tekhnika, 1967

Jane Burbank, Frederick Cooper, *Empires in World History: Power and the Politics of Difference*, Princeton UP, 2010

Jane Burbank, Frederick Cooper, *Post-Imperial Possibilities. Eurasia, Eurafrica, Afroasia*, Princeton UP, 2023

William E Butler, Vladimir G Tunkin (eds) *The Tunkin Diary and Lectures. The Diary and Collected Lectures of G I Tunkin at The Hague Academy of International Law*, Eleven international publishing, 2012

Jean-Yves Calvez, *Droit international et souveraineté en URSS. L'évolution de l'idéologie juridique soviétique depuis la Révolution d'Octobre*, Librairie Armand Colin, 1953

Cosmin Cercel, Gian-Giacomo Fusco, Przemyslaw Tacik (eds), *Legal Form. Pashukanis and the Marxist Critique of Law*, Routledge, 2025

L A Challandes, *Iuridicheskaya priroda terrotorial'noga verkhovenstva. Istoriko-dogmaticheskoe issledovanie* (Legal nature of territorial supremacy. A historical-dogmatic study) Tom 1, Tip. Trenke i Fyuzno, 1903

L A Challandes, *Russkoe gosudarstvennoe pravo* (Russian constitutional law), Tipografia Shnakenburga, 1908

Borislav Chernev, *Twilight of Empire: The Brest-Litovsk Conference and the Remaking of East–Central Europe, 1917–1918*, University of Toronto Press, 2017

Stanislav V Chernichenko, *Teoria mezhdunarodnoga prava* (Theory of international law), Vol II, NIMP, 1999

Wei Chi, *The Soviet Union under the New Tsars*, Foreign Languages Press, 1978

V Chikvadze (ed) *Kurs mezhdunarodnoga prava v shesti tomakh*, Vol II (Osnavnye printsipy mezhdunarodnoga prava), Nauka, 1967

Aminat Chokobaeva, Cloé Drieu, Alexander Morrison (eds) *The Central Asian Revolt of 1916. A Collapsing Empire in the Age of War and Revolution*, Manchester UP, 2019

Benjamin Allen Coates, *Legalist Empire. International Law and American Foreign Relations in the Early Twentieth Century*, OUP, 2016

Ariel Cohen, *Russian Imperialism. Development and Crisis*, Praeger, 1996

Jerome Alan Cohen, Hungdah Chiu, *People's China and International Law. A Documentary Study*, Vol I and II, Princeton UP, 1974

Conférence internationale de la paix, La Haye, 18 mai–29 juillet 1899, La Haye, ministère des Affaires étrangères. Annexes au rapport de la convention pour le règlement pacifique des conflits internationaux. Annexe A, Documents émanés de la délégation russe, 1899

Frederik Dhondt, *Balance of Power and Norm Hierarchy: Franco–British Diplomacy after the Peace of Utrecht*, Brill, 2015

Alton S Donnelly, *The Russian Conquest of Bashkiria 1552–1740. A Case Study in Imperialism*, Yale UP, 1968

V N Durdenevsky, S B Krylov (eds), *Mezhdunarodnoe pravo* (International law), Iuridicheskoe izdatel'stvo ministerstva iustitsii SSSR, 1947

Bernard Dutoit, *Coexistence et droit international a la lumière de la doctrine soviétique*, A. Pedone, 1966

Luis Eslava, Michael Fakhri, Vasuki Nesiah (eds) *Bandung, Global History, and International Law. Critical Pasts and Pending Futures*, CUP, 2017

A.Ya. Esayan, *Nekotorye voprosy teorii i istorii mezhdunarodnoga prava*, Yerevan: Izdatel'stvo Yerevanskogo universiteta, 1977

Alexander Etkind, *Russia Against Modernity*, Polity Press, 2023

Alexander Etkind, *Internal Colonization. Russia's Imperial Experience*, Polity Press, 2011

Jörg Fisch, *The Right of Self-Determination of Peoples. The Domestication of an Illusion*, Translated by Anita Mage, CUP, 2015

Caroline von Gall, *Die Konzepte 'staatliche Einheit' und 'einheitliche Macht' in der russischen Theorie von Staat und Recht. Der Einfluss des Gemeinschaftsideals auf die russische Verfassungsentwicklung*, Duncker & Humblot, 2010

Adom Getachew, *Worldmaking after Empire. The Rise and Fall of Self-determination*, Princeton UP, 2019

Stella Ghervas, *Conquering Peace. From the Enlightment to the European Union*, Harvard UP, 2021

Serge Goriaïnov, *La question d'Orient a la veille du Traité de Berlin (1870–1876), avec une introduction par Boris Nolde*, Institut d'études slaves, 1948
V E Grabar, *The History of International Law in Russia, 1647–1917. A Bio-Bibliographical Study*, translated and edited by W E Butler, Clarendon Press, 1990
Kathryn Greenman, Anne Orford, Anna Saunders, Ntina Tzouvala (eds) *Revolutions in International Law: The Legacies of 1917*, CUP, 2021
Wilhelm G Grewe, *Epochen der Völkerrechtsgeschichte*, Nomos, 1984
Raluca Grosescu, Ned Richardson-Little (eds) *Socialism and International Law. The Cold War and Its Legacies*, OUP, 2025
Kazimierz Grzybowski, *Soviet Public International Law. Doctrines and Diplomatic Practice*, A. W. Sijthoff, 1970
Oona A Hathaway, Scott J Shapiro, *The Internationalists. How a Radical Plan to Outlaw War Remade the World*, Simon & Schuster, 2017
Lene Hansen, *Security as Practice. Discourse Analysis and the Bosnian War*, Routledge, 2006
Rebecca Haynes, Moldova. *A History*, Bloomsbury, 2020
Michael Head, *Evgeny Pashukanis: A Critical Reappraisal*, Routledge, 2008
Olaus Hermelin, *Gerechte Ablehnung derer lasterhafften Beschuldigungen, womit der Moscowitische Czar Seinen Krieg, damit Er Schweden, wieder Eyd, und noch neulich versicherte Treu und Glauben, angegriffen, zu beschönigen gesuchet hat*, nach dem Lateinischen Original übersetzt, Stockholm, 1701
Francine Hirsch, *Soviet Judgment at Nuremberg. A New History of the International Military Tribunal after World War II*, OUP, 2020
Samuel J Hirst, *Against the Liberal Order. The Soviet Union, Turkey, and Statist Internationalism, 1919–1939*, OUP, 2024
Kaj Hobér, *The Perestroika Era and International Law*, Edward Elgar Publishing, 2024
Adam Hohschild, *King Leopold's Ghost: A Story of Greed, Terror, and Heroism in Colonial Africa*, Macmillan, 1998
Thomas Erskine Holland, *A Lecture on the Treaty Relations of Russia and Turkey from 1774 to 1853, delivered at Oxford on April 28, 1877*, Macmillan & Co, 1877
Immanuel C Y Hsü, *The Ili Crisis: A Study of Sino-Russian Diplomacy*, Clarendon Press, 1965
Inge Van Hulle, *Britain and International Law in West Africa. The Practice of Empire*, OUP, 2020
Taras Hunczak (ed) *Russian Imperialism from Ivan the Great to the Revolution*, Rutgers UP, 1974
Hungarian Situation and the Rule of Law, International Commission of Legal Scholars, 1957
M P Iroshnikov, A O Chubarian, *Tainoe stanovitsia iavnym. Ob izdanii sekretnykh dogovorov tsarskogo i vremennogo pravitel'stv* (The secret becomes visible. The publication of secret treaties of the tsarist and provisional governments), Nauka, 1970
S V Ivanenko, *Sankt-peterburgskaya shkola mezhdunarodnoga prava. Mesto i rol' sankt-peterburgskogo universiteta, ego uchenykh i vypusknikov v stanovlenii i razvitii nauki i praktiki mezhdunarodnoga prava. Chast' pervaya 1720–1920-e gg.* (The St Petersburg school of international law. The place and role of St Petersburg university, its scholars and graduates in the formation and evolution of the science and practice of international law), Iuridicheskii tsentr, 2019
Boris Kagarlitsky, *From Empires to Imperialism. The State and the Rise of Bourgeois Civilisation*, Translated by Renfrey Clarke, Routledge, 2014
Jeffrey Kahn, *Federalism, Democratization, and the Rule of Law in Russia* , OUP, 2002
Chiang Kai-shek, *Soviet Russia in China. A Summing Up at Seventy*, China Publishing Company, 1969

Andreas Kappeler, *The Russian Empire: A Multiethnic History*, Routledge, 2013 (2001 Taylor & Francis)

Andreas Kappeler, *Ungleiche Brüder: Russen und Ukrainer vom Mittelalter bis zur Gegenwart*, 6. C H Beck, 2022

Didar Kassymova, Zhanat Kundakbayeva, Ustina Markus, *Historical Dictionary of Kazakhstan*, Lanham: The Scarecrow Press, 2012

Erich Kaufmann, *Das Wesen des Völkerrechts und die clausula rebus sic stantibus*, J C B Mohr, 1911

Firuz Kazemzadeh, *Russia and Britain in Persia, 1864–1914. A Study in Imperialism*, Yale UP, 1968

Christian Kelch, *Liivimaa ajaloo järg* (Continuation of the History of Livonia), Tänapäev, 2024

R L Khachaturov, *Mezhdunarodnye dogovory Rusi s Vizantiei, zakliuchennye v X veke* (International treaties of Rus' with Byzantium concluded in the tenth century), A-prodzhekt, 2015

Jan Klabbers, *International Law*, CUP, 2013

Peter Kleist, *Die völkerrechtliche Anerkennung Sowjetrußlands*, Ost-Europa-Verlag, 1934

Boris M Klimenko, *Gosudarstvennaya territoria. Voprosy teorii i praktiki mezhdunarodnogo prava* (State territory. Questions of theory and practice of international law), Mezhdunarodnye otnoshenia, 1974

Fabian Klose, *In the Cause of Humanity. A History of Humanitarian Intervention in the Long Nineteenth Century*, CUP, 2021

E A Korovin, *Mezhdunardonoe pravo perekhodnoga vremeni* (International law of the transitional period), Gosudarstvennoe izdatel'stvo, 1923

E A Korovin, *Sovremennoe mezhdunarodnoe publichnoe pravo* (Contemporary public international law), Gosudarstvennoe izdatel'stvo, 1926

Evgeny A Korovin, *Iaponia i mezhdunarodnoe pravo* (Japan and international law), Sotsekgiz, 1936

E A Korovin, *Istoria mezhdunarodnogo prava. Vypusk I (ot drevnosti i do kontsa XVIII veka). Posobie k lektsiam* (History of international law. Issue I (from antiquity to the end of the eighteenth century). Lecture manual), Voenno-iuridicheskaia akademia Krasnoi Armii i Vyshaya Diplomaticheskaya Shkola MID SSSR, 1946

Martti Koskenniemi, *From Apology to Utopia. The Structure of International Legal Argument*, CUP, 2006

Martti Koskenniemi, Walter Rech, Manuel Jiménez Fonseca (eds) *International Law and Empire. Historical Explorations*, OUP, 2017

F I Kozhevnikov, *Russkoe gosudarstvo i mezhdunarodnoe pravo (do XX veka)* (Russian state and international law (until the twentieth century)), Zertsalo, 2006 (original: Moscow: Iuridichekoe izdatel'stvo Ministerstva iustitsii SSSR, 1947)

F I Kozhevnikov, *Sovetskoe gosudarstvo i mezhdunarodnoe pravo 1917–1944 gg. (Opyt istoriko-pravovogo issledovania)* (The Soviet state and international law 1917–1944. Experience from historical–legal study), Iuridicheskoe izdatel'stvo ministerstva iustitsii SSSR, 1948

F I Kozhevnikov (ed) *Mezhdunarodnoe pravo* (International law), Moscow: Gosudarstvennoe izdatel'stvo iuridicheskoi literatury, 1957

F I Kozhevnikov, V M Koretsky, D B Levin, G I Tunkin, N A Ushakov, V M Chikvadze, V M Shurshalov (eds), *Kurs mezhdunarodnoga prava v shesti tomakh. Tom VI. Mezhdunarodnoe pravo v otnosheniakh mezhdu sotsialisticheskimi gosudarstvami* (Course on international law in six volumes. Vol VI. International law in relations between socialist states), Nauka, 1973

Petr P Kremnev, *Raspad SSSR: mezhdunarodno-pravovye problemy* (Collapse of the USSR: international legal problems), Zertsalo-M, 2005

Jaan Kross, *Professor Martens' Departure. A Novel*, translated by Anselm Hollo, The New Press, 1994

N B Krylov, *Na vesakh Femidy: SShA i mezhdunarodnoe pravo* (On the scales of Themis: the USA and international law) Molodaya gvardia, 1986 (Series 'Imperializm: sobytia, fakty, dokumenty; 'Imperialism: events, facts, documents')

W L Lakhtine, *Prava na severnye poliarnye prostranstva* (Rights over the Arctic regions), Izdanie litizdata Narodnoga Komissariata po Inostrannym Delam, 1928

Margus Laidre, *Domus belli. Põhjamaade saja-aastane sõda Liivimaal 1554–1661* (Domus belli. The hundred years war of the Nordic countries in Livonia 1554–1661), Argo, 2015

Nikolai Lavrovsky, *O vizantiiskom elemente v iazyke dogovorov russkikh s grekami* (The Byzantine element in the language of treaties of the Russians with the Greeks), Tipografia Imperatorskoi Akademii Nauk, 1853

Dominic Lieven, *Empire. The Russian Empire and Its Rivals*, Yale UP, 2001

C L Lim, *The Aims and Methods of Postcolonial International Law*, The Hague Academy of International Law, Recueil des cours, Vol 437, Brill, 2024

M M Litvinov, *Vneshniaya politika SSSR. Rechi i zayavlenia 1927–1935* (Foreign policy of the USSR. Speeches and announcements 1927–1935), Gosudarstvennoe sotsial'no-ekonomicheskoe izdatel'stvo, 1935

M Litvinov, *Protiv agressii* (Against aggression), OGIZ, 1938

Igor I Lukashuk (ed) *Osnovnye printsipy mezhdunarodnoga prava*, in: V N Kudriavtsev (ed) *Kurs mezhdunarodnoga prava v semi tomakh* (Main principles of international law; in: course on international law in seven volumes), Vol 2, Nauka, 1989

I I Lukashuk, *Mezhdunarodnoe pravo. Obschchaya chast* (International law. General part), 2nd edn, Beck, 2001

N P Lyzhin, *Stolbovskii dogovor i peregovory emu predshestvuyushie* (The Stolbovo peace treaty and its preceding negotiations), Tip Imp Akademii Nauk, 1857

Lauri Mälksoo, *Russian Approaches to International Law*, OUP, 2015

André Mandelstam, *Le sort de l'empire Ottoman*, Librairie Payot & Co, 1917

André Mandelstam, *Mémoire sur la délimitation des Droits de'l État et de la Nation d'après la doctrine du Président* Wilson , Imprimerie Polyglotte Hugonis, 1919

André N Mandelstam, *La Société des Nations et les Puissances devant le Problème Arménien*, A. Pedone, 1926

Kamo Adibekovich Manukyan, *Printsip ravnopravia gosudarstv v mezhdunarodnom prave*, Yerevan: Izdatel'stvo yerevanskogo universiteta, 1975

N Marks (ed) *K tysiacheletiu dogovora Olega 911-go goda. Dogovory russkikh s grekami i predshevstvovavshie zakliucheniu ikh pokhody russkikh na Vizantiu. Chast' pervaia. Vremia Olega; Chast' vtoraya. Vremia Igorya i Sviatoslava* (The millenium of the treaty of Oleg in 911. Treaties of the Russians with the Greeks and the preceding campaigns of the Russians against Byzantium. First part. The era of Oleg. Second part. The era of Igor and Svyatoslav), Moskovski arkheologicheskii institut, 1912

F de Martens, *Traité de droit international*, Tome I, Librairie Marescq Ainé, 1883

F de Martens, *Ėtat indépendant du Congo. Mémoire sur les droits dominiaux de l'état indépendant du Congo*, Hachez, Novembre 1892

F Martens, *Actes concernant le congrès de Teschen, tirés des archives du prince N Repnine*, Tipogr. I N Skorokhodova, 1888

F F Martens, *Sobranie traktatov i konventsii zakliuchennykh Rossieiu s inostrannymi derzhavami* (Collection of treaties and conventions with foreign powers), vol II, Tipografia Bencke, 1875

F F Martens, *Sovremennoe mezhdunarodnoe pravo* tsivilizovannykh narodov (Contemporary international law of civilized nations), Iuridicheskiy kolledzh MGU, vol I, 1995

F F Martens, *Contemporary International Law of Civilized Peoples. General Part*, Translated and edited by W E Butler, The Lawbook Exchange, 2021

Kimitaka Matsuzato (ed) *Imperiology. From Empirical Knowledge to Discussing the Russian Empire*, Slavic Research Center, 2007

Sean McMeekin, *Stalin's War*, Penguin Books, 2021

Edward McWhinney, *'Peaceful Coexistence' and Soviet–Western International Law*, A W Sijthoff, 1964

Boris Meissner, *Die Sowjetunion, die baltischen Staaten und das Völkerrecht*, Verlag für Politik und Wirtschaft, 1956

China Miéville, *Between Equal Rights. A Marxist Theory of International Law*, Brill, 2005

Júlia Miklasová, *Secession in International Law with Special Reference to Post-Soviet Space*, Brill, 2024

Wolfgang J Mommsen, *Theories of Imperialism*, Translated from the German by P S Falla, Random House, 1980

Roger Moorhouse, *Poland 1939. The Outbreak of World War II*, Basic Books, 2020

R A Müllerson, G I Tunkin (eds) *Kurs mezhdunarodnogo prava. Tom 1. Poniatie, predmet i sistema mezhdunarodnoga prava*, in: V N Kudriavtsev (general ed) *Kurs mezhdunarodnoga prava v semi tomakh* (Course on international law, vol 1. Definition, subject, and system of international law, in: Course on international law in seven volumes), Nauka, 1989

Rein Müllerson, *Dawn of a New Order: Geopolitics and the Clash of Ideologies*, I B Tauris, 2017

V A Myakotin, *'Pereyaslavskii dogovor' 1654-go goda* (The 1654 'Pereyaslav treaty'), Izdatel'skoe obshchestvo 'Edinstvo', 1930

N A Narochnitskaya, G A Sanin, I V Nogaev (eds) *Nishtadtskii mirnyi dogovor i rozhdenie Rossiiskoi imperii 1721–2021* (The Nystad peace treaty and the birth of the Russian Empire 1721–2021), Veche, 2021

Benjamin Nathans, *To the Success of Our Hopeless Cause. The Many Lives of the Soviet Dissident Movement,* Princeton University Press, 2024

V A Nezabitovsky, *Uchenie publitsistov o mezhgosudarstvennom vladenii* (Teachings of publicists on international dominion), Kiev, 1862

Friedrich Nietzsche, The *Twilight of the Idols* or, *How to Philosophise with the Hammer*, Translated by Anthony M Ludovici, T N Foulis, 1911 (original German version 1888)

Otfried Nippold, *Le Géorgie du point de vue du droit international*, Édition du Bureau de presses géorgien, 1920

Kwame Nkrumah, *Neo-Colonialism, the Last Stage of Imperialism*, International Publishers, 1965

Boris Nolde, *Ocherki po russkomu gosudarstvennomu pravu* (Essays on Russian constitutional law), Tipografia PRAVDA, 1911

Boris Nolde, *L'Ukraine sous le protectorat russe. Traduit du russe par Maurice Gehri*, Payot, 1915

Georg Nolte, *Eingreifen auf Einladung. Zur völkerrechtlichen Zulässigkeit des Einsatzes fremder Truppen im internen Konflikt auf Einladung der Regierung*, Springer, 1999

John Norton Moore, Robert F Turner, *International Law and the Brezhnev Doctrine*, University Press of America, 1987

P N Ol'shansky, *Rizhskii dogovor i razvitie sovetsko-pol'skikh otnoshenii* (The Riga treaty and development of Soviet–Polish relations), Nauka, 1974

Sven Olsson, *Olof Hermelin. En karolinsk kulturspersonlighet och statsman*, Gleerupska Univ.-Bokhandel, 1953

Alexander Orakhelashvili, *International Law and International Politics. Foundations of Interdisciplinary Analysis*, Edward Elgar Publishing, 2020

Anne Orford, *International Law and the Politics of History*, OUP, 2021

Umut Özsu, *Completing Humanity. The International Law of Decolonization, 1960–82*, CUP, 2024

William Partlett, *Why the Russian Constitution Matters. The Constitutional Dark Arts*, Hart, 2024

William Partlett, Herbet Küpper, *The Post-Soviet as Post-Colonial. A New Paradigm for Understanding Constitutional Dynamics in the Former Soviet Empire*, Edward Elgar Publishing, 2022

E Pashukanis, *Ocherki po mezhdunarodnomu pravu* (Essays on international law), Moscow: Sovetskoe zakonodatel'stvo, 1935; reprinted with a foreword by Theodor Schweisfurth as E B Pašukanis, *Umrisse des Völkerrechts*, Berlin Verlag, 1971

E B Pashukanis, *Imperializm i kolonial'naya politika. Chast' pervaya: ekonomika imperializma. Kurs lektsii, chitannykh v I MGU*, (Imperialism and colonialist politics. First part: the economy of imperialism. Course of lectures read at I Moscow State University), Izdatel'stvo kommunistischeskoy akademii, 1928

Nadezhda Pastukhova, *Soyuz Rossii i Belorussii: istoria, nastoyashchee, perspektivy* (The union of Russia and Belarus: history, nowadays, outlook), Kniga i biznes, 2000

Gegam Petrosyan, *Zakavkaz'e v diplomaticheskikh peripetiakh: stanovlenie armianskoi nezavisimoi gosudarstvennosti (fevral' 1917- iun' 1918 gg)* (Transcaucasia in diplomatic vicissitudes: the formation of Armenian independent statehood (February 1917–June 1918), Izdatel'stvo EGU, 2019

Kaarel Piirimäe, *Roosevelt, Churchill, and the Baltic Question: Allied Relations during the Second World War*, Palgrave Macmillan, 2014

Jennifer Pitts, *Boundaries of the International: Law and Empire*, Harvard UP, 2018

Serhii Plokhy, *Lost Kingdom. The Quest for Empire and the Making of the Russian Nation. From 1470 to the Present*, Basic Books, 2017

William E Pomeranz, *Law and the Russian State. Russia's Legal Evolution from Peter the Great to Vladimir Putin*, Bloomsbury Academic, 2019

Horst Pommerening, *Der chinesisch-sowjetische Grenzkonflikt. Das Erbe der ungleichen Verträge*, Walter Verlag, 1968

Miroslav Potočny, Stanislav Myslil, *Legal Principles of Peaceful Co-Existence*, Translated from Czech by Dr Zdeněk Červenka, Prague: Státni pedagogické nakladatelství, 1968

V V Pustogarov, *Our Martens: F. F. Martens, International Lawyer and Architect of Peace*, edited and translated by W E Butler, Kluwer Law International, 2000

John Quigley, *Soviet Legal Innovation and the Law of the Western World*, CUP, 2007

K B Radek, *Likvidatsia Versal'skogo mira: doklad IV Kongressu Kommunistischeskogo Internatsionala* (Liquidation of the Versailles peace: presentation at the 4th Congress of the Communist International), Izdanie Kommunisticheskogo Internatsionala, 1922

Ignacio de la Rasilla, *International Law and History. Modern Interfaces*, CUP, 2021

D Van Reybrouck, *Congo. The Epic History of a People*, translated from the Dutch by S Garrett, Fourth Estate, 2014

Michael Riepl, *Russian Contributions to International Humanitarian Law. A Contrastive Analysis of Russia's Historical Role and Its Current Practice*, Nomos, 2022

Shabtai Rosenne, *A Guide to the Legislative History of the Vienna Convention*, A W Sijthoff, 1970

Balthasar Russow, *Liivimaa provintsi kroonika* (Chronicle of the province of Livonia), translated by Jüri Kivimäe, Tänapäev, 2022

Ivan Sablin, *The Rise and Fall of Russia's Far Eastern Republic, 1905–1922. Nationalisms, Imperialisms, and Regionalisms in and after the Russian Empire*, Routledge, 2019

Domitilla Sagramoso, *Russian Imperialism Revisited. From Disengagement to Hegemony*, Routledge, 2020

Reza Sardari, *Un chapitre de l'histoire diplomatique de l'Iran. Les Traités entre l'Iran et la Russie depuis le XVIe siècle jusqu'à 1917*, Maurice Lavergne, Imprimeur, 1941

Aleksandr N Savenkov, *Niurnberg. Prigovor vo imia mira* (Nuremberg. Judgment in the name of peace), Prospekt, 2022

Wolodymyr Sawchak, *The Status of the Ukrainian SSR in the View of State and International Law*, Ukrainian Information Service, 1971

Carl Schirren, *Zur Geschichte des Nordischen Krieges.* Rezensionen, Walter G Mühlau, 1913

Carl Schmitt, *Der Nomos der Erde im Völkerrecht des Jus Publicum Europaeum*, 5th edn, Duncker & Humblot, 2011

Willi Schwanitz, *Die hegemoniale Vertragspolitik. Militärpolitik und Völkerrecht*, Berlin Verlag, 1983

Theodor Schweisfurth, *Der internationale Vertrag in der modernen sowjetischen Völkerrechtstheorie*, Verlag Wissenschaft und Politik, 1968

Theodor Schweisfurth, *Sozialistiches Völkerrecht? Darstellung—Analyse—Wertung der sowjetmarxistischen Theorie vom Völkerrecht 'neuen Typs'*, Springer, 1979

P P Shafirov (PS), *A Discourse Concerning the Just Causes of the War Between Sweden and Russia: 1700–1721*, with an introduction by W E Butler, Oceana Publications, 1973

V M Shurshalov, *Osnovania deistvitel'nosti mezhdunarodnykh dogovorov* (Grounds of validity of international treaties), Izdatel'stvo akademii nauk SSSR, Moscow, 1957

V M Shurshalov (ed), *Mezhdunarodno-pravovye formy sotrudnichestva sotsialisticheskikh gosudarstv* (International legal forms of cooperation between socialist states), Izdatel'stvo Akademii nauk SSSR, 1962

Hendrik Simon, *A Century of Anarchy? War, Normativity, and the Birth of Modern International Order*, OUP, 2024

Pierre Singaravélou (ed) *Les empires coloniaux (XIX–XXe siècle)*, Éditions Points 2013

Adamantios Theodor Skordos, *Südosteuropa und das moderne Völkerrecht. Eine transregionale und globale Geschichte im 19 und 20 Jahrhundert*, Wallstein Verlag, 2021

Will Smiley, *From Slaves to Prisoners of War. The Ottoman Empire, Russia, and International Law*, OUP, 2018

Timothy Snyder, *The Road to Unfreedom.* Russia, Europe, America, Blackwells, 2019

Johannes Socher, *Russia and the Right to Self-Determination in the Post-Soviet Space*, OUP, 2021

Peter Alfons Steiniger, *Oktoberrevolution und Völkerrecht: eine populärwissenschaftliche Studie*, Staatsverlag der Deutschen Demokratischen Republik, 1967

Petr I Stucka, *Die revolutionäre Rolle von Recht und Staat—Theorie 1*, Übersetzung und Einleitung von Norbert Reich, Suhrkamp Verlag, 1969

James Summers, *Peoples and International Law*, 2nd revised edn, Brill, 2014

A N Talalaev, *Venskaya konventsia o prave mezhdunarodnykh dogovorov. Kommentarii* (The Vienna Convention on the International Law of Treaties. A commentary), Iuridischekaya literatura, 1997

A N Talalaev, *Pravo mezhdunarodnykh dogovorov. Tom 1. Obshchie voprosy* (Law of international treaties, Vol 1, General questions) Moscow: Zertsalo, 2011 (Originally, Mezhdunarodnye otnoshenia, 1980)

A N Talalaev, *Pravo mezhdunarodnykh dogovorov. Tom 2. Deistvie i primenenie dogovorov. Dogovory s uchastiem mezhdunarodnykh organizatsii*, (Law of international treaties, Vol 2, Validity and application of treaties. Treaties with participation by international organizations) Moscow: Zertsalo, 2011 (Originally, Mezhdunarodnye otnoshenia, 1985)

T A Taracouzio, *The Soviet Union and International Law. A Study based on the Legislation, Treaties and Foreign Relations of the Union of Socialist Soviet Republics*, The Macmillan Company, 1935

Vladislav I Tolstykh, *Kurs mezhdunarodnoga prava* (Course on international law), Prospekt, 2018

Dmitri Trenin, *Novyi balans sil. Rossiia v poiskakh vneshnepoliticheskogo ravnovesia* (New balance of power. Russia in search of foreign policy equilibrium) Alpina Publisher, 2021

Heinrich Triepel, *Die Hegemonie. Ein Buch von führenden Staaten*, W Kohlhammer, 1938

Jan F Triska, Robert M Slusser, *The Law, Theory, and Policy of Soviet Treaties*, Stanford UP, 1962

Arno Trültzsch, *Sozialismus und Blockfreiheit. Der Beitrag Jugoslawiens zum Völkerrecht 1948–1980/91*, Wallstein Verlag, 2021

M A Tsimmerman, *Ocherki novoga mezhdunarodnoga prava. Posobie k lektsiam* (Essays on new international law. Lecture manual), Plamya, 1923

Ntina Tzouvala, *Capitalism as Civilization. A History of International Law*, CUP, 2020

Henn-Jüri Uibopuu, *Die sowjetische Doktrin der friedlichen Koexistenz als Völkerrechtsproblem*, Verlag Notring, 1971

Henn-Jüri Uibopuu, *Die Völkerrechtssubjektivität der Unionsrepubliken der UdSSR*, Springer-Verlag, Wien, 1975

G M Velyaminov, *Sotsialisticheskaya integratsia i mezhdunarodnoe pravo* (Socialist integration and international law), Mezhdunarodnye otnoshenia, 1982

E R Voronin (ed) *Prakticheskoe mezhdunarodnoe pravo i diplomatia F. F. Martensa. Iz dnevnikov, traktatov, konventsii* (Practical international law and diplomacy of F F Martens. From diaries, treatises, conventions), MGIMO-Universitet, 2023

Éric Vuillard, *Congo*, Actes Sud, 2012

M P Vyatkin (ed) *Iz istorii imperializma v Rossii* (From the history of imperialism in Russia), Izdatel'stvo Akademii Nauk SSSR, 1959

A Ya Vyshinsky (ed) *Diplomaticheskii slovar* (Diplomatic dictionary), Vol II, Gosudarstvennoe izdatel'stvo politicheskoi literatury, 1950

Claudia Weber, *Der Pakt. Hitler, Stalin und die Geschichte einer mörderischen Allianz*, C H Beck, 2019

Anton Weiss-Wendt, *The Soviet Union and the Gutting of the UN Genocide Convention*, The University of Wisconsin Press, 2017

Natasha Wheatley, *Life and Death of States: Central Europe and the Transformation of Modern Sovereignty*, Princeton UP, 2023

Karol Wolfke, *Great and Small Powers in International Law from 1814 to 1920. (From the Pre-History of the United Nations)*, Travaux de la Société des sciences et des lettres de Wroclaw, 1961

Georgi Zadorozhny, *Peaceful Coexistence. Contemporary International Law of Peaceful Coexistence*, Progress Publishers, 1968

N V Zakharova, *Vlianie sotsial'noi revoliutsii na silu mezhdunarodnogo dogovora* (The impact of social revolution on the validity of international treaties), Nauka, 1966

Karl-Heinz Ziegler, *Völkerrechtsgeschichte. Ein Studienbuch*, C H Beck, 1994

Journal Articles and Chapters

K A Adzharov, 'V I Lenin i pervye dogovory Sovetskogo gosudarstva so stranami Vostoka' (V I Lenin and the first treaties of the Soviet state with the countries of the East), *Soviet YBIL* 1969, 58–68

O Afanasyeva, 'K istorii shveitsarskogo neitraliteta' (The history of Swiss neutrality), *MZh* No 1, 1956, 78–84

A A Agzamkhodzhaev, 'Sotsialisticheskii federalizm i printsip ravnopravia narodov' (Socialist federalism and the principle of equal rights of peoples), *SGP* No 12, 1972, 52–8

G B Akbarov, 'Iz opyta osuschestvlenia mezhdunarodnykh sviazei Tadzhikskoi SSR' (From experience of implementing international relations of the Tajik SSR), *Soviet YBIL* 1969, 309–14

D V Aleksandrikov, 'Vlianie Velikoi oktiabrskoi revoliutsii na razvitie i utverzhdenie printsipa ravenstva gosudarstv v mezhdunarodnom prave' (The impact of the Great October Revolution on the development and affirmation of the principle of equality of states in international law), *Soviet YBIL* 1968, 106–20

L A Aleksidze, 'Znachenie obrazovania SSSR dlia obespechenia mira i mezhdunarodnoga pravoporiadka' (The meaning of establishment of the USSR for ensuring peace and international legal order), *Soviet YBIL* 1982, 11–28

Levan Aleksidze, 'Mezhdunarodno-pravovaya priroda Georgievskogo traktata 1783 goda' (The international legal nature of the Georgievsk treaty of 1783), in: *International Law and Georgia (From Antiquity to the Present). Selected Papers Published 1957–2012*, Ivane Javakhishvili Tbilisi State University, 2012, 189–219

Antony Anghie, 'Imperialism and International Legal Theory', in: Anne Orford, Florian Hoffmann (eds) *The Oxford Handbook of the Theory of International Law*, OUP, 2016, 156–72

Anonymous, 'Mezhdunarodno-pravovye problemy polnoga zapreshchenia ispytanii iadernogo oruzhia' (International legal problems of complete prohibition of nuclear testing), *SGP* No 11, 1986, 80–5

G Apalin, 'Maoizm—rezerv imperialisticheskoi reaktsii' (Maoism: stockpile of imperialist reaction), *MZh* No 7, 1969, 27–36

G Apalin, F Liev, 'Pekin: kurs na podryv mezhdunarodnoga pravoporiadka' (Beijing: course to disrupt the international legal order), *SGP* No 12, 1977, 76–84

Guido Acquaviva, 'Russia as a State Continuing the Legal Personality of the USSR - An Inquiry into State Identity or Succession', *JHIL* No 23, 2019, 310–53

A Astrakhansky, 'Nerushimaya druzhba velikikh narodov' (Inviolable friendship of great peoples), *MZh* No 2, 1955, 47–55

R Yu Auling, 'Sozdanie i razvitie Sovetskogo gosudarstva v Estonii' (The creation and development of a Soviet state in Estonia), *SGP* No 5, 1955, 24–30

Helmut Philipp Aust, 'From Diplomat to Academic Activist: André Mandelstam and the History of Human Rights', *EJIL* No 25, 2014, 1105–21

'Avakov, Mirza Mosesovich', Russian Wikipedia article https://ru.wikipedia.org/wiki/%D0%90%D0%B2%D0%B0%D0%BA%D0%BE%D0%B2,_%D0%9C%D0%B8%D1%80%D0%B7%D0%B0_%D0%9C%D0%BE%D1%81%D0%B5%D1%81%D0%BE%D0%B2%D0%B8%D1%87

M M Avakov, 'Pravopreemstvo gosudarstv v otnoshenii dogovorov (Venskaya konventsia OON 1978 g) (State succession with respect to treaties (The UN Vienna convention of 1978), *SGP* No 12, 1979, 82–5

M M Avakov, A I Grinberg, 'SShA: kurs na podryv mezhdunarodnoga pravoporiadka' (USA: course to disrupt the international legal order), *SGP* No 6, 1984, 84–92

V Avarin, 'India – velikaya derzhava' (India—a great power), *MZh* No 2, 1956, 16–24

B M Babii, 'Obrazovanie Ukrainskogo Sovetskogo sotsialisticheskogo gosudarstva' (The creation of the Ukrainian Soviet socialist state), *SGP* No 3, 1958, 43–53

B M Babii, V A Chekhovin, 'Vydayusheesya sobytie v istorii nashei Rodiny (K 325-letiu vossoedinenia Ukrainy s Rossiei) (A landmark event in the history of our Homeland. On the 325th anniversary of the unification of Ukraine with Russia), *SGP* No 3, 1979, 26–31

K A Baginyan, Postoiannyi neitralitet, pravo na samooboronu i sistema regionalizma v svete Ustava OON' (Permanent neutrality, the right to self-defense and the system of regionalism in light of the UN Charter), *SGP* No 6, 1956, 102–9

K A Baginyan, 'Printsip nevmeshatel'stva i Ustav OON' (The principle of non-intervention and the UN Charter), *SGP* No 6, 1957, 62–70

A S Bakhov, 'Formy politicheskogo sotrudnichestva evropeiskikh sotsialisticheskikh gosudarstv' (Forms of political cooperation among European socialist states), *SGP* No 3, 1972, 74–8

A S Bakhov, 'Varshavskii dogovor kak faktor mezhdunarodnoi bezopasnosti' (The Warsaw treaty as a factor in international security), *Soviet YBIL* 1980, 12–28

D I Baratashvili, 'Natsional'no-osvoboditel'noe dvizhenie i razvitie mezhdunarodnoga prava' (National liberation movements and development of international law), *SGP* No 9, 1967, 69–75

Yu A Baskin, P V Sovetov, 'Voprosy mezhdunarodnoga prava v dogovornoi praktike i politicheskoi literature Moldavii XIV-XVIII vv' (Questions of international law in the treaty practice and political literature of Moldavia in the 14th–18th centuries), *Soviet YBIL* 1962, 189–210

David J Bederman, 'The 1871 London Declaration, *Rebus Sic Stantibus* and a Primitive View of the Law of Nations', *AJIL* No 82, 1988, 1–40

A Z Begiyan, 'Obrazovanie sovetskikh respublik Zakavkazia—torzhestvo leninskoi natsional'noi politiki i printsipov gosudarstvennoga suvereniteta' (The formation of the Transcaucasian Soviet republics—a celebration of Leninist policies of nationalities and principles of state sovereignty), *SGP* No 2, 1961, 48–58

A Z Begiyan, 'Velikii Oktiabr i sozdanie sovetskoi armianskoi gosudarstvennosti' (Great October and the creation of Soviet Armenian statehood), *SGP* No 7, 1967, 3–9

E D Beishembiev, 'Rapallskii dogovor i ego rol' v razvitii sovremennogo mezhdunarodnoga prava (k 60-letiu podpisania dogovora)' (The Rapallo treaty and its role in the development of contemporary international law. To the 60th anniversary of the treaty), *Soviet YBIL* 1981, 270–6

K Bekher, V V Fomin, 'Perestroika mezhdunarodnykh ekonomicheskikh otnoshenii i strany sotsialisticheskoga sodruzhestva' (Reconstruction of international economic relations and the countries of the socialist commonwealth), *SGP* No 10, 1977, 107–14

Marc Bélissa, 'Peace Treaties, Bonne Foi and European Civility in the Enlightment', in: Randall Lesaffer (ed) *Peace Treaties and International Law in European History. From the Late Middle Ages to World War One*, CUP, 2004, 241–53

Eyal Benvenisti, 'The Resilience of International Law in the Face of Empire', *Just Security*, 17.02.2025, https://www.justsecurity.org/107820/resilience-international-empire/

Oliver Bilger, 'Wir kennen Putin, wir wissen, was er tut', Die Welt, 9.12.2024, https://www.welt.de/politik/ausland/plus254781012/Wladimir-Kara-Mursa-Wir-kennen-Putin-wir-wissen-was-er-tut.html. (Paper edition, Welt am Sonntag 8.12.2024, with a different title: 'Was in Russland passiert, betrifft jeden')

Amir Bilialitdinov, 'Kniaz' Gorchakov kak zerkalo russkoi tsiklichnosti. K 220-letiu so dnia rozhdenia samogo populiarnogo v proshlom ministra inostrannykh del' ('Prince' Gorchakov as a mirror of Russian cyclicality. To the 220th anniversary of the most popular minister of foreign affairs from the past), *MZh* No 8, 2018, https://interaffairs.ru/jauthor/material/2067

I P Blishchenko, 'Zakliuchitel'nyi akt Soveshania po bezopasnosti i sotrudnichestvu v Evrope—dal'neishee razvitie mezhdunarodnoga prava' (Final act of the Organization for Security and Cooperation in Europe—further development of international law), *SGP* No 12, 1976, 82–90

I P Blishchenko, V F Shavrov, 'SShA: doktrina i praktika protiv mezhdunarodnoi zakonnosti' (USA: doctrine and practice against international legality), *SGP* No 10, 1984, 110–16

O V Bogdanov, 'Amerikanskaya mezhdunarodno-pravovaya doktrina na sluzhbe imperialisticheskoi ekspansii' (American international legal doctrine in the service of imperialist expansion), *SGP* No 5, 1952, 70–2

O V Bogdanov, 'Peregovory—osnovnoe sredstvo mirnogo uregulirovania mezhdunarodnykh raznoglasii' (Negotiations: the main means of peaceful settlement of international disputes), *SGP* No 7, 1957, 71–80

O V Bogdanov, 'Sovetskii plan vseobchego razoruzhenia i mezhdunarodnoe pravo' (The Soviet plan for general disarmament and international law), *SGP* No 2, 1960, 46–56

O V Bogdanov, 'Otkaz ot primenenia iadernogo oruzhia – trebovanie vremeni' (Rejecting use of nuclear weapons—current demand), *SGP* No 7, 1977, 132–38

O V Bogdanov, 'Otkaz SSSR ot primenenia pervym iadernogo oruzhia v mezhdunarodnom prave' (The USSR's rejection of being the first to use nuclear weapons in international law), *SGP* No 4, 1983, 89–96

M M Boguslavsky, 'Pravovye voprosy nauchno-tekhnicheskoi integratsii stran-chlenov SEV' (Legal questions concerning the scientfic-technical integration of the member states of COMECON), *SGP* No 9, 1977, 117–24

M M Boguslavsky, V V Tsybukov, 'Novaya kontseptsia o pravopreemstve gosudarstv' (New concept of state succession), *SGP* No 3, 1984, 118–24

S Borisov, 'Neudavshaiasya ataka protiv printsipa edinoglasia velikikh derzhav v Sovete Bezopasnosti' (Failed attack on the principle of unanimity of great powers in the Security Council), *SGP* No 6, 1950, 51–8

S Borisov, 'Protiv proektov peresmotra Ustava OON' (Against projects to revise the UN Charter), *SGP* No 6, 1955, 92–8

E L Borodulin, 'K voprosu o statuse postoyannogo neitraliteta' (The question of the status of permanent neutrality), *Soviet YBIL* 1966/7, 195–202

Bill Bowring, 'The Soviets and the Right to Self-Determination of the Colonized. Contradictions of Soviet Diplomacy and Foreign Policy in the Era of Decolonization', in: Jochen von Bernstorff, Philipp Dann (eds) *The Battle for International Law. South-North Perspectives on the Decolonization Era*, OUP, 2019, 404–25

M Yu Braichevsky, 'O pervykh dogovorakh Rusi s grekami' (On the first treaties of Rus' with the Greeks), *Soviet YBIL* 1978, 264–84

M Yu Braichevsky, 'K voprosu o pravovom soderzhanii pervogo dogovora Rusi s grekami (860–863 gg)' (The legal content of the first treaty of Rus' with the Greeks (860–863), *Soviet YBIL* 1982, 276–97

Herbert W Briggs, 'The Leaders' Agreement of Yalta', *AJIL* No 40, 1946, 376–83

Yu P Brovkva, 'Soyuznaya Respublika—sub'ekt mezhdunarodnoga prava', *SGP* 1972 No 12, 36–42

V T Bulanenkov, Yu D Il'in, 'K razrabotke mezhdunarodno-pravovoga opredelenia agressii' (Development of the international legal concept of aggression), *SGP* No 2, 1974, 78–83

August Bulmerincq, 'Rußland. Die deutschen Ostseeprovinzen', in J C Bluntschli, K Brater (eds) *Deutsches Staatswörterbuch*, Vol 9, Stuttgart: Expedition des Staatswörterbuchs, 1865, 1–63

Erin Burnett (CNN), 'Putin's Latest Move Includes a 17th Century Map', 23.05.2023, https://edition.cnn.com/videos/world/2023/05/23/erin-burnett-monologue-map-putin-ukraine-17-century-ebof-vpx.cnn

N Chelyapov, 'Partia i natsional'nyi vopros' (The party and the national question), SGIRP No 5–6, 1930, 101–21

B S Chimni, 'Anti-Imperialism. Then and Now', in: Luis Eslava, Michael Fakhri, Vasuki Nesiah (eds) *Bandung, Global History, and International Law. Critical Pasts and Pending Futures*, CUP, 2017, 35–47

B S Chimni, 'Inclusion and Exclusion in International Organizations', in: Jan Klabbers (ed) *The Cambridge Companion to International Organizations Law*, CUP, 2022, 76-97

O I Chistyakov, 'Razvitie federativnykh otnoshenii mezhdu USSR i RSFSR (1917–1922 gg)' (Development of federal relations between the USSR and the Russian SFSR (1917–1922), *SGP* No 2, 1954, 14–25

O I Chistyakov, 'RSFSR i obrazovanie Soyuza SSR' (The Russian SFSR and the formation of the Soviet Union), *SGP* No 11, 1972, 3–9

K Ya Chizhov, 'Amerikanskii imperializm – razrushitel' mezhunarodnoga prava' (American imperialism – wrecker of international law), *SGP* No 2, 1953, 52–9

Olga I Chupris, Elena S Smirnova, 'Neitralitet respubliki Belarus kak iuridicheskaya norma' (Neutrality of the Republic of Belarus as a legal norm), *Moscow JIL* No 4, 2017, 107–15

A M Davidovich, 'Sushchnost i evoliutsia samoderzhavia v epokhu imperializma' (Nature and evolution of autocracy during the period of imperialism), *SGP* No 6, 1970, 71–9

G V Degtev, 'Federalizm v sovremennoi Rossii' (Federalism in contemporary Russia), *Moscow JIL* No 2, 2001, 81–94

R V Dekanozov, 'Demilitarizatsia i neitralizatsia Spitsbergena' (Demilitarization and the neutrality of Svalbard), *Soviet YBIL* 1966/7, 181–94

M V Demchenko, 'Dogovor, popustitelstvuyushii agressoru' (An agreement that condones the aggressor), *SGP* No 7, 1979, 121–8

Yu Deporov, 'Agressia SShA protiv Grenady i mezhdunarodnoe pravo' (US Aggression against Grenada and international law), *SGP* No 5, 1984, 80–5

Yu A Dmitriev, V O Mironov, 'Netipichnaya forma gosudarstvennogo ustroistva' (An atypical form of government structure), *GP* No 7, 2012, 82–91

Eric Draitser, 'Ukraine and the March of Empire', in: Immanuel Ness, Zak Cope (eds) *The Palgrave Encyclopedia of Imperialism and Anti-Imperialism*, Vol I, Palgrave Macmillan, 430–45

V A Drozhzhin, 'Byl li Sovetskii Soiuz imperiei?' (Was the Soviet Union an Empire?), *Moscow Journal of International Law*, 1996, 22–7

Arturas Dubonis, 'Dve modeli litovskoi ekspansii na Rusi (XIII-nachalo XIV v). Ovladenia Polotksom i Novogrudkom' (Two models of Lithuanian expansion to Rus (13th–early 14th century). Acquisition of Polotsk and Novogrudok), in: A E Titkov (ed) *Istoricheski vestnik, Tom 7, Litva, Rus' i Polsha XIII–XIX vv* (Historical Courier. Lithuania, Rus' and Poland in the 13th–19th centuries), 2014, 54–85

A Kh Dudaev, 'Sozdanie i razvitie checheno-ingushskoi natsional'noi sovetskoi gosudarstvennosti' (Creation and development of Chechen-Ingush national Soviet statehood), *SGP* No 6, 1964, 117–22

V N Durdenevsky, 'Dogovornyi rezhim Dunaya' (The Danube Treaty regime), *SGP* No 2, 1946, 68–73

V N Durdenevsky, 'Sovetskaya territoria v aktakh mezhdunarodnoga prava za 30 let (1917–1947 gg)' (Soviet territory in international law documents over 30 years (1917–1947)), *SGP* No 12, 1947, 58–65

V N Durdenevsky, 'Neitralitet v sisteme kollektivnoi bezopasnosti' (Neutrality in the system of collective security), *SGP* No 8, 1957, 81–91

V Durdenevsky, S Krylov, 'Narushenie imperialisticheskimi gosudarstvami printsipa sobliudenia mezhdunarodnykh dogovorov' (Violation of the principle of compliance with international treaties by imperalist states), *MZh* No 2, 1955, 64–71

V N Durdenevsky, G A Osnitskaya, 'Neitralitet i atomnoe oruzhie' (Neutrality and nuclear weapons), *SGP* No 2, 1960, 101–5

Editorial, '"Postavit"' iadernoe oruzhie vne zakona' ('Outlawing' nuclear weapons), *MZh* No 5, 1957, 3–7

L M Entin, 'O reaktsionnoi suschnosti burzhuaznykh iuridicheskikh teorii dekolonizatsii' (The reactionary nature of bourgeois legal theories of decolonization), *SGP* No 5, 1959, 108–15

N Fadeev, 'SEV—sotrudnichestvo ravnopravnykh natsii' (COMECON—cooperation among nations with equal rights), No 4, 1967, 8–16

N P Farbegov, 'O edinstve sotsialisticheskikh gosudarstv i svoeobrazii ikh politicheskikh form' (The unity of socialist states and the uniqueness of their political forms), *SGP* No 6, 1957, 40–51

Sergei Fediunin, Hélène Richard, 'La Russie est-elle impérialiste?', *Le monde diplomatique*, January 2024, https://www.monde-diplomatique.fr/2024/01/FEDIUNIN/66451

M M Fedorov, 'V I Lenin i avtonomia Iakutii' (V I Lenin and the autonomy of Yakutia), *SGP* No 4, 1972, 122–5

V N Fedorov, 'Kritika nekotorykh planov peresmotra Ustava OON' (Criticism of certain plans to revise the UN Charter), *SGP* No 4, 1973, 85–91

A Galina, 'Problema neitraliteta v sovremennom mezhdunarodnom prave' (The problem of neutrality in contemporary international law), *Soviet YBIL* 1958, 200–29

G B Gal'perin, 'Voprosy mezhdunarodnopravovoga priznania edinogo rossiiskogo gosudarstva XV–XVI vv' (Questions of international legal recognition of the united Russian state in the 15th–16th centuries), *Soviet YBIL* 1969, 261–77

V V Gavrilov, R M Nurimbetov, 'Istoricheskie prava gosudarstv na morskie akvatorii i pravovoi status Okhotskoga morya' (Historical rights of states to marine waters and the legal status of the Sea of Okhotsk), *Moscow JIL* No 4, 2022, 44–55

Sebastian Gehrig, 'A Socialist Legal Universalism? Cold War Struggles over International Law', in: Raluca Grosescu, Ned Richardson-Little (eds) *Socialism and International Law. The Cold War and Its Legacies*, OUP, 2025, 17–43

L Ya Gintsburg, 'Protiv spekuliatsii imenem sovetskogo uchenoga-iurista' (Against speculation with the name of the Soviet legal scholar), *SGP* No 3, 1973, 102–8

Artem Girsh, 'Putin rasskazal o mine "zamedlennogo deistvia" v Konstitutsiii SSSR' (Putin spoke about the 'time-bomb' in the Constitution of the USSR), *Vedomosti*, 05.07.2020, https://www.vedomosti.ru/politics/news/2020/07/05/833979-putin-rasskazal-o-konstitutsii

S A Gonionski, 'Organizatsia amerikanskikh gosudarstv—orudie monopolii SShA' (The Organization of American States—a weapon of US monopolies), *SGP* No 5, 1953, 144–51

A A Gordienko, 'Samoopredelenie narodov i obrazovanie sovetskoi natsionalnoi gosudarstvennosti v Srednei Azii' (Self-determination of peoples and the formation of Soviet national statehood in Central Asia), *SGP* No 5, 1967, 76–84

L V Grechko, G G Shinkaretskaya, 'Poniatie konferedatsii i SNG' (The definition of confederation and the CIS), *Moscow JIL* 1994, 61–73

Ya A Grigelionis, 'Printsip nerushimosti granits v mezhdunarodnom prave' (The principle of the inviolability of borders in international law), *Soviet YBIL* 1981, 55–70

A A Gromyko-Piradov, 'Suverenitet i konflikty v Rossii v pervoi polovine 1990-kh godov' (Sovereignty and conflicts in Russia during the first half of the 1990s), *Moscow JIL* No 4, 1995, 52–63

L M Gudoshnikov, 'Velikoderzhavnyi shovinizm rukovodstva KNR v voprosakh natsional'no-gosudarstvennogo stroitel'stva' (Great power chauvinism of the leadership of the People's Republic of China in questions of ethnic state formation), *SGP* No 9, 1973, 92–100

L M Gudoshnikov, 'Antinarodnaya konstitutsionnaya deklaratsia maoistov' (Anti-people constitutional declaration by the Maoists), *SGP* No 2, 1976, 95–102

L M Gudoshnikov, 'Tretia konstitutsia KNR' (The third constitution of the People's Republic of China), *SGP* No 1, 1979, 34–9

L M Gudoshnikov, 'O politicheskom rezhime v Kitae' (On the political regime in China), *SGP* No 3, 1982, 111–18

Jens Hacker, 'Die Intervention in Theorie und Praxis', in: Reinhart Maurach, Boris Meissner (Hg) *Völkerrecht un Ost und West*, W. Kohlhammer Verlag, 1967, 154–77

György Haraszti, 'Treaties and Fundamental Change of Circumstances', *RCADI* Vol 146, 1977, 5–93

Ragnhilde Marie Hatton, 'Russia and the Baltic', in: Taras Hunczak (ed) *Russian Imperialism from Ivan the Great to the Revolution*, Rutgers UP, 1974, 106–30

Pierre Hentgès, 'Dunaiskaya konferentsia kak konets "priobretennym pravam"' (The Danube convention as an end to 'acquired rights'), *SGP* No 2, 1949, 47–52 (Originally published in *Democratie nouvelle* 1948 No 9, 480–3)

Vladimir Hrabar, 'Nachalo ravenstva gosudarstv v sovremennom mezhdunarodnom prave' (The beginning of the equality of states in contemporary international law), in: *Izvestia Ministerstva Inostrannykh Del*, Tipografia V O Kirshbauma, 1912, 1–44

Henry R Huttenbach, 'The Origins of Russian Imperialism', in: Taras Hunczak (ed) *Russian Imperialism from Ivan the Great to the Revolution*, Rutgers UP, 1974, 18–44

Maxim A Isaev, 'K voprosu o mezhdunarodno-pravovom statuse Velikoga kniazhestva Finliandskogo' (The issue of the international legal status of the Grand Duchy of Finland), *Moscow JIL* No 2018, 33–43

L A Ivanashchenko, 'Printsip ravnoi bezopasnosti storon i ego znachenie dlia sovremennogo mezhdunarodnoga prava' (The principle of equal security of the parties and its meaning in contemporary international law), *Soviet YBIL*, 1976, 57–68

J.-M. Jadot, 'Martens de, Frédéric', in: *Bibliographie Coloniale Belge*, T. IV (1955), col 574–9

Kaforov Zaver Murad ogly, 'Mezhdunarodno-pravovoe znachenie dogovora o druzhbe mezhdu RSFSR i Afghanistanom' (International legal significance of the treaty of friendship between the Russian SFSR and Afghanistan), *Soviet YBIL* 1982, 302–15

G F Kalinkin, 'Malye gosudarstva: polnopravnye sub'ekty mezhdunarodnoga prava' (Small states: subjects of international law with full rights), *SGP* No 2, 1973, 75–80

L M Karapetian, G M Khachatrian, 'Suverenitet narodov v mnogonatsional'nom gosudarstve' (Sovereignty of peoples in a multinational state), *SGP* 1990, No 11, 3–14

A A Karlov, 'Obrazovanie i razvitie sovetskoi natsional'noi gosudarstvennosti moldavskoga naroda' (The formation and development of the Soviet national statehood of the Moldovan people), *SGP* 1964, No 6, 111–17

A Kemov, 'Sodeistvie vooruzheniu Kitaya: protivopravno' (Assistance to arming China is illegal), SGP No 2, 1980, 57–65

Dzovinar Kévonian, 'André Mandelstam and the Internationalization of Human Rights (1869–1949)', in Pamela Slotte, Miia Halme-Tuomisaari (eds), *Revisiting the Origins of Human Rights*, CUP, 2015, 239–66

Michael Khodarkovsky, 'Between Europe and Asia. Russia's State Colonialism in Comparative Perspective, 1550s–1990s', *Canadian-American Slavic Studies* No 52, 2018, 1–29

V M Khvostov, 'Kitaiski 'schet po reestru' i pravda istorii' (The Chinese 'register account' and historical truth), *MZh* No 10, 1964, 21–7

V Kirillov, 'Narody zhdut soglashenia o prekrashenii iadernykh ispytanii' (Peoples wait for agreement on termination of nuclear tests), *MZh* No 12, 1959, 36–41

G Ya Kliava, V O Miller, 'Slavnoe dvadsatiletie pribaltiiskikh sovetskikh respublik' (Twenty glorious years of the Soviet Baltic States), *SGP* 1960, No 7, 11–21

Robert Know, 'Marxist Approaches to International Law', in: Anne Orford, Florian Hoffmann with Martin Clark (eds) The Oxford Handbook of the Theory of International Law, OUP, 2016, 306–26

Kommentator, 'Parizhskie soglashenia: ugroza bezopasnosti Evropy' (Paris agreements: a threat to the security of Europe), *MZh* No 2, 1954, 15–28

M Korbut, 'Evraziistvo kak beloemigrantski fashizm i ego agentura v SSSR' (Eurasianism as the fascism of the Russian White emigrant movement and its agents in the USSR), SGIRP, No 9, 1931, 110–29 and No 10, 1931, 106–22

V M Koretski, 'Akademik V P Bezobrazov v Institute mezhdunarodnoga prava' (Academician V P Belobrazov at the International Instutute of International Law), *Soviet YBIL* 1973, 190–7

K D Kormasova, 'Sovetskaya natsional'naya gosudarstvennost': vazhnyi faktor internatsional'nogo edinstva narodov SSSR' (Soviet national statehood: an important factor for the international unity of the peoples of the USSR), No 8, 1976, 12–18

E Korovin, 'Rossiya i mezhdunarodnoe pravo' (Russia and international law), *SGP* No 2, 1949, 65–6

E Korovin, 'Problema neitraliteta na sovremennom etape' (The problem of neutrality in today's context), *MZh* No 3, 1958, 48–54

E A Korovin, 'Vazhnyi istoricheskii dokument. (Po povodu spravki Sovinformbyuro 'Falsifikatory istorii') (An important historical document. On the occasion of the enquiry by Sovinformbyuro into "Falsifiers of history"'), *SGP* No 4, 1948, 1–7

E A Korovin, 'K voprosu o roli narodnykh mass v razvitii mezhdunarodnoga prava' (The issue of the role of the popular masses in the development of international law), *SGP* 1956, No 3, 50–60

E A Korovin, 'Protelarskii internatsionalizm i mezhdunarodnoe pravo' (Proletarian internationalism and international law), *Soviet YBIL* 1958, 50–73

E V Korovin, 'Ustav OON i mirnoe sosuschestvovanie' (The UN Charter and peaceful co-existence), *Soviet YBIL* 1960, 28–57

Anastasiya Kotova, Ntina Tzouvala, 'In Defense of Comparisons: Russia and the Transmutations of Imperialism in International Law', *AJIL* No 116, 2022, 710–19

F N Kovalev, 'Korennoe izmenenie obstoyatel'stv (Doktrina i praktika) (Fundamental change of circumstances (doctrine and practice), *SGP* No 3, 1970, 66–74

F I Kozhevnikov, 'I V Stalin ob osnovnykh printsipakh sovremennoga mezhdunarodnoga prava' (I V Stalin on the main principles of contemporary international law), *SGP* No 12, 1949, 95–109

F I Kozhevnikov, 'Nekotorye voprosy mezhdunarodnoga prava v svete truda I V Stalina 'Marksizm i voprosy iazykoznania" (Some questions of international law from the perspective of the work of I V Stalin 'Marxism and linguistic issues'), *SGP* No 4, 1951, 25–36

F I Kozhevnikov, 'Nekotorye voprosy teorii i praktiki mezhdunarodnoga dogovora' (Some questions of the theory and practice of an international treaty), *SGP* No 2, 1954, 62–76

F I Kozhevnikov, A P Movchan, 'Ustav OON—voplyushenie obshepriznannykh printsipov mezhdunarodnoga prava' (UN Charter—incarnation of generally accepted principles of international law), *SGP* No 6, 1955, 3–7

F I Kozhevnikov, I P Blishchenko, 'Sotsializm i sovremennoe mezhdunarodnoe pravo' (Socialism and contemporary international law), *SGP* No 4, 1970, 88–95

F I Kozhevnikov, 'Iz zapisok diplomata', in: A N Vylegzhanin, Yu M Kolosov, E S Krivchikova (eds), *Rossiya i mezhdunarodnoe pravo. Materialy mezhdunarodnoi konferentsii, poskhviachennoi 100-letiu F. I. Kozhevnikova, 15.10.2004* (From a diplomat's notes; Russia and international law. Materials of the international conference dedicated to the centenary of F I Kozhevnikov), Moscow: Izdatel'stvo 'MGIMO-Universitet', 2006, 7–13

A B Kozyrev, 'Politika gegemonizma—ugroza miru i mezhdunarodnomu pravoporiadku' (Politics of hegemonism—a threat to peace and the international legal order), *SGP* No 4, 1982, 85–93

H Kröger, 'Oktiabrskaya revoliutsia, mezhdunarodnoe pravo i bonnskaya "vostochnaya politika"' (The October Revolution, international law, and Bonn's 'Eastern policy'), *SGP* No 12, 1967, 102–10

V A Krutalevich, 'Stanovlenie natsional'noi gosudarstvennosti belorusskoga naroda' (Formation of national statehood of the people of Byelorussia), *SGP* No 12, 1967, 49–57

Serge Krylov, 'Les notions principales du droit des gens (La doctrine soviétique du droit international)', *RCADI* Vol 70, Martinus Nijhoff, 1947

B S Krylov, I N Kuznetsov, N A Mikhaleva, 'Kontseptsia Soyuznogo dogovora' (The concept of the Union treaty), *SGP* No 10, 1990, 3–12

M D Kudryashov, V I Morozov, 'Ustav Soveta Ekomomicheskoi Vzaimopomoshi—pravovoe vyrazhenie ekonomicheskogo sotrudnichestva novoga tipa' (COMECON Charter—legal expression of a new type of economic cooperation), *SGP* No 10, 1960, 22–30

Julian Kulaga, 'Renaissance of the Doctrine of *Rebus Sic Stantibus*?', *ICLQ* No 89, 2020, 477–97

Łukasz Kulesa, 'Contested Intepretations of the Indivisibility of Security', PISM, 03.02.2022, https://pism.pl/publications/contested-interpretations-of-the-indivisibility-of-security

I Kurdov, 'Velikaya derzhava kitaiskogo naroda' (Great power of the Chinese people), *MZh* 1954, No 2, 81–99

Patryk Labuda, 'Memory Wars at the United Nations after Russia's 2022 Invasion of Ukraine', 07.01.2025, Lawfare blog, https://www.lawfaremedia.org/article/memory-wars-at-the-united-nations-after-russia-s-2022-invasion-of-ukraine

M Lachs, 'Varshavskii dogovor i problema kollektivnoi bezopasnosti v Evrope' (The Warsaw Pact and the problem of collective security in Europe), *MZh* No 10, 1955, 55–62

M Lazarev, 'V narushenie suverennykh prav narodov. (O voennykh bazakh USA na inostyrannykh territoriakh)' (In violation of sovereign rights of peoples. US military bases abroad), *MZh* No 10, 1956, 77–88

M I Lazarev, 'Revoliutsennaya Kuba i mezhdunarodnoe pravo' (Revolutionary Cuba and international law), *SGP* 1966, No 7, 70–7

M A Lebedev, 'Nekotorye voprosy pol'zovania inostrannoi territoriei v sovremennom mezhdunarodnom prave' (Some questions on the use of foreign territory in contemporary international law), *Soviet YBIL* 1981, 282–7

Walter Leitsch, 'Russo-Polish Confrontation', in: Taras Hunczak (ed) *Russian Imperialism from Ivan the Great to the Revolution*, Rutgers UP, 1974, 131–66

Erlend M Leonhardsen, 'Pride and Perseverance: Strategic Use of Rebus Sic Stantibus in Russian Foreign Policy 1870–1950', *German YBIL* No 63, 2020, 581–620

I Levin, 'Natsional'nyi vopros v Rumynii' (The issue of nationalities in Romania), SGRP No 10–12, 1931, 186–209

I Levin, 'Natsional'nyi vopros v Evrope i ugroza voiny' (The national question in Europe and the threat of war), *SGP* No 4, 1934, 14–29

I Levin, 'Dogovory o zashchite prav natsional'nykh menshinstv' (Treaties on protection of the rights of national minorities), *SGP* No 6, 1934, 63–6

I Levin, 'Sredniaya Azia—primer konsolidatsii natsii v usloviakh diktatury proletariata' (Central Asia: an example of consolidation of nations under conditions of the dictatorship of the proletariat), *SGP* No 6, 1934, 74–82

I D Levin, 'Rabstvo vo vladeniakh imperializma' (Slavery in the domain of imperialism), *SGP* No 10, 1951, 55–63

B I Levin, 'Sorokoletie Estliandskoi trudovoi kommuny' (Forty years of the Estonian workers' commune), *SGP* No 11, 1958, 19–26

D B Levin, 'Printsip samoopredelenia natsii i likvidatsia kolonializma' (The principle of self-determination of peoples and the liquidation of colonialism), *SGP* No 8, 1962, 90–99

D B Levin, 'Pashukanis kak iurist-mezhdunarodnik' (Pashukanis as an international lawyer), *SGP* No 9, 1981, 96–103

L R Lewitter, 'The Russo-Polish Treaty of 1686 and its Antecedents', IX *The Polish Review* No 3–4, 1964

V I Lisovsky, 'Dogovor getmana Bogdana Khmel'nitskogo s sultanom Turtsii o svobodnom plavanii torgovykh sudov po Chernemu moriu' (The treaty of Hetman Bogdan Khmelnitsky with the Turkish sultan on free navigation of commercial ships in the Black Sea), *Soviet YBIL* 1959, 401–5

Yuri Lotman, 'The Contract and Self-Surrender as Archetypal Models of Culture', in: Marek Tamm (ed) *Juri Lotman—Culture, Memory and History. Essays in Cultural Semiotics*, Translated from the Russian by Brian James Baer, Palgrave Macmillan, 2019, 49–66

I I Lukashuk, 'Nekotorye voprosy kodifikatsii i progressivnogo razvitia prava mezhdunarodnykh dogovorov' (Some questions on the codification and progressive development of the law of international treaties), *Soviet YBIL* 1966/7, 51–71

I I Lukashuk, 'Normotvorcheskaya deyatel'nost' SEV' (Norm-creating activity of COMECON), *Soviet YBIL* 1980, 29–53

I I Lukashuk, 'Mezhdunarodno-pravovoi nigilizm vo vneshnei politike SShA' (International legal nihilism in US foreign policy), *SGP* No 7, 1982, 121–9

M Lvov, 'Atomnuyu bombu—vne zakona!' (Outlaw the nuclear bomb!), *MZh* No 1, 1965, 12–21

S A Malinin, 'Aktual'nye problemy mezhdunarodnoi bezopasnosti v svete reshenii XXVI s'ezda KPSS' (Current problems of international security in light of the decisions of the 26th congress of the Soviet communist party), *Soviet YBIL* 1981, 26–41

L Mälksoo, 'The Legacy of F F Martens and the Shadow of Colonialism', 21 *Chinese JIL* 2022, 55–77

L Mälksoo, 'The Empires: China, Russia, and the Soviet Union in the History of International Law', in: Ignacio de la Rasilla, Jiangyu Wang and Congyan Cai (eds) *Histories of International Law in China. All Under Heaven?* OUP, 2026 (forthcoming)

Maria Mälksoo, 'The Postcolonial Moment in Russia's War against Ukraine', 25 *Journal of Genocide Research* 2022, 471–81

S Malolin, 'O politike neitraliteta v Shvetsii' (On the politics of neutrality in Switzerland), *MZh* No 9, 1955, 84–91

Boris N Mamlyuk, 'The Cold War in Soviet International Legal Discourse', in: Matthew Craven, Sundhja Pahuja, Gerry Simpson (eds) *International Law and the Cold War*, CUP, 2020, 339–75

V V Mamonov, 'Gosudarstvennyi suverenitet i territorial'naya tselostnost' – glavnye printsipy sovremennoi rossiiskoi gosudarstvennosti' (State sovereignty and territorial integrity—main principles of contemporary Russian statehood), *GP* No 4, 2004, 5–12

S Mamulya, 'Review of Kozhevnikov's book Sovetskoe gosudarstvo i mezhdunarodnoe pravo (The Soviet state and international law)', *SGP* No 2, 1949, 67–70

B N Manelis, 'Edinstvo suvereniteta Soyuza SSR i suvereniteta soyuznykh respublik v period razvernutoga stroitel'stva kommunizma' (The unity of the sovereignty of the USSR and the sovereignty of union republics during the period of extensive construction of communism), *SGP* No 7, 1964, 17–26

B L Manelis, 'Protiv burzhuaznoi fal'sifikatsii natsional'no-gosudarstvennogo ustroistva SSSR' (Against bourgeois falsifications of the national-state system of the USSR), *SGP* No 3, 1968, 57–66

F Martens, 'La Russie et l'Angleterre dans l'Asie centrale', *RDILC* 1879

F Martens, 'Le conflit entre la Russie et la Chine, ses origines, son développement, et sa portée universelle', *RDILC* 1880

F Martens, 'La question égyptienne et le droit international', *RDILC* 1882

F Martens, 'La conference de Congo à Berlin et la politique coloniale des États modernes', *RDILC* 1886

Edward McWhinney, '"Peaceful coexistence" and Soviet-Western International Law', *AJIL* No 56, 1962, 951–70

Dmitry Medvedev, 'Rossiya i Polsha: zametki k 4 noyabrya' (Russia and Poland: notes for the 4th of November), *Rossiyskaya Gazeta*, 01.11.2023, https://rg.ru/2023/11/02/rossiia-i-polsha-zametki-k-4-noiabria.html

Boris Meissner, 'Das Wesen und der Geltungsbereich des Völkerrechts', in: Reinhart Maurach, Boris Meissner (Hg) *Völkerrecht un Ost und West*, W Kohlhammer Verlag, 1967, 9–38

D Mel'nikov, 'Problema neitraliteta i sovremennoe mezhdunarodnoe polozhenie' (The problem of neutrality and the contemporary international situation), *MZh* No 2, 1956, 72–80

D Mel'nikov, 'Nezyblemost' evropeiskikh granits' (Inviolability of European borders), *MZh* No 9, 1966, 10–8

V I Menzhinsky, 'Ustav OON i printsip neprimenenia sily' (The UN Charter and the principle of non-use of force), *Soviet YBIL* 1973, 82–99

V I Menzhinsky, 'XXV s'ezd KPSS i printsip neprimenenia sily v mezhdunarodnykh otnosheniakh' (25th congress of the Soviet communist party and principles of non-use of force in international relations), *SGP* No 2, 1977, 106–14

V I Menzhinsky, 'Printsipy mira, bezopasnosti i sotrudnichestva (K 10-i godovshine Khelsinkskoga soveshania) (The principles of peace, security, and cooperation) (To mark the 10th anniversary of the Helsinki Accords), *SGP* No 8, 1985, 89–95

A N Mikhailov, 'Uzbekskaya SSR—ravnopravnyi sub'ekt mezhdunarodnoga prava' (The Uzbek SSR: a subject of international law with equal rights), *Soviet YBIL* 1972, 25–37

A N Mikhailov, 'Iz istorii sovetsko-turetskikh mezhdunarodno-pravovykh otnoshenii (k 60-letiu Sovetsko-turetskogo dogovora 1921.g)' (From the history of Soviet–Turkish international legal relations (To mark the 60th anniversary of the 1921 Soviet–Turkish treaty), *Soviet YBIL*, 1982, 307–15

N A Mikhaleva, 'Pravovye problemy sozdania soyuznogo gosudarstva Rossii i Belarusi' (Legal issues of creation of the Russia–Belarus union state), *GP* 2002, No 6, 14–21

N A Mincheva, 'Karskoe more v mezhdunarodno-pravovoi politike Rossii' (The Kara Sea in Russia's international–legal policy), *Moscow JIL* No 3, 2023, 41–51

Boris Mirkine-Guetzévitch, 'L'influence de la révolution française sur le développement du droit international dans l'Europe orientale', *RCADI* Vol 22, 1929, 295–457

L A Modzhoryan, 'Bor'ba demokraticheskogo lageria za natsional'nuyu nezavisimost' i natsional'nyi suverenitet' (The struggle of the democratic camp for national independence and national sovereignty), *SGP* No 1, 1953, 52–65

L A Modzhoryan, 'Identichnost, nepreryvnost i pravopreemstvo sub'ektov mezhdunarodnogo prava' (Identity, continuity, and succession of subjects of international law), *SGP* 1959 No 9, 61–70

L A Modzhoryan, 'Raspad kolonial'noi sistemy imperializma i Organizatsia Ob'edenennykh Natsii' (The collapse of the colonial system of imperialism and the UN), *Soviet YBIL* 1960, 121–43

L A Modzhoryan, 'Amerikanskie doktriny grabezha i razboya: ot Monroe do Johnsona' (American doctrines of robbery and plunder: from Monroe to Johnson)', *SGP* 1965, No 9, 57–64

S V Molodtsov, 'Pravilo edinoglasia postoyannykh chlenov Soveta Bezopasnosti – nezyblemaya osnova OON' (The rule of unanimity of the permanent members of the Security Council: the unshakable foundation of the UN), *SGP* No 7, 1953, 44–57

S V Molodtsov, 'Raspad sistemy kolonializma i ego vlianie na mezhdunarodnoe pravo' (Collapse of the system of colonialism and its influence on international law), *SGP* No 5, 1956, 79–86

S Molodtsov, 'Granitsy i pravo' (Borders and the law), *MZh* No 4, 1964, 9–17

V M Molotov, 'Vneshnyaya politika Sovetskoga Soyza. Doklad na zasedanii VII Sessii Verkhovnoga Soveta SSSR, 1.08.1940' (Foreign policy of the Soviet Union. Report at the meeting of the 7th session of the Supreme Soviet of the USSR), *SGP* No 8–9, 1940, 3–4

Sergey Monin, '"Delo s Iranom deistvitel'no vyshlo neplokho"' ('The Iran affair actually worked out pretty well'), *MZh* No 8, 2011, https://interaffairs.ru/jauthor/material/518

G I Morozov, 'O novykh planakh revizii Ustava OON' (New plans to revise the UN Charter), *SGP* No 5, 1959, 116–24

V I Morozov, 'Pravovye aspekty deyatel'nosti organov Soveta ekonomicheskoi vzaimopomoshi' (Legal aspects of the work of COMECON organs), *SGP* No 10, 1961, 146–54

A Natalin, 'Protivopravnost' "strategicheskoi oboronnoi initsiativy" SShA' (Illegality of the US 'strategic defense initiative'), *SGP* No 11, 1985, 113–19

A Nikolaev, 'O zalive Petra Velikogo' (The Peter the Great Gulf), *MZh* No 2, 1958, 50–7

K N Nurbekov, 'Obrazovanie kirgizskoi suverennoi sovetskoi sotsialisticheskoi respubliki' (The formation of the Kyrghyz sovereign Soviet socialist republic), *SGP* No 9, 1958, 43–50

Kseniya Oksamytna, 'Russia's Status as a Colonial Power', 01.11.2024, E-International Relations, https://www.e-ir.info/pdf/106552

Stephen C Y Pan, 'Legal Aspects of the Yalta Agreement', *AJIL* No 46, 1952, 40–59

Rose Parfitt, 'Newer is Truer: Time, Space and Subjectivity at the Bandung Conference', in: Luis Eslava, Michael Fakhri, Vasuki Nesiah (eds) *Bandung, Global History, and International Law. Critical Pasts and Pending Futures*, CUP, 2017, 49–65

V V Parkosadze, 'Iz istorii sozdania i razvitia sovetskoi gosudarstvennosti v Gruzii' (From the history of the creation and development of Soviet statehood in Georgia), *SGP* No 1, 1967, 82–7

V V Parkosadze, 'Zakavkazskaya federatsia i ee rol' v razvitii natsionalnoi gosudarstvennosti narodov Zakavkazia' (The Transcaucasian Federation and its role in the deveopment of the national statehood of Transcaucasia), *SGP* No 12, 1972, 66–72

E Pashukanis, 'Mezhdunarodnoe pravo', from: Entsiklopedia gosudarstva i prava (International law; from the encyclopedia of the state and the law), Moscow: Izdatel'stvo kommunisticheskoi akademii,1926, vol 2, 858–74, republished in: Piers Beirne, Robert Sharlet (eds) *Pashukanis: Selected Writings on Marxism and Law*, Translated by Peter B Maggs, London: Academic Press, 1980, 168–82

E Pashukanis, 'Vstuplenie SSSR v Ligu natsii' (The USSR joins the League of Nations), *SGP* No 6, 1934, 23–8

N Pavlovsky, 'Malye strany i NATO' (Small states and NATO), *MZh* No 12, 1961, 88–92

Peredovaya, 'Dukh Bandunga—znamenie natsional'nogo vozrozhdenia' (The spirit of Bandung: sign of national revival), *MZh* No 4, 1957, 9–14

I S Peretersky, 'Znachenie mezhdunarodnoga dogovora dlia tret'ego (ne zakliuchivshego etot dogovor) gosudarstva' (The meaning of an international treaty for a third state non-party to the treaty), *SGP* No 4, 1957, 71–80

E Petrov, 'Amerikanskie imperialisty—zlostnye narushiteli rezhima voennoga plena' (American imperialists—vicious violators of the regime of military captivity), *SGP* No 12, 1952, 48–61

Pärtel Piirimäe, 'Russia, the Turks and Europe: Legitimations of War and Formation of a European Identity in the Early Modern Period', *Journal of Early Modern History* 2007, 63–86

Jaanus Piirsalu, 'Ajaloolane Andrei Zubov: Tartu rahu bolševikega oli Eesti moraalne viga' (The historian Andrey Zubov: the Tartu Peace Treaty with the Bolsheviks a moral mistake by Estonia), Diplomaatia, February 2020, https://diplomaatia.ee/ajaloolane-andrei-zubov-tartu-rahu-bolsevikega-oli-eesti-moraalne-viga/

V V Poznakhirev, 'Osobennosti dogovorov o sdache krepostei (kapituliatsii), zakliuchennykh v khode russko-turetskikh voin XVIII-XIX vv' (Special features of treaties on the surrender of fortresses concluded in the course of the Russian-Turkish wars in the 18th-19th centuries), GP No 12, 2015, 93–101

President of Russia, 'Unveiling of a Monument to World War I Heroes', 1 August 2014, http://en.kremlin.ru/events/president/news/page/627

Vyacheslav Prokopovych, 'The Problem of the Juridical Nature of Ukraine's Union with Muscovy', *The Annals of the Ukrainian Academy of Arts and Sciences in the US* No 4, 1955, 917–80

Vladimir Putin, 'On the Historical Unity of Russians and Ukrainians', 12.07.2021, http://www.en.kremlin.ru/events/president/news/66181

S Radzhapov, 'Etapy razvitia sovetskogo gosudarstvennogo stroya v Srednei Azii' (Stages of development of the Soviet state system in Central Asia), *SGP* No 11, 1948, 61–7

Sarah Rainsford, 'Putin and Peter the Great: Russian leader likens himself to 18th Century tsar', *BBC*, 11.06.2022, https://www.bbc.com/news/world-europe-61767191

M Rapoport, 'Sushchnost sovremennogo mezhdunarodnoga prava' (The nature of contemporary international law), *SGP* 1940, No 5–6, 137–53

Akbar Rasulov, 'Central Asia as an Object of Orientalist Narratives in the Age of Bandung', in: Luis Eslava, Michael Fakhri, Vasuki Nesiah (eds) *Bandung, Global History, and International Law. Critical Pasts and Pending Futures*, CUP, 2017, 215–31

S M Ravin, 'Istoricheskii opyt sovetskogo federalizma' (The historical experience of Soviet federalism), *SGP* No 11, 1957, 74–85

K S Rodionov, 'Pravda o dogovorakh X veka, zakliuchennykh Vizantiei s kievskimi kniaziami Olegom (911 g) i Igorem (945 g) (The truth about the 10th century treaties concluded by Byzantium with the Kiev princes Oleg (911) and Igor (945)), *Russian YBIL* 2019, 284–305

I I Rogachev, 'Interventsia SShA v Paname i mezhdunarodnoe pravo' (The US intervention in Panama and international law), *SGP* No 8, 1990, 109–17

V A Romanov, 'Zaliv Petra Velikogo – vnutrennie vody Sovetskogo Soyuza' (The Peter the Great Gulf – internal waters of the Soviet Union), *SGP* No 5, 1958, 47–55

S L Ronin, 'Konstitutsionnye proekty Vremennogo pravitel'stva' (Constitutional projects of the provisional government), *SGP* No 4, 1947, 45–53

L A Rudzitsky, V A Dorogin, 'Obrazovanie Belorusskoi SSR' (The formation of the Byelorussian SSR), *SGP* No 4, 1957, 12–19

Russian Orthodox Church, 'Sviateishii patriarkh Kirill: Te, kto budut sokhraniat' vernost' dukhovnomu edinstvu nashei Tserkvi, v kontse kontsov pobediat' (Holiest Patriarch Kirill: those who remain faithful to the spiritual unity of our Church will win in the end), 28.08.2024, http://www.patriarchia.ru/db/text/6154796.html

V S Saltanov, Dvustoronnie dogovory sotsialisticheskikh gosudarstv o druzhbe, sotrudnichestve i vzaimnoi pomoshi i ikh mezhdunarodno-pravovoe znachenie' (Bilateral treaties between socialist states on friendship, cooperation, and mutual help and their international legal significance), *Soviet YBIL* 1971, 80–95

G S Sapargaliev, M A Binder, 'Razvitie sovetskoi natsional'noi gosudarstvennosti kazakhskogo naroda' (The development of Soviet national statehood of the Kazakh people), *SGP* No 9, 1970, 24–31

Emanuel Sarkisyanz, 'Russian Imperialism Reconsidered', in: Taras Hunczak (ed) *Russian Imperialism from Ivan the Great to the Revolution*, Rutgers UP, 1974, 45–81

M A Sarsembaev, 'Dobrovol'noe prisoedinenie Kazahstana k Rossii: mezhdunarodno-pravovye aspekty' (Voluntary unification of Kazakhstan with Russia: international legal aspects), *SGP* No 12, 1982, 85–8

Wilfried Schaumann, 'Clausula rebus sic stantibus', in: Hans-Jürgen Schlochauer (ed) *Wörterbuch des Völkerrechts, Erster Band*, de Gruyter, 1960, 289–91

M I Semiryaga, '"Asimmetrichnaya voina". K 50-letiu okonchania sovetsko-finliandskoi voiny (1939–1940 gg)' ('Assymmetric war'. On the 50th anniversary of the Soviet-Finnish war (1939–1940), *SGP* No 4, 1990, 116–23

M I Semiryaga, 'Prestuplenie v Katyni' (Crime in Katyn), *SGP* No 12, 1990, 110–18 and 1991, no 1, 91–102

G V Sharmazanashvili, 'Kolonial'naya voina—gruboe narushenie mezhdunarodnoga prava' (Colonial war: a gross violation of international law), *SGP* 1957, No 10, 55–61

V S Shevtsov, 'Suverenitet v Sovetskom soyuznom gosudarstve' (Sovereignty in the Soviet Union), *SGP* No 6, 1972, 49–58

V S Shevtsov, 'Nekotorye problemy teorii Sovetskogo soyuznogo gosudarstva' (Some issues on the theory of the Soviet Union as a state), *SGP* No 4, 1978, 25–34

G G Shinkaretskaya, 'Problemy pravopreemstva i granitsy Rossiiskoi Federatsii' (Problems of state succession and borders of the Russian Federation), *Moscow JIL* No 4, 1995, 84–105

G G Shinkaretskaya, 'Soyuznoe gosudarstvo Belorussii i Rossii' (The union state of Belarus and Russia), *GP* 2001, No 4, 84–8

Yu Shishkov, 'Novyi etap mezhimperialisticheskikh protivorechii' (New stage of interimperialist contradictions), *MZh* No 3, 1967, 88–99

NShmigol', 'Dogovor velikoy druzhby' (Treaty of great friendship), *MZh* No 2, 1959, 82–5

Artur Simonyan, 'Russia's Counter-revolutionary International law in the Scholarship of Boris Mirkine-Guetzévitch', 35 *EJIL* 2024, 797–804

E I Skakunov, 'Nekotorye aspekty doktrinal'nogo tolkovania instituta samooborony' (Some aspects of doctrinal interpretation of the institute of self-defense), *Soviet YBIL* 1971, 259–65

E I Skakunov, 'Vseob'emliushaya bezopasnost': model perestroiki mezhdunarodnykh otnoshenii' (Comprehensive security: model for reconstruction of international relations), *SGP* No 5, 1987, 102–11

Yu M Skuratov, 'Evraziiskaya paradigma Rossii i nekotorye problemy integratsii na prostranstve Sodruzhestva Nezavisimykh Gosudarstv (SNG) (The Eurasian paradigm of Russia and some issues of integration in the space of the Commonwealth of Independent States), *GP* 2015, No 2, 89–95

Yuri I Skuratov, 'Evraziiskaya kontseptsia "mnogonarodnoi natsii" i ee zhanchenie dlia razvitia Rossiiskoi gosudarstvennosti' (The Eurasian concept of 'multinational nation' and its significance for the development of Russian statehood), *Moscow JIL* No 4, 2019, 18–30

Yuri I Skuratov, 'Evraziiskie osnovy mezhdunarodno-pravovoi politiki Rossiiskoi Federatsii' (Eurasian foundations of the international-legal policies of the Russian Federation), *Moscow JIL* No 1, 2021, 28–45

Timothy Snyder, 'Ivan Ilyin, Putin's Philosopher of Russian Fascism', 16.03.2018, *The New York Review*

V K Sobakin, 'Printsip ravenstva i odinakovoi bezopasnosti' (The principle of equality and equal security), *SGP* No 10, 1982, 85–92

K A Sofronenko, 'Vossoedinenie Ukrainy s Rossiei (1654–1954 gg) (The unification of Ukraine with Russia (1654–1954)), *SGP* No 1, 1954, 55–70

G S Starodubtsev, 'Protivodeistvie falsifikatsii otechestvennoi mezhdunarodno-pravovoi istorii' (Counteracting falsification of the homeland's international legal history), in: B M Ashavskiy, A A Moiseev, *Sovremennoe mezhdunarodnoe pravo. Teoria i praktika. Liber Amicorum v chest Stanislava Chernichenko*, Prospekt, 2015, 353–61

A Stepanov, 'Malye strany pered alternativoi' (Small countries facing an alternative), *MZh* No 4, 1965, 49–56

Williard Sunderland, 'Russian Empire, 1552–1917', in: Philippa Levine, John Marriott (eds) *The Ashgate Research Companion to Modern Imperial Histories*, Surrey, 2012, 223–42

Viatcheslav Svetlichnyi, 'Kratkii ocherk istorii rossiiskogo diplomaticheskogo predstavitel'stva v Krymskom khanstve' (Short essay on the history of Russian diplomatic representation in the Crimean khanate), *MZh* No 12, 2013, https://interaffairs.ru/jauthor/material/997

G T Taimanov, 'Kazakhskaya SSR v Sovetskom mnogonatsional'nom gosudarstve' (The Kazakh SSR in the Soviet multinational state), *SGP* No 4, 1954, 27–38

A N Talalaev, 'Prekrashchenie mezhdunarodnykh dogovorov v istorii i praktike sovetskogo gosudarstva' (Termination of international treaties in the history and practice of the Soviet state), *Soviet YBIL* 1959, 144–57

A N Talalaev, 'Nekotorye voprosy teorii mezhdunarodnogo dogovora na venskoi konferentsii OON' (Some questions on the theory of international treaties at the UN Vienna conference), *Soviet YBIL* 1970, 112–27

A N Talalaev, 'Pravo mezhdunarodnyh dogovorov: istoriko-pravovoi ocherk' (The law of international treaties: historical legal essay), *Soviet YBIL* 1972, 53–67

Michel de Taube, 'L'apport de Byzance au développement du droit international occidental', *RCADI* Vol 67, 1939, 233–339

N Terentyev, 'KVZhD' (Chinese Eastern Railway), *SGP* No 4, 1933, 88–96

The Insider, 'Sovetnik Putina zayavil, shto "SSSR yuridicheskyi prozolzhaet sushchestvovat'", a voina s Ukrainoi—"vnutrennii protsess", 21.05.2025, https://theins.ru/news/281461?fbclid=IwY2xjawKa1NtleHRuA2FlbQIxMABicmlkETFOamwwMTJzdkR1dEp1V2E5AR5oAH0DB0WK7jp_k8lfZua5nHCulLhyOslK9AzlsQzZoyXOwqy8YZSpKKmATg_aem_ocCrFXH1t5tnUgWU0TgGqQ

Yu A Tikhomirov, 'Geopoliticheskie imperativy bezopasnosti rossiiskogo gosudarstva' (Geopolitical imperatives of security of the Russian state), *GP* No 1, 2005, 80–7

T Timofeev, 'O nekotorykh voprosakh proletarskogo internatsionalizma' (Some questions of proletarian internationalism), *MZh* No 5, 1957, 41–51

V G Titov, 'K voprosu sozdania beziadernoi zony na severe Evropy' (The question of creation of a nuclear-free zone in Northern Europe), *Soviet YBIL* 1981, 81–93

P A Tokareva, 'Mezhdunarodnaya ekonomicheskaya organizatsia novoga tipa' (A new type of international economic organization), *SGP* 1959, No 2, 104–11

P A Tokareva, 'Stanovlenie sistemy mezhdunarodnykh organizatsii sotsialisticheskikh gosudarstv' (The formation of a system of international organizations of socialist states), *SGP* No 10, 1967, 64–72

V A Tomsinov, 'Predislovie' (Introduction), in: P P Shafirov, *Rassuzhdenie, kakie zakonnye prichiny Petr I, tsar' i povelitel' vserossiiski k nachatiu voiny protiv Karla XII, korolia shvedskogo, v 1700 godu imel* (A discourse on Tsar Peter I's legal basis for going to war in 1701 against the Swedish King Charles XII), Zertsalo, 2008, vii–xii

I Trainin, 'Antiimperialisticheskie avanposty na Dal'nem Vostoke' (Antiiperialist outposts in the Far East), *SGP* No 4, 1932, 135–56

I Trainin, 'Imperializm na Dal'nem Vostoke i SSSR' (Imperialism in the Far East and the USSR), *SGP* No 7–8, 1932, 147–68

A Sh Tuganbaev, 'Razvitie natsional'noi gosudarstvennosti narodov Srednei Azii i Kazakhstana' (Development of national statehood of the peoples of Central Asia and Kazakhstan), *SGP* No 12, 1972, 59–65

G I Tunkin, 'Parizhskie soglashenia i mezhdunarodnoe pravo' (The Paris agreements and international law), *SGP* No 2, 1955, 13–22

G I Tunkin, 'Novyi tip mezhdunarodnykh otnoshenii i mezhdunarodnoe pravo' (New type of international relations and international law), *SGP* No 1, 1959, 81–94

G I Tunkin, 'Bor'ba dvukh kontseptsii v mezhdunarodnom prave' (The struggle of two concepts in international law), *SGP* No 11, 1967, 140–9

G I Tunkin, 'V I Lenin i printsipy otnoshenii mezhdu sotsialisticheskimi gosudarstvami' (V I Lenin and principles of relations between socialist states), *Soviet YBIL* 1969, 16–32

G I Tunkin, 'Sovetskaya programma mira i nekotorye problemy mezhdunarodnoga prava' (Soviet programme of peace and some issues of international law), *Soviet YBIL* 1971, 13–28

G I Tunkin, V M Shishkin, 'O mezhdunarodno-pravovykh printsipakh novoga mezhdunarodnoga ekonomicheskoga poriadka' (International legal principles of the new economic order), *SGP* No 9, 1980, 88–96

G Tunkin, 'XXVI s'ezd KPSS i dal'neishee razvitie sovetskoi nauki mezhdunarodnoga prava' (26th congress of the Soviet communist party and further development of the Soviet science of international law), *Soviet YBIL* 1981, 12–25

R A Tuzmukhamedov, A L Larionov 'Napadki na printsip samoopredelenia narodov i natsii' (Violations of the principle of self-determination of peoples and nations), *SGP* No 10, 1963, 132–6

R A Tuzmukhamedov, 'Kollektivnaya bezopasnost' v Azii i mezhdunarodnoe pravo' (Collective security in Asia and international law), *SGP* No 4, 1974, 99–105

R A Tuzmukhamedov, 'Afghanskaya revoliutsia i mezhdunarodnoe pravo' (The Afghan revolution and international law), *SGP* No 4, 1984, 85–92

Rais A Tuzmukhamedov, 'Nekotorye mezhdunarodnye i mezhdunarodno-pravovye aspekty sozdania, sushchestvovania i padenia Zolotoi Ordy' (Some international and international–legal aspects of the creation, existence, and fall of the Golden Horde), *Moscow JIL* No 1, 1995, 116–24

O I Tiunov, 'Printsip dobrosovestnogo sobliudenia mezhdunarodnykh obiazatel'stv i doktrina *rebus sic stantibus*' (The principle of conscientious observance of international obligations and the doctrine of *rebus sic stantibus*) *Soviet YBIL* 1978, 101–12

N N Ulyanova, 'Vazhnaya mera povyshenia neprimenenia sily (k voprosu o zakliuchenii Vsemirnogo dogovora o neprimenenii sily' (A necessary measure to promote non-use of force (the issue of concluding a global treaty on non-use of force), *Soviet YBIL* 1981, 41–55

Sh Z Urazaev, 'Rol' RSFSR v sozdanii sovetskoi gosudarstvennoi deyatel'nosti narodov Srednei Azii (1917–1922 gg) (The role of the Russian SFSR in the creation of Soviet state activity of peoples in Central Asia (1917–1922)), *SGP* No 6, 1964, 106–11

E T Usenko, 'Osnovnye mezhdunarodno-pravovye printsipy sotrudnichestva sotsialistichesikh gosudarstv' (Main international legal principles of cooperation among socialist states), *SGP* No 3, 1961, 16–29

E T Usenko, 'Mezhdunarodnoe pravo v vzaimootnosheniakh sotsialisticheskikh gosudarstv' (International law in mutual relations among socialist states), *Soviet YBIL* 1966/7, 30–50

E T Usenko, 'Sotrudnichestvo stran-chlenov SEV i sotsialisticheskii internatsionalizm' (Collaboration among COMECON member states and socialist internationalism), *SGP* No 4, 1970, 79–87

E T Usenko, 'Mezhdunarodnopravovye problemy sotsialisticheskoi ekonomicheskoi integratsii' (International legal problems of socialist economic integration), *Soviet YBIL* 1970, 13–28

E T Usenko, 'Pravovye aspekty kompleksnoi programmy sotsialisticheskoi ekonomicheskoi integratsii' (Legal aspects of the complex program of socialist economic integration), *SGP* No 7, 1973, 63–72

E T Usenko, 'Printsip demokraticheskogo mira – naibolee obshchaya osnova sovremennogo mezhdunarodnoga prava' (The principle of democratic peace: the most general basis of contemporary international law), *Soviet YBIL* 1973, 13–42

E A Usenko, 'O dogovornoi kompetentsii SEV' (The treaty competence of COMECON), *SGP* No 6, 1979, 98–106

E T Usenko, 'Sovet ekonomischeskoi vzaimopomoshi—sub'ekt mezhdunarodnoga prava' (COMECON—a subject of international law), *Soviet YBIL* 1979, 11–44

E T Usenko, 'Mezhdunarodno-pravovye problemy rashirenia i uglublenia sotrudnichestva sotsialisticheskikh gosudarstv' (International legal problems of enlarging and deepening cooperation among socialist states), *Soviet YBIL* 1982, 28–40

N A Ushakov, 'K voprosu o prave "veto" v organizatsii ob'edenennykh natsii' (On the question of the right of "veto" at the UN), *Soviet YBIL* 1959, 212–28

N A Ushakov, 'O narushenii protsedury golosovania v Sovete Bezopasnosti OON' (Violation of the voting procedure at the UN Security Council), *SGP* No 1, 1960, 89–97

N A Ushakov, 'Mezhdunarodno-pravovye aspekty obrazovania Soyuza SSR' (International legal aspects of the formation of the USSR), *Soviet YBIL* 1972, 11–24

Kh P Vakhidov, 'Politicheskie vzgliady prosvetitelei narodov Srednei Azii vtoroi poloviny XIX. v' (Political views of enlighteners of peoples in Central Asia during the second half of the 19th century), *SGP* No 7, 1955, 100–8

G M Velyaminov, 'Soglasovannye predlozhenia i dogovorennosti—pravovye akty v ramkakh SEV' (Agreed proposals and agreements—legal acts in the framework of COMECON), *SGP* No 11, 1990, 107–15

G M Velyaminov, 'Pravopreemstvo mezhdu Rossiiskoi Federatsii i Rossiiskoi imperii, mezhdunarodnye i vnutrennie aspekty' (State succession between the Russian Federation and the Russian Empire, international and domestic aspects), *Moscow JIL* No 3, 1998, 22–6

G M Velyaminov, 'Vossoedinenie Kryma s Rossiei: pravovoi rakurs' (Unification of Crimea with Russia: legal angle), *GP* No 9, 2014, 12–18

S V Vikharev, 'Soyuznaya respublika kak sub'ekt mezhdunarodnoga prava' (Union republic as a subject of international law), *SGP* No 6, 1960, 65–73

N Vinnitsky, A Arkadyev, 'Komu na ruku raskolnicheskaya deyatel'nost' albanskikh rukovditelei' (Who benefits from the divisive moves of the Albanian leadership), *MZh* No 2, 1962, 76–81

V Volgin, '150 let shveitsarskogo neitraliteta' (150 years of Swiss neutrality), *MZh* No 11, 1965, 70–3

L I Volova, 'Mezhdunarodno-pravovoi printsip territorialnoi neprikosnovennosti i nerushimost granits evropeiskih gosudarstv' (The international legal principle of the territorial integrity and inviolability of borders of European states), *Soviet YBIL* 1974, 126–39

P V Voronin, A A Karlov, 'Sozdanie moldavskoi sovetskoi natsional'noi gosudarstvennosti' (The creation of Moldavian Soviet national statehood), *SGP* No 6, 1967, 12–20

E R Voronin, V N Kulebyakin, A V Nikolaev, 'Gosudarstvennyi perevorot v Kieve v fevral'e 2014 g: mezhdunarodno-pravovye otsenki i posledstvia' (Coup d'état in Kyiv in February 2014: international legal assessments and consequences), *Moscow JIL* No 1, 2015, 11–28

A Vyshinsky, 'Osnovnye zadachi nauki sovetskogo sotsialistishcekogo prava' (Main tasks of the science of Soviet socialist law), *Sovetskoe gosudarstvo* No 4, 1938, 4–55

A Ya Vyshinsky, 'Dunaiskaya konferentsia i nekotorye voprosy mezhdunarodnoga prava' (The Danube conference and some questions of international law), *SGP* No 11, 1948, 16–25

S Vyshnepolsky, 'Svoboda morei v epokhu imperializma' (Freedom of the seas during the era of imperialism), *SGP* No 1, 1949, 13–25

S A Vyshnepolsky, 'K probleme pravovoga rezhima Arkticheskoi oblasti' (The issue of the legal regime of the Arctic region), *SGP* No 7, 1952, 36–45

N M Yakovlev, 'Znachenie progressivnogo rossiiskogo zakonodatel'stva dlia Yakutii posle ee prisoedineniya k Rossii' (The significance of progressive Russian legislation for Yakutia after its unification with Russia), *GP* No 10, 2004, 92–9

A Ya Yarmatov, 'Obrazovanie Turkmenskoi SSR i razvitie ee suverennykh prav' (The formation of the Turkmen SSR and development of its sovereign rights), *SGP* No 10, 1974, 27–31

Chen Yifeng, 'Bandung, China, and the Making of World Order in East Asia', in: Luis Eslava, Michael Fakhri, Vasuki Nesiah (eds) *Bandung, Global History, and International Law. Critical Pasts and Pending Futures*, CUP, 2017, 177–95

Yu A Yudin, 'Natsional'no-osvoboditel'naya bor'ba narodov Afriki i manevry imperialistov' (The struggle for national liberation in Africa and maneuvres of imperialists), *SGP* No 6, 1959, 112–23

Yu A Yudin, 'Nekotorye problemy stanovlenia natsional'noi gosudarstvennosti v nezavisimykh stranakh Afriki' (Some issues of formation of national statehood in independent countries of Africa), *SGP* No 2, 1961, 35–47

G Zadorozhniy, 'Amerikanskii zhurnal mezhdunarodnoga prava'—propovednik mezhdunarodnoga razboya i bespravia' (American Journal of International Law: preacher of international robbery and lawlessness), *SGP* No 12, 1952, 80–87

G Zadorozhniy, 'Amerikanskaya pravovaya doktrina—zleishii vrag mezhdunarodnoga prava' (American legal doctrine—evil foe of international law), *SGP* No 1, 1953, 66–74

Victor N Zakharov, 'The Russian Empire: Main Features and Particularities', in: Mary N Harris, Csaba Lévai (eds) *Europe and Its Empires*, Edizioni Plus—Pisa UP, 2008, 47–58

N V Zakharova, 'O poniatii i suschnosti kollektivnoi bezopasnosti' (The definition and nature of collective security), *SGP* No 8, 1958, 47–54

N V Zakharova, 'O mezhdunarodnoi pravosub'ektnosti gosudarstva pri sotsial'noi revoliutsii (nekotorye voprosy pravopreemstva) (The international legal subjecthood of a state in cases of social revolution (issues of state succession)), *Soviet YBIL* 1960, 157–66

N V Zakharova, 'Dvustoronnie dogovory o druzhbe, sotrudnichestve i vzaimopomoshi sotsialisticheskikh gosudarstv' (Bilateral agreements on friendship, cooperation, and mutual help among socialist countries), *SGP* No 2, 1962, 80–91

N V Zakharova, 'Otkaz Sovetskogo gosudarstva ot dogovorov tsarskoi Rossii, narushavshikh prava narodov vostochnykh stran' (Denunciation by the Soviet government of tsarist Russia's treaties violating the rights of peoples in Eastern countries), *Soviet YBIL* 1962, 126–36

N V Zakharova, I Yu Barsegov, 'O tak nazyvaemoi teorii 'ravnovesia sil' (The so-called theory of 'balance of power'), *Soviet YBIL* 1959, 272–82

Ivan S Zhudro, 'Evoliutsia mezhdunarodno-pravovoga rezhima Severnogo Ledovitoga okeana i natsional'nye interesy Rossii' (Evolution of the international legal regime of the Arctic Ocean and national interests of Russia), *Moscow JIL* No 2, 2016, 63–80

E Zhukov, 'Konferentsia stran Azii i Afriki v Bandunge i ee istoricheskoe znachenie' (Conference of the countries of Asia and Africa in Bandung and its historical significance), *MZh* No 5, 1955 18–34

V A Zibarev, 'Natsional'no-gosudarstvennoe stroitel'stvo u narodov Severa' (National state building of the peoples of the North), *SGP* No 12, 1972, 81–7

N M Zolotukhina, 'Iz istorii russkoi politicheskoi mysli kontsa XV-nachala XVI v.: teoria 'Moskva—tretii Rim' (From the history of Russian political thought at the end of the 15th-early 16th centuries: the theory of Moscow as 'the third Rome'), *SGP* No 1, 1977, 100–6

V I Zuev, 'Prioritet russkoi pravovoi mysli v sozdanii i razvitii teorii suvereniteta' (Priority of Russian legal thought in the formation and development of the theory of sovereignty), *SGP* No 3, 1951, 24–37

Other Materials

Arkhiv Vneshnei Politiki Rossiiskoi Imperii (AVPRI; Archive of Foreign Policy of the Russian Empire), Moscow, Martens diaries, Fond No 340, opis no 787

'Exclusive: Tucker Carlson Interviews Vladimir Putin', 6.02.2024, https://www.youtube.com/watch?v=fOCWBhuDdDo

Russian MFA, Press release on adoption of the UNGA resolution on eradicating colonialism in all its forms and manifestations, 5.12.2024, https://mid.ru/en/foreign_policy/news/1985538/

Statement of the Presidium of the Russian Association of International Law, 7.03.2022, http://www.ilarb.ru/html/news/2022/7032022.pdf

The Concept of the Foreign Policy of the Russian Federation, 31.03.2023, https://mid.ru/en/foreign_policy/fundamental_documents/1860586/

UNGA, 15th session, Official records, 869th plenary meeting, 23.09.1960, Speech by Mr Khrushchev, Chairman of the Council of Ministers of the Union of Soviet Socialist Republics, 68–84

UN, 'Delegates Voice Concern over Procedural Aspects, Language of Resolution on Eradicating Colonialism as Fourth Committee Approves 24 Texts, Concluding General Debate', 17.10.2024, https://press.un.org/en/2024/gaspd810.doc.htm

'Zakliuchenie Kommissii po voprosam politicheskoi i pravovoi otsenki narushenia Dogovora mezhdu Gruziei i Sovetskoi Rossiei ot 7 maia 1920 goda', 18.11.1989, in: Levan Aleksidze, *International Law and Georgia (From Antiquity to the Present).* Selected Papers Published in 1957–2012, Ivane Javakhishvili Tbilisi State University, 2012, 715–30

Index

For the benefit of digital users, indexed terms that span two pages (e.g., 52–53) may, on occasion, appear on only one of those pages.

The manufacturer's authorised representative in the EU for product safety is Oxford University Press España S.A. of el Parque Empresarial San Fernando de Henares, Avenida de Castilla, 2 – 28830 Madrid (www.oup.es/en or product.safety@oup.com). OUP España S.A. also acts as importer into Spain of products made by the manufacturer.

www.ingramcontent.com/pod-product-compliance
Ingram Content Group UK Ltd.
Pitfield, Milton Keynes, MK11 3LW, UK
UKHW021137160926
475595UK00021B/148
* 9 7 8 0 1 9 8 9 5 5 9 3 1 *